Heroes and Anti-Heroes in Medieval Romance

Studies in Medieval Romance
ISSN 1479–9308

General Editor
Corinne Saunders

Editorial Board
Siobhain Bly Calkin
Rhiannon Purdie
Robert Allen Rouse

This series aims to provide a forum for critical studies of the medieval romance, a genre which plays a crucial role in literary history, clearly reveals medieval secular concerns, and raises complex questions regarding social structures, human relationships, and the psyche. Its scope extends from the early middle ages into the Renaissance period, and although its main focus is on English literature, comparative studies are welcomed.

Proposals or queries should be sent in the first instance to one of the addresses given below; all submissions will receive prompt and informed consideration.

Professor Corinne Saunders, Department of English, University of Durham, Durham DH1 3AY

Boydell & Brewer Limited, PO Box 9, Woodbridge, Suffolk IP12 3DF

Previously published volumes in the series
are listed at the back of this book

Heroes and Anti-Heroes
in Medieval Romance

Edited by
NEIL CARTLIDGE

D. S. BREWER

© Contributors 2012

All Rights Reserved. Except as permitted under current legislation no part of this work may be photocopied, stored in a retrieval system, published, performed in public, adapted, broadcast, transmitted, recorded or reproduced in any form or by any means, without the prior permission of the copyright owner

First published 2012
D. S. Brewer, Cambridge
Paperback edition 2018

ISBN 978 1 84384 304 7 hardback
ISBN 978 1 84384 495 2 paperback

D. S. Brewer is an imprint of Boydell & Brewer Ltd
PO Box 9, Woodbridge, Suffolk IP12 3DF, UK
and of Boydell & Brewer Inc.
668 Mt Hope Avenue, Rochester, NY 14620–2731, USA
website: www.boydellandbrewer.com

A CIP catalogue record for this book is available
from the British Library

The publisher has no responsibility for the continued existence or accuracy of URLs for external or third-party internet websites referred to in this book, and does not guarantee that any content on such websites is, or will remain, accurate or appropriate

Printed from camera-ready copy supplied by the editor

Contents

Notes on the Contributors — vii

Abbreviations — ix

Introduction — 1
Neil Cartlidge

Part I: Individual Characters

1. Turnus — 9
Penny Eley

2. Alexander the Great — 27
David Ashurst

3. Hengist — 43
Margaret Lamont

4. Harold Godwineson — 59
Laura Ashe

5. Mordred — 81
Judith Weiss

6. Merlin — 99
Gareth Griffith

7. Gawain — 115
Kate McClune

8. Gamelyn — 129
Nancy Mason Bradbury

9. Ralph the Collier — 145
Ad Putter

10. The Anti-heroic Heart — 159
Stephanie Viereck Gibbs Kamath

Part II: Character-Types

11. Crusaders — 173
Robert Allen Rouse

12. Saracens — 185
Siobhain Bly Calkin

13. Ungallant Knights — 201
James Wade

14. Sons of Devils — 219
Neil Cartlidge

Index — 237

Notes on the Contributors

Laura Ashe is a University Lecturer in English at Worcester College, Oxford. She is the author of *Fiction and History in England, 1066–1200* (2007), and co-editor of *The Exploitations of Medieval Romance* (2010). She is currently writing volume 1 of the *Oxford English Literary History (1000–1350)*.

David Ashurst is Lecturer in the Department of English Studies at the University of Durham. He is author of *The Ethics of Empire in the Saga of Alexander the Great* (2009) and co-editor of *The Fantastic in Old Norse/Icelandic Literature* (2006). His research interests include Old Norse, Alexander literature, and the work of William Morris.

Nancy Mason Bradbury is Professor of English at Smith College in Northampton, Massachusetts. Her recent projects include a special issue of *Chaucer Review* on 'Time, Measure, Value' co-edited with Carolyn P. Collette, an entry on 'Popular Romance' for the *Blackwell Companion to Medieval Poetry*, and a forthcoming dual-language edition (Latin and Middle English) of *The Dialogue of Solomon and Marcolf*, co-edited with Scott Bradbury.

Siobhain Bly Calkin is an Associate Professor in the English Department at Carleton University, Ottawa, Canada. She is the author of *Saracens and the Making of English Identity: The Auchinleck Manuscript* (2005) as well as articles on medieval romances and Chaucer. She is currently working on a project about narratives of Christian relics circulating in Muslim contexts.

Neil Cartlidge is Reader in the Department of English Studies at the University of Durham. His publications include: *Medieval Marriage: Literary Approaches 1100–1300* (1997), *The Owl and the Nightingale: Text and Translation* (2001), and *Boundaries in Medieval Romance* (2008).

Penny Eley is Emeritus Professor of Medieval French at the University of Sheffield. She is the author of numerous studies of early Old French romance, including *Partonopeus de Blois: Romance in the Making* (2011).

Gareth Griffith is a Research Assistant in the Department of English at the University of Bristol. His research has focused on early Middle English and the transmission of the Bible in the vernacular. He is the author of forthcoming articles on Laȝamon's *Brut* and the manuscripts of Middle English romance.

Stephanie Viereck Gibbs Kamath is Assistant Professor at the University of Massachusetts, Boston. She studies English and French medieval literature, with particular interests in allegory, translation studies, and the history of the material text. She has published on the medieval circulation and adaptation of poetry composed by Christine de Pizan, Guillaume de Deguileville, and John Lydgate, and she has also completed the first full modern English translation of René d'Anjou's *Le livre du cuer d'amours espris*, co-authored with Kathryn Karczewska.

Margaret Lamont is Head of English Programs at Stanford University's Education Program for Gifted Youth. Among her recent publications are 'Becoming English: Ronwenne's Wassail, Language, and National Identity in the Middle English Prose Brut' (*Studies in Philology*, 2010) and '"Genealogical" History and the English Roll' in 'Medieval Manuscripts, Their Makers and Users' (special issue of *Viator*, 2011).

Kate McClune is Lecturer in Medieval English at Balliol and Wadham Colleges, University of Oxford. Her current research focuses on the depiction of regional loyalties in medieval literature. She is the co-editor, with David Clark, of *Arthurian Literature 28: Blood, Sex, Malory: essays on the 'Morte Darthur'* (2011).

Ad Putter is Professor of Medieval English Literature at the University of Bristol. His books include *An Introduction to the Gawain-Poet* (1997) and (with Judith Jefferson) *Studies in the Metre of Alliterative Verse* (2007). He is co-editor of the *Cambridge Companion to the Arthurian Legend* (2009), and is currently completing the Penguin edition of the Gawain poet's works with Myra Stokes.

Robert Allen Rouse is Associate Professor of English at the University of British Columbia. He is the author of *The Idea of Anglo-Saxon England in Middle English Romance* (2005) and, with Cory J. Rushton, *The Medieval Quest for Arthur* (2005). He is currently completing a study of the medieval geographical imagination.

James Wade is a Research Fellow at Emmanuel College, Cambridge. He is the author of *Fairies in Medieval Romance* (2011).

Judith Weiss is an Emeritus Fellow of Robinson College, Cambridge. Her interests lie mainly in the field of Anglo-Norman romance and historiography. Her publications include a parallel text and translation of Wace's *Roman de Brut* (1999, 2002), translations *Boeve de Haumtone* and *Gui de Warewic* (in one volume, 2008), and *The Birth of Romance* (1992, reissued in 2009).

Abbreviations

AND	*Anglo-Norman Dictionary*
ANTS	Anglo-Norman Text Society
ASC	*Anglo-Saxon Chronicle*
BL	British Library
BNF	Bibliothèque nationale de France
CCCM	Corpus Christianorum: Continuation Mediaeualis
CFMA	Classiques français du moyen âge
CUL	Cambridge University Library
DRSO	*Duke Rowlande and of Sir Ottuell of Spayne*
EETS ES	Early English Text Society, Extra Series
EETS OS	Early English Text Society, Original Series
EETS SS	Early English Text Society, Supplementary Series
F	*Firumbras*
JEGP	*Journal of English & Germanic Philology*
MED	*Middle English Dictionary*
MLR	*Modern Language Review*
MS, MSS	manuscript, manuscripts
n.	note
NS	New Series
ODNB	*Oxford Dictionary of National Biography*
OED	*Oxford English Dictionary*
OF	Old French
OK	*Otuel a Kniȝt*
OR	*Otuel and Roland*
PL	*Patrologia cursus completus: series latina*, ed. J.-P. Migne, 221 vols (Paris, 1844–64)
PMLA	*Publications of the Modern Language Association*
RS	The Rolls Series: *Rerum Britannicarum Medii Ævi Scriptores (Chronicles and Memorials of Great Britain and Ireland during the Middle Ages)*, 99 works in 244 vols (London, 1858–1896)
SB	*The Sowdone of Babylone*
SBB-PK	Staatsbibliothek zu Berlin: Preußischer Kulturbesitz
SF	*Sir Ferumbras*
STS	Scottish Text Society
TEAMS	The Consortium for the Teaching of the Middle Ages

Introduction

Neil Cartlidge

Medieval romances so insistently celebrate the triumphs of heroes and the discomfiture of villains that they discourage recognition of just how morally ambiguous, antisocial or even downright sinister their protagonists can be, and, correspondingly, of just how admirable or impressive their defeated opponents often are. This tension between the heroic and the anti-heroic in romance-texts contributes considerably to the complexity of the reading experience that they generate, but it is not an aspect of the genre that has been much discussed up to now. Part of the reason for this lies in the way that medieval romances still tend to be characterized as ideologically and psychologically naïve texts. Romance, so the argument goes, is a genre that typically prefers simplistic scales of value, intellectual commonplaces and easy stereotypes; and it relentlessly depicts the victories and happy endings of its chivalric protagonists only as a means of asserting the intrinsic superiority of the social and ethical ideals that they embody. Viewed in this way, it would perhaps be the very last literary genre in which anyone would expect to find either depth or complexity of characterization, let alone any figures interesting enough to be described as 'anti-heroes'. Medieval romances may not aspire to the illusion of three-dimensional characters whose motives and emotions are complete enough to seem entirely realistic, but this certainly does not mean that they are incapable of sustaining any ambivalence towards their heroes, or towards the idea of heroism. Indeed, it could be argued that, far from simply underwriting the idealization of heroism, romances actually derive much of their imaginative power and appeal from the very contradictions implicit within it.

'Anti-hero' is not a medieval expression, of course – but then neither is its simplex, 'hero', which has long been used in medieval studies, and often in ways that make it a highly value-laden term. In a medieval context, heroism is always complicit, to some extent, with such values as chivalry, aristocracy, loyalty, masculinity and militarism; and anti-heroism is perhaps so prominent in medieval romance precisely because it provides a means of challenging or examining these values. If heroism is the paradigm to which the protagonists of romance-texts are expected to conform, then it is entirely logical to describe the various ways in which they fail to conform to it – or in which they reveal fundamental contradictions within it – as anti-heroism. Yet anti-heroism in medieval romance is not just about ideological or moral values: it is also very largely to do with literary effect. Medieval writers and their audiences seem to have been attracted to anti-heroes, very often not because of any real anxiety about the meaning of heroism, but simply because of the dramatic possibilities that anti-heroism creates. In other words, the concept is useful because it helps to explain the various different ways in which medieval narratives invite admiration of figures who are obviously either flawed, failed, sinister or destructive. They do so, perhaps, precisely because its effect is so unsettling. Anti-heroes compel attention even when – and perhaps especially when – the narratives in which they appear in other respects follow conventional and predictable patterns.

Each of the following chapters is focused on one character or character-type with a significant presence in romance-texts, in such a way as to present a series of separate case-histories, each providing its own perspective on what constitutes heroism or anti-heroism in medieval texts. What we have aimed at throughout is thought-provoking concision, rather than exhaustive elaboration. The challenge implicit in such an approach is that most of the contributors have had to be very selective in their choice of material, for the literary traditions conveying the characters and character-types chosen are, in most cases, very substantial, and in some cases (such as those of Merlin, Gawain or Alexander the Great) enormous. Even in the case of characters and character-types that have relatively distinct and continuous literary traditions of their own, different texts can tell very different stories about them, in such a way as to make it rather problematic to think of any given character as being 'the same' throughout the tradition of texts in which he appears. In effect, such figures have two-dimensional biographies – one dimension being intradiegetic, the story of their lives within texts; and the other being literary-historical, how that story changes from text to text. So, for example, some of the most challenging aspects of the character of Gawain, say, are an effect, not just of one text, but of a dialogue between texts – in the sense that each new depiction of Gawain inevitably develops, modifies or contradicts some of the depictions that previously existed. From this perspective, 'Gawain' is not just a figure within certain individual texts, but an accumulation of impressions generated by a tradition of texts – which means, in turn, that his status either as hero and/or as anti-hero is to some extent an effect of this complex literary-historical continuity. In some cases, pursuing such continuities necessarily means going well beyond medieval romance itself – for example, into the realm of historical fact, as in the case of those figures in romance who also have a place in history (such as Harold Godwineson, Alexander, Hengist or Richard the Lionheart), or into a number of other literary genres besides romance, such as epic, chronicle, ballad, prophecy, drama and fabliau. In other words, we have sometimes found it helpful to connect our shared interest in the workings of medieval romance to an investigation of the wider contexts that often (but by no means always) define the cultural impact of individual characters or character-types. At the same time, it is worth emphasizing that, despite the various directions in which our studies have led, the principal figures addressed in each chapter can certainly be said to exist prominently in medieval romance, even if their existence is not, at the same time, wholly limited to medieval romance.

No attempt has been made here to impose or contrive any fixed or final definition of medieval anti-heroism (or indeed of romance). The studies presented here are intended to be suggestive and selective: they address a wide range of different kinds of (anti)hero in a wide range of different kinds of literary text (although with a recurring emphasis on texts generally described as romance), and they reach a correspondingly wide range of different conclusions about the ways in which characters in such texts might validly be described as (anti)heroic. Penny Eley's contribution to this book (Chapter 1) shows how the *Roman d'Eneas* deliberately departs from its source, Virgil's *Aeneid*, in its treatment of the hero, Turnus. Whereas Virgil is prepared to describe Turnus specifically as a hero ('heros'), despite the role that he is condemned to play as an obstacle on the way to Aeneas's greatness, the *Roman d'Eneas* instead subjects Turnus to a 'thorough-going character assassination'. Eley suggests that one of the reasons why he is treated in this way is to block any possible comparison with historical figures like Eustace of Blois or Harold Godwineson, who (like Turnus) were notoriously victims of regime-change. As it happens, Harold gets his own chapter later on in this book, written by Laura Ashe (Chapter 4), because of the complex way in which his reputation evolved after his death at the Battle of Hastings in 1066, culminating in a kind of rehabilitation in the tropes of romance. As Ashe shows, no one could deny either Harold's force of character or the completeness of ultimate failure, so that he is an almost inevitably paradoxical figure, 'an unanswered question, symbol of an alternative and counterfactual history'. Hengist, too, seems to be in certain ways at odds with history, even though, unlike Harold, he was one of history's victors, in that he was one of the leaders of the successful Anglo-Saxon invasions of England. However, as Margaret Lamont observes in Chapter 3, he owes much of his literary prominence to Geoffrey of Monmouth's resolutely pro-British (and correspondingly anti-Anglo-Saxon and anti-English) romanticization of the island's history, in such a way as to make him troublingly ambiguous. It is apparently from the profound ethnic tension at the very heart of Geoffrey's text that Hengist's anti-heroism is generated.

In the Arthurian legend that Geoffrey of Monmouth did so much to popularize, it is the character of Mordred who is typically condemned to play the role of traitor, and ultimately to kill, or to cause the death of, his uncle, King Arthur. It is not a role that leaves very much room for redemption, but as Judith Weiss shows in Chapter 5, even Mordred is nevertheless sometimes allowed by medieval writers to have redeeming features. This tends to occur most often in those texts that are also most prepared to see the seeds of Arthur's destruction as lying either in his own character, or in the values espoused by his court, or in the exigencies of fate. Some of the romance-figures discussed in this volume can be regarded as anti-heroes in the sense that, even if they fight for the right cause and do so effectively (unlike Mordred), they are nevertheless disappointing at some other level. In other words, they are 'heroes' who fail to live up to the very definition of heroism suggested by the texts in which they appear. In this category belongs the protagonist of Rene d'Anjou's *Livre du Cuer*, who (despite being an allegorical representation of the author's own heart) ultimately serves not as a type of the successful lover-knight, but rather as a means of questioning the very idealization of courtly love and aristocratic knighthood, as Stephanie Viereck Gibbs Kamath explains in Chapter 10. The Arthurian hero Sir Gawain, too, is often a significant 'failure', as Kate McClune shows in Chapter 7. He is repeatedly depicted falling short, not just of the avowed moral standards of the Arthurian court, but also of his own reputation. As to the several 'ungallant knights' discussed by James Wade in Chapter 13 – who include Sir Gyngeleyne (from *Libeaus*

Desconus) and Thomas of Erceldoune – they turn out to be guilty of behaviour that would be conspicuously reprehensible by any standards, let alone those of medieval courtliness or chivalry. However, Wade suggests that they might have seemed to medieval readers all the more conspicuously 'ill-behaved' because of the rather moralistic context in which their stories tend to appear in the extant medieval manuscripts.

Some of the heroes discussed in this book create discomfort as a result of the way in which they represent ethical and political values very different from those that are generally regarded as acceptable in the modern world. This applies with particular force to those figures whose heroism depends on political and cultural aggression – as in the case of the imperial ambitions of Alexander the Great (discussed by David Ashurst in Chapter 2), and of the xenophobia, violence and savagery that marks the activities of some of the crusaders who appear in romance (as discussed by Robert Allen Rouse in Chapter 11). However, as Ashurst and Rouse make clear, it is not only from a modern perspective that such heroes – or anti-heroes – can appear problematic, since a certain ambivalence towards such figures often seems to be written into the medieval narratives that describe them. Similarly, several of the Saracens discussed by Siobhain Bly Calkin in Chapter 12 are made to seem so admirable in comparison with the heroes of Christendom that they pose a kind of implicit moral challenge to the values that they are supposed to represent, or at least a recognition of the social costs and potentially destructive effects of heroic action. There are also some figures discussed in this book who are anti-heroes in the sense that, even though the texts in which they appear clearly invite us to admire them as heroes, they possess characteristics that are not normally compatible with heroic status in romance. Despite romance's characteristic preference for aristocracy, Gamelyn and Ralph the Collier (discussed by Nancy Mason Bradbury and Ad Putter in Chapters 8 and 9 respectively) are heroes whose identity is emphatically defined by their low social status; and as such they necessarily pose something of a challenge to what medieval romance generally understands as 'heroic'. Both Gamelyn and Ralph are more than merely uncourtly: they are, in fact, positively brusque and churlish – and, in Gamelyn's case, gleefully lavish with violence – to the extent that they remain rather forbidding figures, however much we might approve of the social egalitarianism that they seem to embody. Even more forbidding still are the romance-heroes who are explicitly depicted as sons of devils, in particular the great seer and magician of the Arthurian tradition, Merlin (discussed by Gareth Griffith in Chapter 7), and his rather more destructive (but eventually penitent and saintly) relatives, Robert le Diable and Sir Gowther (for whom see my own contribution, Chapter 14). It says something for the sheer elasticity of medieval romance's definition of heroism that it can create heroes even out of men whose very being derives from the Devil.

This sketch of the book's contents illustrates, I hope, how wide is the variety of different anti-heroic characters and character-types that have been chosen for it; but it has to be acknowledged, in the end, that it by no means exhausts the scope of anti-heroism as a phenomenon in medieval romance. There are clearly a number of other figures who might have lent themselves just as readily to the kind of critical approach that is taken here. The Arthurian tradition offers an abundance of potential anti-heroes, including Lancelot, Tristram and King Arthur (besides the three Arthurian characters who do appear here in chapters of this book: Mordred, Merlin and Gawain). There are also other categories of hero/anti-hero that we might have considered – such as the outlaw-heroes Fulk Fitzwarin, Eustace the Monk and Hereward, or the werewolf-heroes William of Palerne and Mélion – to name just a few possibilities. But this only underlines the general point that this volume is intended to make – which is that even among the repeatedly triumphant heroes of medieval romance, it is not difficult to find figures who are implicitly self-contradictory, ambivalent, destructive or just plain unpleasant, whatever else they manage to achieve. The same could perhaps be said of many of the hero*ines* of medieval romance, but this is not an issue that the current volume is intended to explore. The reason for this is that gender is clearly a very significant factor in determining the range of possible ways in which individuals might be cast as heroic or anti-heroic. Just as medieval heroism is defined, to some extent, by the particular opportunities and responsibilities typically associated with masculinity (and with knighthood in particular), so too it is perhaps a distinctively masculine set of failings that tends to shape the construction of anti-heroism. 'Anti-heroinism' is therefore an essentially different phenomenon – and one complex enough to require a book of its own.

The idea for *Heroes and Anti-Heroes in Medieval Romance* emerged at the 8th Biennial Conference on Medieval Romance, which took place at Durham University in 2002. I am particularly grateful to Caroline Palmer, of Boydell and Brewer, for supporting this project from the very outset, and for keeping faith with it in all the years since then. Durham University is now my own home-institution (as it was not in 2002). This makes it all the more pleasing to be able to acknowledge the support of Durham's Department of English Studies, which, among other things, has provided help with the costs of the index (compiled with customary efficiency by Tom Norton). Thanks are also due to the current Head of the Department, Corinne Saunders (who, as it happens, was also the organiser of the 2002 conference). All of the contributors have been tolerant and efficient at all times, but I owe thanks particularly to Laura Ashe (for her advice at several key stages in the project's development) and to my colleague David Ashurst for being willing to contribute at such very short notice. Finally, I should mention my family: Kate Thomas – for supportiveness of all kinds; and our daughters Carrie and Jen Thomas – simply for being themselves.

Part I
Individual Characters

1

Turnus

PENNY ELEY

On the face of it, Turnus should have been a character that a mid-twelfth-century audience could have identified with and admired. Virgil's 'ingens Turnus' ('mighty Turnus', XII, 927)[1] stands poles apart from the villains of the first phase of Old French literature, who are generally constituted as such by their status as traitors (Ganelon in the *Chanson de Roland*, Modret in Wace's *Brut*, Hoel in *Ille et Galeron*, numerous antagonists of the Normans in Benoît's *Chronique de ducs de Normandie*), cowards (Tedbalt and Esturmi in the *Chanson de Guillaume*), perjurers (Etioclés in the *Roman de Thèbes*), or outsiders whose beliefs and/or values place them firmly beyond the pale of courtly Christian society (the Saracen leaders of the early *chansons de geste*, plus the *fils à vilain* figures of *Partonopeus de Blois* and the Alexander romances). As a man who attempts to defend his homeland against alien incomers and his own honour against an outrageous breach of faith by his overlord, Turnus would appear to conform to the vernacular audience's conception of a hero rather than its opposite. Virgil himself calls Turnus a hero,[2] and it is not hard to imagine the Rutulian prince portrayed in Books VII to XII of the *Aeneid* as the protagonist of a *chanson de geste* from the *cycle des barons révoltés*, resisting injustice and a royal volte-face after the fashion of Girart de Roussillon. And yet, when an Old French poet came to adapt Virgil's epic into octosyllabic rhyming couplets some time in the 1150s or early 1160s,[3] his public was presented with an entirely different Turnus, one whose words and actions were at odds with some of the most fundamental values of their society. No longer a figure whom the great Virgil scholar Brooks Otis described as 'struggl[ing] with pathetic heroism in a most unequal combat with fate',[4] this Turnus

---

[1] All quotations from and translations of the *Aeneid* are taken from *Virgil*, ed. and trans. H. Rushton Fairclough, revised edition, 2 vols, Loeb Classical Library, 63 & 64 (Cambridge, MA, 1932).
[2] Robert M. Boltwood, 'Turnus and Satan as Epic "Villains"', *The Classical Journal* 47 (1952), 183–86, at p. 183. It is particularly significant that the term *heros* is used to describe Turnus during his final, desperate struggle with Aeneas (XII, 902).
[3] *Eneas, roman du XIIe siècle*, ed. by J.-J. Salverda da Grave, 2 vols, CFMA, 44 & 62 (Paris, 1925 & 1929). All references here will be to the CFMA edition unless otherwise indicated; English translations are my own. The most generally accepted date of composition for *Eneas* is 1155–60; Jean-Charles Huchet makes a case for dating the romance more precisely to 1156: see *Le Roman medieval*, Littératures modernes 36 (Paris, 1984), p. 13.
[4] *Virgil: A Study in Civilized Poetry* (Oxford, 1963), p. 313. Cf. also Boltwood's comment that both Virgil's Turnus and Satan 'are engaged in mighty efforts to make their own strongly held

was a character whose death at the hands of Eneas must have struck knights, lords and their ladies as exactly what he deserved, a cause for celebration untinged with regret for the loss of a noble warrior. In the process of adaptation, Turnus had been transformed from a hero into an anti-hero, a figure whose noble qualities had been systematically undermined and whose fate now lacked any sense of tragic dignity. How – and perhaps more importantly why – the Old French Turnus became almost the negative image of his Virgilian counterpart provides a fascinating study in medieval vernacular rewriting.[5]

It must be said at the outset that the *Eneas* poet does not bear sole responsibility for blackening the image of Turnus. The transformation began in late antiquity with Fulgentius's *Expositio continentiae Virgilianae secundum philosophos moralis* (*Exposition of the Content of Virgil according to Moral Philosophy*).[6] Following in the footsteps of Aelius Donatus, Fulgentius adopted an allegorical reading of the *Aeneid*, seeing it as a model of human life from birth to adulthood. He re-interpreted the principal characters with whom the hero interacts as universal abstractions such as Time (Charon), representative types such as the Good Man (Evander), or human vices and virtues such as Vainglory (Misenus). In this schema Turnus is identified with Rage (*furibundus sensus, furor animi*), which must be overcome on the path to true maturity, along with its allies such as Drunkenness (Metiscus) and Impiety (Mezentius).[7] Since Wrath had been firmly established as one of the Seven Deadly Sins even before Pope Gregory I drew up his definitive list in the late sixth century, any Christian reader of Virgil who was schooled in the Fulgentian tradition could scarcely have avoided coming away from the text with a more negative vision of Turnus than the original audience.[8] Other strands in the exegetical tradition may also have contributed to a general darkening of readers' perceptions of the character. By the time our poet came to compose his adaptation, the *Aeneid* was also being interpreted as a paradigmatic story of human fall and redemption, with parallels being drawn between the hero and both Adam and Christ.[9] Such readings inevitably create an expectation that one or more of the protagonists will fulfil the role of the arch-enemy Satan. Daniel Poirion suggested

---

conceptions of justice and right prevail in a sordid atmosphere of personally experienced injustice' (p. 183).

[5] 'L'*Enéas* apparaît comme un miroir déformant où l'original latin contemple moins son image qu'il ne s'y perd. La copie se veut réécriture' (Jean-Charles Huchet, 'L'*Enéas*: un roman spéculaire', in *Relire le Roman d'Enéas*, ed. Jean Dufournet (Paris, 1985), pp. 63–81, at p. 64). Despite the proliferation of studies of the romance as *translatio* over the last thirty years or so, very little critical attention has so far been focused on Turnus.

[6] Fabius Planciades Fulgentius, *Opera*, ed. R. Helm (Leipzig, 1898), pp. 81–107.

[7] Fulgentius, *Opera*, ed. Helm, pp. 105 and 106. See also Domenico Comparetti, *Vergil in the Middle Ages*, trans. by E.F.M. Benecke (London, 1908), pp. 107–111, and Francine Mora-Lebrun, *L'Enéide médiévale et la chanson de geste*, Nouvelle Bibliothèque du Moyen Age 23 (Paris, 1994), p. 64.

[8] The influence of Fulgentius can be seen in the early twelfth-century commentary on the first six books of the *Aeneid* traditionally attributed to Bernard Sylvestris (but which may well have been written by Bernard of Chartres), which indicates that the author intends to approach Books VII to XII as a psychomachia. John of Salisbury was also reading Virgil's poem as an allegory of human life at the period when he composed his *Policraticus*. See Francine Mora-Lebrun, *L'«Enéide» medieval et la naissance du roman*, Perspectives littéraires (Paris, 1994), pp. 76 and 109.

[9] Philippe Logié, *L'Enéas, une traduction au risque de l'invention*, Nouvelle Bibliothèque du Moyen Age 48 (Paris, 1999), pp. 201–202 and 297–99.

that our poet's decision to include the story of the Judgement of Paris as a prelude to the main action casts Paris in the role of the great tempter, re-enacting the offer of an apple that led to Adam's expulsion from Eden.[10] The devil remains active in the world after the Fall, however, and it is easy to see how this association might have been transferred unconsciously from Paris to Turnus, who does everything he can to thwart the progress of Eneas and engages in a climactic struggle with him for the future of civilisation. An educated twelfth-century French adapter might very well have approached the *Aeneid* already conditioned to read the worst into some aspects of the hero's principal opponent. To a certain extent, then, our poet's negative rewriting of the character and motivation of Turnus can be seen as a natural consequence of the reinterpretation of Virgil's text by the Christian Middle Ages.

Fall-out from the *Expositio* and other exegetical approaches to Virgil is not enough, however, to account for the thorough-going character assassination suffered by Turnus in the vernacular romance. It is clear from the first mention of his name that a more deliberate, conscious strategy of rewriting is at work. Virgil introduces Turnus in the context of a narratorial intervention that immediately invests the Rutulian with a certain status within the story, as well as foregrounding his good looks and noble lineage. He is the only one of Lavinia's many suitors to be singled out for such attention:

> Multi illam magno e Latio totaque petebant
> Ausonia. Petit ante alios pulcherrimus omnes
> Turnus, avis atavisque potens, quem regia coniunx
> Adiungi generum miro properabat amore.   (VII, 54–57)

Many wooed her from wide Latium and all Ausonia, yet goodliest above all other wooers was Turnus, of long and lofty ancestry, whom the queen-mother yearned with wondrous passion to unite to her as son.

This initial portrait is then followed by a detailed account of the portents and prophesies that force Latinus to reconsider the future of his kingdom and offer his daughter in marriage to Aeneas instead of this admirable local suitor. In the Old French version, the portents are omitted altogether, while the preamble is reduced and transferred piecemeal into the account of Eneas's arrival in Latium and the king's response to his envoys. As a result, Turnus is introduced not by the narrator, but by Latinus, in a speech that immediately associates him with questionable activities:

> 'Molt sui vialz on, si n'ai nul oir,
> Ne mes que sol une meschine
> De ma moillier, qu'a nom Lavine.
> Ge l'ai promise estre mon gré
> Et ancontre ma volanté
> A un prince de cest païs;
> Turnus a a non li marchis;
> Ma moillier vielt qu'il ait mon regne,
> Et Lavine ma fille a fegne.'   (lines 3230–38)

---

[10] 'L'Ecriture épique: du sublime au symbole', in *Relire le Roman d'Enéas*, pp. i–xiii (p. x).

'I am a very old man, and I have no heirs other than a single daughter by my wife, whose name is Lavine. I have promised her in marriage reluctantly and against my will to one of the local princes. The name of this baron is Turnus; my wife wants him to have my kingdom and have my daughter Lavine as his wife.'[11]

Such telescoping might be unremarkable for a minor character, but in the case of the hero's principal opponent, this mode of presentation immediately raises doubts about the narrator's attitude towards the character.[12] The omission of the prophecies is perhaps to be expected, given the adaptor's overall strategy of reducing the role of pagan deities and the practices associated with their worship. Nevertheless, the way in which our poet has reconfigured the narrative around this cut is highly significant for the subsequent portrayal of Turnus. In place of the picture of a devout monarch seeking to establish the will of the gods and then bowing to their command, we find the Old French Latinus welcoming the arrival of the Trojans as a justification for ending a commitment that had been imposed on him when he was too vulnerable to resist.

This version of events begs the question of who had forced the old king into an agreement against his will, and suggests that dark forces may be at work, manipulating the rightful ruler for their own selfish ends. Virgil's Latinus had yet to make up his mind about which of Lavinia's many suitors would succeed him, and so was not guilty of an explicit breach of promise when he chose Aeneas instead of a local candidate. In presenting Turnus as the beneficiary of a contract that has already been finalised, and is then deliberately broken, the Old French poet could have strengthened his case for audience sympathy. A few deft touches could have transformed the Rutulian into an innocent victim of double-dealing on the part of an unscrupulous monarch; this in turn could have provided a compelling justification for his subsequent actions. Instead, by suggesting that the venerable Latinus has been the victim of coercion, the author himself manages to pull off a remarkable double. One small addition to his source enables him not only to present Eneas as a saviour-figure who can prevent an injustice from being committed, but also to impute unworthy motives to the person or persons who had brought undue pressure to bear on an elderly man. Suspicion inevitably falls on Turnus, who stands to profit from the agreement. However, it is clear that Latinus's wife is also implicated, and further rewritings of the figures of the classical gods provide an opportunity for the poet to develop her role in ways that cast an increasingly negative light on Turnus.

In the *Aeneid*, news of Latinus's change of heart is brought to Turnus by the Fury Allecto, who appears to the sleeping youth in the form of the aged priestess Calybe. Still apparently asleep, Turnus laughs and tells the old woman not to meddle in men's

---

[11] My translation attempts to retain the emphasis given in the original to the idea of possessing both the land and the woman who is identified with it. On the identification of *feme* and *terre* in *Eneas*, see Christiane Marchello-Nizia, 'De l'*Enéide* à l'*Eneas*: les attributs du fondateur', in *Lectures médiévales de Virgile. Actes du Colloque organisé par l'Ecole française de Rome (25–28 octobre 1982)*, ed J.-Y. Tilliette (Rome, 1985), pp. 251–66, at pp. 252–54.

[12] It is worth comparing this with the introduction of Aeneas's ally Pallas (*Aeneid*, VIII, 102–12; *Eneas*, lines 4644–60). In this case, the Old French poet respects the order of Virgil's text, Pallas is named by the narrator, and the force of the complimentary epithet *audax* is retained in line 4659.

affairs. It is only when Allecto throws off her disguise and hurls her torch at him that he is overcome by the rage that will lead him to declare war on Aeneas. He immediately summons his men, who rally to his cause out of admiration for Turnus's 'peerless beauty', his ancestry, and his achievements as a warrior (VII, 413–74). In *Eneas*, there is no divine intervention at this point: Turnus hears the news from a messenger sent by the queen, who arrives just as he has finished dining. The queen's message is articulated twice, first in indirect speech as she briefs her squire on what to say to Turnus (lines 3386–98), and then in direct speech when the messenger arrives in his castle (lines 3410–56). These passages reproduce the content of Allecto's speech to Turnus quite faithfully, but the technique of doubling has the effect of turning the Fury's exhortations into a series of royal commands, the most important of which are to raise an army and to conduct a private war against the Trojans. Turnus responds immediately and enthusiastically to the message, declaring that Latinus is too old and weak to ensure that the Trojans will prevail if he takes up arms to assert his rights. As Baswell notes, 'private war, skipping over any legal recourse that might be available (however weak), was the aristocratic course to justice in the earlier feudal period'. In cases where a contractual obligation had been breached, such feuding could also be categorised as 'just war'.[13] Although attitudes were beginning to change by the time *Eneas* was composed, Turnus's response to the situation might have seemed quite appropriate to many members of the audience – were it not bound up with the morally and politically dubious action of the queen.

The final words of the squire's speech – '"la raïne et li baron/ t'otroient bien tote l'enor"' ('the queen and the barons willingly grant you the whole territory', lines 3450–51) – are the verbal equivalent of Allecto's torch, driving Turnus into military action, but they also carry an ethical payload that is absent from Virgil's text. The vernacular audience is well aware that neither Latinus nor the queen has had the time to consult the barons and establish whether or not they would support the king's change of policy; lines 3450–51 therefore convey the idea of a deliberate manipulation of the truth on her part. Moreover, Latinus had already made it quite clear to his wife that his decision in respect of Lavine's marriage to Eneas was beyond appeal (lines 3337–50), while she had privately declared her intention to thwart Eneas:

> 'Ge li ferai oïr novelles,
> Bien tost li cuit movoir tel guerre,
> Qu'il nos an guerpira la terre
> Ou il an perdra tost la vie.' (lines 3372–75)

'I will make sure he hears unwelcome news; before very long I intend to provoke such hostilities against him that he will either quit this land of ours or quickly lose his life.'

The queen's message thus represents a direct challenge to her husband's authority and an incitement to Turnus to follow suit. The clear implication of the Old French poet's rewriting of Allecto is that the queen in *Eneas* has her own agenda for Latium,

---

[13] Christopher Baswell, 'Men in the *Roman d'Eneas*: The Construction of Empire', in *Medieval Masculinities: Regarding Men in the Middle Ages*, ed. Clare A. Lees, Medieval Cultures 7 (Minneapolis, 1994), pp. 149–68, at pp. 157 and 158–59.

which Turnus is unable or unwilling to question.[14] His reaction to her intervention creates a very different impression from the equivalent scene in the *Aeneid*. Instead of Virgil's self-confident young man, ready to send the priestess packing and find his own solution to the Trojan problem, we find a self-interested vassal who is only too happy to accept orders that hold out the prospect of political advancement. The recontextualisation of the message and reply also removes any possible mitigating circumstances for the Old French Turnus: unlike his Virgilian counterpart, he is fully awake, relaxed and well-fed, and in complete possession of his faculties. If this man takes up arms in response to what he hears, it is not because he is the helpless victim of an irresistible Fury, but because he has decided to throw his lot in with the queen. Virgil had hinted in the 'miro [...] amore' of VII, 57 at something unnatural in Amata's feelings towards the prince she wanted as her son-in-law.[15] The Old French poet retains the idea of a transgressive relationship, but defines it in moral rather than in sexual terms (which may, incidentally, explain why the queen is never named in *Eneas* – it is possible that the poet wanted to avoid the sexual overtones of the name Amata, 'the beloved woman'). His Turnus comes across here not as the queen's lover-in-waiting, but as her potential puppet, whose accession to the throne would give her unrivalled power in Latium.[16] Turnus's speedy compliance with her 'advice' invites the audience to see in him an unprincipled vassal who will sacrifice everything, including his masculine honour, in pursuit of his ambition.

Final confirmation that we are dealing with a deliberate negative rewriting of Turnus, rather than the unintended consequence of a decision to write out pagan deities, can be found in two crucial modifications to the concluding scene of this episode. Firstly, while Virgil's Turnus makes a dramatic, emotional appeal to his men to defend their homeland, culminating in the ringing cry of 'tutari Italiam' ('save Italy', VII, 469), his vernacular counterpart is credited with no such patriotic impulse. The Old French Turnus puts his own grievance first, complaining to his *amis privez* (his inner circle of relatives and supporters) about the king's failure to honour their agreement (lines 3491–94). There is no reference to saving their homeland; the emphasis is rather on settling personal scores and finding a legitimate pretext for war with Eneas. Secondly, the Rutulians' reaction to this appeal is completely omitted in

---

[14] There is an interesting parallel to this in a passage of commentary added to a twelfth-century manuscript of the *Aeneid* (London, BL MS Additional 32319A), which summarises the cause of the war as follows: 'Hearing of Eneas's arrival, Latinus immediately promised him the hand of his daughter, *whom her mother had earlier promised to Turnus*' (my emphasis; quoted from Baswell, p. 153). The portrayal of the Old French Amata supports Karen Pratt's argument that ambiguous presentation of literary queens focalises 'political and gender anxieties' experienced by male poets and the male-dominated context within which they worked. See 'The Image of the Queen in Old French Literature', in *Queens and Queenship in Medieval Europe*, ed. Anne Duggan (Woodbridge, 1997), pp. 235–59, at p. 236.

[15] See Sarah Mack, 'The Birth of War: A Reading of *Aeneid* 7', in *Reading Vergil's 'Aeneid': An Interpretive Guide*, ed. Christine Perkell, Oklahoma Series in Classical Culture 23 (Norman, OK, 1999), pp. 128–47, at p. 143.

[16] Mora-Lebrun argues that the character of Murman in Ermold le Noir's *In honorem Hludowici imperatoris* (early 9th century) is deliberately assimilated to Turnus, and notes that as well as endowing his hero's antagonist with potentially admirable aggression, Ermold is at pains to blacken Murman's character with accusations of his being under the pernicious influence of a woman (*L'Enéide médiévale et la chanson de geste*, pp. 130–31). This suggests that the relationship between Turnus and Amata was already being reinterpreted to the detriment of the former well before *Eneas* was composed.

Eneas: there is no mention of their admiration for Turnus, no allusion to his beauty or prowess, no implication of collective ownership of the action that follows. While reducing the role of the gods inevitably places moral responsibility more squarely on the shoulders of human protagonists than in Virgil, our poet deliberately narrows the focus of this scene so that responsibility attaches to one man rather than to a group of like-minded individuals. The proliferation of third-person singular verbs in lines 3495–524 identifies the Old French Turnus as the prime mover of the war that cost so many lives, an impression that is reinforced by the description of him thinking night and day about how to find an *acheison* (a legally defensible pretext) for attacking the Trojans and taking control of Latium.

This obsession with surface legitimacy was one of the factors that led Cormier to see Turnus as the representative of a conservative, materialistic and legalistic form of feudalism that was being deliberately contrasted with a new political order embodied in the figure of Eneas.[17] Baswell also identifies Turnus with an older social model that is challenged by the hero, although he locates the contrast in two different systems of conflict resolution: on the one hand, the archaic world of chaotic private war, and on the other, the more structured approach of the Normans and Angevins, who strove to replace feuding first with judicial combat and then with a system of legal inquiry (pp. 156–60). Both these approaches are illuminating, but neither takes into account the moral (or rather immoral) dimension of Turnus, which is brought into sharper focus in the scene that follows the killing of Silvia's pet stag and the outbreak of hostilities between Latins and Trojans. His *acheison* in place thanks to this unfortunate incident, Turnus travels to Laurente to confront Latinus, and it soon becomes clear that he has already taken matters into his own hands. Without asking for his grievance to be properly considered by the court, Turnus informs the king that he has seized control of Latium, taken over the castles, mustered an army and received homage from the barons (lines 3855–58). Before Latinus has even had time to respond, Turnus effectively declares war on his own overlord as well as the Trojans:

> 'Ge sui pieça saisiz de tot,
> Ne m'en puez pas rien retolir,
> Ne ge n'en voil ploin pié guerpir,
> Et li tolirs n'est pas legier:
> Ainz an morront mil chevalier.
> Ou bien te poist ou bel te soit,
> Saches que ge tendrai mon droit.' (lines 3867–68)

'I have already taken possession of the whole country, and you cannot wrest any part of it back from me, nor will I give up a single foot of land; taking it off me will not be easy: a thousand knights will die before that happens. Whether you like it or not, know that I will not give up what is rightfully mine.'

Deprived of the support of his barons by this pre-emptive strike, Latinus withdraws, declaring that 'the woman and the land' will go to whoever can prevail on the field of

---

[17] Raymond J. Cormier, *One Heart, One Mind: The Rebirth of Virgil's Hero in Medieval French Romance*, Romance Monographs, 3 (University, MS, 1973), pp. 191–95.

battle. While this royal declaration (which does not feature in the *Aeneid*) might appear to sanction Turnus's actions, it actually has the opposite effect. By allying himself with a disloyal queen and forcing Latinus into an impasse, Turnus fatally undermines his own moral claim to the throne of Latium. How could a man who refuses to respect the king's authority and invests himself with the land *before* marrying the heiress ever be anything but a bad ruler? Eneas, meanwhile, finds his status enhanced by Turnus's *de facto* coup d'état. No longer just a foreign leader whose men have killed some local inhabitants, he becomes a legitimate contender for the throne, and one who holds out the promise of better governance than the home-grown candidate.

The subtlety of the Old French poet's rewriting of Turnus is underlined in the subsequent episode, which recounts the arrival of his allies in preparation for war against the Trojans. We have already noted that positive epithets and descriptive phrases concerning Turnus's valour and physical beauty are omitted from both the initial presentation of the character and the scene in which he takes counsel with his *privez*. This process continues in the description of the allies. Virgil's comment that Mezentius's son Lausus was the most handsome of all the warriors except for Turnus (VII, 649–50) is replaced by two couplets that make no mention of the Rutulian: in this version, Lausus's beauty is unrivalled (lines 3913–16). The Old French text likewise omits the portrait of Turnus 'of wondrous frame, holding sword in hand, and by a whole head o'ertopping all' (VII, 783–84) at the head of a 'cloud of infantry' (VII, 793) covering the plain. In the *Aeneid*, this portrait provides a fitting climax to the account of the massing of Turnus's male allies, and ensures that the prince is not overshadowed by the description of Camilla that follows. This careful balancing is deliberately written out in *Eneas*, where a passing reference to Turnus's having assembled a huge army (line 3956) leads into a vastly expanded portrait of Camille (148 lines, as opposed to Virgil's fifteen) that threatens completely to eclipse the nominal leader of the allied forces.[18] Moreover, Camille is explicitly credited with qualities that are by implication lacking in Turnus:

> A mervoille par estoit bele
> Et molt estoit de grant poeir;
> Ne fu fame de son savoir.
> Molt ert sage, proz et cortoise
> Et molt demenot grant richoise;
> A mervoille tenoit bien terre. (lines 3962–67)

She was extraordinarily beautiful and had great authority; never was there a woman of her intelligence. She was possessed of wisdom, valour and courtliness and wielded power magnificently; she governed her lands extraordinarily well.[19]

---

[18] The definitive analysis of the figure of Camille remains Aimé Petit, 'La reine Camille dans le *Roman d'Enéas*', *Les Lettres Romanes* 36 (1982), 5–40. Petit notes that 'nous avons moins affaire à une amplification qu'à une authentique recréation' (p. 6).

[19] *Richoise* has connotations of both wealth and power: lines 3966–67 imply that Camille establishes her authority as a ruler by the judicious display of material wealth (such as her incomparable mantle) as well as by appropriate political and military action.

It would have been easy enough for our poet to mark Turnus out as the villain of the piece by attaching a range of negative epithets to his name, a technique that Benoît de Sainte-Maure was to adopt with devastating effect for the opponents of William the Conqueror in his *Chronique des ducs de Normandie*.[20] Yet if Turnus had been described from the outset by the narrator as 'orgoillos e felon' like Roger de Tosny and his sons, Eneas's victory would have been diminished by the obvious unworthiness of his opponent, and some of the force of the political lesson that it conveys would have been lost. The vernacular text relies instead on the power of implicit contrast, by stripping out some of the positive elements of Virgil's characterisation and setting Turnus alongside a leader whose superlative qualities remind us that we have not heard similar praise of her fellow combatant.

This dual strategy – of inviting reflection on Turnus's errors of judgement while foregrounding virtues in others that are conspicuously absent from his make-up – is sustained throughout the long account of the war for control of Latium, in a series of both major and minor modifications of Virgil's text. Two examples, one from the beginning and one from the end of the conflict, illustrate the way in which direct speech, in particular, is used as a tool for conditioning our perceptions of the character. In *Eneas*, the description of Turnus's allies is followed by a council scene that has no counterpart in the *Aeneid*. Over the course of 136 lines, the Rutulian prince sets out his grievances and the barons debate whether to hold talks with the Trojans or to attack them the next morning. This scene reminds the Old French audience that war is still not inevitable, and in so doing lays responsibility for the ensuing carnage firmly at the door of those who turn their backs on negotiation. Turnus's address to the barons is skilfully designed to undermine the reader's faith in his integrity by presenting a version of previous events that we know to be untrue. We have been told that Turnus seized control of Latinus's territory before confronting him, and we know that he never formally asked the king to honour their agreement. The allies hear a rather different story. According to Turnus, the old king invested power in him when he promised him Lavine's hand in marriage:

> 'Sa fille m'a doné a fene
> Et sa terre tot ansement,
> Sanz nul autre retenement;
> Otroié l'ont tuit li baron;
> Il n'a chastel, tor ne donjon
> Dont il ne m'a pieça saisi.'   (lines 4130–35)

'He has bestowed his daughter on me in marriage, and likewise his whole territory, without any exclusions, and all the barons have given their approval; there is not a single castle, tower or keep that he has not already invested me with.'

The spin continues as the speaker goes on to claim that he sought redress in vain for the breaking of the agreement:

> 'Toz mes covenanz me retrait

---

[20] See Penny Eley, 'L'image du Conquérant et de ses opposants chez Benoît de Sainte-Maure' in *Guillaume le Conquérant face aux défis: Actes du colloque de Dives-sur-Mer des 17 et 18 septembre 2005*, ed. Huguette Legros, Medievalia 66 (Orléans, 2008), pp. 17–30, at pp. 26–28.

> Et tot l'otroi qu'il m'avoit fait.
> Ge l'an ai puis asez requis.'   (lines 4153–55)

'He is withdrawing the agreement he made with me, and everything that he had granted to me. I have subsequently sought from him extensive redress.'

The use in line 4155 of the polysemous adverb *asez*, which can be translated as either 'at length' or 'many times' or 'sufficiently', suggests that Turnus is deliberately encouraging his hearers to believe that he has taken a measured approach, making adequate or more than adequate representations to Latinus before finally mustering his army. The extradiegetic audience is invited to gauge the distance between this image of Turnus and the picture already painted by the narrator, and to draw their own conclusions as to his fitness to rule.

Some apparently minor changes to the confrontation between Turnus and Drances in *Aeneid* XI have a similar effect of implying that Turnus is lacking in key personal qualities required by a would-be king. This confrontation takes place during the deliberations that follow the death of Pallas; in *Eneas*, it leads to the decision to settle the outcome of the conflict between Latins and Trojans by single combat between the two opposing chieftains. Virgil makes it clear that Drances is a longstanding critic of Turnus, whose opposition to the war is motivated by envy of the Rutulian's achievements in battle as well as by his own shameful lack of prowess (XI, 336–39). The Old French text makes no mention of previous hostility between the two men, and omits any reference to envy: the narrator notes that Drances 'n'estoit pas chevaleros' ('was not a man of valour', line 6642), but does not link his anti-war stance to resentment of Turnus's success. In this version of the council scene, Drances represents a point of view that is not undercut from the outset by a history of bad feeling towards an estimable Turnus. Moreover, our poet develops Virgil's brief description of Drances's skills as a speaker and a counsellor into eight lines of praise for his *sagesse*, articulateness and good judgement (lines 6636–42):

> Drancés s'an est an piez levez,
> Un riches hom bien anparlez
> Et qui molt ert de halt parage;
> Nan ot an la cort nul plus sage,
> Ne miauz saüst an cort parler,
> Ne un bien grant consoil doner,
> Ne mialz contast raisnablement,
> Ne mialz feïst un jugement.   (lines 6633–40)

At this, Drancés rose to his feet. He was a powerful, very articulate man who came from a very high-ranking family. No one in the court was wiser than him, nor better able to express himself in court, nor to give good counsel in weighty matters; no one was better at setting out a reasoned argument or delivering a judgement.

Within the context of the binary opposition between Drances and Turnus as proponents of peace and war respectively, such insistence on the intellectual qualities of the former underlines the extent to which the latter is lacking in such talents. By presenting a more positive picture of Drances, the poet recontextualises Turnus's response so as to bring out the negative aspects of his determination to fight on. The

Old French Turnus may be a fierce warrior, but by leaping forward aggressively and accusing Drances of cowardice, rather than making a rational counter-argument, he reveals his own deficiencies. This Turnus comes across as a hothead rather than the level head that Latium will need to ensure its future success. Unlike Eneas, Turnus will never achieve the synthesis of *prouesse* and *sagesse* that makes for an model ruler.[21]

One of the most significant changes that the *Eneas* poet made to his source was to develop a full-blown love affair between his hero and Lavine. The hero of the *Aeneid* experiences passion with Dido, but his pursuit of Latinus's daughter is motivated by political considerations rather than love. In Virgil's narrative it is Turnus who is the victim of love, which combines with his *furor* to bring him to a tragic end on the battlefield. In this conceptual world, love is a disruptive force best avoided by those who are destined for leadership.[22] For the twelfth-century audience, things were very different. By the time *Eneas* was composed, troubadour poetry, Geoffrey of Monmouth's *Historia regum Britanniae* and Wace's *Brut* had already begun to popularise a different vision of love, as a positive social force that could ennoble the individual and inspire acts of greatness on the field of battle. Within this cultural context, if Eneas is to triumph over Turnus in the final combat, then he, rather than his opponent, must be motivated by a true and honourable love for Lavine. The Old French poet does not go so far as to remove all the references to Turnus's passion;[23] instead, he cleverly rephrases Virgil so as to suggest that the true object of the Rutulian's affections is not the young woman herself, but the wealth and power that will accrue to her husband. In the *Aeneid*, Turnus's feelings are unambiguous: during the deliberations that precede the final day of fighting, he is 'thrown into turmoil by love' (XII, 71), looks at Lavinia, and his eagerness for battle is redoubled. In the equivalent scene in *Eneas*, Lavine is not present, and Turnus declares his readiness to meet the Trojan leader in single combat in these terms:

> 'L'enor et la terre d'Itaire
> O Lavine quite li claing,
> Ce est la riens que ge plus aing;
> Tot li lais quite et tot lo prenge,
> Se m'en defail, sanz nul challenge.'   (lines 7748–52)

'If I default and offer no challenge, I will relinquish any claim to the throne and the land of Italy, together with Lavine – the thing that I love most – and I will cede everything to him and let him take it all.'

The syntax of lines 7748–50 is less straightforward than either Salverda da Grave's punctuation or my English translation might imply. We could equally well put

---

[21] This point is further underlined after the death of Camille, when our poet adds a short passage (lines 7262–70) describing how the knights, barons and peasantry from the countryside near Laurente offer their support to Eneas because they fear persecution if Turnus wins the war. On the importance of *savoir* and *sagesse* in the portrayal of Eneas, see Virginie Dang, 'De la lâcheté du guerrier à la maîtrise du prince: Eneas à la conquête du pouvoir', *Le Moyen Age* 107 (2001), 9–28, at pp. 20–26.

[22] 'Amour et fondation sont exclusifs l'un de l'autre dans l'œuvre de Virgile' (Marchello-Nizia, p. 252). The same point was made by Marianne McDonald, 'Aeneas and Turnus: *labor* vs. *amor*', *Pacific Coast Philology* 7 (1972), 43–48, at pp. 44 and 46.

[23] Although there is no equivalent in *Eneas* to Virgil's description of Turnus being torn between feelings of shame, grief and love before the final encounter with Aeneas (XII, 666–68).

commas after *Itaire* and *Lavine*, which would make the reference to Latinus's daughter more clearly parenthetical and reinforce the idea that 'ce est la riens que ge plus aing' applies to the kingdom – which is, significantly, the first thing that Turnus mentions in the Old French text – rather than to her.

This passage is at best ambiguous about Turnus's priorities and at worst another invitation to the audience to see him as a man driven by greed and ambition rather than by any finer feelings.[24] Read in the light of his recent reaction to the killing of Camille, these lines force us to consider whether there is any substance to his 'love' for Lavine at all. As Petit has noted, Turnus's response to the news of the Volscian queen's death and the *planctus* that he pronounces over her body are expressed in terms more appropriate for a distraught lover than a comrade in arms.[25] An impression is deftly created in these two scenes that the Rutulian's heart has always belonged to Camille, with the consequent implication that his pursuit of Lavine must be motivated by desire for her inheritance rather than true love. The treatment of Virgil's poetic comparisons provides further evidence for a conscious strategy in *Eneas* of associating Turnus with the sin of greed. Isidore of Seville identified greed as a key characteristic of the wolf, and Salisbury argues that the wolf was cast as the villain in medieval fables 'not because he was a predator, but because he was excessively greedy'.[26] It cannot be a coincidence, then, that the only simile to be retained in *Eneas*, out of the dozens deployed throughout the *Aeneid*, is the one that likens Turnus circling the Trojan encampment to a hungry wolf prowling around a sheepfold (*Aeneid* IX, 59 and 564; *Eneas*, lines 5370–90).[27]

The undercutting of Turnus's feelings for Lavine acts as a prelude to the development of a genuine romance between his rival and his betrothed. The council scene leads into a long amplification that describes how Lavine and Eneas see one another and fall in love. In the course of this episode, Eneas acquires the status of Lavine's *ami* (line 8383) and her *dru* (line 9123), while she in turn becomes his *amie* (line 9056), who inspires in him a love that is qualitatively different from what he had experienced with Dido in Carthage (lines 9038–45).[28] Lavine's love for Eneas is so central to her existence that she rejects her mother's pleas to accept Turnus, ignores the threat of being disowned if she does not comply, and resolves to commit suicide rather than marry the Rutulian if he should be victorious:

> Se Eneas i est conquis

---

[24] I disagree here with Michel Rousse, who takes Salverda da Grave's punctuation as read, and concludes that the war between Turnus and Eneas is presented primarily as a contest between love-rivals rather than as a struggle for political power: see 'Le Pouvoir, la prouesse et l'amour dans l'*Enéas*', in *Relire le Roman d'Enéas*, pp. 149–67, at pp. 163–66.

[25] 'La Reine Camille', pp. 32–34.

[26] Isidore of Seville, *Etymologiae*, ed. W.M. Lindsay, 2 vols (Oxford, 1911), XII.2, 23–24; Joyce E. Salisbury, *The Beast Within: Animals in the Middle Ages* (New York, 1994), p. 130.

[27] See *Eneas*, ed. Jacques Salverda da Grave, Bibliotheca Normannica, IV (Halle, 1891), p. xxxvi. The French poet also uses this simile to foreshadow the final defeat of Turnus, by remarking that he, like the wolf, risks losing his skin if he persists in attacking the Trojans.

[28] We should note, however, that the term *fin'amor* is never used in the original version of the text: it appears only in a later addition found in MS D. See Aimé Petit, 'Eneas dans le *Roman d'Eneas*', *Le Moyen Age* 96 (1990), 67–79, at pp. 77–78, and Valerie Gontero, 'De l'amor celé au semblant d'amor: l'échange des anneaux dans l'épisode final du manuscrit D du Roman d'Eneas (ms. B.N.F. fr. 60)', *Littératures* 48–49 (2003), 5–17.

> O par mesaventure ocis,
> Ocirrai mei, ge n'en sai plus;
> Ja vive ne m'avra Turnus.' (lines 8745–48)

'If Eneas is defeated or killed by some mischance, I will kill myself, I have no alternative; Turnus will never have me alive.'

By the time Eneas finally meets and kills his rival in single combat, Turnus has been irrevocably cast in the role of the enemy of love, a victory for whom would be unthinkable: this new, Ovidian style of love has to carry all before it.

The scene of Turnus's death has provoked more controversy among modern critics than almost any other part of the *Aeneid*, with arguments ongoing as to whether Aeneas's action is justified or whether his refusal to spare his defeated opponent contravenes the moral values inculcated in him by Anchises.[29] The twelfth-century audience of *Eneas* would have found little to quibble about. The Old French poet's rewriting of Virgil's doomed general as a man of no integrity, a bad ruler and an obstacle in the path of true love means that death is the only possible outcome for his story. Once Eneas has learned from his past mistakes and has become a model hero, the binary opposition of good and bad embodied in himself and Turnus cannot be resolved by some kind of compromise between the two: the anti-hero has to be eliminated. The victory of *Amor* would likewise be undermined if Eneas's opponent survived to haunt his relationship with Lavine like one of the *losengiers* of lyric poetry. Logically, the Old French Turnus has to die at the hands of his rival, despite his offer to renounce his claim to Lavine and do homage to the victor. That the fatal blow is motivated by the hero's desire to avenge the death of Pallas surely makes the outcome more, rather than less, satisfactory for a knightly audience. As connoisseurs of the *chansons de geste*, whose code of honour requires a man to avenge the death of a companion-in-arms, they could not but have applauded Eneas's refusal to grant his opponent's plea for mercy. In the hierarchy of feudal values, magnanimity towards a defeated enemy ranks lower than the absolute duty of just revenge.

This analysis of some of the aspects of the *Eneas* poet's rewriting of the *Aeneid* points to several overlapping answers to the question of why Turnus was transformed from a 'splendid barbarian' into a medieval anti-hero.[30] The first is related to the overall problem of how to negotiate the role played in Virgil's epic by the pagan gods. In a Christian context, responsibility for Turnus's downfall cannot be attributed solely to Jupiter and his divine associates; the heroic status of Eneas would be compromised if his success were due to the activities of beings whom St Augustine had taught were to be seen as demons.[31] So the Old French Turnus cannot fail simply because he opposes the will of the gods. Our poet implies instead that his defeat is due in part to his opposing a force that came to replace the agency of the gods in the *romans d'antiquité*, namely love. Poirion suggested that the gods in

---

[29] R.J. Tarrant, 'Poetry and power: Virgil's poetry in contemporary context', in *The Cambridge Companion to Virgil*, ed. Charles Martindale (Cambridge, 1997), pp. 196–87, at p. 181.

[30] The description is taken from C.M. Bowra, 'Aeneas and the Stoic Ideal', *Greece & Rome* 8 (1933–34) 3–21, repr. in *Oxford Readings in Vergil's 'Aeneid'*, ed. S.J. Harrison (Oxford, 1990), pp. 363–77, at p. 376.

[31] 'Omnes dii gentium daemonia' ('all the heathen gods are demons'), Augustine, *Enarrationes In Psalmos*, XLVII: 15, XLIX: 2, and LXXVI: 15, in Migne, *PL* 36.

Eneas take on a moral rather than a religious significance, as the collective expression of a destiny to be obeyed.[32] I would argue that the transformation of their role goes further than this. The ineluctability of Fate metamorphosises into the irresistible power of Love, which forces Lavine to set her heart on Eneas ('voillë o non, amer l'estuet', line 8061; 'she had to love him, whether she wanted to or not'), gives the Trojan no choice but to risk everything in the battle for Latium, and bestows on him the strength of two men, thus sealing Turnus's doom:

> 'Se Turnus la vuelt desraisnier
> Molt le cuit forment chalengier,
> Molt li cuit rendre grant estor;
> Quatre mains m'a doné amor.' (lines 9057–60)

'If Turnus wants to contest my claim to her [Lavine], I intend to mount the fiercest of challenges against him, I intend to do the greatest of battles with him; love has given me four hands to fight him with.'

In this version of the story, Love has chosen Eneas as its champion, and has rejected Turnus as unworthy: if he loves at all, his feelings can never be reciprocated, by either Camille or Lavine.

A second possible answer emerges from reading *Eneas* against the historical context in which it was composed. There was a strong tendency amongst vernacular historiographers and their publics to read the past through the present, establishing webs of correspondence between figures from more remote and more recent periods.[33] Like Wace's *Brut*, *Eneas* stands at the meeting-place of historiography and fiction, and such legendary history was no doubt subject to the same strategies of reading as the chronicles of the time. There are some uncomfortably close parallels between the Italian episodes of the *Aeneid* and the events that brought William, duke of Normandy to the throne of a contested kingdom. It would not have been difficult for the twelfth-century audience to map Latinus onto Edward the Confessor, an ageing king who was believed to have designated William as his successor in preference to the 'local' candidate Harold Godwineson. Harold himself might then have been identified with Turnus, while William the Bastard would correspond to Aeneas, whose divine parentage could certainly have been seen as a form of illegitimacy – and we should not forget that the Normans claimed Trojan ancestry via the figure of Antenor.[34] If our romance was indeed composed for William the Conqueror's great-grandson Henry II, then it would have been a risky strategy to present the Harold figure in *Eneas* as a credible alternative to the incomer, and thereby appear to question the legitimacy of Norman rule in England. It would hardly be surprising if a poet working within this milieu were to create a more polarised contrast between the successful Trojan 'invader' and his principal antagonist.

---

[32] Daniel Poirion, 'De l'*Enéide* à l'*Eneas*: mythologie et moralisation', *Cahiers de Civilisation Médiévale* 19 (1976), 213–29, at pp. 217–18.
[33] On this approach, see Catherine Hanley, 'Reading the past through the present: Ambroise, the Minstrel of Reims and Jordan Fantosme', *Mediaevalia* 20 (2001), 265–71.
[34] R.H.C. Davis, *The Normans and their Myth* (London, 1976), p. 55.

Parallels might also have been drawn between Aeneas's victory and the accession of Henry II himself in 1154, when the sixty-year-old Stephen of Blois was replaced not by one of his own immediate kin but by the son of an ex-German empress and the count of Anjou. Here, too, a positive – or even neutral – portrayal of Turnus in the Old French text might have fed into the belief that Henry was a usurper rather than a legitimate successor to the throne of England. In this case, Latinus maps readily on to Stephen, seen by contemporaries as an ineffectual ruler whose realm stood in need of renewal and good government after the ruinous civil war against Henry's mother Matilda and her supporters.[35] If *Eneas* was written shortly after Henry's marriage to Eleanor of Aquitaine in 1152, it would be possible to read Turnus as Henry's rival Eustace, Stephen's elder son and heir apparent, and the romance as a prediction that Henry's claim to the throne of England will prevail, perhaps by force of arms. If, as seems more likely, the romance was composed after Eustace's death in 1153, it is less easy to equate Turnus with a real-life obstacle to Henry's ambitions, since negotiations to bring an end to hostilities by having Stephen recognise Henry as his successor took place later that year. While there is almost certainly some association between the composition of *Eneas* and regime change in England, it may be overly reductive to try to establish precise correspondences between characters inherited from a Latin epic and players in the real-life drama of 1152–54. The fact that the Old French narrative appears to mirror the events of the previous century as well invites a more fluid form of glossing, in which echoes of past and present situations combine to create a broader political meta-narrative.

We have already noted that Eneas seems to dramatise not only the hopes of peace and prosperity invested in the young king(s) of England, but also a new and improved form of political action. By the same token, our twelfth-century Turnus appears to embody both the real or perceived shortcomings of the previous regime(s) and an older feudal order that is no longer fit for purpose. The thematics of political renewal do not, however, require him to have the serious moral flaws that we have identified, nor do they call for such radical elaboration of the embryonic villain inherited from the exegetical tradition. The vernacular Turnus could serve as an effective foil to Eneas without losing either his honour or his integrity. Mora-Lebrun's reading of the second half of *Eneas* as a *miroir de prince* for Henry II more easily accommodates this negative portrayal of Turnus than the structuralist approach of either Baswell or Cormier. According to her analysis, the Old French narrative eventually provides in its hero a *summa* of the qualities required for good government and the foundation of a strong dynasty. In order to achieve this exemplary status, Eneas has to overcome his initial 'fault' (the reputation for cowardice and treachery inherited from Dares the Phrygian's retelling of the Fall of Troy) and reinvent himself as an ideal ruler. One aspect of this process is the casting of another character, Dido, in the role of a bad ruler. Not only is Dido a woman, she is also a slave to her desires, which Mora-Lebrun sees as a transposition of the key vice of *avaritia* (greed, selfishness and cupidity) that makes an individual unfit to

---

[35] The Anglo-Saxon Chronicle entry for 1137, written after Stephen's death in 1154 and so exactly contemporary with *Eneas*, describes him as a kindly but weak monarch who squandered the royal treasure and whose failure to impose his authority led to nineteen years of terrible suffering for his subjects: see *The Anglo-Saxon Chronicle*, ed. and trans. G.N. Garmonsway (London, 1953), pp. 263–64.

govern, according to the political theories of writers such as John of Salisbury.[36] I would take this analysis further and suggest that Dido is only a first sketch of an inherently defective – as opposed to outmoded – monarchy. The more compelling counter-example to Eneas is Turnus, who, as we have seen, is swiftly revealed to be a potentially disastrous king of Latium in the eyes of the medieval audience. Comparing Eneas with a female ruler is tantamount to damning him with faint praise, since by reason of her sex, Dido offers only a weak contrast to the virtues of the hero.[37] Good practice by a male leader needs to be judged in relation to bad practice by another man of equivalent rank and power; the role of Turnus is thus to complete the picture that was left unfinished in Carthage.

If our poet's *miroir* is to project a lesson in governance fit for an inexperienced ruler, it needs to magnify rather than reflect Virgil's subtle contrasting of Aeneas and his rival. As a result, his portrayal of Turnus is forced towards the other pole in the binary opposition between good and bad monarchy, Christ and Satan, virtue and vice. As a negative exemplum, the Old French Turnus will have to demonstrate the most fundamental flaws of twelfth-century leadership; this in turn helps to explain the particular orientation of our poet's rewriting of the *Aeneid*. His omission of any physical or moral portrait of Turnus removes some of the constraints inherited from Virgil, and opens up a space for reconfiguring Eneas's opponent in terms of key transgressions of the feudal value-system. This man's subservience to the queen threatens to place Latium at the mercy of pernicious feminine influence; by relying on her support and advice rather than that of his *privés* (whom he consults only *after* he has replied to the queen's proposal), Turnus undermines the mutual bond of *consilium et auxilium* that should exist between a feudal ruler and his vassals. Like the wolf to which he is assimilated, Turnus also becomes the embodiment of *avaritia*: his selfish greed for land and power leads to contempt for due legal process and coercion of his rightful overlord. And if that were not enough to damn him in the eyes of the courtly audience, his dealings with Drances point unmistakably to a fatal lack of *sagesse* and sound judgement in personal relationships as well as in affairs of state.

The factors that we have identified here all seem to have shaped the transformation of Turnus from a noble victim of forces beyond his control into an anti-hero whose own moral shortcomings are responsible for his downfall. Unlike Virgil's prince, the Old French character cannot be shown to struggle honourably against the Fates nor lose the struggle for supremacy because the gods have willed that Eneas should found a new civilisation in Italy. Nor can Eneas triumph simply because of the moral superiority attached to his Latin counterpart's lack of *furor*, that 'desire for battle-glory […] or for plunder, the satisfaction of revenge or hatred, the sheer lust of conquest' that characterises the Turnus of the *Aeneid*.[38] The desire for glory on the field of battle is a positive trait in medieval heroes, as is the fulfilment of

---

[36] *L'«Enéide» medieval et la naissance du roman*, pp. 187–205.
[37] Dang notes how the *Eneas* poet uses the reactions of the Trojan envoys to foreground the fact that Carthage does not have a 'proper' ruler, only '[une] femme exerçant la royauté' (p. 19). Petit argues that Camille functions as the antithesis of Dido while offering a more nuanced contrast with Pallas ('La Reine Camille', pp. 21–25). He does not, however, discuss the way in which Camille also serves as a foil to Turnus.
[38] Otis, p. 315.

feudal obligations inherent in acts of vengeance. Turnus's failure therefore has to be motivated in terms that are as compelling for the twelfth-century audience as these were for Virgil's, yet he must also remain a worthy adversary for a hero who has still to prove himself as a military commander and thereby establish his fitness to rule. Superficially, the Old French Turnus is an accomplished warrior who follows very much the same trajectory as the Turnus of the *Aeneid*, but his words and actions point to a different underlying story. Looking behind the surface narrative, we find that his role is progressively recontextualised so that any claim to heroic status on his part is undermined and the audience is left to reflect on the image of a thoroughly bad prince whose failure throws the success of Eneas into even sharper relief.

2
Alexander the Great

David Ashurst

Quo tendit tua, Magne, fames? quis finis habendi,
Querendi quis erit modus aut que meta laborum?
Nil agis, o demens. licet omnia clauseris uno
Regna sub imperio totumque subegeris orbem,
Semper egenus eris.[1]

Great One, where will your hunger lead? What end
will come of grasping? Pray, what bounds are set
unto your search? Where stands your labor's goal?
Madman, your works are naught. Though you enclose
all kingdoms in one empire, and subdue
the entire world, a pauper you remain
forever.[2]

Thus Walter of Châtillon, writing in the period 1171–81, upbraids Alexander the Great in what proved to be one of the most successful long Latin poems composed in the Middle Ages, the *Alexandreis*.[3] At this point in the account of his career, Alexander has returned to Babylon after conquering Asia and is poised to begin a new campaign in the west, after which, as he has told us earlier in the poem (in IX.563–70), he intends to seek the other world of the Antipodes because one world alone is too small for him. Walter's censure runs on for fourteen lines in all, ringing the changes on the madness of never being satisfied, and culminating in the ironic

---

[1] Walter of Châtillon, *Galteri de Castellione Alexandreis*, ed. Marvin L. Colker (Padua, 1978), X.191–95.
[2] Walter of Châtillon, *The Alexandreis of Walter of Châtillon*, trans. David Townsend (Philadelphia, 1996), p. 175. Townsend provides the most readable English translation of the poem; the wording is at times closer to that of the Latin original in the prose version found in Walter of Châtillon, *The Alexandreis*, trans. R. Telfryn Pritchard (Toronto, 1986).
[3] Maura K. Lafferty, *Walter of Châtillon's* Alexandreis: *Epic and the Problem of Historical Understanding*, Publications of the Journal of Medieval Latin 2 (Turnhout, 1998), offers a significant study; for the dating of the poem, see pp. 183–89. The success of the *Alexandreis* in the Middle Ages is indicated by the survival of more than two hundred medieval manuscripts of the work (listed in Colker's edition, pp. xxxiii–xxxviii) and the existence of medieval translations in Spanish, German, Dutch, Czech and Norse; for details of the translations see George Cary, *The Medieval Alexander*, ed. D.J.A. Ross (Cambridge, 1956), pp. 64–66. David Ashurst, *The Ethics of Empire in the Saga of Alexander the Great*, Studia Islandica 61 (Reykjavik, 2009), offers a recent study of the Norse translation and its Latin source.

announcement that a single drink will soon put an end to all Alexander's desires, for a plot to poison him is already afoot. At this point, however, Walter performs a startling *volte-face* and berates the gods and Fortune for the madness of permitting the death of such a man by such a means (X.205–206):

> Quis furor, o superi? quid agis, Fortuna? tuumne
> Protectum tociens perimi patieris alumpnum?

> O gods, O Fortune! What mad course is this?
> Will you permit your scion's death, whom you
> have so long shielded?   (trans. Townsend, pp. 175–76)

The correspondences in these two adjacent passages, most notably in the phrases 'nil agis, o demens' and 'quis furor... quid agis', show that Walter is drawing attention to two moral judgements that seem to be in conflict but which are to be held simultaneously: the first condemns Alexander as insatiable, a man who goes beyond all reason in his pursuit of further gains and yet more self-aggrandizement; the second affirms his superlative greatness by decrying his fall as an affront to reason, an event that cannot adequately be explained other than by recourse to the caprice of fortune or the malevolence of inscrutable powers. Taken together the twin apostrophes form a vivid and arresting example of a split judgement on Alexander, hero and anti-hero; it is one that appears again and again in the vast bulk of medieval romance and related literature about this most fascinating and extreme of figures.

The split runs through much of the *Alexandreis* itself. In the section of Book X that precedes the passages just mentioned, for example, Walter is at pains to distance Alexander from divine judgement by presenting his downfall as the result of actions taken by the anarchs of the underworld on the basis of rumour and misunderstanding: it has been suggested to them that Alexander is so powerful that he may eventually lead an assault on the infernal regions when there is nothing else left to conquer (X.95–100); they are aware of a prophecy that one day a certain man will harrow their realm by means of a wooden object (this would be understood by medieval audiences as a reference to Christ and the Cross), so they agree to destroy him in case he proves to be that man (X.134–42). Thus Alexander is cut down by God's enemies, who mistake him for a possible saviour of mankind. Despite these narrative manoeuvres designed to head off the facile conclusion that Alexander is struck down as a righteous punishment for hubris, however, Walter does not draw back, later in the same book, from allotting Alexander a deathbed speech in which the king rationalizes his imminent demise by saying he has been called to share the government and defence of Olympus with the senile Jupiter and inadequate Mars (X.405–17); for any Christian audience this must have appeared, at worst, as outrageous blasphemy or, at best, as the pitifully comic ravings of a man dying of poison, but in any case as evidence of deluded pride. Admiration for Alexander's sheer splendour and dash, nevertheless, is the motive force behind the writing of the *Alexandreis*, and it comes across in line after line, most famously at a point where Walter marvels at the achievements of this pagan conqueror and reflects ruefully that if God would only grant the French such a king, the true faith would soon shine throughout the whole world (V.491–520).

As it happens, medieval English literature, which will be the primary focus of this chapter, does not boast a translation of the *Alexandreis*, but Walter's poem was well known in England, as it was across Europe: as early as 1189, for example, lines X.448–50, to the effect that a small patch of earth now suffices the man for whom the world was not enough, appear to have been imitated in the epitaph of the English king Henry II, with whose court Walter may indeed have been associated; the poem was also used as a source of material used for decoration or as a check on veracity in *Kyng Alisaunder*, the earliest Middle English verse romance on Alexander that has come down to us; and Chaucer seems to have had the *Alexandreis* in mind, on the evidence of the whole group of particulars taken together, when writing the Alexander section of 'The Monk's Tale'.[4]

Chaucer, in fact, makes only sparing use of the Alexander legend across the whole corpus of his work: he makes a passing reference to Alexander as a paragon of excellence in *The Book of the Duchess* (ll.1059–60), brackets him with Hercules in *The House of Fame* (line 1413), and in 'The Manciple's Tale' makes a mere jest of a well-known anecdote about Alexander's encounter with a pirate (*The Canterbury Tales*, IX.226–34), a story that equates piracy with conquest and which in other hands could be used to undermine the legitimacy of imperial rule. It is Chaucer, nevertheless, who has bequeathed to us, in a manner that befits the greatest poet of the age, the pithiest summing up of medieval attitudes towards Alexander. In a mere forty lines of 'The Monk's Tale', which consists of a series of 'tragedies', i.e. stories of how the good fortune of the great suddenly turns bad, he touches lightly on most of the major issues that make up the fabric of medieval Alexander literature (but there is a striking omission, which will be discussed below). Everyone has heard of Alexander's luck, the monk says (*The Canterbury Tales*, VII.2631–33); he subdued the world either by conquest or because people were glad to submit in the face of his power (VII.2634–36); he brought low the pride of men everywhere (VII.2637–38); there was no one to compare with him (VII.2639–41); he was the acme of knighthood and generosity (VII.2642); Fortune adopted him as her own (VII.2643); nothing could weaken his resolve except wine and women (VII.2644–46); he defeated Darius and many other kings, bringing them to grief (VII.2647–50); he reigned for just twelve years after succeeding Philip, his father (VII.2655–57); he was poisoned by his own men (VII.2657–60), and thus Fortune at last, in the game of dice, changed his six to a one (VII.2661–62). After this, it remains for Chaucer to glance back over his own review in a lament of marvellous lyrical power (VII.2663–67):

> Who shall me yeven teeris to compleyne
> The deeth of gentillesse and of franchise,
> That al the world weelded in his demeyne,
> And yet hym thoughte it myghte nat suffise?

---

[4] On the epitaph, see Colker's edition of the *Alexandreis*, p. xix; for evidence of Walter's association with the court of Henry II, see Lafferty, pp. 191–93. *Kyng Alisaunder*, ed. Geoffrey V. Smithers, 2 vols, EETS OS 227 and 237 (London, 1952–57); see vol. 2, p. 15; all further citations of *Kyng Alisaunder* refer to this edition, quotations being taken from the B text (Oxford, Bodleian Library MS Laud Misc. 622). Geoffrey Chaucer, *The Canterbury Tales*, in *The Riverside Chaucer*, ed. Larry D. Benson, 3rd edn (Boston, 1987), VII.2631–70; all further citations of Chaucer refer to this edition; for the use of Walter in this passage, see Cary p. 252, but it is reasonable to be less tentative than Cary, given the collocation of themes.

So ful was his corage of heigh emprise.

What is most striking in this passage, apart from the keen sense of the glory that has departed and of the way life somehow destroys greatness of heart, is the insouciance with which the monk alludes to the theme of Alexander's insatiability, here construed as high knightly courage ('emprise') rather than greed. It indicates a willingness to make the best of Alexander on the basis of received material that, as the monk says, is so well-known that everyone has heard something if not all about his fortune. In the section as a whole, in fact, the only concession to definite criticism is the admission, in VII.2644–45, that Alexander sometimes showed a weakness for wine and women, and even this is passed over swiftly in a way that throws emphasis on the fact that nothing else could soften his will to continue with the serious business of empire building. The emphasis on a positive estimation of Alexander accords, indeed, with the passing references to his glory and might in *The Book of the Duchess* and *The House of Fame*. The deflection of a potentially devastating criticism, which we see in connection with the idea that Alexander could not be satisfied even by possessing the whole world, however, resembles the re-channelling of the pirate story in the 'The Manciple's Tale' inasmuch as both references unavoidably, or perhaps slyly, draw attention to the criticism through the very act of neutralising it. All in all, therefore, it would be fair to say that Chaucer, through his various personae, makes light of the darkness in the Alexander legend; but the darkness is there. The split judgement noted in connection with Walter of Châtillon is in evidence even here although the split has been subject to partial mending.

One of the points likely to create the greatest difficulty for the modern reader who wishes to develop a proper appreciation of medieval accounts of Alexander is the assertion that the Macedonian king became sole ruler of the entire world. However absurd the idea may seem to us, it loomed large in medieval minds: Chaucer, for example, alludes to it no less than four times in the forty lines of the relevant section of 'The Monk's Tale', noting in VII.2634–36 in particular that although Alexander did not win every part of the world by direct conquest, such was his fame that all the remaining nations subjected themselves to him in return for peace. The story of the capitulation is told fully by Walter of Châtillon in the *Alexandreis* X.216–48, where it forms part of the elaborately contrived climax of the poem. It would be a mistake, however, to regard the episode as a mere flight of poetic fancy, since Walter's source, as revealed by Colker's *apparatus fontium* for the relevant lines, was the *Epitoma historiarum Philippicarum* of Justinus.[5] This was a respected work of historiography, probably composed in the second or third century: in England it formed a major source of Ranulf Higden's very successful Latin *Polychronicon*, a universal chronicle finished ca. 1362 and translated into English by John Trevisa in 1385–87, the English version being printed by Caxton in 1482.[6] The

---

[5] Marcus Junianus Justinus, *M. Iuniani Iustini Epitoma historiarum Philippicarum Pompei Trogi*, ed. Otto Seel (Leipzig, 1935); for the account of the capitulation see XII.xiii.1–2.

[6] *Polychronicon Ranulphi Higden Monachi Cestrensis, Together with the English Translations of John Trevisa and an Unknown Writer of the Fifteenth Century*, ed. Churchill Babington and Joseph R. Lumby, 9 vols, RS 41 (London, 1865–86). For a discussion of historical writing on Alexander see Gerrit H.V. Bunt, *Alexander the Great in the Literature of Medieval Britain*, Mediaevalia Groningana 14 (Groningen, 1994), pp. 35–42, from which the information on Higden and Trevisa here has been taken.

main account of Alexander's career in Higden comes in III.27–30 and displays a critical tone adopted from Justinus, but references to Alexander in other parts of the work do not always reveal a negative attitude; so the split judgement on Alexander is apparent again. It is observable, indeed, in Justinus himself when he expresses a kind of exasperated wonder at the relatively modest forces with which Alexander set out from Macedonia, and remarks that he cannot decide which is the more worthy of admiration, that Alexander subdued the whole world with so small an army, or that he dared to attack it in the first place (XI.vi.3, echoed in the *Alexandreis* I.263–67).

Although Justinus was a significant influence in his own right, it was via the work of the Christian polemicist Paulus Orosius, who used the *Epitoma* as a major source, that he had the greatest effect on medieval Alexander literature, not least in England. In the early fifth century, when Rome had been sacked by Goths and Vandals, an idea gained currency that this catastrophe and other disasters had come upon the Roman world because of the abandoning of pagan worship in favour of Christianity; it was in response to this idea that Orosius wrote his *Historiarum adversus Paganos Libri Septem*, the purpose of which was to demonstrate that the pagan centuries had been at least as miserable as the Christian era.[7] The result is an exceptionally jaundiced and skewed overview of history, which condemns Alexander as a tyrant driven by bloodlust (III.18.10) but praises the Roman emperors Vespasian and Titus, father and son, for killing more than a million Jews who had offended the Father and the Son (VII.9.7–8). Despite its vituperative nature, the book was widely disseminated and details from it were incorporated into works that are not generally hostile to Alexander, especially the twelfth-century Latin version of the (Greek) Alexander Romance known as the J2 version of *Historia de Preliis*, which itself became the major source for the Middle English alliterative poems *Alexander A* and *Alexander B*, the former of which also uses Orosius directly. In addition, perhaps most significantly, Orosius was rendered into Old English at the behest of Alfred, king of Wessex, at some point in the late ninth century, most probably in the period 890–91 since a brief passage not found in the original Orosius refers to short-lived foreign incursions in a way that suggests Viking raids and may imply that the translation was completed before the arrival of the Danish Great Army in 892 posed a more serious threat to Alfred's kingdom.[8] In any case it is certain, and significant, that this Old English narrative, featuring a prominent account of Alexander as one of the supreme threats to the security of mankind, was produced in the context of Alfred's long-term struggle against Viking incursions.

The Old English Orosius is a translation in the medieval sense of the term, i.e. it paraphrases the original whilst making numerous adjustments. In general it preserves the criticisms aimed at Alexander in the Latin text and sometimes intensifies them, as is the case when Orosius (III.15.1) declares Alexander to have been even worse than

---

[7] The standard edition is *Pauli Orosii Historiarum adversus Paganos Libri VII*, ed. Carl Zangemeister (Leipzig, 1889).

[8] *Historia Alexandri Magni (Historia de Preliis). Rezension J2 (Orosius-Rezension)*, ed. Alfons Hilka, 2 vols, Beiträge zur klassischen Philologie 79, 89 (Meisenheim am Glan, 1976–77). *The Gests of King Alexander of Macedon: Two Middle-English Alliterative Fragments*, Alexander A *and* Alexander B, ed. Francis P. Magoun (Cambridge, MA, 1929); see pp. 19 and 21. *The Old English Orosius*, ed. Janet Bately, EETS SS 6 (London, 1980); for the dating see p. xcii; for the passage referred to, see p. 83.

his appalling father, and the Alfredian version adds a pejorative reference to Alexander as 'that drunkard' (*se swelgend*, p. 66) – thus combatively foregrounding a topic that Chaucer's monk alludes to so briefly and apologetically, as mentioned above. Orchard has listed and analysed several of what he sees as similar points at which the Old English account accentuates or adds to Orosius' negative portrayal of Alexander;[9] his statement that 'at every point, Alexander is depicted in the vernacular translation as much more bloodthirsty and unreasonable than in the Latin original' (p. 122), however, must not go unchallenged, for *The Old English Orosius* shows a markedly greater admiration than does the Latin text for the kind of bloodthirsty and unreasonable behaviour that accompanies courage and heroic prowess. An example is in the passage where Alexander finds himself cornered and alone in a hostile city and is wounded by an arrow but manages not only to defend himself until help arrives but to fight his way through crowds of enemies in order to kill the man who had shot him: here the Old English text (p. 73) considerably expands the Latin (III.19.9–10) in order to emphasize not only the loyalty of Alexander's men and their love for their lord but also Alexander's own courage, resilience and pugnacity. In this respect, therefore, the split attitude towards Alexander found in this work might be said to be the reverse of that noted in connection with Chaucer, for here the dark aspects of the Alexander legend are wilfully made predominant and yet the light of Alexander as hero glints through.

A rather different kind of alteration to the significance of the Alexander material in the source text is made by the Alfredian translator in connection with the capitulation of all the still unconquered nations just prior to Alexander's death, which Orosius (III.20.1–3) adapts from Justinus. Responding in particular to the narrative of this event but also reviewing the whole history of Alexander as it has just been told, *The Old English Orosius* ends the section in a notably different way by emphasising the need for courage and pugnacity (the virtues which, as mentioned in the previous paragraph, the translator admires in Alexander himself): whilst the Latin text (III.20.5–13) is content to draw its oft-repeated moral that people suffered more in the past than in the present, the Alfredian version (p. 74) notes that whereas people in the past feared Alexander so much that they were willing, shamefully, to cross the earth from the West to the East in order to sue for peace, people in the present are too afraid either to travel far or to defend their farms, even when enemies come upon them at home. Thus Alexander may be condemned for rapacity, but those who negotiated a tactical surrender when danger was far off are condemned more, and those who give up when war is on their doorstep receive the greatest condemnation of all.

At this point it is now possible for us to see three distinct responses to the idea that Alexander became the lord of all mankind through the self-surrender of all who had not been subjugated by force: Chaucer's monk claps his hands for the man before whom all the world quaked in dread; Orosius wrings his fingers at the thought that Alexander, more than anyone else, shows that the world has always been a bad place; but the Old English translator balls his fists in the knowledge that the courage and pugnacity of a man like Alexander must be met with equal courage and resolve.

---

[9] Andy Orchard, *Pride and Prodigies: Studies in the Monsters of the* Beowulf-*Manuscript* (Cambridge, 1995; repr. Toronto, 2003), pp. 121–25.

That everyone with any awareness had heard something or all about Alexander's fortune, as Chaucer's monk asserts, is evidenced by the Old English poem 'Widsið', which is found in the tenth-century manuscript known as the Exeter Book but which is likely to be a good deal older than the extant copy.[10] Here the poet refers to 'Alexandreas' and remarks that he was 'ealra ricost/ monna cynnes, ond he mæst geþah' ('of all mankind the most powerful [or richest], and he prospered the most', lines 15–16). The unusual spelling of the name, perhaps conflating 'Alexander' and 'Andreas', suggests that the poet or scribe knew little of the Macedonian king, as Hill notes in her edition (p. 96); but the one thing he did know and communicated to his audience is that things worked out better for Alexander than for anyone else in the whole world. What he does not mention, and perhaps did not know, is what the Middle Ages came to see as the corollary to this success, the sudden reversal of his luck that changed his dicing score from six to one, as Chaucer has it, and brought about a swift shameful end to his life. The idea of this reversal, which is what caused Chaucer to include Alexander in his list of 'tragedies', became one of the great clichés of medieval literature, a topos that could be alluded to even when nothing else concerning Alexander was mentioned. Thus Malory, to name only one example from almost the other end of the timeline of medieval English literature from 'Widsið', makes Sir Lancelot invoke the name and fate of Alexander to comfort himself for being forced to leave Britain:[11]

> But fortune ys so varyaunte, and the wheele so mutable, that there ys no constaunte abydynge. And that may be preved by many olde cronycles, as of noble Ector of Troy and Alysaunder, the myghty conquerroure, and many mo other; whan they were moste in her royalté, they alyght passyng lowe. And so faryth hit by me.

Taking logical priority here and chiming with Lancelot's sense of himself as a worshipful knight is the overarching background image of Alexander's majesty and power, but the foreground concept, the characteristic idea, is simply an image of a tremendous loss; it may indeed have its ethical complexities, just as Lancelot's predicament with Arthur and Guenivere has its ethical dimension, but fundamentally it is a loss that appears senseless, something that just happens and yet has such vast consequences that it cries out for rationalization or for some meaning to be found in it.

Authors writing about Alexander *in extenso* naturally wanted to surround the conqueror's unheroic death with meaning even if they could not, or would not, pin a clear meaning on the death itself – hence, for instance, Walter of Châtillon's elaborate manoeuvres, noted above, that involve the powers of the underworld while casting accusations against Fortune. A far more natural and humane treatment of the death can be found in the anonymous Middle English *Kyng Alisaunder*, which probably dates to the early fourteenth century; though taking the *Alexandreis* as a

---

[10] 'Widsið' is in *Old English Minor Heroic Poems*, ed. Joyce Hill, 3rd ed. (Durham, 2009), pp. 31–36; the quotation is from this edition. For the dating, see R.D. Fulk and Christopher M. Cain, *A History of Old English Literature* (Oxford, 2005), p. 219, where it is noted that the Age of Bede in the early eighth century is at least as likely a time as the tenth century for a monkish poet to have culled names from Latin as well as other sources, as is the case in this poem.

[11] Sir Thomas Malory, *Works*, ed. Eugène Vinaver, 2nd edn (London, 1971), p. 697.

minor source as previously mentioned, it is based primarily on a significant Alexander poem known as *Le roman de toute chevalerie*, written in Anglo-Norman towards the end of the twelfth century by one Thomas of Kent, who is otherwise unknown.[12] An especially attractive feature of *Kyng Alisaunder* are the so-called headpieces, i.e. brief passages of mixed description and comment that introduce the many sub-sections of the work and which may or may not be relevant to what comes next in the story; in the case of the section relating Alexander's death the headpiece is certainly pertinent and prepares for what is to follow by emphasising the simple fact that all power and beauty passes away (lines 7829–30):

> So strong, so fair, neuere non nas
> Þat he ne shal passe wiþ 'allas!'

As Alexander feels the poison take effect and death approach he laments for the effect this will have on the world, on his mother and sister, and above all on his men (lines 7853–61):

> 'Allas!' he seide, 'Ich am neiȝ ded!
> Drynk ne shal neuere efte more
> Do to þis werlde so mychel sore
> As þis drynk ha[þ y]do.
> Allas! Allas! what me is [w]o
> For my moder Olympias,
> And for my suster, þat so fair was,
> And for myne barouns, al þing aboue,
> Þat Ich miȝth in herte loue!

These are surely the thoughts of a loving and responsible ruler; and if the reader is inclined to view the lament as an example of Alexander's arrogance, since it assumes that the world will be far worse off without him, the poet rebuts this with his brief account of the woe and conflict (line 8012) that ensues once Alexander is dead, and by this final remark (lines 8016–19):

> Þus it fareþ in þe myddelerde,
> Amonge þe lew[ed] and þe lerde!
> Whan þe heued is yfalle,
> Acumbred ben þe membres alle.

Hence, in his very last comment, the poet reflects not on the existential meaning of the hero's fall but on its social significance, and in doing so he sums up both the strength and the weakness of Alexander's empire.

With regard to the fact of acquiring an empire by bloody conquest, *Kyng Alisaunder*, like many another text of the Middle Ages, takes a boldly approving stance, as is shown by one of the most delightful headpieces (lines 1573–82), where the sequence of thought is that there is banqueting, the storyteller is well-fed, Alexander is a noble man and lots of kings surrender to him:

---

[12] For the date of *Kyng Alisaunder*, see Bunt, p. 20. Thomas of Kent, *The Anglo-Norman Alexander = Le roman de toute chevalerie, by Thomas of Kent*, ed. Brian Foster with Ian Short, 2 vols, (London, 1976–77).

> Noyse is gret wiþ tabour and pype,
> Damsoysels playen wiþ peren ripe.
> Ribaudes festeþ also wiþ tripe;
> Þe gestour wil oft his mouþe wype.
> Alisaunder is a noble man –
> His ost telle no wiȝth ne can.
> Hij shippen alle in shippes gode;
> Þe cee ferd also a wode.
> Kynges, princes, of fele londes,
> Quyk hem ȝolden to his hondes.

As already seen, Chaucer's monk takes much the same sanguine if not positively sanguinary view, cheerfully noting that Alexander humbled the pride of men everywhere (*The Canterbury Tales*, VII.2637–38) and brought many kings to grief (VII.2647–50). Gower, in contrast, condemns Alexander as a warmonger in his poem 'In Praise of Peace' (lines 36–49 and 281–84) and makes room in the vast bulk of the *Confessio Amantis* for a good deal of criticism of Alexander, particularly in the summary of his wars and death (III.2438–80), which emphasizes Alexander's supposed greed, pride and unreasonable nature; it is perhaps surprising, then, that Gower also praises Alexander, elsewhere in the *Confessio*, as the worthiest man ever known, as regards conquest and chivalry (VI.2087–89).[13] Likewise Lydgate, in his huge poem *The Fall of Princes*, dwells with great vehemence on Alexander's killing of Callisthenes and Clitus (IV.1107–449), and although the section on the wars with Darius (IV.1604–2002) naturally places the emphasis on the downfall of the Persian king, this being the theme announced by the title of the poem, Alexander is not spared censure for unprovoked aggression (IV.1804–806) or for claiming divine status (IV. 1870–83); yet in this same section Lydgate admires Alexander for being peerless in knighthood (IV.1818), calls him 'this manli kyng' (IV.1863) and makes Darius thank him for 'his hih noblesse' (IV.1926). In his 'Ballade to King Henry VI', furthermore, Lydgate prays for the king to be given Alexander's magnanimity and conquests (lines 61–62).[14]

The connection between conquest and the manners that came to be seen as qualities appropriate for a chivalric hero – the features that even Gower and Lydgate found it in their interest to praise from time to time – is much in evidence in medieval treatments of a scene, encountered in versions of the Alexander Romance, in which the victorious Macedonian discovers Darius at the point of death from wounds inflicted by his own traitorous retainers. A relatively plain telling, translated from the J3 version of the *Historia de Preliis*, appears in the early fifteenth-century *Prose Life of Alexander* (p. 54):[15]

---

[13] John Gower, *The English Works of John Gower*, ed. George C. Macaulay, 2 vols, EETS ES 81, 82 (London, 1900–1901); all citations refer to this edition.

[14] John Lydgate, *Lydgate's Fall of Princes*, ed. Henry Bergen, 4 vols, EETS ES 121–24 (London, 1924–27). 'Ballade to King Henry VI' in John Lydgate, *The Minor Poems*, ed. Henry N. MacCracken, vol. 2, EETS OS 192 (London, 1934).

[15] *Die Historia de Preliis Alexandri Magni Rezension J3*, ed. Karl Steffens, Beiträge zur klassischen Philologie 73 (Meisenheim am Glan, 1975). *The Prose Life of Alexander, from the Thornton MS*, ed. John S. Westlake, EETS OS 143 (London, 1913); for the dating, which is not certain, and the

And than he went to þe chambre þare Darius laye halfe dede. And alsone als he saw hym he hadd grete rewthe & compassion of hym, and he tuke off his awenn mantill & couerd [hym] þarewit, & went and graped his wondes and wepid for hym riȝt tenderly, & said un-til hym. 'Rise vp, sir Darius,' quoþ he, '& be of gude comforthe. And als frely as euer þou reioysede thyn Empire, so mot þou ȝitt do, And be als myghty, & als gloryouse as euer þou was.

All the key details of this passage are in fact already present in the ancient Alexander Romance, but it is easy to see that a medieval audience would interpret as specimens of knightly courtesy the compassion for a defeated but noble foe, the freely shed tears, Alexander's removal of his own mantle so that he can use it to comfort the suffering man, the carefully respectful address to 'Sir Darius', and even the gesture of making the impossible offer to restore the dying man's kingdom if he can rally and survive.[16] Modern readers may find it difficult to see the passage as anything other than an ironic depiction of behaviour that is either absurd or appallingly insincere, and indeed some medieval writers were willing to exploit the ironies of the situation: Walter of Châtillon, for example, is surely making a pointed comment, in a corresponding but not precisely analogous scene, when he makes his Alexander weep over the corpse of Darius and then dry his tears on cloth of imperial purple (*Alexandreis*, VII.354). Whatever its inherent ironies may be, however, the scene in the *Historia de Preliis* and its derivatives is best approached in a way that takes it seriously and at face value, as it clearly was by the highly accomplished poet of *The Wars of Alexander*, who works hard to adumbrate its horror and pathos.[17] Basing his text on J3 like the writer of the *Prose Life*, he describes Darius lying amid his palace with terrible wounds 'Gird[and] out as gutars in grete gill-stremes' (i.e. pouring out like rivers in great streams from a gorge, line 3359). For a moment Alexander is transfixed by pity, but then he goes into action as we have already seen (lines 3364–67):

> Þan nymes he fra his awyn neke an emperoures mantill,
> And þat he couirs ouire þe kyng & clappis him in armes,
> With grym gretyng & gro[ne] & grysely terys,
> Bad, 'Comfurth þe, sire conquirour, & of þi care ryse.'

Certainly there is a controlled deployment of irony here, but unlike Walter's it is used to sharpen the pathos and take the audience deeper into the scene rather than to make the reader stand aloof in judgement. Thus the added detail of the *emperor*'s mantle serves here to emphasize what Darius has lost to Alexander, even as Alexander tries to give it back; and the fact that Alexander seeks to encourage Darius by addressing him as 'Sir Conqueror' reminds us that the Persian king was indeed a conqueror until the greater man appeared. The death speech that Darius then makes is the inevitable meditation on mutability, but it leads, as in the source, to the giving

---

dialect of the translation, see Gerrit H.V. Bunt, 'The Art of the Medieval Translator: The Thornton *Prose Life of Alexander*', *Neophilologus* 76 (1992) 147–59, at 147 and 156.

[16] For the ancient version of the scene, see *The Greek Alexander Romance*, trans. Richard Stoneman (London, 1991), II.20 (p. 109).

[17] *The Wars of Alexander*, ed. Hoyt N. Duggan and Thorlac Turville-Petre, EETS SS 10 (London, 1989). All citations here refer to this edition. The poem cannot be dated more accurately than to between ca. 1350 and ca. 1450; see p. xlii.

of his daughter to his courteous foe, thus confirming him as his son and successor. Hence a courteous response to Alexander's courteous behaviour eases the transition to a new political reality, which Darius, as death comes upon him, foresees and approves (line 3440): 'Lat þan oure kyngdomes acorde & cock we na langir' (i.e. let our kingdoms then be reconciled, and let us fight no longer).

An aspect of Alexander that makes him unusual among heroes is his explicit involvement with philosophy and philosophers, which goes back to the historical reality of his being the pupil of Aristotle and to the condemnation of him by the Greek philosophical community following his killing of the sophist Callisthenes, supposedly for refusing to worship him as a god, an event that prompted a symbolic opposition between the more extreme of Alexander's heroic ideals and the views of those who claimed to advocate reason, measure or asceticism. This is the important topic, alluded to above, that is not mentioned by Chaucer's monk, whose mind runs rather on the externals of being a noble hero – on *puissance* and fine manners. In medieval literature, in fact, Alexander has many a conversation with philosophers and holy men, sometimes getting the better of them and sometimes being worsted, and in various texts he also becomes, after a fashion, a philosopher in his own right. The culmination of this development, it might be said, is *The Dicts and Sayings of the Philosophers*, to give it its English title, a work that was originally composed in Arabic, probably in the middle of the eleventh century, was translated into Spanish, from Spanish into Latin and from that into French; it reached English from French in the middle of the fifteenth century.[18] The popularity and importance of the work is indicated by the fact that one of several English translations was edited by Caxton and became, almost certainly, the first book ever to be printed in England. The longest of its twenty-three sections, each of which offers a somewhat fantastical life of a particular philosopher followed by a set of his supposed sayings, is devoted to Alexander, who also appears in the sections on Aristotle and Diogenes.

In the section on Aristotle (pp. 149–77), which precedes that on Alexander, the future king is suitably presented as the boy who must grow, under the philosopher's tutelage, into the wise monarch. This is also the theme of a separate and influential book known as the *Secretum Secretorum*, which purports to be educational material offered by Aristotle to Alexander, who appears in only two episodes, apart from which he functions merely as the recipient of Aristotle's wisdom, which ranges across kingship, military leadership and various medical issues; numerous English translations were made at various times, including one by Lydgate in collaboration with Benedict Burgh.[19] It should be noted, too, that Book VII of Gower's *Confessio Amantis* offers a different account of Aristotle's supposed advice to Alexander, so attractive was the general idea. The Diogenes section of *Dicts* (pp. 63–73) takes another line and presents Alexander, briefly, as a rich and powerful lord who must be

---

[18] For full information see *The Dicts and Sayings of the Philosophers*, ed. John W. Sutton (Kalamazoo, 2006); and *The Dicts and Sayings of the Philosophers: The Translations Made by Stephen Scrope, William Worcester and an Anonymous Translator*, ed. Curt F. Bühler, EETS OS 211 (London, 1941), pp. ix–lxii. All citations refer to the Helmingham Hall version in Bühler, which is printed on odd-numbered pages only.

[19] *Secretum Secretorum: Nine English Versions*, ed. M.A. Manzalaoui, EETS OS 276 (Oxford, 1977). *Lydgate and Burgh's Secrees of Old Philisoffres: A Version of the Secreta Secretorum*, ed. Robert Steele, EETS ES 66 (London, 1894).

told that his love of riches and power effectively makes him a servant, whereas Diogenes, according to Diogenes himself, is 'lorde aboue all couetise' and needs nothing that Alexander could give him (pp. 63–65). The philosopher also reminds Alexander that good works matter more than good looks (p. 67); he tells him that he can gain the grace of God by doing good deeds (p. 73); and he refuses to listen to a minstrel who is praising Alexander too fulsomely (p. 69). The Alexander revealed in the section of *Dicts* devoted to him (177–225), however, has little need of the reproofs directed at him by the likes of Diogenes, for here he is a deeply pious and moral king, marked by his Islamic origins though doubtless informed also by crusading ethics. Accordingly he tells Porus, king of the Indians, that God has enabled him to subdue many lands in order to avenge unbelief (p. 197); and to the Brahmans he says, 'My God hathe sente me to enhaunce his lawe in this worlde and to destroye the mysbeleuers' (p. 201). His piety nevertheless has its limits proper to a man of action, as shown by his remark on hearing a sermon that goes on too long: 'The predycacion is nat to be allowed that is ouer the powere of the herers' (p. 221).

It is essentially Alexander's nature as a man of action, albeit a thoughtful one, that puts him at odds with the Gymnosophists, the naked philosophers, when he confronts them, and with Dindimus, king of the ascetic Brahmans, when he exchanges letters with him, in sundry versions of the *Historia de Preliis* and elsewhere. This comes across well in *Alexander B*, also known as *Alexander and Dindimus*, a fragment from a Middle English paraphrase of J2 probably written in the middle third of the fourteenth century.[20] Since the paraphrase is close, the deviations from the Latin text reveal interesting ways in which the poet subtly tilts the argument in Alexander's favour.[21] In the opening section of the fragment, for example, the poet twice calls the Gymnosophists 'proude' (lines 5 and 11), thus going flat against what is said in the Latin text. 'Proude' is not necessarily a term of opprobrium, but its presence here does prompt the attentive reader to think of several possible lines of criticism against naked men who specialize in lowliness. In the same section the poet calls Alexander 'schamlese' (line 20): here the adjective, which is an addition to the Latin, is part of an alliterative phrase and probably has the positive meaning of 'unsullied by any shameful deed', paralleling the term 'makelese' (i.e. peerless) in line 1130, which is similarly an addition partly governed by the needs of alliteration; as such, 'schamlese' indicates the poet's approval for Alexander, but its allusion to shame also throws into an interesting perspective the fact that the people whom the Macedonian is about to parley with are nudists. Later – to take one more example, this time from the exchange of letters with Dindimus – when Alexander has been roundly criticized and abused by the Brahman king from an extreme back-to-nature standpoint, he says the following (lines 872–73):

> ȝif we lengede in ȝoure land – ful loþ were oure bestus
> To ben so simple as ussilf and suffre þat tene.

[20] For the dating, see Magoun's edition, pp. 100–101. For a general discussion, see Frank Grady, 'Contextualising *Alexander and Dindimus*', *Yearbook of Langland Studies* 18 (2004), 81–106.
[21] Magoun prints the Latin at the foot of each page. For a discussion of the poet's divergence from the Latin text, different from the one here, see K.H. Göller, 'Alexander und Dindimus: West-östlicher Disput über Mensch und Welt', in *Kontinuität und Transformation der Antike im Mittelalter*, ed. W. Erzgräber (Sigmaringen, 1989), pp. 105–19.

This remark about animals, which is an addition to the Latin, serves as a stinging riposte to the many insults Alexander has received, but it also gets to the heart of the intellectual debate, for it acts as a reminder that, to a man of the active life, ascetic saints only succeed in making themselves less, not more, than human.

Subsidiary to the topic of Alexander as a man of thought is that of him as an explorer, as a seeker of facts about the world, its fauna and especially its peoples. It is the aspect of Alexander that links his intellectualism with his restlessness, his intrepidity, his desire for ever-extending conquests, and ultimately with his fate as the man for whom the world was not enough. That the medieval interest in Alexander's explorations, and the medieval appetite for details of the strange animals and stranger peoples he discovered, was strong and constant throughout the period is shown above all by the popularity of the supposed letter Alexander wrote to Aristotle, his erstwhile teacher, giving him information about his campaigns in India, with much emphasis on the wonders he found there. The Latin *Epistola Alexandri ad Aristotelem* is first known as an interpolation in early versions of the Alexander Romance and thus forms part of the *Historia de Preliis* in its various redactions, but it also had currency as a separate and highly influential work.[22] The unique copy of a translation into Old English survives in one of the most important English literary manuscripts, the Nowell Codex, where it immediately precedes *Beowulf*. The copy, which is dated to around the year 1000, is West-Saxon but shows many signs of descent from an Anglian precursor, for the date of which there is no strong evidence; however, the work is in any case the earliest surviving translation of the *Epistola* into a vernacular.[23] There is also a fifteenth-century translation into Middle English.[24] Of the many texts that make use of the material in the various forms of the *Epistola* and supplement it with data of a similar kind, one could point especially to *Kyng Alisaunder*, which falls into two main sections, the second of which, announced in line 4747 and running to 8021, deals largely with Alexander's adventures in the distant east and contains much information on the wonders to be found there. The sheer bulk and density of this material, with its long lists of peoples and beasts, relative to the other narrative substance of the section, is eloquent testimony to the medieval interest in this aspect of the Alexander legend.

To return, in conclusion, to Walter of Châtillon and the split judgement on the Macedonian conqueror: the *Alexandreis* provides what is perhaps the most complex treatment of the theme of Alexander as intrepid explorer. It was noted above that in IX.563–70 Alexander declared a wish to visit the peoples who may inhabit the

---

[22] See Bunt, *Alexander the Great in the Literature of Medieval Britain*, pp. 6–7. For an extensive discussion of the *Epistola*'s history, see L.L. Gunderson, *Alexander's Letter to Aristotle about India*, Beiträge zur klassischen Philologie 110 (Meisenheim am Glan, 1980). The standard edition of the Latin text is *Epistola Alexandri ad Aristotelem*, ed. Walther W. Boer, Beiträge zur klassischen Philologie 50 (Meisenheim am Glan, 1973).

[23] The standard edition is in *Three Old English Prose Texts in MS Cotton Vitellius A XV*, ed. Stanley Rypins (London, 1924) but a more accessible version, with a Modern English translation on facing pages, can be found in Orchard, pp. 224–53. Concerning the Anglian element, see Rypins, p. xli; cf. Fulk and Cain, p. 161. As regards dating, Kenneth Sisam, *Studies in the History of Old English Literature* (Oxford, 1953), p. 85, takes the view that 'a certain uncouthness in the translation' points to an early date; however, the problems with such reasoning are obvious.

[24] *The Middle English 'Letter of Alexander to Aristotle'*, ed. Vincent DiMarco and Leslie Perelman, Costerus, New Series 13 (Amsterdam, 1978).

opposite side of the globe once he had subdued the world, i.e. the northern hemisphere; the latter aim achieved, he repeats the declaration, urging his men to accompany him in seeking the peoples of the Antipodes ('queramus…/ Antipodum populos', X.314–15) and telling them, in the true style of an heroic leader who is about to take his followers into the unknown, that no land will be inaccessible to them while he is at their head ('Me duce nulla meis tellus erit inuia', X.318). For good measure he explains that his basis for wanting to make this expedition is the fact that ancient authorities affirm that there are more worlds than one (X.320). By this time, however, Nature herself has taken offence at Alexander's plans, which she considers as a threatened rape, a ransacking of her secret parts (X.6–10); so she visits the ruler of the underworld to enlist his help (X.74–106). Thus it is she who makes the suggestion that Alexander might one day attack the regions of the dead, and who therefore prompts the infernal powers to set afoot the plot that brings about Alexander's death, as discussed above.

Does this mean, then, that Alexander, whatever the ethical status of his explorations and conquests may have been until this point, is now about to transgress a moral and physical boundary in such a way as to outrage the natural order? Does it signify that his courage has become an appalling insolence, that his confidence has become overweening pride, that his love of achievement has become a self-destructive urge to attempt the impossible, that in wishing to see and to know all things in the world he has lost his understanding of the world's nature, that in coming to rule the world he has forgotten how to rule himself? Is this what his heroic qualities have brought him to? Doubtless Orosius would say yes, but Chaucer's monk, if he knew the *Alexandreis* well enough and cared about its niceties, might say no. For at a point before Alexander embarks on his expedition against Persia, Walter contrives to have him visited by the Christian God, or someone who speaks with the authority of God, who commands him to leave his homeland and who promises to make him ruler of all peoples. The wording is important: 'omnemque tibi pessundabo gentem' ('and I shall subject to you every nation', I.533).[25] The terms of this divine promise beget the question whether the 'populi Antipodum', whom Alexander wishes to visit, are *gentes*: if they are, they are Alexander's by divine right and must be conquered. Augustine, as it happens, denied the possibility of their existence, on the grounds that the descendants of Adam could not have traversed the vast tracts of ocean separating the northern landmasses from whatever continent may be in the southern hemisphere;[26] from this it could also be inferred that if any sentient antipodeans existed, they could not be human. Not all medieval Christians agreed with Augustine, however, nor did they all think that human beings were the only *gentes* that inhabited the earth. If Chaucer's monk believed there were no peoples in the southern hemisphere, he would think Alexander was about to embark on a fool's errand, but he might also reflect that the

---

[25] The story descends from one in the *Jewish Antiquities* of Josephus; see *Josephus*, ed. H.StJ. Thakeray et al., 13 vols, Loeb Classical Library (Cambridge, Mass., 1926–65), 11.333–44. The usual wording of God's promise is to the effect that Alexander will subdue all Asia. For a fuller treatment of the story and its implications, see Ashurst, pp. 157–64, 231–33 and 248–50.

[26] See Aurelius Augustinus, *Sancti Aurelii Augustini episcopi De civitate Dei libri XXII*, ed. Bernard Dombart, 3rd ed., 2 vols (Leipzig, 1918–21), XVI.9.

pagan king, on the basis of his ancient authorities and the limited revelation granted to him by the divine visitant, would be bound in all piety to seek for other worlds where the promise of God might yet await fulfilment. If, on the other hand, he believed that the antipodeans existed, he would see that Alexander's intentions were fully covered by the divine promise and that Alexander would be continuing to act in accordance with God's will; but then he would be forced to acknowledge that within the logic of the poem the death of Alexander proves that God's promise had already been fulfilled and that there are therefore, according to Walter, no peoples of the Antipodes, in which case he would be able to fall back on the position already discussed. In this way Walter has confronted us with two possibilities concerning Alexander's intention to campaign beyond the confines of this world of humankind: either Alexander's heroic virtues have simply turned into the corresponding heroic vices listed above, or his virtues have been maintained even though they are now exercised in a way that is against Nature, and they continue to be energized by a real but now mistaken faith in the mission he has been given by God. If we choose the latter possibility (but really there is hardly a basis for choice), we must see that the problem of Alexander comes down to the problem of his being an exemplary pagan hero in the framework of Christian romance. Putting this a different way, it might be said that Walter is again drawing attention to the problem confronting the Middle Ages in dealing with Alexander, which is that the man whom the Christian God appointed to achieve more than any Christian king was not a Christian.

3
Hengist

MARGARET LAMONT

Hengist's Afterlives

Hengist enters medieval literature as one of its great villains in the ninth-century *Historia Brittonum* attributed to Nennius, as leader of a people 'amicialiter locuti, in mente interim vulpicino more agebant' ('friendly in their words, but wolfish in heart and deed').[1] In all versions of his story, he arrives with his brother Horsa and their men on the shores of Britain (sometimes by invitation and sometimes not) and serves as mercenary for the British king Vortigern against his northern enemies. He becomes so indispensable to the unpopular Vortigern that he acquires lands in Britain, after which he steadily widens the sphere of Saxon power and influence until he and his Saxons finally slaughter their British hosts in the infamous 'Eu, nimet saxas' ('take out your knives') episode,[2] turning the formalities meant to cement a peace treaty between the two peoples into a massacre. Yet by the post-medieval period this villain had become a heroic figure in English literature. A short survey, moving backward in time from the nineteenth century, conveys the sea-change in Hengist's reputation.

John Lesslie Hall's (1856–1928) poem 'The Calling of Hengist and Horsa' (1899) participates fully in the nineteenth-century vogue for 'Germanic Philology', which came to full flowering in Britain with the establishment of the Philological Society in 1842 and the Early English Text Society in 1864. Hall's poem presents a bard singing:

> Of earlmen of old, athelings, mighty ones,
> Sons of the gods, scions of Woden;
> [The bard] Urged the brave earlmen ever to mind them
> From whence sprang they; sped them on their journey,

---

[1] John Morris, ed. and trans., *Nennius: British History and The Welsh Annals* (London, 1980), p. 73 (Latin text), p. 32 (English translation).
[2] In the *Historia Brittonum*, this episode takes place at a feast. In its most widely disseminated form, it occurs after Hengist and the Saxons have been driven out of Britain by Vortigern's son Vortimer. They return after Vortimer's death, and Vortigern and Hengist arrange a truce to be confirmed at a meeting of the two armies. Hengist secretly instructs his men to hide long knives in their clothes, and at a pre-arranged signal (usually reported in distinctively Saxon language) to draw their knives and slaughter the Britons next to them. The successful ruse allows the Saxons to defeat the Britons and drive them, at least temporarily, into Wales. This version of the episode occurs in Geoffrey of Monmouth's *Historia regum Britanniae* and most Brut texts.

> Urged them to Albion, isle of the sea-foam,
> Land all lovely with leaves, blossoms,
> Forests and flowers, fairest and winsomest
> Island that ocean ever embraceth,
> Bountiful, beauteous; bade them possess it.[3]

Hall's attempt to revive Old English alliterative verse forms and his use of archaic diction such as 'earlmen' and 'atheling' correspond with his celebration of the Anglo-Saxon past and the Saxon conquest of 'Albion'. Early readers of Nennius would be astonished at this representation of Hengist's relationship to their island. Later readers of the many Brut legends of medieval England, too, would be startled by Hall's equivalence of the Saxon *adventus* to Brut's prophetic vision of the island of Albion which was destined for him and his Trojans – not to Hengist and the Saxons.[4]

Eighteenth-century treatments are equally enthusiastic. William Julius Mickle's (1735–88) poem 'Hengist and Mey: A Ballad' (1772) presents a love affair between the British Mey and the Saxon Hengist, here 'Offa's eldest son' (line 57).[5] Mey rapturously describes Hengist:

> 'His hair, as black as raven's wing;
> His skin – as Christmas snow;
> His cheeks outvie the blush of morn,
> His lips like rose-buds glow.
>   'His limbs, his arms, his stature, shap'd
> By Nature's finest hand;
> His sparkling eyes declare him born
> To love, and to command.'   (lines 37–44)

Also in the second half of the eighteenth century, Thomas Jefferson proposed that Hengist and Horsa be depicted on the Great Seal of the newly formed United States as 'Saxon chiefs, from whom we claim the honour of being descended'.[6] Finally, William Hamilton's 1793 painting of Vortigern and Rowena demonstrates just how much the Saxons' reputation had improved by this period:

> Hamilton's Rowena differs from the bare-bosomed, reclining temptress of the earlier canvases: here, she appears in a high-necked virginal white gown, with her hair tumbling around her shoulders, further signifying her virginity. She no longer acts as a passive tool of Saxon diplomacy; instead, she represents both Saxon womanhood and Saxon sacrifice, two qualities that are mutually inclusive in her story. Hengist and Horsa do not enjoy a secret

---

[3] John Lesslie Hall, *Old English Idyls* (Boston, 1899), p. 10.
[4] For the goddess Diana's prophecy to Brutus that the island of Albion was destined for him, see *Geoffrey of Monmouth: The History of the Kings of Britain*, ed. Michael D. Reeve, trans. Neil Wright (Woodbridge, 2007), pp. 19–21.
[5] Thomas Evans, ed., *Old Ballads, Historical and Narrative* (London, 1784), pp. 181–87.
[6] See *The Letters of John and Abigail Adams*, ed. Frank Shuffelton (New York, 2004), p. 212. The letter is dated August 4, 1776. For a fuller discussion of Thomas Jefferson's promotion of Anglo-Saxon language and culture, see Peter Thompson, '"Judicious Neology": The Imperative of Paternalism in Thomas Jefferson's Linguistic Studies', *Early American Studies: An Interdisciplinary Journal* 1 (2003), 187–224.

triumph as Vortigern falls in their trap; instead, they slump over the banquet table, looking as if they regret the sacrifice they must make of their favourite daughter.

But this sacrifice seems to have divine inspiration. Rowena is bathed in a radiant white light that emanates from her.[7]

By the late eighteenth century, then, Hengist was established as a sympathetic rather than a villainous figure in British history.

Even as early as Samuel Drayton's *Poly-Olbion* (1612), the attitude toward Hengist's arrival in Britain could be quite sanguine. In the Eleventh Song of the poem, Drayton writes:

> Nor could our men permit the Britans to descend
> From Jove or Mars alone; but brought their blood as high,
> From Woden, by which name they styled Mercury.
> Nor were the race of Brute, which ruled here before,
> More zealous to the Gods they brought unto this shore
> Than Hengist's noble heirs; their idols that to raise,
> Here put their German names upon our Weekly days.
> These noble Saxons were a nation hard and strong;
> On sundry lands and seas in warfare nuzzled long;
> Affliction throughly knew; and in proud Fortune's spite,
> Even in the jaws of Death had dar'd her utmost might:
> Who under Hengist first, and Horsa, their brave Chiefs,
> From Germany arriv'd.   (lines 172–84)[8]

The frontispiece to the 1612 edition further reinforces Hengist's elevated place in Drayton's historical poem. A female figure representing Britain occupies the centre of the page, and each of the four corners features one of the conquerors of Britain: Brutus, Julius Caesar, Hengist, and William the Conqueror. Though Drayton's cheerful assessment is not shared by John Foxe's *Acts and Monuments* (1570), Edmund Spenser's *Faerie Queene* (1590), or Thomas Middleton's play *Hengist, King of Kent, or The Mayor of Quinborough* (c. 1615–20), Drayton's poem suggests that by the early modern period Hengist's reputation had begun its ascent.[9]

We know some of the trends that influenced Hengist's more and more favourable portrayal over time, even prior to the rise of 'Germanic Philology' in the nineteenth century. Many of the founders of the United States of America saw in the Anglo-Saxons the roots of their most cherished political institutions, as Thomas Jefferson indicated when he argued that Hengist and Horsa should adorn the Great Seal because they represented the 'political principles and form of government we have

---

[7] Juliet Feibel, 'Vortigern, Rowena, and the Ancient Britons: Historical Art and the Anglicization of National Origin', *Eighteenth-Century Life* 24 (2000), 1–21, at p. 15.
[8] Rev. Richard Hooper, ed., *The Complete Works of Michael Drayton, Volume II* (London, 1876; repr. Charleston, SC, 2008).
[9] John Foxe, *Acts and Monuments* [...], 1570 edition <http://www.johnfoxe.org>, Book II, pp. 161–68; Edmund Spenser, *The Faerie Queene*, ed. Thomas P. Roche, Jr. (London, 1978), II.x.65–67; Thomas Middleton, *The mayor of Quinborough a tragedy* [...] (London, 1661).

assumed'.[10] Jefferson even believed that the Anglo-Saxon language itself was conducive to republican sentiments.[11] Such ideas can be traced back at least to Sir John Fortescue's fifteenth-century *De Laudibus Legum Angliae*, which argued for a continuous tradition of common law from the Anglo-Saxon period through to Fortescue's present. Influential English writers such as John Milton further popularized this point of view. In addition, Reformation thinkers like John Bale pointed to the Anglo-Saxon church as a precedent for a national English church largely independent of Rome, another idea taken up by Milton.[12]

The question arises: Are the seeds of Hengist's transformation from villain to hero present in nascent form in the early Middle Ages, or was his transformation the product of fifteenth-, sixteenth-, and seventeenth-century movements in political and religious philosophy? To answer this question, this essay attends to representations of Hengist in the most romance-like of British 'histories', Geoffrey of Monmouth's twelfth-century *Historia regum Britanniae*, and Wace's translation and adaptation, the *Roman de Brut*. Both these works, I will show, create Hengist as hybrid, neither hero nor villain, but occupying an in-between space that mirrors his position as both ancestor and enemy for many of Geoffrey and Wace's early readers.

Hengist and other Anti-heroes in the *Historia regum Britanniae*

By all appearances, the *Historia regum Brittaniae* – dedicated to Norman patrons, presenting a glorious history for the Britons, and virulently anti-Saxon – was written for a Norman and Welsh audience, not for those who identified themselves primarily as Anglo-Saxon or English. Yet, paradoxically, the most enthusiastic adopters of Geoffrey's material, outside of the Arthurian sections, were those who identified themselves as 'English'.[13] For evidence one only need look to the Brut narratives that multiply throughout the thirteenth, fourteenth, and fifteenth centuries in Latin and in all of the vernaculars of Britain. Such works include not only Wace's *Roman de Brut* (ca. 1155), but also *Laʒamon's Brut* (ca. 1200), Robert of Gloucester's *Chronicle* (ca. 1300), Peter Langtoft's *Chronicle* (ca. 1294), Robert Mannyng's *Chronicle* (ca. 1338), Castleford's *Chronicle* (ca. 1327), the seven versions of the *Short English Metrical Chronicle* (late-thirteenth to early-fourteenth century), the Anglo-Norman prose *Brut* (earliest version ca. 1272, later versions ca. 1333), the Middle English prose *Brut* (ca. 1380), and Higden's *Polychronicon* (ca. 1330). English Brut narratives continued well into the early modern period with Holinshed's *Chronicles* and Stowe's *Chronicles*, and legendary characters such as Brutus, Corineus, and the giant Gogmagog appeared in royal and civic pageantry throughout the period. Thus the reception of the *Historia*

---

[10] Shuffelton, p. 212.
[11] Thompson, 'Judicious Neology', p. 210.
[12] For Milton's representation of the Saxons and a general overview of Reformation English attitudes toward the ancient British and Anglo-Saxon past, see Nicholas von Maltzahn, *Milton's 'History of Britain': Republican Historiography in the English Revolution* (Oxford, 1991), especially the chapters 'Culture and Conquest: Milton and the Saxons' (pp. 166–97) and 'The Reticent *History*: Milton, the Ancient Constitution, and the Feudal Law' (pp. 198–223).
[13] Material from Geoffrey's *Historia* was also very popular in Wales. More than fifty manuscripts of Welsh versions of the *Historia regum Britanniae* survive; these versions are titled *Brut y Brenhinedd*. See *Brut y Brenhinedd: Cotton Cleopatra Version*, ed. and trans. John Jay Parry, (Cambridge, MA, 1937); also *Brut y Brenhinedd: Llanstephan MS 1 Version*, ed. Brynley F. Roberts (Dublin, 1971).

regum, as suggested by changes made in these later texts, should form part of our understanding of the processes at work in transforming Hengist from Nennius's villain to the nineteenth century's hero. In particular, they point us to aspects of the *Historia* that were ripe for reworking or expansion.

Even in Geoffrey's *Historia*, where relations between the Britons and the Saxons swiftly sour along the pattern of Nennius's account, Hengist makes a good first impression. He and Horsa appear in Britain as 'duos germanos; nam ipsi prae ceteris et nobilitate et decore praeminebant' ('two brothers, who, noble and handsome, stood out from their men').[14] Elsewhere I have discussed how Saxon good looks in Brut narratives often foreshadow their later conversion to Christianity, motivated by Gregory the Great's appreciation of their angelic beauty.[15] Here, it is simply relevant to note that neither Gildas nor Nennius gives any indication of Hengist's noble bearing and handsome good looks, nor does the Anglo-Saxon Bede. Though Geoffrey's Saxons later degenerate into a 'nefandam gentem' ('a terrible people'),[16] we may perhaps see the germ of their later transformation in his noble and handsome brothers. It remains, however, only a germ, because Hengist rapidly deteriorates into a man who employs – even embodies – 'noua proditione' ('unheard-of treachery').[17]

However, for readers of Geoffrey's *Historia* who identified themselves wholly or in part as Anglo-Saxon English, Hengist was not just a villain but also a distant ancestor. For Bede and his early readers, the Saxons' conversion to Christianity marked a radical transformation that rendered their pre-Christian past more or less irrelevant. So for Bede, Hengist's character was not terribly important. Indeed, since Bede attributed the triumph of the pagan Saxons over the Christian Britons to God's desire to punish the Britons for their sins, Hengist's treachery even appears as part of God's plan for Britain. By contrast, Geoffrey's entire *Historia*, and the secular Brut narratives to which it gave rise, spring from the premise that ancestry, here embodied in the ancient deeds of the Britons, matters.[18] For Geoffrey himself, and certainly for those of his readers who identified themselves as Welsh, the pre-Christian British kings whose lives he describes were a source of pride. Readers of the *Historia* who identified themselves as English, however, would see themselves reflected as much, or more, in the villainous Hengist.

Geoffrey presents the Saxons as dangerous outsiders who are unconnected – and intrinsically hostile – to the Britons. But another group in the *Historia*, the Romans, elicits from the Britons the same feeling of simultaneous familiarity and hostility that the Saxons might elicit from later English readers who saw themselves as, in some

---

[14] Reeve and Wright, pp. 124–25.
[15] See Margaret Lamont, 'Becoming English: Ronwenne's Wassail, Language, and National Identity in the Middle English Prose *Brut*', *Studies in Philology* 107 (2010) 283–309, at p. 292 and footnote 12.
[16] Reeve and Wright, p. 137, translation mine.
[17] Reeve and Wright, pp. 134–35.
[18] For the rise of genealogical models of history in the twelfth century, see especially R. Howard Bloch, *Etymologies and Genealogies: A Literary Anthropology of the French Middle Ages* (Chicago, 1983); Gabrielle Spiegel, *Romancing the Past: the Rise of Vernacular Prose Historiography in Thirteenth-Century France* (Los Angeles, 1993); and Francis Ingledew, 'The Book of Troy and the Genealogical Construction of History: The Case of Geoffrey of Monmouth's *Historia regum Britanniae*', *Speculum* 69 (1994), 665–704.

measure, descended from those very invaders. An examination of Geoffrey's portrayal of the Romans opens up a number of new interpretive possibilities for later readers troubled by a sense of ancestral relationship to the Saxons.

Romans enter the *Historia* as blood relatives to the Britons. As Julius Caesar exclaims, 'ex eadem prosapia nos Romani et Britones orti sumus, quia ex Troiana gente processimus' ('we Romans and the Britons share a common ancestry, being both descended from the Trojans'). The British king Cassibellaunus concurs: 'communis nobilitatis uena Britonibus et Romanis ab Aenea defluat et eiusdem cognationis una et eadem catena praefulgeat, qua in firmam amicitiam coniungi deberent' ('Briton and Roman share the same blood-line from Aeneas, a shining chain of common ancestry which ought to bind us in lasting friendship').[19] Yet, as with the Saxons later in the *Historia*, these blood relatives (of Geoffrey's Welsh readers) bring not friendship but war and conquest to Britain.

Conquest, first by the Romans and later by the Saxons, follows a similar pattern in the *Historia*. In each case, the invaders come in waves, first repulsed by the Britons and finally triumphant as a result of internal British strife. Twice the Britons beat Julius Caesar back from Britain to Gaul, reducing him from one who 'prius leonina feritate fulminans ipsis omnia abstulerat nunc mitis agnus humili uoce balans omnia posse reddere laetatur' ('formerly [...] had taken everything from them and roared like a savage lion, [to one who] now bleated meekly like a harmless sheep, happy to return it all').[20] Only after Cassibellaunus alienates one of his own lords, duke Androgeus, do the Romans win a decisive victory. Androgeus sends Caesar a letter proposing an alliance and, with his help, Caesar finally conquers Cassibellaunus's forces. From this point forward in the *Historia*, the Britons owe a yearly tribute to Rome that entangles them in Roman politics, culture, and bloodlines.

The generations that follow bring frequent intermarriages between Britons and Romans. King Arviragus marries Claudius Caesar's daughter Gewissa; the Roman Severus takes a British wife, and fathers King Bassianus; Coel's daughter Helena marries the Roman Contantius, and their son Constantine becomes first king of Britain and later emperor of Rome; Octavius's daughter marries the half-Roman, half-British Maximianus. Even Arthur's wife is 'ex nobili genere Romanorum editam' ('a woman of noble Roman ancestry').[21]

With many good British kings fostered in Rome or half-Roman by blood, Geoffrey's attitude toward the Romans becomes increasingly ambivalent. King Arthur's final confrontation with the Romans, in which he defeats them decisively on the battlefield but is called back to Britain before he can conquer the city of Rome itself, is an almost perfect microcosm of the entire portrayal. Rome is at once cousin, enemy, Britain's double, and a measure of worldly power that remains frustratingly beyond the Britons' ability to match.

The same ambiguity cannot be said to mark Geoffrey's portrayal of the Saxons, but the general pattern of invasion is similar nonetheless. Like Julius Caesar, Hengist is driven from Britain only to return and, ultimately, to secure a lasting presence for his people on the island. As with Cassibellaunus, Vortigern's poor choices as a ruler

---

[19] Reeve and Wright, pp. 68–69.
[20] Reeve and Wright, pp. 72–73; my alterations in brackets.
[21] Reeve and Wright, pp. 204–205.

lead to the Britons' capitulation to the invaders. And readers of the *Historia* were only too aware that Saxons and Britons came to mix their bloodlines, as had the Romans and the Britons before them and the Normans, Saxons, and Welsh after them. Though Geoffrey's overt attitude toward each invading people differs, the similarities between the two invasion sequences suggest interpretive parallels that Geoffrey left dormant but later writers exploited.

Hengist and other Anti-heroes in the *Roman de Brut*

Wace's *Roman de Brut* demonstrates how these parallels between Romans and Saxons might be further developed, and Hengist made less of a villain and more of an anti-hero. His poem also shows what I argue is a peculiarly Anglo-Norman response to the mixed bloodlines and hybridization that characterize Brut narratives. Unlike Geoffrey, who appears deeply troubled by British hybridization with Rome, which he ultimately rejects, Wace embraces the Romans – like, one assumes, his Anglo-Norman patrons – and he seems largely untroubled by frequent changes in language, place-names, and bloodlines over the course of his poem.

In the *Roman de Brut*, Romans are unambiguously positive. Not for Wace Geoffrey's vacillation between approval of British kings who pay the tribute to Rome and scorn for Romans who try to impose their will on Britain (most famously, the emperor Lucius, who tries to force Arthur to pay tribute). Instead Julius Caesar enters the *Roman de Brut* as 'Li forz, li pruz, li conqueranz,/ Ki tant fist e tant faire pout,/ Ki tut le mund conquist e out' ('the noble, the strong, the brave, the conqueror who did, and could do, so much and who conquered and possessed the whole world', lines 3834–36) and a 'Savies huem… e bon donere' ('wise man… and a generous giver', line 3840).[22] Wace describes Caesar, even when fighting a losing battle against the Britons, as 'li pruz e li hardiz, / Ke unches ne fu esbaïz' ('the brave and bold Caesar, never disconcerted', lines 4291–92). Not only does Caesar appear positively heroic, but Cassibellaunus seems even worse than in Geoffrey's *Historia*; here he is known to be 'mult cruel' ('very cruel', line 4400).

Wace also condemns later British rulers who try to hold back Rome's rightful tribute, while Geoffrey often expresses admiration for them. For example, Wace describes how King Arviragus:

> a merveille se preisa
> E a merveille s'orguilla.
> Le treü as Romans veia
> Ne d'els tenir rien de deinna. (Wace, *Brut*, lines 5101–104)

had an exceedingly high opinion of himself and became exceedingly proud. He refused to pay tribute to the Romans and did not deign to hold any lands from them.

Geoffrey's claim that this same proud king 'coepit sensum et probitatem habere coepitque ciuitates et oppida reaedificare populumque regni tanta iusticia coercere ita ut longe positis regibus timori esset' ('began to show judgement and ability and to rebuild cities and towns, displaying such justice towards his people that foreign kings

---

[22] *Wace's 'Roman de Brut': A History of the British: Text and Translation*, ed. and trans. Judith Weiss, rev. edn (Exeter, 2002).

feared him')[23] disappears from Wace's account entirely. In both the *Historia* and the *Roman de Brut* Arviragus is eventually reconciled with Rome. But, characteristically, Geoffrey emphasizes British superiority to Rome by describing how 'diligebant eum Romani et timebant ita ut prae omnibus regibus sermo de eo apud Romam fieret' ('the Romans so respected and feared him that no king was more talked about in Rome')[24] while Wace, by contrast, paints a picture of peaceful cooperation with Rome:

> Arviragus, tut sun vivant,
> Tint as Romains lur covenant;
> Unc puis de rien ne lur falsa,
> Ainz les servi e eshauça
> Pur l'amistied de la reïne
> Ki nee esteit de lur orine. (Wace, *Brut*, lines 5147–52)

Arviragus kept the agreement with the Romans all his life; never again untrue to them in any way; instead he served them and advanced their cause, through affection for the queen who originally belonged to them by birth.

For Wace, unlike Geoffrey, political and genealogical mixture with Rome is entirely laudable.

As Julius Caesar and the Romans transform from Geoffrey's ambiguous figures to Wace's exemplary ones, so too Hengist and the Saxons move from nefarious villains to much more ambiguous, and sometimes even positive, figures. Wace goes far beyond Geoffrey's concession, cited above, that Hengist and Horsa are 'duos germanos; nam ipsi prae ceteris et nobilitate et decore praeminebant' ('two brothers, who, noble and handsome, stood out from their men').[25] When the Saxons first land in Britain, Wace reports that they are 'genz estranges.../ Od bels viaires, od gent cors' ('strangers... with handsome faces and fine bodies', lines 6706–707). He goes on to describe Hengist and Horsa as 'dous freres/ As cors bien faiz, as faces cleres,/ Ki plus grant erent e plus bel/ Que tuit li altre juvencel' ('two brothers, with their shapely bodies and fine faces, who were taller and more handsome than all the other young men', lines 6723–26). Wace adds that, as a result of letting the Saxons remain in Britain, 'Sempres fu la curt replenie / De mult gente bachelerie' ('before long the court was full of fine young men', lines 6815–16). Thus the *Roman de Brut* expands exponentially upon the germ of a positive portrayal of Hengist and the Saxons in the *Historia regum Britanniae*. Even when Hengist begins to scheme for more land and power, Wace notes approvingly, 'D'avancier sei s'entremeteit,/ Cume chescuns fere devreit' ('He began to advance himself, as everyone should try and do', lines 6847–48).

While Hengist eventually betrays the Britons, as he does in all accounts, he remains a more sympathetic figure in the *Roman de Brut* than he is in the *Historia regum* because he stays personally loyal to Vortigern. After defeating the Britons through the usual 'Nem eure sexes!' (line 7245) treachery, and thereby displaying what even

---

[23] Reeve and Wright, pp. 84–85.
[24] Reeve and Wright, pp. 86–87.
[25] Reeve and Wright, pp. 124–25.

Wace calls a 'quer felun' ('wicked heart', line 7207), Hengist prevents the Saxons from killing Vortigern. As Wace relates:

> Saissun voldrent le rei tuer,
> Mais Henguist lur prist a crier :
> 'Laissez le rei, maint bien m'ad fait,
> E maint travail ad pur mei trait.
> Guarder le dei cume mun gendre...' (Wace, *Brut*, lines 7277–81)

The Saxons wanted to kill the king, but Hengist shouted to them: 'Leave the king, he has done much for me and endured much hardship on my account. I should protect him, as my son-in-law...'

Thus, even at his worst, Hengist displays some good qualities, such as a measure of personal loyalty. No parallel speech occurs in Geoffrey's *Historia*.

Wace's more tempered account of Hengist's character and actions opens up new interpretive possibilities for medieval readers, and arguably makes him an anti-hero rather than an outright villain. The *Roman de Brut* invites readers to admire Hengist's good looks, intelligence, fierceness in battle, and personal loyalty. In so doing, they might just find themselves admiring his cunning also, or sympathizing with his frustration at the Britons' insistent refusal to grant him a permanent place in their land. He has nowhere else to go.

Anti-heroic Foundations in Medieval British Romance

Implicit behind Romans and Saxons in the *Historia regum Britanniae* and the *Roman de Brut* are the Normans who are the newest and most immediately relevant conquerors of the island of Britain in the twelfth century when both works were composed. If Hengist is, at best, an anti-hero in these works, then what of the Normans?

Francis Ingledew, in his influential article 'The Book of Troy and the Genealogical Construction of History', argues that Geoffrey of Monmouth implicitly presents the Norman Conquest as a triumphant return of the Trojan bloodline to rule in Britain through the Normans' Trojan ancestor Antenor.[26] In support of Ingledew's claim, 151 manuscripts of the *Historia regum* carry dedications to Anglo-Norman nobles, and none to Welsh patrons; it would be hard to argue that Geoffrey's narrative is so pro-Welsh as to be anti-Norman.[27] At the very least, the mere existence of the Normans' myth of Trojan ancestry set them apart from the Anglo-Saxons, with their ancestor myth of the pagan god Woden.

But if we accept, or are at least willing to consider seriously, Ingledew's arguments about the Normans as a return of Trojan rule to Britain, we must ask also whether Geoffrey's *Historia* promotes implicit links between Normans and Saxons. For Dudo of Saint-Quentin's *De moribus et actis primorum Normanniae ducum*, which first introduces a Trojan strain into Norman ancestry, also presents a story of Norman wanderings remarkably similar to that of Hengist. As Amanda Hingst explains in *The Written World*:

---

[26] Ingledew, p. 687.
[27] For a discussion of the dedications, see Julia C. Crick, *The 'Historia Regum Britannie' of Geoffrey of Monmouth IV: Dissemination and Reception in the Later Middle Ages* (Cambridge, 1991), pp. 113–20.

Denmark did not have enough land to satisfy the restless inhabitants, and so, returning to Dudo's account, 'according to a very ancient rite, a multitude of young men is gathered by lot and they are thrust out into the kingdoms of foreign nations, in order to acquire through battle a realm for themselves'. The first of these exiled Danes to be named by Dudo was Hasting, a mythical figure who along with the various 'vagabond nations' that he had gathered into his band laid waste to Francia before deciding to take his chances at 'the head of the world', the city of Rome itself.[28]

Hengist's description of his wanderings echoes Dudo's account of the early Normans:

> Fueramus etenim expulsi a patria nostra nec ob aliud nisi quia consuetudo regni expetebat. Consuetudo namque in patria nostra est ut cum habundantia hominum in eadem superuenerit conueniunt ex diuersis prouinciis principes et tocius regni iuuenes coram se uenire praecipiunt ; deinde, proiecta sorte, potiores atque fortiores eligunt qui extera regna petituri uictum sibi perquirant et patria ex qua orti sunt a superflua multitudine liberetur. Superfluente igitur nouiter in regno nostro hominum copia, conuenerunt principes nostri sortemque proitientes elegerunt iuuentutem istam quam in praesentia tua cernis praeceperuntque ut consuetudini ab antiquo statutae parerent.[29]

Perhaps it is a stretch to imagine that readers of Geoffrey's *Historia* would have made this same connection, or that Geoffrey himself had Dudo's Hasting in mind when he expanded Hengist's backstory to address why he came to Britain in the first place. But, coupled with implicit parallels between Romans and Saxons in the *Historia*, this possible link between Normans and Saxons suggests that Geoffrey may have been groping toward an accommodation with the Saxons, one that later Anglo-Norman writers developed more fully. After all, as Hingst points out, Hasting is a destroyer of lands and peoples, but his descendants improve.

What is certain is that from at least the twelfth century onward medieval British literature shows a propensity for an anti-hero of a very particular kind – the anti-heroic founding national figure. To Hengist and Julius Caesar might be added the Danish King Cnut, the Norman William the Conqueror, and, one of the most surprising foundation figures of all, the Greek or Syrian Albina. Though Cnut drives out the Anglo-Saxon king Æthelred and schemes to rid himself of the young sons of Edmund Ironside (always a heroic figure), he also shows great courtesy to his

---

[28] Amanda Hingst, *The Written World* (Notre Dame, IN, 2009), p. 25. The quotation from Dudo is from *De moribus*, i.1: 'collecta sorte multitudine pubescentium, veterimo ritu, in externa regna extruduntur nationum, ut acquirant sibi præliando regna' (Hingst, note 32). For Dudo of Saint-Quentin, see *De moribus et actis primorum Normanniae ducum*, ed. Jules Lair (Caen, 1865) and *History of the Normans*, trans. Eric Christiansen (Woodbridge, 1998).

[29] 'We have been exiled from our land, but only because the custom of our kingdom demanded it. For it is the practice in our country, whenever it becomes overpopulated, that our leaders come from its various provinces and order all the young men of the entire realm to assemble before them; they then cast lots and choose the best and bravest to support themselves by going to foreign lands, thus relieving their native country of its excessive population. When such overpopulation recently occurred in our own province, the chiefs met, cast lots, chose these young men you see before you and ordered them to obey our ancient custom' (Reeve and Wright, pp. 124–25).

enemies, so much so that Geffrei Gaimar's *Estoire des Engleis* refers to him as 'li bon rei Cnuth' and the Middle English prose *Brut* as 'gode Kyng Knoght'.[30] William the Conqueror, despite the circulation of various stories about the valiant Hereward the Wake and other Anglo-Saxon resistance fighters, remains a dominating figure in medieval English culture. Royal genealogical roles accord him a prominent place, families traced their ancestors to those who had accompanied William across the channel from Normandy, and the phrase 'after the Conquest' was used prominently in dating. Finally, Albina plots to murder her husband (in some accounts she succeeds), suffers exile from her homeland as a result, and, together with her sisters, gives birth to the race of giants that populate Britain before the Trojans arrive. Nevertheless, she also represents the first human inhabitant of the island of Britain and gives it one of its enduring names, Albion.[31]

Such problematic 'national' founders are common, of course. Brutus himself is a patricide, even if an unwilling one – a fact that medieval and early modern Scots were happy to point out.[32] For the Normans, Dudo of Saint-Quentin's choice of Antenor as their progenitor links them to the Trojans but associates them also with Antenor's dubious reputation as the betrayer of Troy (a reputation he shared, in some accounts, with the Britons' distant ancestor Aeneas). In France, Melusine's monstrous body problematises her role as the founder of the house of Lusignan. Even today, we can find a parallel in the Mexican foundation narrative of the conquistador Hernán Cortés and his Native American interpreter and mistress, Malinche. And it is this last, modern parallel that best dramatizes the pressures of a hybrid national identity, a feature pervasive in the literature of medieval England, particularly after the Norman Conquest (though not necessarily restricted to that period).

Genealogical Amalgamation, Anti-heroes and Medievalists in the Americas

A feeling of connection to both the oppressor and the oppressed or, to put it another way, to both the winners and the losers of a major cultural confrontation, characterizes both modern Mexican cultural identity and post-Conquest medieval

---

[30] Geffrei Gaimar, *Estoire des Engleis*, ed. and trans. Ian Short (Oxford, 2009), line 4350; and *The Chronicles of England*, ed. Friedrich Brie, EETS OS 131 (London, 1906), p. 125.

[31] The Albina narrative began as an independent Anglo-Norman poem *Des Grantz Geanz*, which is thought to have been composed in the late thirteenth or early fourteenth century to explain the origin of the giants who inhabit Britain before the arrival of the Trojans in Geoffrey's *Historia*. The poem was appended to the Anglo-Norman prose *Brut* and, during the revisions of the Anglo-Norman prose *Brut* into the Long and Short Continuations to 1333, was rewritten in prose. This prose version was subsequently translated into Middle English as the prologue to the Middle English prose *Brut*. For a fuller treatment of the Albina legend, see Lesley Johnson, 'Return to Albion', *Arthurian Literature* 13 (1995), 19–40; and James P. Carley and Julia Crick, 'Constructing Albion's Past: An Annotated Edition of *De Origine Gigantum*', *Arthurian Literature* 13 (1995), 41–114.

[32] See, for example, the Asloan manuscript, which describes Brutus as descended from '[th]e falss tratouris of troye' (*The Asloan manuscript: a miscellany in prose and verse written by John Asloan in the reign of James the Fifth*, Vol. 1, ed. W.A. Craigie (Edinburgh and London, 1923), p. 198). My thanks to Jaclyn Rajsic for bringing this passage to my attention. For a fuller discussion of Scottish resistance to English historiographical claims, see Katherine H. Terrell, '"Lynealy discendit of þe devill": Genealogy, Textuality, and Anglophobia in Medieval Scottish Chronicles', *Studies in Philology* 108 (2011), 320–344.

English identity. As Martha J. Cutter explains, 'Entrenched accounts portray La Malinche as a betrayer of her own people who facilitated Cortés's colonization of Mexico and then mothered a race of bastardized mestizos that eventually displaced the "pure" indigenous native population of Mexico.'[33] Here a medievalist might recall Geoffrey of Monmouth's plaintive description of how the Saxons diluted the purity of British blood: 'iam nesciebatur quis paganus esset, quis Christianus, quia pagani filias et consanguineas eorum sibi associauerant' ('no one knew who was pagan and who Christian, since the pagans had married their daughters and relatives').[34] Many medieval readers of Geoffrey of Monmouth would have identified themselves as just such a mixed people, whether they saw themselves as Norman (famously a community with a sense of mixed ethnicity), Norman-English, English, Welsh, or some combination of them all. Yet there is another side to Malinche's significance, and that of the anti-heroic national figures like Hengist that I have examined here. As Rachel Phillips explains, 'She [Malinche] disturbs the easy dichotomies into which, without her, the Spanish conquest of Mexico could be resolved [...] she made impossible in Mexico the easy dualism of Spaniard versus Indian.'[35] Instead of dualism, the dominant Mexican national narrative is one of *mestisaje*, or cultural and genealogical mixture. The final section of this essay turns to this push against simple duality and towards *mestisaje*, as manifested in Geoffrey of Monmouth's *Historia regum Britanniae* and Wace's *Roman de Brut*.

Genealogical mixture was indeed a hallmark of medieval English self-conception, as a number of scholars have demonstrated in recent years. Prominent among these is Andrew Galloway, who claims that

> Variable identity, a troubling feature of Englishness as Higden overtly states [in the *Polychronicon*], is seized on by many late-fourteenth-century vernacular writers as their common bond [...] They thus contribute to Higden's project of defining an inclusive contemporary cultural identity of 'England' in terms of the very problem of national identity that Higden so steadily contemplated.[36]

What Higden does is transform an ostensible force for disunity – England's experience of multiple conquests and the reality of multiple ethnicities on the island of Britain – into a force for unity. As Galloway explains, 'Higden's intense and self-consciously textual debate *about* England keeps and deepens the focus *on* England.'[37] The Normans, as Marjorie Chibnall has convincingly shown, brought a myth of themselves as a mixed people with them to the lands that they conquered, and it seems reasonable to make some connections between this Norman cultural attitude and later English developments.[38] But we should not forget that even before the Conquest, Anglo-Saxon England made a number of gestures toward a more inclusive

---

[33] 'Malinche's Legacy: Translation, Betrayal, and Interlingualism in Chicano/a Literature', *Arizona Quarterly* 66 (2010), 1–33, at p. 1.
[34] Reeve and Wright, pp. 130–31.
[35] 'Marina/Malinche: Masks and Shadows', in *Women in Hispanic Literature: Icons and Fallen Idols*, ed. Beth Miller (Berkeley, 1983), 97–114, at pp. 113–14.
[36] 'Latin England', in *Imagining a Medieval English Nation*, ed. Kathy Lavezzo (Minneapolis, 2004) pp. 41–95, at pp. 70–71.
[37] Galloway, p. 62 (emphasis original).
[38] Marjorie Chibnall, *The Debate on the Norman Conquest* (Manchester, 1999), p. 127.

Englishness. The English church always presented itself as a unifying, but also specifically English, force among the various Anglo-Saxon kingdoms. Bede's *Historia ecclesiastica* progressively conflates the Angles, Saxons, and Jutes into a single *Angelcynn*, while, as Kathy Lavezzo argues, Ælfric's *Catholic Homilies* 'circulated throughout England, from Canterbury to Exeter to Worcester and as far north as Durham [...so that] at the very least we can speculate that on some Sundays and holidays throughout the country the English laity heard in their native tongue the same sermon, one geared toward their English tastes'.[39] More recent scholarship has shown that later Anglo-Saxon kings also conceived of an 'Albion' over which they aspired to rule that included not only Anglo-Saxon English but also Danes, Welsh, and Scots.[40]

National anti-heroes like Hengist remind us that medieval English *mestisaje*, if one may borrow the term from modern Mexican usage, was a pervasive cultural concept in medieval English literature. While certain ethnic groups may have resisted such cultural amalgamation within the expanding and acquisitive medieval English state – the Welsh, the Scots, the people of Aquitaine – it remained a dominant trend in literature as variable as Brut narratives, the legends of Havelok, and many of the various Arthurian stories with their multinational Knights of the Round Table.

Perhaps no text better demonstrates the sheer scope of genealogical amalgamation in medieval English literature than the Auchinleck manuscript's version of the *Short English Metrical Chronicle*. In an inversion of William Caxton's later transformation of King Arthur of the Britons into an Englishman, the Auchinleck's Hengist becomes a Briton.[41] The resulting figure is almost – but not quite – unrecognizable:

> To þe riche he was gode
> & wiþ þe pouer mild of mode.
> Of godenes was al his fame,

---

[39] *Angels on the Edge of the World: Geography, Literature, and English Community 1000–1534* (Ithaca, 2006), p. 34. For a discussion of Bede's role in creating an idea of a unified 'English' people, see especially Nicholas Brooks, 'Bede and the English', Jarrow Lecture, 1999. See also Patrick Wormald, *Legal Culture in the Early Medieval West* (London and Rio Grande, 1999), especially the chapter 'Engla Lond: the Making of an Allegiance'. Wormald writes, 'There is [...] even more significance than is generally appreciated in the well-known fact that a single English kingdom was anticipated by a single English Church. The very name "English" was one of its fruits. Another side-effect of more than merely spiritual moment was the remarkably consistent festal cycle celebrated throughout the Anglo-Saxon Church by the tenth and eleventh centuries' (p. 374). In the *Anglo-Saxon Chronicle*, too, the different kingdoms of the Heptarchy increasingly come under the rubric of *Angelcynn* as the history progresses (Lavezzo, p. 8).

[40] Anke Bernau, 'Beginning with Albina: Remembering the Nation', *Exemplaria* 21 (2009) 247–273; Julia Crick, in 'Albion before Albina: the Scottish question', a paper delivered at the 83rd Annual Meeting of the Medieval Academy of America, Vancouver, 4 April 2008.

[41] The Auchinleck manuscript's version of the *Short English Metrical Chronicle* devotes more than 220 lines to this Hengist. To access a full transcription as well as images from the manuscript, see the National Library of Scotland's Auchinleck Manuscript site (http://digital.nls.uk/auchinleck/). In his prologue to *Le Morte Darthur*, Caxton laments that 'it is a meruayl why he [Arthur] is nomore renomed in his owne contreye', for volumes about him 'been not had in our maternal tongue / but in walsshe ben many & also in frensshe' (Sir Thomas Malory, *Le Morte d'Arthur*, ed. William Caxton, ed. H. Oskar Sommer (London: 1889), p. 2).

> Sterne in wretþe & glad in game.
> Of belding he was wise man:
> Lyncoln first he bigan,
> Herforþ & Wircestre,
> Schrowesbirye, Staford & Chestre,
> Oxenford & Reding;
> Of Walingford he made þe gining,
> Grauntebrige & Huntingdone,
> Bedeford & Norhamtone,
> Gloucester & Þrekingham,
> Dudele & Euesham.
> Hingist wan to his hond
> Inglond, Wales & Scotlond.
>
> (*Short English Metrical Chronicle*, lines 661–76)

This British king, known for his 'godenes' and for his building of cities rather than his sacking of them, shares with the more familiar Saxon Hengist a status as conqueror: 'Into þis lond come a conquerour,/ Hingist, þe strong king,/ Wele doinde in al þing' (lines 656-59). Indeed, the poem does not make clear where exactly this Hengist comes from, though it inserts him into the usual genealogy of British kings between Belin and Leir, who according to the poem is Hengist's son. Yet this quasi-British Hengist is associated also with distinctly Saxon terms: 'He made boþe hundred & schire' (line 696). And he has recognizably Anglo-Norman ambitions; the French king yields to him 'al Gascone/ & Normundye also' (lines 794–95). In fact, the Auchinleck Hengist ends up holding all of the lands that English kings claimed in the late medieval period: England, Scotland, Wales, Normandy, and Gascony. Later in the poem, astonishingly, Uther – in most texts a famous fighter of Saxons – desires 'to hauen in weld/ Þat his auncestres held:/ Gascoyne & Normondye,/ As Hingist it wan wiþ meistri' (lines 999–1002). Complicating genealogical lines even further, during the reign of Seberd (recognizably Anglo-Saxon) appears Inge, an Anglo-Norman speaking woman who carries out the 'Eu, nimet saxas' trick using the Anglo-Saxon word 'wassail' as her signal to begin the slaughter of her hosts (lines 1263–1344). We might simply dismiss this poem as hopelessly confused were it not so inventive and did it not flow so well as a narrative, however atypical its content is among Brut texts. More fruitfully, we can see in the Auchinleck's *Short English Metrical Chronicle* the tendency toward cultural and genealogical amalgamation in medieval English literature taken to its extreme limit.

To return to the question with which this essay opens, it appears that the germ of Hengist's later portrayal as a cultural hero does indeed exist in medieval texts. Like their medieval counterparts, these later Hengists fluctuate in significance, sometimes representing racial purity or impurity – as Thomas Jefferson's ideas and Geoffrey of Monmouth's *Historia regum* seem to suggest – and sometimes representing a genealogical mixture to be celebrated – as in the 'Ballad of Hengist and Mey', Drayton's *Poly-Olbion*, and Wace's *Roman de Brut*. But the dominant medieval portrayal of Hengist was as anti-hero. And medieval England's literature was full of such anti-heroes, it seems, because there were so many different 'English' peoples to be incorporated into the fabric of both history and romance. These anti-heroes shaped understandings of what it meant to be English, which was to be related to both the conquered and the conquerors of historical struggles both ancient and more recent.

For us today, as much as for our medieval and early modern predecessors, representing Hengist poses a challenge and an opportunity. For Americans (as I am), especially those of us teaching near our borders at a time marked by an acute sense of rapidly shifting ethnic and cultural admixture, this history of Hengist as both ancestor and conqueror is compelling. Since the country's foundation, ideas about Hengist and the Saxons have percolated from Britain to the United States. As antihero instead of hero or villain, Hengist connects us to a cultural heritage of *mestisaje* rather than exclusion, one that we can share with students whose encounters with the English language and English literature are, arguably, as marked by cultural domination and exclusion as those of the medieval Welsh. In the very languages of medieval narratives of Hengist, such students discover a history of admixture and change that has often been obscured for them by the English language's dominance in North America. We can find, that is, a prehistory of the inclusion that still struggles to become our defining national characteristic.

4

Harold Godwineson

Laura Ashe

The reputation of the last Anglo-Saxon king of England has perhaps never been higher than it was some eight centuries after his death, when Edward Freeman produced his magisterial work on the Norman Conquest. For him, Harold was an essential pillar in the meaningful structure of English history, as he elaborated when recounting the passage of Edward I's body through Waltham on its way to Westminster in 1307; for Waltham was supposedly the site of Harold's burial:[1]

> But for a while the two heroes lay side by side – the last and the first of English Kings, between whom none deserved the English name or could claim honour or gratitude from the English nation. The one was the last King who reigned purely by the will of the people, without any claim either of conquest or of hereditary right. The other was the first King who reigned purely as the son of his father, the first who succeeded without competitor or interregnum. But each alike, as none between them did, deserved the love and trust of the people over whom they reigned. With Harold our native kingship ends ... the Crown, the laws, the liberties, the very tongue of Englishmen, seem all fallen never to rise again. In Edward the line of English Kings begins once more. ... The King with whom England fell might greet his first true successor in the King with whom she rose again.[2]

This stirring passage is an idealized sublimation of the pre-Conquest English king and the man chosen as his metaphorical successor, 'native' kings of England. In writing thus of Harold, Freeman binds him to 'the will of the people' and the fate of the nation, indeed to some essence of Englishness; as such, he demonstrates the enduring symbolic importance which Harold Godwineson can be made to possess, as the 'last English king'.[3] However, this is evidently not an identity to which Harold aspired, and it is one of those historical categories which only gains reality in

---

[1] Early Norman sources suggested that he was buried on the cliffs of the English shore, but these were superseded by the claims of Waltham Abbey: *The Waltham Chronicle: An account of the discovery of our holy cross at Montacute and its conveyance to Waltham*, ed./trans. Leslie Watkiss and Marjorie Chibnall (Oxford, 1994), pp. xliii–xlvi.

[2] Edward A. Freeman, *The History of the Norman Conquest of England*, 3 vols (Oxford, 1869), 3:521–22.

[3] Cf. some popular recent historical biographies and novels: Peter Rex, *The Last English King: The Life of Harold II* (Stroud, 2008); Ian W. Walker, *Harold, the Last Anglo-Saxon King* (Stroud, 1997); Julian Rathbone, *The Last English King* (London, 1997).

retrospect, anachronistically; it cannot take us closer to the historical individual. In his own time, Harold had painstakingly made himself the most important nobleman in England, and he moved decisively for the crown when the moment came, in a political world fraught with faction and internecine strife.[4] It had not been a smooth path; in 1051 Harold's father Earl Godwine and the whole family had been forced into exile after their relations with Edward the Confessor had broken down.[5] Commenting on these apparently momentous events, a chronicler observed that 'it would have seemed remarkable to everyone who was in England, if anyone earlier told them that it should turn out thus, because [Godwine] was formerly so very much raised up, as if he ruled the king and all England; and his sons were earls and the king's favourites; and his daughter was married and espoused to the king'.[6] They were indeed not so easily dispensed with, and returning under arms in 1052 were restored to all their lands and offices; Harold resumed his place as earl of East Anglia until his father's death in 1053, when he was given the vast earldom of Wessex, and became the second most powerful man in the kingdom.

The power and influence of the Godwines can be read in the disparities between different manuscripts of the Anglo-Saxon Chronicle; the version most consistently favourable to the family asserts that they came before Edward in 1052 and successfully cleared themselves of all guilt.[7] But they had come with an army, and two less partisan manuscripts of the Chronicle explained the king's reconciliation with Godwine and his sons as a matter of expediency and national loyalty: 'it was abhorrent to almost all of them that they should fight against men of their own race, because there was little else of any great value except English men on either side; and also they did not want that this country should be the more greatly laid open to foreign nations, should they themselves destroy each other'.[8] This alignment of shared English loyalties in opposition to *utlendiscum þeodum* was no doubt sharpened by the recent experience of Danish conquest and rule, but such ready identifications were themselves fictional. Godwine had thrived under Cnut, marrying the king's

---

[4] See N.J. Higham, 'Harold Godwineson: the Construction of Kingship', in *King Harold II and the Bayeux Tapestry*, ed. Gale R. Owen-Crocker (Woodbridge, 2005), pp. 19–34.

[5] See Ann Williams, 'Godwine', *ODNB*.

[6] 'Þæt wolde ðyncan wundorlic ælcum men þe on Englalande wæs, gif ænig man ær þam sæde þæt hit swa gewurþan sceolde, for ðam þe he wæs ær to þam swyðe up ahafen swylce he weolde þæs cynges 7 ealles Englalandes, 7 his sunan wæron eorlas, 7 þæs cynges dyrlingas, 7 his dohtor þæm cynge beweddod 7 beæwnod': *The Anglo-Saxon Chronicle, a Collaborative Edition, Volume 6: MS. D*, ed. G.P. Cubbin (Cambridge, 1996), s.a. 1051 (p. 71); trans. Michael Swanton, *The Anglo-Saxon Chronicles* (London, 2000), p. 176.

[7] *The Anglo-Saxon Chronicle, a Collaborative Edition, Volume 7: MS. E*, ed. Susan Irvine (Cambridge, 2004), s.a. 1052 (p. 84). On MS E's bias in favour of the Godwine family see D.N. Dumville, 'Some Aspects of Annalistic Writing at Canterbury in the Eleventh and Early Twelfth Centuries', *Peritia* 2 (1983), 23–57, at p. 25; Stephen Baxter, 'MS C of the Anglo-Saxon Chronicle and the Politics of Mid-Eleventh-Century England', *English Historical Review* 122 (2007), 1189–1227, at pp. 1190–91.

[8] 'hit wæs heom mæst eallon lað þæt hig sceoldon fohtan wið heora agenes cynnes mannum, for þan þar wæs lyt elles þe aht mycel myhton buton englisce men on ægþer healfe, 7 eac hig noldon þæt utlendiscum þeodum wære þes eard þurh þæt þe swiðor gerymed, þe hi heom sylfe ælc oðerne forfore.' *The Anglo-Saxon Chronicle, a Collaborative Edition, Volume 5: MS. C*, ed. Katherine O'Brien O'Keeffe (Cambridge, 2001), s.a. 1052 (p. 113); trans. Swanton, p. 180; cf. *ASC MS. D*, pp. 72–73.

sister's husband's sister;[9] one historian has argued that an informal part of Harold's claim to the English throne might have lain in his connections with the Danish royal house.[10] Meanwhile, Edward the Confessor's affinity with the Normans was to provide William with material for his own claim, as Edward's mother Emma of Normandy was the sister of Duke Richard II, William's grandfather;[11] Edward himself had spent the many years of his exile in Normandy, and the immediate cause of the dispute in 1051 was Edward's decision to make the Norman Robert of Jumièges archbishop of Canterbury.[12]

To say the least, then, mid-eleventh-century politics were dangerous and complex; matters only worsened with the growing succession crisis, fired by Edward's lack of an heir and his apparent failure consistently to establish and promote any single claimant.[13] In this context one might observe that, blood aside, in 1065 Harold was as good a candidate as any; he had proved his military capacity in the Welsh borders and his political nous in the royal court;[14] he was earl of Wessex and the south-west Midlands, his brother was earl of East Anglia, his sister was Edward's queen, and he had just forged a marriage alliance which made the earls of Mercia and Northumbria his brothers-in-law. He had served Edward efficiently and kept rebellion in check on his behalf;[15] he was the second man in the land to the king, called by one twelfth-century chronicler *subregulus*, the 'underking'.[16] And it seems probable that on his deathbed Edward nominated Harold as his successor.[17] There was no precedent in English history for a king to grant the kingdom in this manner to someone not of the royal line,[18] but Harold was there, and he had himself crowned;[19] he then raised the army and prepared to face successive invasions. In a great victory at Stamford Bridge he defeated King Harald Hardrada of Norway, who

---

[9] See *English Historical Documents vol. II: 1042–1189*, ed. David C. Douglas and George W. Greenaway (New York, 1953), genealogical tables 3 and 7 (pp. 984, 988).

[10] Ian Howard, 'Harold II: A Throne-Worthy King', in *King Harold II and the Bayeux Tapestry*, ed. Owen-Crocker, pp. 35–52.

[11] *EHD* genealogical table 2 (p. 983).

[12] On Edward's exile see Simon Keynes, 'The Æthelings in Normandy', *Anglo-Norman Studies* 13 (1990), 173–205; on the disputed archbishop see H.E.J. Cowdrey, 'Robert of Jumièges', *ODNB*.

[13] For a recent analysis of Edward's conduct see Stephen Baxter, 'Edward the Confessor and the Succession Question', in *Edward the Confessor: the Man and the Legend*, ed. Richard Mortimer (Woodbridge, 2009), pp. 77–118.

[14] Cf. the judgement of William of Malmesbury, *Gesta regum Anglorum*, ed./trans. R.A.B. Mynors, R.M. Thomson and M. Winterbottom, 2 vols (Oxford, 1998), 1:420.

[15] In 1065 he was sent by Edward to calm rebellion in the north, which he did by acceding to the Northumbrians' demands to replace his brother Tostig with Morcar as earl, and 'renewing the laws of Cnut': *ASC MS. D*, p. 78; *MS. E*, p. 86; cf. *MS. C*, p. 118.

[16] *The Chronicle of John of Worcester*, ed./trans. R.R. Darlington, Jennifer Bray and P. McGurk, 2 vols (Oxford, 1995), 2:600.

[17] *ASC MS. C*, p. 119; *MS. D*, p. 79; *MS. E*, p. 86; *Vita Ædwardi: The Life of King Edward*, ed./trans. Frank Barlow, 2nd edn (Oxford, 1992), p. 122; *John of Worcester*, 2:600; the Norman apologist William of Poitiers does not dispute the fact of this grant, but rather its validity: *The Gesta Guillelmi of William of Poitiers*, ed./trans. R.H.C. Davis and Marjorie Chibnall (Oxford, 1998), pp. 118, 140–42.

[18] Baxter, 'Edward and the Succession', pp. 113–14.

[19] On the advantages of being on the spot at the crucial moment see Higham, p. 23; George Garnett, *Conquered England: Kingship, Succession, and Tenure, 1066–1166* (Oxford, 2007), pp. 136–42.

had invaded in alliance with Harold's own treacherous brother Tostig; less than three weeks later, in the third major battle on English soil within a month, he fell at Hastings.

In the morass of eleventh-century politics Harold thus cuts an impressive figure, albeit ultimately an unfortunate, perhaps even a poignant one. The Anglo-Saxon Chronicle acknowledged this, breaking into verse on the occasion of Edward's death:

> Englas feredon
> soþfæste sawle innan swegles leoht.
> 7 se froda swa þeah befæste þæt rice
> heahþungenum menn, Harolde sylfum,
> æþelum eorle, se in ealle tid
> hyrde holdlice hærran sinum
> wordum 7 dædum, wihte ne agælde
> þæs þe þearf wæs þæs þeodkyninges.

7 Her wearð Harold eac to kynge gehalgod, 7 he lytle stillnesse þar on gebad þa hwile þe he rices weold.[20]

Angels conveyed the righteous soul into heaven's light. However, the wise man committed the kingdom to a distinguished man, Harold himself, a princely earl, who at all times loyally obeyed his superior in words and deeds, neglecting nothing of which the nation's king was in need. And here also Harold became consecrated as king, and he experienced little quietness in it while he ruled the kingdom.

There it ends; and this laconic annal is indicative of the most serious and enduring challenge to Harold's literary afterlife: his irreparable failure. The Victorian historian could regard this loss as a melancholy tragedy; but for medieval chroniclers, history was an expression of divine judgement. As such, any attempt to romanticize or celebrate King Harold is compromised, even crushed, by the brevity of his reign and the finality of his defeat. This essay will trace Harold's uneven path through the medieval chronicles, his appearances in hagiography and saga, and his development as the subject of a unique romance. In his various incarnations he is both hero and anti-hero, protagonist and foil; and above all, he is an unanswered question, symbol of an alternative and counterfactual history. Each author strives to negotiate with history to create a meaningful identity for England's lost king; and each text betrays the difficulty of sustaining the memory and vision of a hero whose tragedy was as ignominious as it was complete.[21]

Harold in Chronicle and Hagiography

Medieval chroniclers who sought to write fairly of Harold's character, qualities and achievements thus faced this apparently insuperable difficulty, that God had damned him to shameful defeat and death, and with that fall had come the subjection and

---

[20] ASC *s.a.* 1065: *MS. C*, p. 119; *MS. D*, p. 79; trans. Swanton, p. 194.
[21] On the difficulties of celebrating the figure of the warrior hero throughout the period, see also Laura Ashe, 'The Hero and his Realm in Medieval English Romance', in *Boundaries in Medieval Romance*, ed. Neil Cartlidge, Studies in Medieval Romance 6, (Cambridge, 2008), pp. 129–47.

degradation of the English people. This man could not, therefore, be in the right; perhaps he could not be morally admirable at all, and the Conqueror's most partisan Norman historian asserted simply that Harold's end was more than sufficient proof of his perfidy and treachery in usurping the throne from William, the rightful king.[22] Those willing to praise Harold found it necessary to suspend their providential understanding of history in order to do so, or alternatively to shape their account of events around the revelations of hindsight. William of Malmesbury, the Anglo-Norman historian who most prided himself on his balanced account of the past,[23] analysed Harold's earlier achievements as a property of his (ultimately unlawful) ambition:

> ut non celetur ueritas, pro persona quam gerebat regnum prudentia et fortitudine gubernaret, si legitime suscepisset; denique uiuente Eduardo quaecumque contra eum bella incensa sunt, uirtute sua compressit, cupiens se prouintialibus ostentare, in regnum scilicet spe prurienti anhelans. (I. 420–21)

> Not to conceal the truth, he might well have ruled the kingdom, to judge by the figure he cut in public, with prudence and fortitude, had it come to him lawfully. For example, during Edward's life, whatever wars were kindled against him, it was Harold's valour that extinguished them, for he was always trying to impress public opinion, being of course consumed with ambition to be king.

And when it came to judging the man in terms of his end at Hastings, the conclusion was inevitable:

> leui uidelicet belli negotio sed occulto et stupendo Dei consilio, quod numquam postea Angli communi prelio in libertatem spirauerint, quasi cum Haroldo omne robur deciderit Angliae, qui certe potuit et debuit etiam per inertissimos soluere penas perfidiae. (I. 422–23)

> The war itself was a mere trifle; it was God's hidden and stupendous purpose that never again should Englishmen feel together and fight together in defence of their liberties, as though all the strength of England had fallen away with Harold, who could and should have paid the penalty for his perfidy even through the agency of utter cowards.

In contrast, William's contemporary John of Worcester eschewed such providential explanations in his chronicle, and in the process of translating the Anglo-Saxon annals made his own, notable additions, offering unqualified praise of Harold's brief kingship:

> Qui mox ut regni gubernacula susceperat, leges iniquas destruere, equas cepit condere, ecclesiarum ac monasteriorem patronus fieri, episcopos, abbates, monachos, clericos colere simul ac uenerari, pium, humilem, affabilemque se bonis omnibus exhibere, malefactores exosus habere, nam ducibus, satrapis, uicecomitibus et suis in commune precepit ministris fures, raptores, regni

---

[22] William of Poitiers, *Gesta Guillelmi*, pp. 140–42.
[23] 'Ego autem, quia utriusque gentis sanguinem traho, dicendi tale temperamentum seruabo' ['For my part, having the blood of both nations in my veins, I propose in my narrative to keep a middle path']: *Gesta regum Anglorum*, 1:424–25.

disturbatores comprehendere, et pro patrie defensione ipsemet terra marique desudare.[24]

> He soon, when he had undertaken the government of the realm, destroyed iniquitous laws, and set about establishing just ones; becoming patron of churches and monasteries, cultivating and venerating at the same time bishops, abbots, monks and clerks; showing himself pious, humble and affable to all good men; detesting malefactors, for he ordered the earls, ealdormen, sheriffs, and his own officers generally to seize thieves, robbers, and disturbers of the realm, and to exert themselves by land and sea for defence of their country.

This approbation is matched by John's view of Harold's eventual defeat, which is presented as the sad end of a king whose nation suffered too many enemies without and traitors within. In the immediate aftermath of victory at Stamford Bridge, Harold hears of William's arrival on the south coast:

> Vnde rex statim uersus Lundoniam suum mouit exercitum magna cum festinatione, et licet de tota Anglia fortiores quosque preliis in duobus bene sciret iam cecidisse, mediamque partem sui exercitus nondum conuenisse, quam citius tamen potuit in Suthsaxonia suis hostibus occurrere non formidauit ... Sed quia arto in loco constituti fuerant Angli, de acie se multi subtraxere et cum eo perpauci constantes corde remansere. Ab hora tamen diei tertia usque noctis crepusculum suis aduersariis restitit fortissime et se ipsum pugnando tam fortiter defendit et tam strenue ut uix ab hostili interimi posset agmine. At postquam ex his et illis quamplurimi corruere, heu, ipsemet cecidit crepusculi tempore. (II. 604–605)

> Whereupon the king at once moved his army to London in great haste, and although he knew that all the more powerful men from the whole of England had already fallen in two battles, and that half of his army had not yet assembled, yet he did not fear to go to meet his enemies in Sussex with all possible speed ... But because the English were drawn up in a narrow place many slipped away from the battle-line, and very few of a constant heart remained with him. However, from the third hour of daylight until dusk he resisted his enemies most stoutly, and defended himself by fighting so strongly and so vigorously that he could scarcely be slain by the enemy line. But afterwards, when very many had fallen on both sides, he himself fell, alas, at dusk.

That is the whole of Harold's story, in the most sympathetic chronicle of all; it leaves us with a lost hero, whose premature end might provoke some speculation on what could have been, had events fallen out differently. But these are characteristically modern musings. In the twelfth century John of Worcester is a lone voice in praising Harold's qualities and heroism without reference to God's judgement upon him. Even Wace, whose *Roman de Rou* is notorious for its refusal to judge the moral rights

---

[24] *John of Worcester*, 2:600–601. The editors comment: 'This eulogy seems JW's, and contrasts with the staccato sentence with which the annal for 1065 ASC CD ends' (p. 600, n. 3).

of situations,[25] comments simply on the battle of Hastings that 'Heraut out grant pople e estult, / de totes parz en i vint mult, / mais multitude petit valt / se la vertu del ciel i falt' ['Harold had many bold men and they came in great numbers from all directions, but a multitude is not worth much if the favour of heaven is lacking'].[26]

Within a few years of the Conquest Norman historians and administrators had taken this providential judgement to its fullest extent, eliding Harold's kingship from history entirely. The argument was that he had never been a lawful king, never more than a perjured usurper of William's rightful throne.[27] In Domesday Book, that great, unprecedented, unmatched, and final statement of Norman ownership of the land, Harold's brief reign was omitted from legal record; the marker of pre-Conquest land ownership was laid down as 'T. R. E.', *tempore regis Edwardi*, 'in the time of King Edward'. Every landholder at the time of the survey in 1086, *tempore regis Willelmi*, was the lawful successor of his antecessor in 1065, T. R. E. Thus, with the exception of two moments which can probably be regarded as scribal errors, Harold appears throughout only as 'earl', *comes*: 'he had never been a king'.[28] This astonishing feat of legal revisioning was not sustained in narrative accounts of the Conquest. But with greater distance from the event, as the Norman and then Angevin kings cemented an apparently permanent dynasty, such legalistic precision on Harold's kingship in any case became unnecessary; what remained was ambivalence about the conduct and fate of this short-lived king.

A part of that ambivalence lay in Harold's relationship with other historical figures. William of Poitiers had justified Harold's death not only as a divine judgement on his seizure of the throne, but also as a price paid for his father Godwine's most notorious crime;[29] a recurring trope of historiography was the rottenness of the entire family, sometimes with the miraculous exception of Edward's queen Edith.[30] But beyond the Godwines, Harold's posthumous reputation was inevitably involved with that of Edward the Confessor. The latter was to be celebrated by the Normans as a great, law-giving and just king; to be canonized within a century; and then to be adopted by Henry III as the king's own patron saint.[31] The implications of this for Harold were not, however, as straightforward as

---

[25] As in for example his dual account of the English succession dispute: Wace, *Roman de Rou*, ed./trans. Anthony J. Holden and Glyn Burgess (St Helier, 2002), III. 5588–604 (pp. 220–21); see Laura Ashe, *Fiction and History in England, 1066–1200* (Cambridge, 2007), pp. 70–72; Jean Blacker, *The Faces of Time: Portrayal of the Past in Old French and Latin Historical Narrative of the Anglo-Norman Regnum* (Austin, 1994), pp. 102–104.

[26] *Roman de Rou*, III. 7777–80 (pp. 264–65).

[27] See *Gesta Guillelmi*, pp. 100; 140–42; Garnett, pp. 9–10, 23, 37.

[28] Garnett, pp. 18–19, at p. 19.

[29] The blinding and death of Alfred Ætheling, brother of Edward the Confessor, were popularly believed to have been Godwine's doing: *Gesta Guillelmi*, pp. 5–7; *ASC* s.a. 1036: MS. C, pp. 105–106; John of Worcester, II. 522–23; Henry of Huntingdon, *Historia Anglorum: The History of the English People*, ed./trans. Diana Greenway (Oxford, 1996), pp. 384–85.

[30] See William of Malmesbury's summation of the family, *Gesta regum Anglorum*, I. 354, pp. 362–64. Edith is a 'rose among thorns' in Ailred of Rievaulx, *Vita S. Edwardi regis*, in *PL* 195.737–90 (col. 747C–D), quoted verbatim in *La Estoire de Seint Aedward le rei* attributed to Matthew Paris, ed. Kathryn Young Wallace (London, 1983), lines 1175–76. The author of the *Vita Haroldi*, discussed below, uses the same metaphor to praise Harold himself: *Vita Haroldi*, ed./trans. Walter de Gray Birch (London, 1885), pp. 16, 116.

[31] See Frank Barlow, 'Edward', *ODNB*; Bruce R. O'Brien, *God's Peace and King's Peace: The Laws of Edward the Confessor* (Philadelphia, 1999); Edina Bozoky, 'The Sanctity and Canonisation of

one might expect; it is not always the case that Edward's sanctity demanded a narrative counterpart in Harold's perfidy. Indeed, one of the earliest accounts of the saintly Edward's miracles included a story in which Harold plays the part of pious recipient of favour. Osbert of Clare was prior of Westminster Abbey, and by 1138 he had produced a *Vita* of Edward which clearly aimed to further the king's cult and support his canonization.[32] One of the miracle stories he recounts is 'De uisione quam quidam abbas uidit, et de mandato quod a rege sancto ad Haroldum accepit'[33] ['Of the vision which a certain abbot saw, and of the command which he received from the saintly king for Harold']. It is 1066; Harald Hardrada's army has just invaded the north when the abbot of Ramsey receives a vision of Edward in a dream, in which the dead king commands him to go to Harold, 'et dic ei ut contra iminentem exercitum festinet ad prelium' (114) ['and tell him to hurry to battle against the impending army']. Edward promises Harold divine favour in the fight: 'de Dei adiutorio certus et de me confisus secure contra Aquilonalium regem Haroldum pulcra uenustate crinitum exeat ad bellum, et precedentibus aquilis reportabit hoste prostrato triumphum' (115) ['let him march to war against the northern king Harald Fairhair, with God's aid and my assurance certain and free from care, and he will carry off the victory with the leading eagles of his defeated enemy'].[34] Harold obeys the command, and we are told that he succeeds 'uiriliter' ['manfully'] at the battle of Stamford Bridge.

But at this point, Osbert begins to enjoy the contradictory turns of God's providence, and to explore the paradoxes of Harold's position:

> Sic uictor triumphat effectus, qui paucis post diebus occubuit uictus, et qui eos uicit qui contra iusticiam Dei inmerito in regnum irruerant alienum, eum iuste oppressit periurium quod Willelmo fecerat duci Normannorum. ... In eo enim ei successit uictoria ubi pro patrie libertate non iniuste pugnauit; et cum deuio errore exorbitaret a iusticia, iuste peremtus rex iniustus occubuit. (115)

> Thus he was made a triumphant conqueror, who within few days lay dead and conquered; and he who undeserving conquered those who against God's justice had invaded a foreign land, was himself justly brought down by the perjury he had committed against William, duke of the Normans. ... In him therefore, alas, victory lodged when he fought not unjustly for the freedom of his country; and when with deviant error he strayed away from justice, justly killed, the unjust king lay dead.

Osbert's text is thus equivocal about Harold's personal qualities, which are incidental to the story; he is used as an example both of Edward's miracles and the saint's care for England, and of the minute and inevitable workings of the judgements of God.

Edward the Confessor', in Mortimer, *Edward the Confessor*, pp. 173–86; David Carpenter, 'Henry III and Saint Edward the Confessor: The Origins of the Cult', *English Historical Review* 122 (2007), 865–91.

[32] See Frank Barlow, 'Osbert of Clare', *ODNB*.

[33] Marc Bloch, ed., 'La Vie de S. Édouard le Confesseur par Osbert de Clare', *Analecta Bollandiana* 41 (1923), 5–131, at pp. 114–15.

[34] Harald 'Fairhair' is Harald Harfarger, the first king of Norway and a legendary hero, an error for Harald Hardrada (1015–66): see Bloch, 115, n. 1.

In Ailred of Rievaulx's adaptation of the tale for his definitive and influential *Vita* of 1162–63, Harold's role is reduced and the man himself diminished: he is 'ille coelesti promissione factus audacior'[35] ['made braver by this heavenly promise'], and the episode's conclusion is made to be merely the confirmation of a prophecy uttered by Edward many years earlier, that the young sons of Godwine would one day kill one another.[36] This interpretation is followed in Matthew Paris's *La Estoire de Seint Aedward le rei*, written around 1240, at the height of Henry III's celebration of Saint Edward:

> Li rois Haraudz de la victoire
> A seint Aedward rent graces e gloire.
> Ke mortz est par Haraud Tostin
> De cest cunte prove la fin,
> Cum mustra la desestance
> Ki fu entre eus en lur enfance.
> Acumpli fu tut, mes k'a tart,
> K'out dit avant li rois Aedward. ...
> Pecchee tapist au cumençail,
> Mais trop mustre mal au finail.[37]

King Harold gave the glory and thanks for the victory to Saint Edward. That Tostig was killed by Harold proves the point of this story, just as the discord between them was demonstrated when they were children. Everything happened in due time as Edward had said earlier. ... At the beginning, sin hid, but evil indeed showed itself at the end.[38]

Matthew Paris then manipulates time to create some unspecified weeks or months between Stamford Bridge and William's invasion, during which Harold becomes 'Si orgoillus, si fers e baudz, / Si fruiz e si cuveitus ... Marchant semble u usurer / Plus ke prince u chivaler' (4284–306) ['So arrogant, so cruel and proud, so violent and so covetous ... He resembled a merchant or a usurer more than a prince or knight']. Edward 'mut l'enchastie' (4300) ['many times reproached him'], repeatedly appearing to him in dreams and visions, while a sorrowful William sends him numerous letters of warning; but all is to no avail. As a representation of Harold's character, this is the narrative equivalent of Domesday Book's conclusion that he had never been a king: for Paris, as a perjured usurper stylized as Edward's aesthetic opposite, Harold could not be seen to possess any positive qualities at all.[39] This amounts to no more than Harold's being ground under the wheels of Edward's canonization, providing a

---

[35] Ailred, *Vita S. Edwardi regis*, col. 778B.
[36] *Vita S. Edwardi*, col. 778C: because Tostig fell alongside Harald Hardrada. Edward's prophecy of fratricide is at cols. 765D–766B.
[37] *La Estoire de Seint Aedward le rei*, lines 4253–64.
[38] *The History of Saint Edward the King by Matthew Paris*, trans. Thelma S. Fenster and Jocelyn Wogan-Browne (Tempe AZ, 2008), pp. 108–109.
[39] On Paris' 'literary crusade against Harold' see Rebecca Reader, 'Matthew Paris and the Norman Conquest', in *The Cloister and the World: Essays in Medieval History in Honour of Barbara Harvey*, ed. John Blair and Brian Golding (Oxford, 1996), 118–47, at p. 126.

counterpoint to Edward in creating an idealized model of saintly kingship for Henry III.[40]

In the saint's life Matthew Paris thus necessarily exonerates Edward of all responsibility in Harold's seizure of the throne.[41] But in chronicles, despite the available providential Norman master narrative, the succession question did not go away. Writing his verse chronicle at the end of the thirteenth century, Peter Langtoft drew upon a number of different sources for English history.[42] His portrayal of the succession is brief, and focuses on Edward's actions rather than Harold's:

> Countes et barouns devaunt ly appelayt,
> A Harald fiz Godewyn sun regne devisayt,
> Le duk de Normendye ublyez avayt,
> Du covenaunt k'il ly fist nul ly mentyvayt. ...
> Après la mort Eduuarde, Harald est elu
> Ray par la commune, la coroune ad resceu;
> En drayture et ley leaus est-il tenu.[43]

He called earls and barons before him, granted his kingdom to Harold son of Godwine; he had forgotten the duke of Normandy; no one reminded him of the promise he had made to him. ... After Edward's death Harold is chosen king by the people, he has received the crown; he is held legitimate in right and law.[44]

Peter Langtoft's Chronicle was popular and influential,[45] and it was translated into English verse by Robert Mannyng of Brunne within a few decades. Mannyng's English history is in the main a close translation from Langtoft's French, but its most recent editor comments that 'his emphasis is often different',[46] and this is one such occasion. Langtoft's neutral presentation of the episode evidently troubled Mannyng, who had also read some version of Edward's *vita*, and he altered his text with a significant, moralizing addition of twenty-eight admonitory lines, including a direct challenging of his source:

> Þe barons befor him kald & said vnto þam alle,
> 'Tille Harald, Godwyn sonne, þe regne wille best falle.'
> Me meruailes of my boke, I trowe he wrote not right,
> þat he forgate Wiliam, of forward þat he him hight;

---

[40] On the usefulness of Edward to Henry III see David Carpenter, 'Kings, Magnates and Society: The Personal Rule of King Henry III, 1234–1258', *Speculum* 60 (1985), 39–70, at pp. 59–62; Paul Binski, 'Reflections on *La estoire de Seint Aedward le rei*: hagiography and kingship in thirteenth-century England', *Journal of Medieval History* 16 (1990), 333–50; Carpenter, 'Henry III and Saint Edward'.

[41] *Estoire de Seint Aedward*, lines 3859–948; *History of Saint Edward*, pp. 103–104.

[42] Including Henry of Huntingdon, William of Malmesbury and John of Worcester: see *The Chronicle of Pierre de Langtoft*, ed. Thomas Wright, 2 vols (London, 1866–68), 1:xviii.

[43] Peter Langtoft, *Chronicle*, I. 398.

[44] *leaus* here means lawful, rightful (king): *AND s.v.* 'leal' (3); not, as Wright offers, 'loyal'; cf. Mannyng's translation at line 1628, below. However, for a different interpretation see Helen Young, 'Correction to Translation of Piers Langtoft's Chronicle', *Notes & Queries* 57 (2010), 320–21.

[45] See J. C. Thiolier, 'Langtoft, Peter', *ODNB*.

[46] Idelle Sullens, ed., Robert Mannyng of Brunne, *The Chronicle* (Binghamton, NY, 1996), p. 58.

> neuerles þe forward held, what so was in his þouht.
> I wote wele criste it wild þat Edwardes wille wer wrouht.
> Who so lokes his life & redis his vision,
> what vengeance ordeynd was on Inglond to be don;
> of princes of þe lond it sais of þam þis sawe
> þat þei dred no þing god no ȝemed euenhed of lawe.
> Bot felawes vnto þefes to robbours of ilk cuntre,
> þar wilkednes was fulfilled, venged behoued it be. ...
> God has sette þat ȝere a day þer in salle falle;
> þe Inglis salle go to suerd, to pyne þar soules alle.
> Dede & fire salle fede þe scheperdes & þare schepe;
> þis vision is ȝit to drede, þink & gif gode kepe.
> I trowe it is ouergone þorgh William conqueroure.
> He com & slouh ilkone þo wikked men in stoure
> & sette vs in seruage, of fredom felle þe floure;
> þe Inglis þorgh taliage lyue ȝit in sorow fulle soure. ...
> After Saynt Edward, Harald kyng þei ches
> þorgh conseile of þam alle, & he þe scheld les.
> In right & in lawe, þe barons held him trewe,
> neuerles his falshed brouht vs sorowe alle newe.[47]

The sorrowful tone holds an uneasy balance; Harold's 'falshed brouht vs sorowe', but his act of perjury is not the primary cause of the Conquest: 'vengeance ordeynd was on Inglond to be don'. Such an analysis makes God's terrible judgement on the English more tolerable; it redirects the burden of guilt away from Harold alone, making him the instrument by which all the English people can be punished for their impiety and wickedness. This recalls Henry of Huntingdon's famous summation of the Conquest at the end of William's life:

> Anno uigesimo primo regni Willelmi regis, cum iam Domini iustam uoluntatem super Anglorum gentem Normanni complesent, nec iam uix aliquis princeps de progenie Anglorum esset in Anglia, sed omnes ad seruitutem et ad merorem redacti essent, ita etiam ut Anglicum uocari esset obprobrior, huius auctor uindicte Willelmus uitam terminauit. Elegerat enim Deus Normannos ad Anglorum gentem exterminandam.[48]

> In King William's twenty-first year [1087], when the Normans had fulfilled the just will of the Lord upon the English people, and there was scarcely a noble of English descent in England, but all had been reduced to servitude and lamentation, and it was even disgraceful to be called English, William, the agent of this vengeance, ended his life. For God had chosen the Normans to wipe out the English nation.

The implication of both these analyses, written perhaps two hundred years apart, is that Harold's fall marked the beginning of a period of degradation and subjugation for the English. This necessarily poses our next serious question about Harold: does

---

[47] Robert Mannyng, *Chronicle*, Part II, lines 1592–1629 (pp. 528–30).
[48] Henry of Huntingdon, *Historia Anglorum*, pp. 402–403.

that collocation of events make him a national, an English hero, whose tragic defeat brought all England's defeat? Or contrarily, might it even make him a national scapegoat, an English *anti*-hero, who shaped and carried the people's dreadful fate in his own moral failings and corruption? In the end, and whatever its moral weighting, does Harold carry the symbolism of national, English identity?

Some more or less isolated texts sought to suggest as much. Harold is stoutly defended in the *Waltham Chronicle*, which gives an adulatory account of his part in the foundation and patronage of that abbey, and celebrates the burial and veneration of his body there. Separate from the *Chronicle*'s historical account, however, the manuscript's praise of Harold culminates in a poetic eulogy, added immediately following the *Chronicle* by the same scribe, entitled *Versus Circa Tumbam Haroldi Regis* ['Verses upon the tomb of King Harold']:

> Macte pater patrie, meritis insignis Harolde,
>   Parma, pugil, gladius: te tegit hic tumulus. ...
> In hoc mausoleo fortis requiescit Haroldus
> qui fuit Anglorum gentis rex inclitus olim,
> cui fauor imperium species natura potestas
> contulit et regnum, dans cum dyademate sceptrum.
> Dum pugil insignis proprias defendere gentes
> nititur, occubuit Francorum gente peremptus.
> Huius nobilibus successibus inuida fata
> quem nequeunt saluare necant fraudemque sequuntur.[49]

Blessed father of our country, Harold marked out by your merits; you, our shield, fist, and sword: now a mound covers you ... In this tomb brave Harold rests who once famed king of England was, on whom renown, mien, character and authority conferred power and a kingdom, a sceptre and a crown as well. Until he strove, a famed warrior, to defend his very own people, but died, slain by the men of France. The Fates, so envious of his noble conquests, kill him they cannot save, and pursue deceit.

In comparison with the usual historiographical interpretations of Harold's fall, invoking the classical Fates is a clever poetic manoeuvre which sidesteps the question of providence.[50] The *Waltham Chronicle* manuscript was written to celebrate and support the abbey's historical rights and claims, and the possession of Harold's body was still important to them in the 1170s. The chronicler tells us that he himself was present at one of three separate twelfth-century translations of Harold's remains, which, as Alan Thacker observes, gives the strong impression that 'something approaching cultic honours were being paid' to him before the house was refounded by Henry II.[51]

---

[49] *Waltham Chronicle*, Appendix II, pp. 90–91.
[50] Cf. Robert W. Hanning, *The Vision of History in Early Britain: From Gildas to Geoffrey of Monmouth* (New York, 1966), pp. 125–26.
[51] *Waltham Chronicle*, pp. xxxi–xxxiv, 56–57; Alan Thacker, 'The Cult of King Harold at Chester', in *The Middle Ages in the North-West*, ed. Tom Scott and Pat Starkey (Oxford, 1995), pp. 155–76 (159–60). Waltham was refounded as a house of Augustinian regular canons as one of Henry's acts of penance for Becket's murder: see also W.L. Warren, *Henry II* (London, 1977), 538, n. 1; Frank Barlow, *Thomas Becket* (London, 1986), p. 272.

Harold also makes a brief and striking appearance in the *Life* of St Wulfstan of Worcester, as recounted in the *South English Legendary*:

> Harold was þo riȝhtest eyr : for non oþur þere nas;
> Þe croune he bar of Enguelonde : ȝwuche ȝwile so it was.
> For willame Bastard, þat was þo : Eorl in Noremaundie,
> Þouȝte to winne Enguelond : þoruȝ strencþe and tricherie ...
> No strencþe ne hadden þis straunge men : þat were i-come so newe,
> Aȝeinest heom of enguelonde : þe ȝwyle huy wolden beo trewe.
> Ake alas þe muchele tricherie : þat þo was, and ȝeot is,
> þat brouȝte þo Enguelond : al-to grounde i-wis!
> For þe englische barones bi-comen some : on-treowe and false also
> To bi-traiȝe heom-seolf and heore kyng : þat so muche heom
>   truste to. ...
> For þulke þat þe king truste to : failleden him wel faste;
> So þat he was bi-neoþe i-brouȝt : and ouer-come atþe laste
> And to grounde i-brouȝt, and alle his : and al Enguelond also,
> In-to vnecouþe mannes honde : þat no riȝht ne hadden þar-to;
> And neuer-eft it ne cam a-ȝein : to riȝhte Eyres none –
> Vnkuynde Eyres ȝeot huy beothþ : ore kingues echone,
> And neiȝh-ȝwat alle þis heiȝe Men : and of þe loȝwe al-so.[52]

However, there are some nuances in this passage which complicate both its apparent clarity of national identity and antipathy, and Harold's place in that encoding of English and foreign. Some cracks are plausibly the result of genuine historical confusion or ignorance, such as the fact that there certainly was another available heir in 1066, Edgar Ætheling, and indeed he was of the Old English royal line.[53] Secondly, the declared treachery of the English nobility is evidently troubling for anything other than a self-flagellating national reading; it is also quite possibly a literary invention, the betrayal from within which preserves the moral integrity of the fallen hero.[54] Finally, writing at the close of the thirteenth century, the English poet betrays some confusion about the composition and identity of his society as a whole; not only are the Plantagenet kings 'unnatural heirs', but also 'nearly all the high men' and, it emerges, 'among the low too'.

The *Life*'s defence of Harold is in any case subordinate to its purpose of establishing the horrors of the Conquest and William's harsh rule; Wulfstan is then praised as 'þe cuyndeste englische man' because 'he was so luyte a-drad of him' (106–108). This is a nationalistic reading imposed upon a potentially much more ambiguous character; Wulfstan was that rare Englishman who retained his land, position and power after the Conquest. Wulfstan's life and history are indicative of the bonds and bargains which forged the new Anglo-Norman kingdom; he used his

---

[52] *The Early South-English Legendary or Lives of the Saints I: MS. Laud, 108*, ed. Carl Horstmann (London, 1887), 'St Wolston', 70–77, lines 61–91.
[53] See Nicholas Hooper, 'Edgar Ætheling', *ODNB*.
[54] Alternatively it is possible that this is a shadowy reference to earls Eadwine and Morcar, who fought at Fulford Gate and survived Hastings; the Anglo-Saxon Chronicles are silent on their actions in the interim, but John of Worcester suggests that they deserted Harold on the battlefield: 2:604.

position to support the continuity of English learning and religious practice in the church, while benefitting from Norman support and advancement.[55] In that context the miracle subsequently recounted in the *Life* is tendentiously nationalistic; Wulfstan is supposedly under attack from Norman opponents keen to deprive him of his bishopric, and a miraculous sign at the tomb of King Edward causes a shamed William the Conqueror to reconfirm his rights.[56] But in the context of the *Life*'s praise of King Harold a few lines earlier, this miracle is itself an important choice. Harold may be mourned in the text, but it is the Normans' chosen saint King Edward who holds power. The *Life* attempts to deny that Wulfstan was bishop of Worcester by the gift of William the Conqueror, but when it does so with the miracle at Edward the Confessor's tomb, it is subtly and unavoidably engaged in a negotiation and reconciliation with the Anglo-Norman kings, Edward's 'successors'. Indeed, Wulfstan was himself adopted as a favoured saint by King John, who saw in this miracle a useful claim that kings, not the pope, held the right to appoint bishops.[57] One might see such developments as ironic; or they could equally be seen as simply the warp and weft of a new hybrid kingdom. But by either view, in the Anglo-Norman world, there is no space left for Harold.

A Hero in the Margins

This discussion has begun to illuminate a quality fundamental to Harold's literary afterlife: his marginality, or liminality. In the chronicles, whether praised or blamed, he occupies a dead end in history; in saints' lives he plays the role of foil or villain. Waltham Abbey had the greatest reason to celebrate Harold, but even there he was with 'prudent restraint' gradually edged out of the record.[58] The Normans' enthusiastic legal and literary appropriation of Saint Edward the king not only elides Harold's reign, but has the further effect of robbing Harold of his status as the last symbol of native English freedom; when pre-Conquest Englishness is idealized, it is located in Edward. Thus the saintly Confessor is made to be the last icon of English kingship, not Harold, and it is Edward who is able to aid Wulfstan in his role as pious English instructor of his Norman successor. Edward even takes over Harold's greatest achievement, in being held responsible for the victory at Stamford Bridge. Meanwhile, when *post*-Conquest Englishness is idealized, it is located in those who reach a reconciliation with the new regime, as in the saintly bishop Wulfstan; even the rebel Hereward ultimately comes to honourable terms with the Conqueror. Perhaps the long-held English virtue of loyalty to one's lord was too powerful to be resisted, as the most famous statement in the eighth-century annals of the Chronicle asserts: 'him nænig mæg leofra nærre þonne heora hlaford'[59] ['no kinsman could be dearer to them than their lord']. Within a decade of the Conquest the Anglo-Saxon Chronicle described the remaining English rebels in 1075 as *swican*, 'traitors' to *heora*

---

[55] See Emma Mason, 'Wulfstan', *ODNB*.
[56] On the origins of this story, not present in William of Malmesbury's influential *Vita Wulfstani*, see William of Malmesbury, *Saints' Lives*, ed. M. Winterbottom and R.M. Thomson (Oxford, 2002), pp. xxxiii–iv.
[57] Emma Mason, 'St Wulfstan's staff: a legend and its uses', *Medium Ævum* 53 (1984), 157–79.
[58] *Waltham Chronicle*, xiii–xiv.
[59] ASC s.a. 755: *MS. C*, p. 47; *MS. D*, p. 13; *MS. E*, p. 38.

kynehlaford, 'their royal lord'.[60] God had given England to the Normans, and this providential understanding of events was too great to be resisted. Inevitably, then, Harold is confined to the edges and shadows of historiography.

But Harold's liminality also has a genuinely historical aspect, in his lasting presence in the borders of the realm. His numerous military victories in the Welsh marches were apparently remembered long after his death, as Gerald of Wales observed at the end of the twelfth century:

> respice reges Anglicos Normannis priores. Qui, quoniam hac solum insula Britannica contenti fuerant, et tantum his debellandis operam dabant, eosdem pene penitus saepe deleverant. ... Et sicut longe plenius Haroldus ultimus: qui, pedes ipse, cumque pedestri turba, et levibus armis, victuque patriae conformi, tam valide totam Kambriam et circuivit, et transpenetravit, ut in eadem fere mingentem ad parietem non reliquerit. In cujus victoriae signum, perpetuamque memoriam, lapides in Wallia more antiquo in titulum erectos, locis plerisque in quibus victor extiterat, literas hujusmodi insculptas habentes plurimos invenies, HIC FUIT VICTOR HAROLDUS.[61]

> Consider the English kings before the Normans came. They gave their whole attention to the island of Britain, and they made such a determined effort to subdue the Welsh that they destroyed them almost to a man. ... And last of all, and by far the greatest, came Harold. He advanced into Wales on foot, at the head of his lightly clad infantry, lived on the country, and marched up and down and round and about the whole of Wales with such energy that he 'left not one that pisseth against a wall'. In commemoration of his success, and to his own undying memory, you will find a great number of inscribed stones put up in Wales to mark the many places where he won a victory. This was the old custom. The stones bear the inscription: HIC FUIT VICTOR HAROLDUS.[62]

Nevertheless, Harold's enduring fame in the borderlands was not confined to his historical exploits. The remainder of this essay will discuss the flowering of an astonishing, pseudohistorical myth, denied or doubted in almost all surviving writings, and yet clearly ineradicable as oral legend: the story that he had survived the battle of Hastings, and had come in secret to live in the Welsh borders as a hermit, before dying and being buried at Chester.

Gerald of Wales is one of the earliest surviving witnesses to assert that Harold's body was at Chester, and the story held currency for hundreds of years.[63] The Chester monk Ranulf Higden's mid-fourteenth-century *Polychronicon*, which was rapidly translated into English by John Trevisa,[64] recounts the accepted history of

---

[60] ASC *s.a.* 1076 (for 1075): *MS. D*, pp. 87–88.
[61] Gerald of Wales, *Descriptio Kambriae*, ed. James F. Dimock, in *Giraldi Cambrensis: Opera*, 8 vols (London, 1861–91), 6:217. Cf. John of Salisbury's description of Harold's Welsh victories as an example of great military leadership: *Policraticus*, trans. Cary J. Nederman (Cambridge, 1990), pp. 113–14; *PL* 199, cols. 598C–599D.
[62] Gerald of Wales, *The Journey Through Wales and The Description of Wales*, trans. Lewis Thorpe (Harmondsworth, 1978), p. 266: *Here Harold was victorious.*
[63] *Itinerarium Kambriae*, ed. Dimock, in *Giraldi Cambrensis: Opera*, 6:140; trans. Thorpe, pp. 198–99. See Thacker, 'Cult of King Harold'.
[64] See John Taylor, 'Higden, Ranulf'; Ronald Waldron, 'Trevisa, John', *ODNB*.

Harold's burial at Waltham Abbey and then records the alternative story as a matter of current popular belief:

> Vult autem Giraldus Cambrensis in suo itinerario quod Haraldus multis confossus vulneribus, oculoque sinistro sagitta perdito, ad partes Cestrenses victus evasit, ubi sancta conversatione vitam ut creditur anachoritam in cella Sancti Jacobi juxta ecclesiam Sancti Johannis feliciter consumavit, quod ex ejus ultima confessione palam fuit. Huic et opinioni attestatur fama publica in urbe...[65]

> Bote Giralde Cambrensis in his book þat hatte Itinerarius wolde mene þat Harald hadde many woundes and loste his left yȝe wiþ a strook of an arwe, and was overcome, and scapede to þe contray of Chestre, and lyvede þere holily, as me troweþ, an ankers lyf in Seint Iames celle faste by Seint Iohn his chirche, and made a gracious ende, and þat was i-knowe by his laste confessioun; and þe comyn fame accordeþ in þat citee to þat sawe.[66]

The story is in essence a survival legend, endowing Harold with a pseudohistorical pious afterlife, and something close to posthumous sanctity after his eventual death. Evidently an oral, popular myth, the tale is occasionally referred to and then immediately excluded from the mainstream of English historiography;[67] as such, it is aptly located in the Welsh marches. A closely contemporary Welsh annal for 1332 records the exhumation of his body at Chester: 'And his body and his crown and his raiment and his leathern hose and his golden spurs were found as whole and smelling as good as on the day they were buried.'[68] These are tellingly mixed symbolic signals, of the royal and military body with the purity and incorruption of the saint. In the historical circumstances Harold can neither be canonized nor fully celebrated as a warrior king, but he can be associated with the values of both; he is himself at this point almost a blank, available as a focus for the oppressed, useful to those who feel themselves to be on the margins of Anglo-Norman England. Medieval Chester was regarded by its own chroniclers as a land apart, neither English nor Welsh; it had probably been Harold's base for his greatest victories in the region; it rebelled in 1069–70 and suffered punitive destruction as a consequence; and its twelfth-century earls asserted their independence from the king at every opportunity.[69] This is fertile ground for the liminal figure of Harold Godwineson.

However, before discussing the fullest flowering of this Chester legend, it is worth juxtaposing Harold's Welsh, borderland reputation with another aspect of his

---

[65] *Polychronicon Ranulphi Higden monachi Cestrensis*, ed. C. Babington and J.R. Lumby, 9 vols (London, 1865–86), 7:244.

[66] John Trevisa's 1380s translation, in *Polychronicon Ranulphi Higden*, VII. 245.

[67] Ailred of Rievaulx refers to the survival rumour in tones of indifference: 'aut misere occubuit, aut ut quidam putant poenitentiae tantum reservatus evasit' ['either died wretchedly, or as some think, escaped to live out his life in penitence']: *Vita S. Edwardi regis*, col. 766B; Ralph of Coggeshall recounts it as popular falsehood: *Chronicon Anglicanum*, 1; the *Waltham Chronicle* dismisses it, 'quicquid fabulentur homines' ['whatever stories men may invent']: pp. 54–57.

[68] *Brut y tywysogyon, or, The chronicle of the princes: Peniarth MS. 20 version*, trans. Thomas Jones (Cardiff, 1952), p. 127; Thacker, 'Cult of King Harold', p. 164.

[69] See Thacker, 'Cult of King Harold', pp. 164–68; Alan Thacker, 'The Earls and their Earldom', *The Earldom of Chester and its Charters: Journal of the Chester Archaeological Society* 71 (1991), 11–18, at p. 17.

identity which also overlaps and interacts with his putative 'Englishness': his Danishness. He was a grandson of the Danish *Jarl* Thorgils, and thus a cousin of King Swein Ulfsson of Denmark, and potential claimant to the throne of England by virtue of his Danish predecessors.[70] And Harold was remembered in the Scandinavian world; three Norse sagas record the legend of his survival at the battle of Hastings.[71] The most extensive of these is notable for its fully-fledged sanctification of the penitent Harold, who is said to have lived as an anonymous hermit at Canterbury. His death brings about a posthumous reconciliation with William the Conqueror, who reveres his sweet-smelling, holy body, and gives him an honourable, royal burial in London.[72] The two shorter accounts also present his holy afterlife as a pilgrim and hermit,[73] and there are evident parallels with the survival legends which attended upon the memory of the heroic Norwegian king Olaf Tryggvason.[74]

Thus while King Harold is systematically damned by, diminished in, or excluded from the mainstream of post-Conquest English historiography, he holds a place on the margins, in the Anglo-Danish and the Anglo-Welsh literary and geographical borderlands. However, paradoxically enough, Harold's legendary afterlife takes on its fullest potential in an early thirteenth-century text which was most likely written at Waltham Abbey; certainly it was copied there, as its sole witness is that same manuscript which contains the abbey's *Chronicle* and relic lists.[75] Sitting alongside the account of Harold's death and burial at Waltham, then, is this work known as the *Vita Haroldi*, which effectively denies the presence of Harold's body at the abbey, instead siting him anonymously in Chester. But in elaborating and celebrating the holiness of Harold the hermit, the *Vita* perhaps aided Waltham's cause better than the corpse of a usurper ever could, despite all the chronicler's attempts to salvage his reputation in verse. As the years passed, the abbey made less and less of its possession of Harold's body.[76]

---

[70] For the fullest exposition of this case see Howard, 'A Throne-Worthy King'.
[71] See Gillian Fellows-Jensen, 'The Myth of Harold II's Survival in the Scandinavian Sources', in *Harold II and the Bayeux Tapestry*, ed. Owen-Crocker, pp. 53–64; Marc Cohen, 'From Throndheim to Waltham to Chester: Viking- and post-Viking-Age attitudes in the survival legends of Óláfr Tryggvason and Harold Godwinson', in *The Middle Ages in the North-West*, ed. Scott and Starkey, pp. 143–53; Christine Fell, 'English history and Norman legend in the Icelandic saga of Edward the Confessor', *Anglo-Saxon England* 6 (1977), 223–36, at pp. 233–34.
[72] *Hemings þáttr Áslakssonar*, ed. Gillian Fellows-Jensen (Copenhagen, 1962); the relevant passages are translated in Margaret Ashdown, 'An Icelandic Account of the Survival of Harold Godwinson', in *The Anglo-Saxons: Studies in Some Aspects of their History and Culture presented to Bruce Dickins*, ed. Peter Clemoes (London, 1959), pp. 122–36.
[73] *Játvarþar Saga*, in *Icelandic Sagas and other historical documents relating to the settlements and descents of the Northmen on the British Isles*, ed./trans. Gudbrand Vigfusson and George W. Dasent, 4 vols (1887–94) 1:388–400 (p. 397), 3:416–28 (pp. 424–25); and *Fornmanna Sögur*, 12 vols (Copenhagen, 1825–37), 10:372–73.
[74] Cohen, 'From Throndheim to Waltham to Chester'; Oddr Snorrason, *Óláfs saga Tryggvasonar*, ed. Finnur Jónsson (Copenhagen, 1932); trans. Theodore M. Andersson, *The Saga of Olaf Tryggvason* (Ithaca, 2003).
[75] *Waltham Chronicle*, pp. l–lii.
[76] Cf. Thacker, 'Cult of King Harold', p. 159.

The Latin prose *Vita Haroldi* has the approximate form of a saint's life, albeit with some key omissions;[77] it can equally be regarded as a kind of romance, sharing multiple tropes with closely contemporary vernacular romances.[78] In sum, the *Vita* recounts chosen vignettes from the historical life and pseudohistorical afterlife of Harold Godwineson.[79] His early achievements and victories over the Welsh are closely tied to his pious devotion to Waltham and its holy cross; repeatedly he prays to it and his prayers are answered. He survives the battle of Hastings, and is rescued and healed by a Saracen lady in Winchester. He then briefly attempts to raise support to retake the kingdom, before receiving a revelation which gives him a repentant change of heart, after which he transforms himself into a pilgrim. He travels across Europe and to the Holy Land in anonymity, before returning to England to live as a humble hermit in the Welsh borders. Here he is frequently assaulted by the people over whom he had once been victorious, until they learn to venerate him as holy; he then moves to a hermitage in Chester where he ends his days unknown, revealing his identity only on his deathbed.

This brief summary immediately shows the text's shared cultural field with contemporary romance; and, indeed, the insular romance's close relationship with hagiography.[80] The grand transformation of a noble warrior into a wandering pilgrim, and finally a hermit, is the central plot motif of *Gui de Warewic*;[81] and the fleeting reference to the care of the Saracen lady glances toward that recurring romance theme, most fully developed in *Boeve de Haumtone*, of the powerful heathen princess who aids (and usually loves) the hero.[82] Echoed in those romances and in numerous others, however, is the most important structuring principle of the *Vita*, which is to present Harold throughout his life, both before and after Hastings, as the pious recipient of divine favour. This takes on particular importance in the author's innovative adaptation of the miraculous vision of Edward which heralds his victory

---

[77] Chiefly a list of miracles and a final resting place for the saint's body: the observation is Cohen's (p. 150).

[78] It has also frequently been termed as such, as in its 1885 editor's subtitle, 'The Romance of the Life of Harold'; see also Robert M. Stein, 'The Trouble with Harold: The Ideological Context of the *Vita Haroldi*', *New Medieval Literatures* 2 (1998), 181–204, at p. 197.

[79] On the *Vita Haroldi*'s provenance, structure and purposes see Stephen Matthews, 'The Content and Construction of the *Vita Haroldi*', in *King Harold II and the Bayeux Tapestry*, ed. Owen-Crocker, pp. 65–73; Thacker, 'Cult of King Harold'; for an alternative reading of the text, see Stein, 'Trouble with Harold'.

[80] See in general Andrea Hopkins, *The Sinful Knights: A Study of Middle English Penitential Romance* (Oxford, 1990), and the references in n. 81, below.

[81] *Gui de Warewic: Roman du XIIIe siècle*, ed. Alfred Ewert, 2 vols (Paris, 1933); trans. Judith Weiss in *Boeve de Haumtone and Gui de Warewic: Two Anglo-Norman Romances* (Tempe, AZ, 2008), pp. 97–243. On Gui's conversion see Susan Crane, *Insular Romance: Politics, Faith and Culture in Anglo-Norman and Middle English Romance* (Berkeley, 1986), pp. 101–15; Neil Cartlidge, *Medieval Marriage: Literary Approaches, 1100–1300* (Cambridge, 1997), pp. 99–106; Paul Price, 'Confessions of a Godless Killer: Guy of Warwick and Comprehensive Entertainment', in *Medieval Insular Romance: Translation and Innovation*, ed. Judith Weiss, Jennifer Fellows and Morgan Dickson (Cambridge, 2000), pp. 93–110; Judith Weiss, 'The Exploitation of Ideas of Pilgrimage and Sainthood in *Gui de Warewic*', in *The Exploitations of Medieval Romance*, ed. Laura Ashe, Ivana Djordjević and Judith Weiss (Cambridge, 2010), pp. 43–56, and n. 85, below.

[82] *Boeve de Haumtoune*, ed. Albert Stimming (Halle, 1899); trans. Judith Weiss in *Boeve de Haumtone and Gui de Warewic*, pp. 25–95. See Judith Weiss, 'The Wooing Woman in Anglo-Norman Romance', in *Romance in Medieval England*, ed. Maldwyn Mills, Jennifer Fellows and Carol M. Meale (Cambridge, 1991), pp. 149–61.

at Stamford Bridge. In Osbert's and Ailred's versions discussed above, Edward gives the abbot proof of his supernatural knowledge by revealing that he knows Harold had suffered from a terrible pain in his leg, about which he had told no one, and which had abated with prayer.[83] Here, the pain is now daringly recast as a temporary punishment for Harold's breaking his oath to William in seizing the throne:

> Quod preter divinitatis nutum minime accidisse: celitus post in brevi fuerat declaratum. cum enim rex Norwagensis classe advectus numerosa intrasset Angliam ... illique rex novus coacto exercitu sestinaret occurrere tybie subito unius vehementissimo cepit dolore constringi. ... noctem pene totam suspiriis et precibus agentes insompnem familiarem sancte crucis expecierat subvencionem. In ipsa vero nocte astitit in visione servo Domini Elsino abbati Ramesiensi sanctus et vigil propugnator suorum rex Edwardus predecessor viri merentis et afflicti... "Surgens vade et annunciabis regi vestro ex me quia et presentis sui doloris medelam et imminentis belli me interveniente Deus ei concessit victoriam." ... Rex itaque ut paucis utamur divinis curatur beneficiis exhilaratur oraculis.

> But that this had not happened with the divine Will had been declared a little time after from heaven. For when the Norwegian king, sailing with a numerous fleet, had made an entry into England ... and the newly-elected king was hastening to meet him with an army he had collected, he was suddenly seized with a most violent pain in his leg. ... Passing nearly the whole night without sleep in sighs and prayers, he begged for the familiar assistance of the Holy Cross. In the same night there appeared to that servant of the Lord, Elsin, the abbot of Ramsey, King Edward, the holy and watchful defender of his people, the predecessor of our sorrowing and afflicted hero ... 'Rise, go and tell your king from me the remedy for his present pain and the threatened war, that, at my intercession, God has granted him the victory. ... So the king, to speak briefly, is cured by divine favour, and is exhilarated by heavenly messages.[84]

The effect is to redirect the spiritual force of the miracle from Edward back to Harold, and (not incidentally) to clear Harold of the traditional guilt of his usurpation, by having him serve a limited penance demonstrably accepted as sufficient. This done, the author's representation of Harold's defeat at Hastings and subsequent change of life works supremely against the grain of the usual providential reading. Despite dramatizing a central scene of repentance after Hastings, when he realizes that he must no longer strive to retake the kingdom, the *Vita* actually shows Harold throughout his life as a consistently humble and pious character, a man who had always sought to serve God in the appropriate manner. This man had lacked guidance in the aftermath of Hastings, but now it is forthcoming:

> Tandem vero in se reversus Haroldus et quasi a fantastico quo diucius sompnio sibi redditus ad cor suum totus convertitur. Intelligit vel sero obsistentem sibi in via hac qua inaniter ambulabat Deum. ... Apertisque

---

[83] 'La Vie de S. Édouard', pp. 114–15; *Vita S. Edwardi regis*, cols. 778A–B.
[84] *Vita Haroldi*, pp. 54–55, 156–57.

mentis sue oculis aliud de cetero sibi genus eligendum videt preliorum alia requirenda presidia. Respexerat enim oculo jam propicio crucifixus rex regis dejecti labores et longos cruciatus. nec ulterius paciebatur peculiarem vexilli sui cultorem tanti meroris abysso demergi involvi laberinto. ... spem vero et studium regnandi non deponeret sed mutaret. ... cepit regni longe felicioris faciliorem multo viam agnoscere ... Intuetur jam qualiter Dominus mundi mundanum cum esset in mundo sprevit imperium. qui et quesitus in regem: fugerit. et milibus obsequencium turbis solitarie orationis secessum pretulerit. Reminiscitur datam huic per passionis dure et mortis dire supplicium omnem in celo et in terra potestatem. (38–39)

Now Harold, coming at length to himself, and returning, as it were, from his fantastic dream, is completely changed in his heart. He perceives, though late, that it was God who was opposing him in the way in which he was so fruitlessly walking... and the eyes of his understanding being opened, he sees that he must choose another kind of warfare, and that other kinds of defences would be required. For the crucified King had looked upon the toils and long-sufferings of the dethroned king with a regard already favourable to him, and would not further suffer the special devotee of His banner to be engulphed in the depths, or be overwhelmed in the maze of so great an affliction. ... yet He had not deprived him of the hope and desire of ruling, but had changed the nature of his desire. ... he begins to find that the path to a more blessed kingdom is far easier ... He now sees how the Lord of the world, when He was in the world, despised a worldly kingdom; and, when they sought to make Him a King, fled, and preferred the retirement of a solitary life to a throng of followers. He remembers that all power was given to Him in heaven and earth by the humiliation of a bitter passion and a cruel death. (139–40)

The key to this moment of transformation is its surprising lack of any real change.[85] Harold has long been favoured by God, and now in his sufferings he is compared directly to Christ. He had wanted a kingdom; now he realizes there is a better kingdom to seek. He had wanted power; now he sees that power is gained in a different way. In this re-reading, the defeat at Hastings is no longer a divine punishment for Harold's sins. Ultimately, and against all expectation, it becomes a sign of divine *favour*.

The *Vita Haroldi* thus strives to transform Harold's historical marginality into chosen spiritual exile; his exclusion from the secular, political world is reshaped, into the powerful figure of the holy man who is very properly a 'stranger' to this world. Eremitism was a phenomenon of growing importance in the high middle ages; across Europe the period saw a flowering in multiple forms of religious and spiritual life, in the centres and on the margins of society.[86] The hermit's reclusive and enclosed life

---

[85] For a fuller discussion of this including a comparative analysis of *Gui de Warewic*, see Laura Ashe, '*Mutatio dexterae Excelsi*: Narratives of Transformation after the Conquest', *JEGP* 110 (2011), 141–72.

[86] See e.g. several chapters in *The Cambridge History of Christianity vol. 4: Christianity in Western Europe c.1100–c.1500*, ed. Miri Rubin and Walter Simons (Cambridge, 2009): Henrietta Leyser, 'Clerical purity and the re-ordered world', pp. 11–21; Beverly Mayne Kienzle, 'Religious

functions as an allegorical nexus in which marginality, humility and exclusion are recast as idealized spiritual states; and in this, the fictional Harold is not alone. As Henry Mayr-Harting has shown, the twelfth-century English hermit was a powerfully important figure in the landscape; he was a focus for religious devotion, but also a practical source of advice and guidance, an aid to the local population in all matters of daily life.[87] Such men gained great importance in the world by their decision to reject it, and they were turned to by aristocratic patrons, visited and supported by royalty, and consulted by senior clergy. All known recluses in the period were of native birth and English mother tongue, and as Hugh Thomas has suggested, their active spiritual status must have bridged gaps between the local English and the French-speaking higher aristocracy.[88]

The holy recluse is thus by nature a conciliating figure in a community. And in the *Vita*'s great recuperation of Harold, it is important to note the price which is paid in the process: Harold is explicitly not a hero for the English, or a figurehead of English identity. The author emphasizes this in a disagreement with his source, who has apparently speculated that Harold must have returned from the Holy Land out of a love of his country:

> Dicit igitur memoratus vir de sancto tunc peregrinante ita. Postmodum quia natalis soli semper dulcis esse solet inhabitacio: ad Angliam cujus antea rex extiterat concito properavit. Cum autem sapientum diffinicione tritum sit: quia infirmus est adhuc cui patria sua dulcis est. fortis vero jam. cum omne solum patria est. perfectus quoque cui omne solum exilium est. cui non pateat absurde dici virum ut ipse dicit senectute aridum. diuturnitate itineris utique religiosi confractum. natalis soli ut repatriaret dulcedine attractum? Dicente insuper Domino ad Abraham: *Ingredere de tera tua.* itemque in psalmo. *Obliviscere populum tuum et domum patris tui.* Quem etate minorem animi firmitate. et sanctitate meriti. inferiorem pariter et imbecilliorem. tenere non potuit terre sue. populi sui. domusque paterne dulcedo aut memoria duceret jam vel attraheret in omnibus hiis quo provecciorem eo proculdubio et perfecciorem. (88–89)

> Thus the aforesaid man says of the saint who was then on his journeyings, as follows: 'Afterwards, because to live on one's own native soil is always pleasant, he made all haste to England, where he had formerly been King, that he might spend there the remainder of his days.' But since it is a trite saying of the wise that that man is yet weak who holds his fatherland dear, but still strong when he makes any land his fatherland, and even perfect when

---

poverty and the search for perfection', pp. 39–53; Walter Simons, 'On the margins of religious life: hermits and recluses, penitents and tertiaries, beguines and beghards', pp. 311–23.

[87] Henry Mayr-Harting, 'Functions of a Twelfth-Century Recluse', *History* 60 (1975), 337–52. See also Peter Brown, 'The Rise and Function of the Holy Man in Late Antiquity', *Journal of Roman Studies* 61 (1971), 80–101; Susan J. Ridyard, 'Functions of a Twelfth-Century Recluse Revisited: the Case of Godric of Finchale', in *Belief and Culture in the Middle Ages: Studies presented to Henry Mayr-Harting*, ed. Richard Gameson and Henrietta Leyser (Oxford, 2001), pp. 236–50.

[88] Hugh M. Thomas, *The English and the Normans: Ethnic Hostility, Assimilation, and Identity 1066–c.1200* (Oxford, 2003), pp. 208–209, 222–23; Mayr-Harting, pp. 344–45, 350.

every land is a land of exile to him; who does not see that it is absurd that a man withered with old age, as he himself says, and broken down by the length of his journey, religious though it was, should be declared to have been attracted by the sweetness of his native soil to seek a fatherland again in it? And does not the Lord say to Abraham, 'Get thee out of thy country;' and again in the Psalm, 'Forget thine own people and thy father's house'? And if the sweetness or recollection of his land, his people, and his father's house could not hold him of less age or inferior strength of mind, or holiness of purpose, would it lead or would it attract him to all these things whereby the more he advanced the more perfect he became? (192–93)

Thus Harold's exclusion from the world, his marginality in history, has become a positive good: an ever-increasing perfection of soul. And most importantly, this is a cultic interpretation of Harold which empties out his ambivalent symbolic associations. It does not focus upon his Englishness; instead, it sweeps away all nationalistic concerns in favour of conciliatory holiness; even the fierce, 'brutish' Welsh, his former enemies, learn to venerate him.[89] Concomitantly, it ignores his status as a symbol of conquest and oppression.

The *Vita Haroldi* has thus performed an audacious transformation upon the historical Harold; but the substance of this change is not, in fact, the conversion of the sinful warrior to a religious life. Harold is not represented as a shamed penitent, living miserably in the hope of purging his terrible sins: that would only accord with the triumphalist Norman myth of his perjury and damnation. Instead, he is a consistently pious servant of God, who suffers a reversal in this world, and is gifted with a revelation of the route to sanctity. Along this route he becomes ever *perfeccior*. Finally, Harold is 'omnium hostium suorum victor' ['the conqueror of all his enemies'],[90] as an anonymous, stateless, holy man; and this victory has very little to do with his former identity, or his nation, or even with the uniqueness of individual experience. He is less and less Harold, son of Godwine, king of England; but that identity, like all worldly rank and status, is in any case fleeting, and gone.

---

[89] *Vita Haroldi*, pp. 73–75, 176–78.
[90] *Vita Haroldi*, pp. 99, 203.

5
Mordred

JUDITH WEISS

The Origins of Mordred

Mordred is one of literature's greatest traitors.[1] Moreover, his treachery is compounded by sexual sins that are not its necessary or usual corollaries: adultery and incest. However, the first text in which he appears, the Welsh Annal for the year 537 (which may itself be no older than middle of the tenth century), refers to 'the battle of Camlann in which Arthur and Mordred fell' ('Gueith Camlann in qua Arthur et Medrait corruerunt') only in a way that seems to be entirely neutral.[2] It is not obvious that he was on the opposite side to Arthur at the sixth-century battle; and the two men may well have fought and died together.[3] References to Mordred in twelfth-century Welsh texts are positive: his valour and good nature form a standard for the praise of others.[4] Arthur and Mordred – although not originally related, as far as we can tell – might thus be said to be warriors 'on the same side' and from the same place. In this essay, I propose to discuss how Mordred came to be such an paradigmatically evil figure, to the point where he is used as a template for villainy in other later texts. At the same time, I also want to consider the survival of those admirable aspects in his characterization that ultimately make him a figure of considerable ambivalence: simultaneously both anti-hero and hero.

In the extant medieval texts, it is Geoffrey of Monmouth who first associates the name Modred with a wicked deed.[5] The *Historia* gives no reason why Arthur's

---

[1] Dante places Mordred in one of the lowest circles of Hell: *Inferno*, canto 32, lines 61–62 (*The Divine Comedy of Dante Alighieri: Inferno*, trans. John D. Sinclair (New York, 1939, repr. 1978).

[2] See Thomas Charles-Edwards, 'The Arthur of History', in *The Arthur of the Welsh*, ed. Rachel Bromwich, A.O.H. Jarman and Brynley F. Roberts (Cardiff, 1991), pp. 15–32 (p. 25), and O.J. Padel, *Arthur in Medieval Welsh Literature* (Cardiff, 2000), p. 10.

[3] Where Camlann was is unknown; it is Geoffrey of Monmouth who first gives a very similar name, Camblan, to a river in Cornwall. See Geoffrey of Monmouth, *The Historia Regum Britanniae I: Bern, Bürgerbibliothek MS 568* (i.e. the 'Vulgate' Version), ed. Neil Wright (Cambridge, 1984), 11.178, p. 250; O.J. Padel, 'Geoffrey of Monmouth and Cornwall', *Cambridge Medieval Celtic Studies* 8 (1984), 1–27, at p. 13; it may be the river Camel. Welsh Triads later allude to Camlann: see Rachel Bromwich, *The Triads of the Island of Britain*, 3rd edition (Cardiff, 2006), p. 167.

[4] Padel, *Arthur in Medieval Welsh Literature*, p. 113.

[5] See Padel, *Arthur in Medieval Welsh Literature*, p. 113 and chapter 2, 'Dynastic Chronicles' (by W.R.J. Barron, Françoise Le Saux and Lesley Johnson) in *The Arthur of the English*, ed. W.R.J. Barron (Cardiff, 2001), p. 16. I have used 'Modred' here because it is the form used by the

nephew,[6] once he is left in charge of Britain in his uncle's absence on the Continent, should decide to usurp the crown and marry the queen, but it is careful *not* to suggest that Ganhumara is certainly complicit, which would mean she would share responsibility. The particular use of verb-forms in the ablative absolute and perfect passive infinitive suggests otherwise:

> ...nuntiatur ei Modredum nepotem suum cuius tutele permiserat Britanniam eiusdem diademate per tyrannidem et proditionem insignitum esse reginamque Ganhumeram uiolato iure priorum nuptiarum eidem nephanda uenere copulatam fuisse. (*Historia*, 10.176; p. 249)

> ...the news was brought to him (Arthur) that his nephew Modred, in whose care he had left Britain, through tyranny and treachery, had placed the crown on his own head and queen Ganhumara was married (to him) in abominable passion in violation of her former marriage.[7]

What also suggests that Ganhumara is a victim, rather than an agent, is her desperate and frightened flight from York to Caerleon when she hears Modred has recovered from defeat and is marching into Winchester (*Historia*, 11.177; p. 130). This was significantly changed in the first Variant Version of the *Historia*: her flight is postponed until after Arthur's successful siege of Winchester and Modred's escape to Cornwall; in other words, when Arthur looks as if he is winning, she flees, as if in guilt.

Wace, some seventeen years later, drawing on both Vulgate and Variant versions, considerably enlarged on this hint. As he informs us of Modred's prior secret love for the queen, now a motive for his behaviour, the poet raises the emotional

---

Historia and in Wace's *Roman de Brut* but in general will use the later form, Mordred, except when discussing texts where the form is rather different.

[6] Both the Vulgate and the First Variant Version of Geoffrey's *Historia* give a contradictory picture of Modred's relationship to Arthur. First Loth becomes Arthur's brother-in-law by marrying Arthur's sister Anna, daughter of Uther and Ygerna (*Historia* I, viii, 139, 138): her future sons will be Arthur's nephews. But next Loth marries the (unnamed) sister of Aurelius, brother of Uther, and thus becomes Arthur's uncle by marriage; Loth's two sons Gawain and Modred are thus Arthur's cousins (*Historia* I, ix, 152; *The 'Historia Regum Britanniae' of Geoffrey of Monmouth: II: the First Variant Version*, ed. Neil Wright (Cambridge, 1988)). Anna is also confusingly given another marriage, to Budicius king of Brittany; their son is Hoel, another nephew for Arthur (*Historia* I, ix, 144). Wace tries to sort out the confusion; though he repeats the information about Hoel, Budicius and Anna (lines 9140–42) at line 9635, he omits all mention of Aurelius's sister's marriage and tells us that Loth is Arthur's brother-in-law. Here he mentions Walwein as Loth's son – though not Mordred. *The Anonymous Short English Metrical Chronicle* calls Moddred Arthur's 'cosyn', 291, but this may merely mean 'relative' as in Robert Mannyng's *Chronicle*, c. 1303–38 (line 11745). See Wace, *Roman de Brut: A History of the British*, text and translation by Judith Weiss, revised edition (Exeter, 2002), *The Anonymous Short English Metrical Chronicle*, ed. Ewald Zettl, EETS OS 176 (London, 1935), and Robert Mannyng of Brunne, *The Chronicle*, ed. Idelle Sullens (Binghamton, 1996).

[7] Grammatically, *Uiolato* is ablative absolute, indicating a completed event, and is not an active verb; *copulatam fuisse*, the perfect passive infinitive, indicates that Ganhumara is an object, passively being wed. (*Copulo* is probably from *copulare* and not from the deponent verb *copulor*.) I am grateful to Naomi Weiss for her help with this. A later history of Britain by a Fleming, Sire Jehan de Wavrin's *Recueil*, begun c. 1455, tried to clear Guenevere's name by asserting that her marriage to Mordred was a forced one: see Robert Huntington Fletcher, *The Arthurian Material in the Chronicles Especially Those of Great Britain and France* (Boston, 1906), pp. 225–29.

temperature and finally laments in such a way as to suggest that she is already complicit:

> Modret esteit de grant noblei
> Mais n'esteit pas de bone fei.
> Il aveit la reine amee,
> Mais co esteit chose celee;
> Mult s'en celout; e ki quidast
> Que il feme sun uncle amast,
> Maismement de tel seinnur
> Dunt tuit li suen orent enur;
> Feme sun uncle par putage
> Ama Modret si fist huntage.
> A Modret e a la reine –
> Deus! tant mal fist cele saisine –
> Comanda tut fors la corune. (*Roman de Brut*, lines 11177–89)

Modret was of noble birth, but disloyal. He was in love with the queen, but this was not suspected. He kept it very quiet; and who would have believed he could love his uncle's wife, especially the wife of such a lord, whose kin all held him in honour? Modret loved his uncle's wife shamefully and was dishonourable. To Modret and to the queen – alas! how unfortunate that he gave [them] this possession! – Arthur entrusted everything but the crown.

Wace's repeated emphasis here is on Modred's incestuous desire – for loving one's uncle's wife would in the Middle Ages have been regarded in that light.[8] His next comment both insists on the horror of this and equates land and queen as bodies both 'occupied':

> Deus, quel hunte, Deus, quel vilté,
> Sis niez, fiz sa sorur, esteit,
> E en guarde sun regne aveit;
> Tut sun regne li ot livré
> E en guarde tut cumandé.
> E Modred li volt tut tolir
> E a sun ues tut retenir...
> Empres ceste grant felunie
> Fist Modred altre vilainie,
> Kar cuntre cristiene lei
> Prist a sun lit femme lu rei,
> Femme sun uncle e sun seignur
> Prist a guise de traitur. (*Roman de Brut*, lines 13016–30)

God, what shame, God what disgrace! He was his nephew, his sister's son, and had the care of his kingdom; Arthur had entrusted the whole realm to him and put it all in his charge. And Modred wanted to take it all away from

---

[8] See Helen Cooper, 'Counter-Romance: Civil Strife and Father-Killing in the Prose Romances', in *The Long Fifteenth Century: Essays for Douglas Gray*, ed. Helen Cooper and Sally Mapstone (Oxford, 1997), pp. 141–62, at pp. 153–54.

him and keep it all for his own use ... After this act of great wickedness, Modred did another evil deed, because against Christian law he took to his bed the king's wife; he treacherously took the wife of his uncle and lord.

At the queen's flight (lines 13201–222) her compliance with Modred's desire is finally beyond doubt: she is guilty of *vilainie*, of tarnishing her honour for Modred's sake, putting Arthur to shame by desiring his nephew. As a result, she is *mult avilee* ('badly degraded', line 13212). Wace thus took a decisive step in blackening Guinevere's reputation – and also very slightly diminished Modred's responsibility for his crime (because the queen returned his passion). Again embroidering on the *Historia*, he also shows us a usurper who is fertile (Modred has two sons) in contrast to a barren royal couple:

> entr'els dous n'orent nul eir
> Ne ne porent emfant aveir.   (*Brut*, lines 9657–58)

The two of them had no heir, nor could they have a child.

This barrenness is almost certainly Wace's invention, but it is unclear whether he is doing so to discredit either the king or the queen, or both.

Both the *Historia* and Wace depict Modred as being supported by heathen allies in his conflict with Arthur. This suggests he is as good as a renegade to the Christian faith; worse, perhaps, is his bringing back into the land those enemies previously routed by Arthur, the Saxons and their leader Childric (*Historia* 11.177, p. 248; and *Roman de Brut* lines 13054–70). This is an element that is long-lived in the Arthurian chronicle tradition, as far as the Alliterative *Morte Arthure* (c. 1400–02), but it does not appear in the fourteenth-century Stanzaic *Morte Arthur* or in Malory's *Morte Darthur* (where it was important to depict the final struggle specifically as a civil war). Modred's seizure of the opportunity to rebel when his uncle is abroad indicates unscrupulousness as well as a certain cowardice: in the Alliterative *Morte* he is sufficiently scared of Arthur to change his heraldic device in their last battle; in the Stanzaic *Morte* he flees, terrified, when his brother Agravain is slain by Lancelot.[9]

Ancestry and Incest

Several Arthurian narratives portray Mordred as a knight with a fine appearance and some chivalric talent, both in keeping with his lineage; but at odds with it are his arrogance and fear of confrontation:

> Il atendrent un chevalier ... et estoit cil chevaliers apelez Mordrez, et estoit frère monseignor Gauven, et estoit auques bons chevaliers, mes mout i avoit a dire, car il estoit fel e orgueillous. Il ne reperoit adonc mie a la cort, car li rois avoit dit qu'il corroceroit Mordre s'il le tenoit. Por doutance de celi corroz ne reperoit mie Mordrez a la cort...[10]

> They awaited a knight ... and this knight was called Mordred and was the brother of my lord Gawain; he was a rather good knight, but there was much

---

[9] *Morte Arthure*, ed. Edmund Brock, EETS OS 8 (London, 1865, repr. 1961), lines 4180–86; *Le Morte Arthur*, ed. P.F. Hissiger (The Hague and Paris, 1975), lines 1862–63.

[10] *Le Roman de Tristan en Prose*, ed. Renée L. Curtis, 3 vols (Leiden, 1963–85), vol. 2 (1976), cap. 668, p. 239.

wanting in him because he was wicked and proud. So he did not return to the court because the king had said he would chastise Mordred if he found him. For fear of his anger Mordred did not return to court.

The Vulgate Cycle's *Lancelot* has one of the most extended portraits of Mordred, which suggests that his good looks raise expectations of correspondingly virtuous behaviour, but also emphasizes that he does not take after other members of his family:

> Et neporquant il estoit grans chevaliers et lons; si ot les chevels crespes et blons et fust trop seant de vis, s'il n'eust la regardeure si felenesse. Et de ce ne resambloit il mie mon signor Gauvain, son frère.[11]

> And yet he was a big and tall knight; he had blonde, curly hair and would have been very handsome of face had he not had such a wicked expression. And in this he did not resemble my lord Gawain, his brother.

Though Lancelot later congratulates Mordred on being true to his lineage (*Lancelot*, cap. xcvi, 5:215), this turns out to be the opposite of the truth when a hermit reveals that he is not Loth's son but the serpent of Arthur's dream, which will destroy many men. Mordred promptly beheads the hermit in shame and anger (*Lancelot*, cap. xcvi, 5:222). So untrue to his family origins is he that in the Alliterative *Morte*, where he is labelled Mordred the Malebranche,[12] it is his hand that kills his brother Gawain.[13] The *Suite Merlin* (after 1230) possibly prepares us for this action: Mordred is shown as having a great scar from a wound on his forehead 'qui puis i parut tous les jours de sa vie' ('which afterwards was apparent there for his whole life')[14] – a wound that reminds us of the mark of Cain, even if the apparent cause is a bump on the head when he was a baby.

Whoever invented the story that Mordred killed his brother was clearly inspired to do so by the tradition that he would kill his father, and the story of the end of Arthur benefits immensely from this personalized aspect of his death. Already Laȝamon's *Brut* intensifies the emotional aspect of the close uncle-nephew relationship between Arthur and Mordred, thereby heightening the pathos of the betrayal. That he is a 'sister's son' is constantly emphasized (lines 12715, 13973, 14027, 14051) and Arthur refers to Anna's children as 'children alre leofest' ('most beloved of children', line 11081).[15] However, it is in the Vulgate *Lancelot* that the idea of Mordred actually being Arthur's son first appears, though not yet incestuously. The author first tells us that Mordred and his uncle will die in the carnage which Mordred starts (*Lancelot*, cap. lxix, 2:411), but it is the hermit who reveals to Mordred the secret of his

---

[11] *Lancelot*, ed. Alexandre Micha, 9 vols (Geneva, 1978–1983), cap. lxix, 2:408.
[12] Lines 4062 and 4174. Benson translates this as 'ill-begotten': see *King Arthur's Death*, ed. Larry D. Benson (Exeter, 1986), while Hamel glosses it as a child who turns against its parents and betrays its upbringing: see *Morte Arthure*, ed. Mary Hamel (New York, 1984), p. 387.
[13] In Laȝamon's *Brut*, Gawain is killed by 'a Saxon earl'; in *Le Mort Artu* (the source for Malory here) he dies from a wound inflicted on him earlier by Lancelot. See *Laȝamon's Arthur: the Arthurian Section of Laȝamon's Brut*, ed. and trans. W.R.J. Barron and S.C. Weinberg (Harlow, 1989), lines 14140–41, and *La Mort Le Roi Artu*, para. 175, p. 224.
[14] *La Suite du Roman de Merlin*. ed. Gilles Roussineau, 2 vols (Geneva, 1996), cap. 2, para. 76, 1:57.
[15] On the special relationship between mother's brother and sister's son, see Tomas Ó Cathasaigh, 'The Sister's Son in Early Irish Literature', *Peritia* 5 (1986), 128–60.

illegitimate birth (while not disclosing Arthur's name) and his real father's dream of the destructive snake which issues from him. It is Lancelot, however, who – by means of a piece of paper in the dead hermit's hand – learns that this father is Arthur. This knowledge is not revealed to Mordred at this point in the Cycle, but by the time of the *Mort Artu*, the Vulgate's third romance, he appears to have discovered it.[16]

Given that Mordred is the unquestioned son of Loth's wife, the queen of Orkney, it did not take long for post-Vulgate narratives, influenced by the contemporary fashion for stories of incest,[17] to put two and two together: Anna (called Morcades in later narratives)[18] is Arthur's sister and Mordred's mother, so that Arthur has slept with her (though, improbably, neither realized their relationship at the time), and by her incestuously conceived his son Mordred. The thirteenth-century *Estoire del Saint Graal,* the *Estoire de Merlin* and the *Suite du Merlin* (the latter two deriving from the late twelfth or early thirteenth century *Merlin* by Robert de Boron), all contain this revelation, given to Arthur by Merlin, and the *Suite* makes a point of emphasising both the incest and Arthur's crime:

> Adont conut li frères carneument sa serour et porta la dame chelui qui puissedi le traist a mort...

> [Merlin to Arthur:] '...tu ies dyables et anemis Jhesucrist et le plus desloial chevalier de ceste contree, car tu ies rois sacres...Artus, tu as fait si tres grant desloiaute que tu as geu carnelment a ta serour germaine que tes peres engenra et ta mere porta, si as engenre un fil qui iert teuls coume Diex set bien, car par lui verra moult de grant mal en terre.'[19]

> Then the brother carnally knew his sister and the lady bore the one who later would mortally betray him...

> 'You are a devil and an enemy of Jesus Christ and the most disloyal knight in this land, for you are a consecrated king ... Arthur, you have committed such great disloyalty because you have lain carnally with your blood sister, engendered by your father and borne by your mother; you have begotten a son who will be such as God very well knows, for through him will be seen much evil in the land.'

---

[16] Mordred forges a letter from the supposedly dead Arthur to the English barons telling them to take Mordred as their king and drops a strong hint that he is more than a nephew: 'por pes vos pri ge que vos Mordret que ge tenoie a neveu – mes il ne l'est pas – que vos en faciez roi de la terre de Logres' ('for the sake of peace I beg you that you make Mordred, whom I treated as my nephew – but he is not – king of the land of Logres': *Mort Artu*, para. 135, p. 172).

[17] Elizabeth Archibald, 'Arthur and Mordred: Variations on an Incest Theme', *Arthurian Literature* 8 (1989), 1–27 (pp. 4–6).

[18] E.g. the *Enfances Gauvain*: see *Arthurian Literature in the Middle Ages*, ed. Roger Sherman Loomis (Oxford, 1959), pp. 360–61.

[19] *Suite du Merlin*, cap. I, para. 3, 1:2; cap. I, para 11, 1:8.

Mordred

The incestuous begetting of Mordred appears in late English texts too, but with much less emphasis than in French ones. There is an oblique reference to it in the Alliterative *Morte*, when Gawain expresses his hatred of Mordred:

> 'May I that traytoure ouer-take torfere hyme tyddes,
> That this tresone has tymbyrde to my trew lorde.
> Of siche a engendure fulle littylle joye happyns'
> (Alliterative *Morte*, lines 3741–43)[20]

There is also a more explicit reference in the Stanzaic *Morte*:

> That fals traytour, Syr Mordreid,
>   The kynges soster sone he was
> And eke hys owne sonne, as I rede
>   Therefore men hym for steward chase,
> So falsely hathe he Yngland ledde,
>   Wete yow wele, withouten lese,
> Hys eme-is wyffe wolde he wedde,
>   That many a man rewyd that rease.
> (Stanzaic *Morte*, lines 2954–61)

It is as if the incestuous birth of Mordred retrospectively explains his incestuous desire for his father's wife. A horror of forbidden sexuality and its dire consequences surfaces through Arthur's dream of the snake[21] (or dragon, in the *Suite Merlin*) that issues from him. It is consistent with the development of Mordred in thirteenth-century texts into a figure not just overcome by passion for Guinevere but casually lecherous even in his younger days. In the prose *Lancelot* he sleeps with the *amie* of a knight who has received him hospitably (*Lancelot*, cap. 8, 2:412–18); in the *Prose Tristan* (ca. 1215–35) he would like to abduct the demoiselle accompanying Brun le Noir.[22] Even the love he feels for the queen is in some texts inextricably mixed with political ambition, as is seen in his manipulation of the barons in the *Mort Artu*. As Dominique Boutet pointed out, while only four pages describe Arthur's Roman wars (which in chronicle tradition lengthily preceded the king's downfall), thirty-five concern Mordred's usurpation of the throne.[23] By comparison, his 'deep love' for the queen is mentioned only once (para. 134, p. 171); after that, it is more a matter of capturing her as the figurehead for a rebellion against Arthur (para. 142, p. 179). Mordred's sexuality has consequences: from the *Historia* onwards we know that he has two sons (though by whom is unknown). In the Alliterative *Morte* incest with Guinevere has actually resulted in a child (lines 552, 3576).

---

[20] According to Hamel (p. 377), this is 'carefully ambiguous': *engendure* can mean both 'origin, source' and has the root sense of 'the act of begetting'; 'Gawain perhaps implies that his brother is illegitimate, as a way of rejecting his own kinship to him.' She thinks only a very oblique reference to Arthur's incestuous siring of Mordred can be seen here. See also Cooper, 'Counter-Romance', p. 151, n. 18.
[21] *Lancelot*, cap. xcvi, 5: 221; *Mort Artu*, para. 164, p. 211.
[22] *Tristan en Prose*, ed. Curtis, cap. 669, 2: 240.
[23] Dominique Boutet, 'La Fin des Temps Arthuriens, du *Roman de Brut* au *Lancelot-Graal*: Critique Esthetique et Critique Historique', in *Lancelot-Lanzelet Hier et Aujourdhui*, ed. Danielle Buschinger and Michel Zink (Greifenwald, 1995), pp. 39–52 at p. 45.

However, Mordred's incestuous relationship to the king also has the effect of exculpating him in some measure from his future wickedness – and at the very least explaining it. Elizabeth Archibald sees the story of the incestuous relationship between Arthur and Mordred as 'an unusual variation on traditional story patterns'. She has drawn attention to its similarities with the legends about Judas and Pope Gregory that began to be popular and to circulate in written form in the twelfth century.[24] Gregory is supposedly the fruit of an incestuous affair between siblings; Judas kills his father; both marry their mothers and both are cast adrift as babies on a boat. But while, in the case of Judas, such a back-story 'can be used to blacken an already accepted villain',[25] it does not do so in the case of Gregory, and in Mordred's case its effect is more complicated still. To a large extent, it is the explanation for why he is doomed to choose evil in the first place.

Mordred as Murderer

While Mordred's treachery is the cause of his father's death from the outset of the story, it is not clear who actually kills Arthur in the *Historia* or Wace's and Laʒamon's *Bruts*,[26] and it is rather late in the tradition that the king's nephew/son is portrayed as intent on performing the deed himself. The *Mort Artu* introduces a splendid build-up to Arthur's death by emphasizing his tragic decision to continue fighting Mordred despite all warnings; finally Arthur mortally wounds his son, who retaliates in kind: 'Einsi ocist li peres le fill, et li filz navra le pere a mort' ('In that way the father killed the son and the son gave his father a mortal wound', para. 191, p. 245).[27] The Stanzaic *Morte*, drawing on the *Mort Artu*, introduces by a stroke of genius the adder, the element of chance or Fortune, which co-operates with Fate and human choice (lines 3340–49), but the actual mutual slaying is something of an anti-climax. The Alliterative *Morte* is better; it portrays the mutual, fatal wounding with satisfying amounts of gore, each blow being described in great detail (lines 4236–48).

Malory takes the prize, however, for dispensing with too much bloody detail in order to concentrate on the true horror and pathos of the scene, emphasizing that Mordred increases the extent of his own fatal wound in order to make sure he mortally wounds his father:[28]

> Than the kynge gate his spere in bothe hys hondis, and ran towarde sir Mordred, crying and saying,
>
> 'Traytoure, now ys thy dethe-day com!'

---

[24] Elizabeth Archibald, 'Arthur and Mordred', pp. 4–5, and *Incest and the Medieval Imagination* (Oxford, 2001), p. 218.

[25] Archibald, *Incest*, p. 132.

[26] Though Laʒamon introduces a magnificent dream in which Arthur sees Mordred hacking at the posts of the hall on whose roof the king sits, we are not told who kills Arthur in the final battle.

[27] These words closely (and deliberately) repeat those uttered in the Vulgate *Lancelot*, cap. xcvi, 5: 220.

[28] See Rosemary Morris, *The Character of King Arthur in Medieval Literature* (Cambridge, 1982), p. 132: 'Malory succeeds in a scene which ranks supreme.' See also M. Victoria Guerin, *The Fall of Kings and Princes: Structure and Destruction in Arthurian Tragedy* (Stanford, CA, 1995), p. 263, n. 113.

And whan sir Mordred saw kynge Arthur he ran untyll hym with hys swerde drawyn in hys honde, and there kyng Arthur smote sir Mordred undir the shylde, with a foyne of hys speare, thorowoute the body more than a fadom. And whan sir Mordred felte that he had hys dethys wounde he threste hymselff with the might that he had upp to the burre of kyng Arthurs speare, and right so he smote hys fadir, kynge Arthure, with hys swerde holdynge in both hys hondys, upon the side of the hede, that the swerde perced the helmet and the tay of the brayne. And therewith Mordred daysshed downe starke dede to the erthe.[29]

Mordred's Ambivalence

However, there are other more ambivalent, or even more sympathetic, portrayals of Mordred in medieval literature. Even though Geoffrey of Monmouth made him wicked, as we have seen, other twelfth-century Welsh texts associated his name with bravery and good nature,[30] and that name was used as an ordinary personal one in Brittany and Cornwall,[31] so very unlikely to carry evil connotations. Though those Welsh Triads which are influenced by the *Historia* mention Medrawd as 'a man of shame', violent and treacherous, they also several times allude in a casual and neutral manner to him, and even praise him for beauty and wisdom.[32] Laȝamon's *Brut* shows Arthur entrusting his kingdom to a *selcuþe cnihte* (line 12709), a 'remarkable [or 'outstanding'] knight'.[33] Laȝamon of course realized that the tragic fall of Arthur and Modred would be more impressive if he emphasized Modred's previous good qualities, as well as his affectionate relations with his uncle (line 12722).

Mordred continues to be an energetic and determined warrior, no coward, in both the *Mort Artu* and in Scots tradition; in the latter, he was even portrayed as the kingdom's legitimate heir by John of Fordun (1385) and subsequent Scottish historians.[34] His relationship to his close kin, and his chivalric behaviour, is also in

---

[29] *The Works of Sir Thomas Malory* ed. Eugene Vinaver (London, 1962), xxi, 4.
[30] See Bromwich, *The Triads*: 'we have no evidence that Medrawd's treachery formed any part of the pre-Geoffrey tradition. References by the poets suggest the contrary' (on Triad 54a, p. 151); Padel gives details of Gruffudd ap Cynan and Madog ap Maredudd being compared to Medrawd (*Arthur in Medieval Welsh*, p. 113).
[31] See Padel, *Arthur in Medieval Welsh*, p. 114 and Brynley F. Roberts, 'Geoffrey of Monmouth's *Historia* and *Brut Y Brenhinedd*', in *The Arthur of the Welsh*, pp. 98–113, at p. 112.
[32] Padel, *Arthur in Medieval Welsh*, pp. 114–15 and Bromwich, *The Triads*, pp. 138, 153, 268; she quotes (p. 445) T. Gwyn Jones's assertion that Medrawd 'was traditionally regarded as a paragon of valour and courtesy'.
[33] Laȝamon further describes Modred as *wunder god and he hefde swiþe muchel mod* ('an extremely bold [or brave] knight who had a tremendous spirit', line 12714). Translations are taken from Rosamund Allen, *Lawman: Brut* (London, 1992) and G.L. Brook, *Selections from Laȝamon's Brut* (Oxford, 1963).
[34] See John of Fordun, *Chronica genti Scotorum* (Chronicle of the Scottish Nation) trans. Felix J.H. Skene, facsimile reprint, 2 vols (Edinburgh, 1993): 'Arthur by the contrivance of certain men succeeded to [Uther's] kingdom; which, nevertheless, was not lawfully his due, but rather his sister Anna's, or her children's. For she was begotten in lawful wedlock, and married to Loth...and of her he begat two sons – the noble Galwanus and Modred – whom, on the other hand, some relate, though without foundation, to have had another origin', vol. 1, Book 3, chapter xxiv. See Karl Heinz Göller, 'König Arthur in den schottischen Chroniken', *Anglia* 80 (1962), pp. 390–404; Fletcher, *The Arthurian Material*, pp. 241–47; and Flora Alexander, 'Late Medieval Scottish Attitudes to the Figure of King Arthur: A Reassessment', *Anglia* 93

several texts initially good,³⁵ and his later conduct can even be seen as partially excused through his family's own behaviour. We can see this best through considering his relations with Arthur, with Guinevere and with his brothers. In the non-cyclic *Prose Lancelot* Mordred appears as a good-looking youth – *uns vallez et jones enfes, si estoit mout biaus* – and affectionate towards Gawain.³⁶ Even though Mordred kills this same brother in the Alliterative *Morte*, he repents of it, gives him a moving elegy (lines 3874–85), and weeps for his 'sybb-blode':

> 3it that traytour alls tite teris lete he falle,
> Turnes hym further tite, and talkes no more,
> Went wepand a-waye, and weries the stowndys,
> That euer his werdes ware wroghte siche wandrethe to wyrke:
> Whene he thoghte on this thynge, it thirllede his herte;
> ffor sake of his sybb blode sygheande he rydys;
> When that renayede renke remembirde hym seluene,
> Of reuerence and ryotes of the Rownde Table,
> He remyd and repent hyme of alle his rewthe werkes...
>   (Alliterative *Morte*, lines 3886–94)³⁷

Mordred's initial relationship with Arthur is (as we have seen) that of nephew, since he is the legitimate son of Loth, and this relationship is not cancelled out by later narratives saying that he is the king's son. The Alliterative *Morte* – though it may hint once at a different link (see above, pp. 86–87) – emphatically plays up the closeness of uncle and nephew, Arthur addressing Mordred as his foster-son, carefully reared:

> Thowe arte my neuewe fulle nere, my nurrree of olde,
> That I haue chastyede and chosene, a childe of my chambyre.
>   (Alliterative *Morte*, lines 689–90)

The king's constant praise and recommendation of his nephew to his barons and queen (see lines 644–45, 650, 709–12) carries of course a bitter irony: in view of his later actions, Mordred cannot be what he seems to be, but his reluctance to accept the regency seems unfeigned – there is no hint of pretence:

(1975), 17–34, who says (p. 19) that by the start of the fourteenth century the Scots were asserting in the *Processus Baldredi Contra Figmenta Regis Angliae* that Arthur was illegitimate. See also Eithne O'Sharkey, 'King Arthur's Prophetic Dreams and the Role of Modred in Laȝamon's *Brut* and the Alliterative *Morte*', *Romania* 99 (1978), 347–62, at p. 361.

³⁵ 'Il commença bel, mais ne le maintint mie loialment' and 'El commancement de ta chevalerie [...] as esté debonnaires et piteux' ('He started well, but did not continue loyally' and 'At the start of your knighthood [...] you were kind and compassionate': Vulgate *Lancelot*, cap. 7, 2: 411 and cap. 25, 5: 221). See also 'Cil ne fist onques bien fors les .II. premiers ans qu'il porta armes' ('He never did any good except for the first two years when he bore arms': cap. 7, 2: 411).

³⁶ *Lancelot do Lac: The non-cyclic Old French prose romance*, ed. Elspeth Kennedy, 2 vols (Oxford, 1980), 2:416, lines 35–36: he laments Gawain's supposed death through giving his blood to heal Agravain (2:417, lines 6–12). In the *Prose Tristan* there is also a nuanced view of Mordred: he pities the Cote Mal Taille (Brun le Noir) and defends him from slander, recognising good qualities when he sees them (*Tristan en Prose*, ed. Curtis, cap. 680, 3:6).

³⁷ In Robert Mannyng's *Chronicle* Mordred also recognizes his misdeeds: 'he wist himself so coupabille... he had misdone, the kyng he dred' (lines 13527, 13618).

> Than sir Modrede fulle mildly meles hym seluene,
> Knelyd to the conquerour and carpes thise wordez,
> 'I be-seke ȝow, sir, as my sybbe lorde,
> That ȝe wille for charyté cheese ȝow a-nother;
> Ffor if ȝe putte me in this plytte, ȝowre pople es dyssauyde;
> To presente a prynce astate my powere es simple.
> Whene other of were wysse are wyrchipide here-aftyre,
> Thane may I for-sothe be sette bott at lyttille.
>
> (Alliterative *Morte*, lines 679–86)

As Hamel points out, Arthur pressurizes Mordred into accepting the regency through an 'occasionally threatening tone' (p. 277).[38] But that he is the best person for the job has already been suggested in Robert de Boron's *Merlin*, which shows us that Mordred has been regent once before, during Arthur's conquest of France: he joyfully greets the king on his return.[39] There is a strand in a fifteenth-century portrayal of Mordred which even suggests that compared to Arthur he is seen as a better ruler, one more inclined to peace: the Stanzaic *Morte* depicts the populace criticising the (supposedly) dead Arthur as a king who 'lovyd noght but warynge', whereas Mordred brings them 'joy and wele' (lines 2974–77, 2964). While this also reveals Mordred's's successful manipulation of a fickle people, it chimes interestingly with the Alliterative *Morte*'s portrait of Arthur 'the conquerour' whose martial successes lead him into pride and excess.[40]

Certainly some texts portray Morded's adulterous and incestuous father in a manner that tilts the balance in favour of the son.[41] In many texts Arthur displays a violent and vengeful streak towards the adult Mordred, culminating in a determination to cut down the traitor personally. Interestingly this first appears in an early Arthurian text, Henry of Huntingdon's *Epistola ad Warinum* (1139), where Henry summarizes the contents of Geoffrey's *Historia*, which he has just read at the abbey of Bec. His 'summary' contributes some interesting additions, the most dramatic of which is an account of Arthur angrily pursuing Mordred into Cornwall, seizing him and severing his head 'at a stroke like a blade of corn'.[42] This action is repeated in

---

[38] See lines 669–75 and especially 691–92: 'ffor the sybredyne of me, fore-sake noghte this office/ That thow ne wyrk my wille, thow watte whatte it menes'.

[39] *Merlin and the Grail: Joseph of Arimathea, Merlin, and Perceval, attributed to Robert de Boron*, trans. Nigel Bryant (Cambridge, 2001), pp. 157–61.

[40] Critics have varied in their accounts of how far the portrait of Arthur in the *Morte* is denigratory, but the philosopher's words to him do suggest a criticism: 'Thow has schedde myche blode, and schalkes distroyede,/ Sakeles, in cirquytrie, in sere kynges landis' (lines 3398–99). See, on the one hand, William Matthews, *The Tragedy of Arthur* (Berkeley CA, 1960), pp. 125–28 and, on the other, Juliet Vale, 'Law and Diplomacy in the Alliterative *Morte Arthure*', *Nottingham Medieval Studies* 23 (1979), 31–46, at p. 39.

[41] See Morris, *Character of Arthur*, on Mordred's 'initial innocence' in the post-Vulgate narratives which 'proclaims that it is wrong to visit the sins of the fathers upon the children' (p. 108), and Matthews, *Tragedy of Arthur*: 'In some respects [Mordred] is as much a victim of Arthur as Arthur is of him' (p. 123).

[42] Neil Wright, 'The Place of Henry of Huntingdon's *Epistola ad Warinum* in the text-history of Geoffrey of Monmouth's *Historia Regum Britanniae*: a preliminary investigation', in *France and the British Isles in the Middle Ages and Renaissance*, ed. Gillian Jondorf and D.N. Dumville (Woodbridge, 1991), pp. 71–113 (Appendix, p. 104, para. 9). Wright thinks Henry invented these details himself, pp. 83–90.

Robert of Gloucester's *Metrical Chronicle* (ca. 1300).[43] In the *Suite du Merlin*, once Arthur knows a child born in May will destroy him, he attempts to dispose of him, even if in the end he is persuaded not to kill all the May children he has collected (vol. 1, caps. 73–85); and his actions provoke in Loth lifelong hostility. Malory takes this further: Arthur becomes a Herod-figure and actually does massacre all the children – except Mordred who has escaped the danger. The idea that Arthur killed his own son actually appears very early: the *Historia Britonum* (ninth century), recording the 'Mirabilia' of Britain, describes the tomb of Amr: 'He was a son of the warrior Arthur, and he killed him there and buried him.'[44]

Describing the final battle on Salisbury plain, Malory makes it very clear, unlike his immediate sources, that since Arthur at the end has the numerical odds, he also has a choice, to pursue his vengeance or to abstain:

> 'Sir, latte hym be,' seyde sir Lucan, 'for he ys unhappy. And yf ye passe this unhappy day, ye shall be revenged…And for Goddes sake, my lorde, leve of thys, for, blyssed be God, ye have won the fylde: for yet we ben here three on lyve, and with sir Mordred ys nat one of lyve. And therefore if ye leve of now, thys wicked day of Desteny ys paste!'[45]

Arthur, in choosing vengeance, carries responsibility for his own death. However, the doomed innocence of Mordred is nowhere better captured than in the *Anturs of Arther* (late fourteenth century). The adults in the Arthurian court – Guinevere, her mother (now a ghost), Arthur, even Gawain himself – have all been guilty of crimes and misdemeanours, which continue even up to the end of the poem when Arthur is still disposing of other people's land. Future retribution is only glimpsed through the small Mordred playing with his toy:

> In kyng Arthers halle
> The child playes atte the balle,
> That outray schall yo alle
> Derfely that daye.[46]

Mordred as Adulterer

As we have seen, Arthur's queen, from the First Variant Version of the *Historia* onwards, and predominantly in the chronicle tradition, has often shared responsibility with Mordred for the fall of Arthur and his kingdom. The most frequent charge is that she shares, or comes to share, his adulterous passion. A

---

[43] *The Metrical Chronicle of Robert of Gloucester*, ed. William Aldis Wright, 2 vols (London, 1887), lines 4574–78.

[44] Nennius, *British History and the Welsh Annals*, ed. and trans. John Morris (London, 1980), p. 42, section 73. The *Anonymous Short English Metrical Chronicle*, in London, BL MS Royal 12. C.XII (c. 1312), preserves a tradition that Mordred was innocent of parricide: he slept with Guinevere but never killed Arthur who, having taken England back, lived for another ten years: lines 291–304, pp. 69–70.

[45] Malory, *Works*, ed. Vinaver, xxi, 4.

[46] *Ywain and Gawain, Sir Percyvell of Gales, The Anturs of Arther*, ed. Maldwyn Mills (London, 1992), lines 308–11. See Krista Sue-Lo Twu, 'The description of the traitor, Mordred… as a little boy playing with his toys is unique among medieval treatments of the Arthurian cycle': 'The Awntyrs Off Arthure at the Terne Wathelyne: Reliquary for Romance', *Arthurian Literature* 20 (Cambridge, 2003), 103–22, at p. 121.

lecherous Guinevere is a feature of other Arthurian narratives where Mordred (or Lancelot for that matter) does not even appear, or barely appears: she fails the test of the horn in *Le Lai du Cor*; she propositions Lanval; Launfal and other knights know that she has affairs; and in the *Anturs* she is warned against 'luf paramourus' by her mother's fate.[47] The 'hore' and the 'luþer quene', as Robert Mannyng (line 13481) and Robert of Gloucester (line 4537) call her, advises Mordred to usurp the kingdom (Robert of Gloucester, *Metrical Chronicle*, line 4503); she goes to warn him, because he is 'dearest of men to her', in Laȝamon's *Brut* (line 14101); she has heaped praise upon him to Arthur in the past, and even hands over to the usurper Arthur's own sword, entrusted to her keeping (Alliterative *Morte* lines 711, 4202–17). In romances, Guinevere usually gets a better press, despite the examples above. With the rise of the Lancelot story, her passion is half excused by being given to a good rather than a bad man. As Archibald observes, where Mordred is portrayed as a nephew – mostly in the chronicle tradition, to which the Alliterative *Morte* belongs, despite its hint at Mordred's 'engendure' – Guinevere succumbs to him (and so is 'bad'); where he is portrayed as a son – in the romances – she resists (and so is 'good').[48] In the end, the chronicle tradition gives Mordred more reasons for his behaviour – his reciprocated passion *and* his political ambition (as the *Brut* puts it, he 'wolde haue hade þe lande to his owen vse')[49] – whereas the romances give us less reason, indeed in some ways accentuate the oddity of a member of so excellent a family behaving in this horrifying way. The principal 'reason' thus becomes the pressure to do evil resulting from Mordred's illegitimacy and his incestuous birth, a pressure resisted by the analogous and heroic Roland and Gregorius.

Mordred, Cornwall and Treachery

Cornwall has a lengthy association, from early on, with both Mordred and Arthur. At first, it is Arthur who preponderantly has connections to the county,[50] and Hermann of Laon's account of the journey of the Laon canons to Bodmin in 1113 supplies us

---

[47] *The Anglo-Norman Text of Le Lai du Cor*, ed. C.T. Erickson, ANTS 24 (Oxford, 1973), lines 268–370; *Lanval*, lines 267–68, in Marie de France, *Lais*, ed. A. Ewert (Oxford, 1944; repr. 1963); *Sir Launfal*, lines 44–48, in *Middle English Verse Romances*, ed. Donald B. Sands (Exeter, 1986; repr. 1997); *Anturs*, lines 190–216.

[48] Archibald, 'Arthur and Mordred', p. 22. The exception is in Robert de Boron, where Mordred is Arthur's nephew but the queen does not succumb to his love (trans. Bryant, p. 166).

[49] *The Brut or The Chronicle of England*, ed. Friedrich W.D. Brie, EETS OS 131, 136 (London, 1906), cap. 87, 1:88. See also the mid-thirteenth-century *Gesta Regum Britannie*, which pointedly refers to Mordred as 'infected with so great a longing to rule' and ruled by 'the angel of ambition': *Gesta Regum Britannie*, ed. and trans. Neil Wright (Cambridge, 1991), IX, para. 178, lines 215–16, pp. 242–43.

[50] Five dynasties come from Cornwall, including those of Corineus, Constantine son of Cador, and of course Arthur himself who, born in Cornwall, is half-Cornish (through his mother Ygerne), whose wife is raised by Cador, and who is the *aper cornubiae* (boar of Cornwall) in Merlin's Prophecies. According to *Culhwch and Olwen* Arthur has his court at Kelli wic ('forest grove') in Cornwall, and in an early Welsh poem, the mid-twelfth century *Dialogue of the Eagle*, he is addressed as 'chief of the hosts of Cornwall'. See Padel, 'Geoffrey of Monmouth and Cornwall', pp. 19–20, and *Culhwch and Olwen*, ed. Rachel Bromwich and D. Simon Evans (Cardiff, 1992), line 261, and n. on p. 91. Thirteenth-century Welsh Triads also gave Arthur a court in Cornwall, as well as ones in Wales and Scotland: Padel, 'Nature of Arthur', p. 30.

with an indication of the passionate Cornish interest in him.[51] But Mordred's connection with Cornwall is also of long duration; his name was in use there in the ninth and tenth centuries.[52] The *Historia* depicts him fleeing Arthur and eventually ending up in Cornwall where the last battle occurs by the river Camblan. The version of the story in the *Gesta Regum Britannie* conveys the sense of Cornwall's geographical isolation: 'the rebel army has reached Cornwall; and here it remains because it can go no further' ('nec habens quo prodeat ultra,/ Restat ibi').[53] French Arthurian narratives from Robert de Boron onwards start to phase out Cornwall as the venue for the last battle in favour of Ireland[54] or the more long-lasting Salisbury Plain. The English chronicle tradition, however, retains Cornwall as the place to which the traitor flees and where he raises an army.[55] *Arthour and Merlin*, the Stanzaic *Morte* and Malory preserve only faint traces of this[56] but the Alliterative *Morte* places the last battle in Cornwall, even if oddly it is by the river Trent (line 4054) rather than Camble or Tambre.[57] In Cornwall, Robert of Gloucester's Arthur (as in Henry of Huntingdon's *Epistola*) cuts off Mordred's head; Thomas Gray's *Scalacronica* (1355–69) retains the location too.[58]

Could there have been a reason for this continuing insular perception that Cornwall was a place capable of harbouring a traitor and joining his rebellion? From early on it seems to have been considered, in Michele Warren's words, as 'an unstable margin of British identity,' which was 'both tantalizingly familiar and bafflingly strange'.[59] Its rulers were often in conflict with the Crown, its people resistant to the

---

[51] Hermann of Laon wrote an account in ca. 1145 of the canons' visit, during which they heard of the strong belief that Arthur would return: O.J. Padel, 'The Nature of Arthur', *Cambrian Medieval Celtic Studies* 27 (1994), 1–31, at p. 9.

[52] See n. 32, above.

[53] *Gesta Regum Britannie*, IX, para. 178, lines 257–59, pp. 244–45.

[54] Bryant, *Merlin and the Grail*, p. 171.

[55] Robert Mannyng's *Chronicle*, line 13628; Laȝamon's *Brut*, line 14217, p. 90: Mordred assembles 'al þe folc of Cornwayle and hade peple wiþoute nombre'. The last battle is still located in Cornwall in a 'feudal manual' on a roll written in Edward I's reign (Oxford, Bodleian Library MS Bodl. E. 14, m.3r.). See John Spence, 'Re-imagining History in Anglo-Norman Prose Chronicles', unpublished doctoral dissertation (Cambridge, 2005), p. 111), who has also pointed out to me that the battle is described as being *sur le ewe de Cambre en Cornwayle* (by the river of Cambre in Cornwall) in Christian Foltys's *Le Livere de Reis de Brittannie*, whose manuscript is of a similar date.

[56] *Arthour and Merlin* is unfinished anyway, but sounds geographically confused, in that Saracen invaders disembark at 'Arundel in Cornwaile' (line 7685). In the Stanzaic *Morte* Mordred hopes Arthur will give him 'Cornwale and Kente' (lines 3267, 3275, 3295) during their truce, something which Malory retains: see Vinaver, *Works*, xxi, 3:866.

[57] Wace, *Roman de Brut*, Camble in line 13253, MS D; it is Cambre in MSS C and P and Tanbre in MSS A, K and R. See Weiss, *Roman de Brut*, pp. 332–33. Laȝamon has Tambre by Camelford (line 14244), interpreted by Barron and Weinberg as Tamar; Robert of Gloucester follows suit with 'Tamer', line 4558). The river Tamar was traditionally the border between Cornwall and England.

[58] See notes 41 and 42 and Thomas Gray, *Scalachronica*, ed Joseph Stevenson (Edinburgh, 1836), Appendix I, p. 260.

[59] Michele R. Warren, *History on the Edge* (Minneapolis, 2000), p. 36; Michael W. Anderson, '"The honour of bothe courtes be nat lyke": Cornish Resistance to Arthurian Dominance in Malory', *Arthuriana* 19 (2009), 43–57, at p. 43), quoting from Laurie A. Finke and Martin B. Schichtman, *King Arthur and the Myth of History* (Gainesville FL, 2004), p. 108. See also James Vernon, 'Border Crossings: Cornwall and the English (imagi)nation', in *Imagining Nations*, ed. Geoffrey Cubitt (Manchester, 1998), pp. 153–72, at p. 153.

imposition of order and of a different language and culture. Its pre-Norman earldom was held by Cadoc or Condor (possibly the origin of the *Historia*'s Cador?), who was replaced after the Conquest by Count Brian of Brittany. Brian, however, soon joined a baronial revolt against William in 1075 and the earldom went to William's half-brother, Robert of Mortain, one of the wealthiest landowners in England.[60] Robert in turn rebelled against William Rufus in 1088, joining Robert Curthose, and though he was soon pardoned, the reputation of Cornwall's rulers for resisting the Crown was maintained by Robert of Mortain's son William, who also joined Curthose and fought at Tinchebrai against Henry I; in punishment he forfeited his earldom of Cornwall and went into exile.[61] As Brian Golding puts it, in the years after the Conquest the South-West 'proved to be a focus for rebellion'; Cornwall 'could be regarded as [a] frontier lordship' (p. 129). In Stephen's reign, there was a breakdown of central authority in the county, with feudal lords building castles, which threatened regal control.[62]

Cornwall was again associated with disaffection in the late twelfth and early thirteenth centuries. Henry II had intended its earldom for John; though he never received it, he was allowed its revenues, and given absolute control over it when Richard went on Crusade. John began intriguing, and won support from some of the Cornish barons when he rebelled in 1193.[63] But in turn, a Cornish lord, Robert Fitz Walter, was one of the leaders of the baronial revolt against John in 1215.[64] A rather different, though unmerited, picture of an earl of Cornwall as untrustworthy and seditious emerges later in the century, in the powerful figure of Richard of Cornwall (1209–72, earl from 1225), brother to Henry III. Richard fell out with Henry on several occasions and, though he finally became a king's man, sided with the baronial cause three times over some thirteen years. This probably led to the popular perception of him as treacherous.[65] Henry III nevertheless valued his administrative talents and made him Regent during his absences abroad, as in 1252 when the realm was left in his hands and the queen's.[66] Though it is nowadays thought that Richard did not have his eyes on the crown, contemporary rumours 'ascribed his perceived disloyalty towards the king to dynastic ambition'.[67]

---

[60] Philip Payton, *Cornwall* (Fowey, 1996), p. 91; Frank Barlow, *William Rufus* (London, 1983), p. 92.
[61] Brian Golding, 'Robert of Mortain', *Anglo-Norman Studies* 13 (1991), 119–44, at pp. 121–22); L.E. Elliott-Binns, *Medieval Cornwall* (London, 1955), p. 74; C. Warren Hollister, *Henry I* (New Haven, 2001), p. 144.
[62] Elliott-Binns, p. 76.
[63] F.E. Halliday, *A History of Cornwall* (Letchworth, 1959; 2nd edn, 1975), p. 114; Elliot-Binns, p. 79.
[64] Elliott-Binns, p. 80; Fitz Walter had inherited part of the Cornish fief of his uncle, Richard de Lucy, the Younger. See also Halliday, p. 114.
[65] As in the contemporary songs 'Richard, þah þou be euer trichard...' and 'Or vint la tens de May' (Song of the Peace with England) in *Thomas Wright's Political Songs of England*, with a new introduction by Peter Coss (Cambridge, 1996), pp. 69–71 and 63–68. See Adrian Jobson, 'Richard of Cornwall and the Baronial Opposition in 1263', in *Thirteenth Century England* 12, ed. Janet Burton, Phillipp Schofield and Björn Weiler (Woodbridge, 2009), pp. 61–74.
[66] T.W.E. Roche, *The King of Almayne* (London, 1966), p. 119.
[67] Jobson, pp. 63–64, citing Gervase of Canterbury and the Burton Annalist; many of Richard's retinue of knights in 1257 later supported the baronial cause (pp. 67–74).

Mordred as Archetype

The linkage of Cornwall at this period to such a powerful figure closely related to royalty and perceived to be coveting the throne may thus have fuelled a persistent perception that Cornwall could be used in narrative as the home of a traitor and a rebel because of its history of revolt and disaffection from 1066 onwards.[68] The association between Mordred as traitor and Cornwall as a disorderly and rebellious region continued to influence romances in both Anglo-Norman and English. His name appears in various forms, given to disloyal or downright evil characters, sometimes with no motive given for their actions. The most recognizably indebted to the Arthurian story is the figure in the Anglo-Norman *Gui de Warewic* (1205–15) of the 'old and wicked' Duke Modred, 'the liege-lord of Cornwall', who, when Athelstan's court considers how to deal with the imminent Danish invasion, attacks the king for trusting the advice of Heralt, Gui's steward. Having accused Heralt of treachery, Modred himself is guilty of it: he gathers a Cornish army and besieges Heralt's fief of Wallingford during the steward's absence, but is unsuccessful and has to return to Cornwall.[69] This figure recurs in the English *Guy of Warwick* too, with the names further removed from the original, as Medyok (in the Auchinleck MS) and Merof (in CUL MS Ff 2. 38, the fifteenth-century version).[70] It looks as if the English adapters of the story of Gui were no longer entirely familiar with the traitor's name, but still knew that he was linked to Cornwall.

Less close is the figure of Modard, the king of Almayne (the title actually assumed by Richard of Cornwall), in *King Richard*.[71] He hates Richard Coeur de Lion for no obvious reason and captures him and his companions when they are crossing his realm, a clear memory of the historical imprisonment of Richard in 1192 by Duke Leopold of Austria. The Anglo-Norman *Waldef* (1200–10) introduces a minor character late in the romance, one Moderet, who is the only follower of the emperor Guiac (one of Waldef's sons) to launch an accusation of betrayal against him.[72] With

---

[68] The reputation of the county as remote, isolated and forbidding, and its people as unfriendly, even hostile, and fiercely independent, continued, preserved in the complaint of its Archdeacon, Adam de Carleton, who resigned in 1342: 'the folk of these parts are quite extraordinary, being of a rebellious temper and obdurate in the face of attempts to teach and correct'. See Payton, p. 104, and Mark Page, 'Cornwall, Earl Richard, and the Barons' War', *English Historical Review* 115 (2000), 21–38, at p. 21. The Cornish attempts to gain greater autonomy, and their 'lawless independence,' continued into Henry VII's time, with Cornwall supporting the rebellions of Perkin Warbeck and Thomas Flammock: see Page, p. 22; Payton, *Cornwall*, p. 120. It is also reflected in Malory's work, even if he follows his French romance source, the *Mort Artu*, in locating the final battle in Salisbury Plain rather than Cornwall. See Peter Field, in the Introduction to *Re-Viewing Le Morte Darthur*, ed. K.S. Whetter and Raluca L. Radulescu (Cambridge, 2005), p. 5, and Robert L. Kelly, 'Malory's "Tale of King Arthur" and the Political Geography of Fifteenth-century England', in the same volume, pp. 80–93 (p. 85).

[69] *Gui de Warewic*, ed. Alfred Ewert, 2 vols (Paris, 1933), lines 9157–392.

[70] *The Romance of Guy of Warwick: The First or 14th-century version, edited from the Auchinleck MS in the Advocates' Library, Edinburgh, and from MS 107 in Caius College, Cambridge*, ed. Julius Zupitza, EETS ES 42, 49, 59 (London, 1883, 1887, 1891), stanzas 20–27; *The Romance of Guy of Warwick: the Second or 15th-century Version, edited from the paper ms Ff.2.38 in the University Library, Cambridge*, ed. Julius Zupitza, EETS ES 25, 26 (London, 1875–76), lines 8563, 8727–28.

[71] See *Der Mittelenglische Versroman über Richard Löwenherz*, ed. Karl Brunner (Vienna, 1913), line 1423 (in the College of Arms MS but missing in the Auchinleck MS). This name is interestingly read as Modred by Bradford B. Broughton in his *Legends of King Richard I, Coeur de Lion* (The Hague, 1966), p. 66.

[72] *Waldef*, ed. A.J. Holden (Cologny-Geneva, 1984), lines 21713–807.

only the first syllable surviving, the names of villains such as Morgadoure (in *Gui*, 3263), a treacherous steward, and Mordoure, the wicked stepfather of the hero in *Beues of Hamtoun*, are perhaps less clearly indebted to that of the Arthurian traitor.[73]

Mordred's position and plot – someone much trusted by a king who betrays and rebels against him – have a noticeable influence on several romances that do not try to imitate his name. Chronologically the first of these must be *Cligés*, in which Count Angrés of Windsor is entrusted with England, on the unanimous advice of the barons, while king Arthur is away in Brittany.[74] Subsequently messengers bring the news of his rebellion and Arthur has to return; Angrés flees from London to Windsor where the king besieges him, and is captured when secretly stealing away from the battle. The various retreats of Modred before Arthur, invented by Geoffrey's *Historia* and added to by the Variant Version of the *Historia* and Wace, are obviously imitated here.[75]

The Haveloc story, which first appears in Gaimar's *Estorie des Engleis*, c. 1138–40, very close to the date of Geoffrey's *Historia*, alludes to Arthur and Modred at the start (Modred as king gives land to his Saxon allies and is killed by Arthur).[76] It may also have been influenced by Arthurian narratives in its account of Argentille: her uncle, Edelsi, usurps her kingdom of Norfolk entrusted to him by her father (lines 75–88), and betrays her by marrying her to a scullion. The English romance of *Havelok* (c. 1290) makes a significant addition to this plot: the name of the English traitor is not Edelsi but Earl Godrich of Cornwall, who by the advice of the king's barons is made regent of all England (lines 169–209).

The Anglo-Norman *Waldef* uses two pieces of the Mordred story, the first of them reminiscent of the Haveloc tale. Early in the poem king Bede, father of Waldef, dies, having entrusted, in an assembly of all his barons, the kingdom, his wife and his son to his steward Frode. Frode usurps power and forcibly marries the queen, whom he then imprisons (lines 2112–52). At the other end of the romance, the traitors Brand and Hildebrand mimic Mordred's movements in Wace's *Brut* by fleeing from London to Winchester, where Waldef besieges them, and then to Southampton.[77]

The English *Havelok*'s addition of Cornwall serves once again to show its continuing association with villainy. We have seen this happen in *Gui/Guy* (see above), and it also occurs in *Beues of Hamtoun*, though not in its Anglo-Norman source. In the Auchinleck MS, an addition to the original story has a steward at king Edgar's court, 'the worste frend of alle' (lines 4305–306), urge that Beues be hanged as a traitor; he later stirs up the city of London against the hero. In the fifteenth-

---

[73] In *Beues*, MS M and the printed versions. On this and the printed versions of Beues, see Jennifer Fellows, 'Bevis: A Textual Survey', in *Sir Bevis of Hampton in Literary Tradition*, ed. Fellows and Ivana Djordjević (Cambridge, 2008), pp. 93–94, n. 62, and pp. 96–98, 109–113.

[74] Does the barons' advice slightly lessen the responsibility of both Arthur and Mordred for the ensuing rebellion? In *Cligés* Arthur certainly suggests the barons are at fault through poor judgement (lines 1059–71). It looks as if that is an element in the *Lai d'Havelok*, *Waldef* and *Havelok*.

[75] *Cligés*, ed. Alexandre Micha (Paris, 1957), lines 422–34, 1045–97, 1199–1227, 1778–2029.

[76] Geffrei Gaimar, *Estoire des Engleis*, ed. A. Bell (Oxford, 1960), lines 9–10, 4316, 37–38.

[77] Wace, *Roman de Brut*, lines 13131–79. The *Historia* does not have London or Southampton, towns which Wace adds, probably following the Variant Version which adds Southampton. See *The 'Historia Regum Britanniae' of Geoffrey of Monmouth: II: the First Variant Version*, ed. Wright, para. 177, p. 173.

century printed versions of the romance, this figure has been changed to 'Sir Bryane of Cornwall.'[78] As with the English Guy, so here too the detailed knowledge of Mordred may have faded, but the feeling that somehow Cornwall could supply unpleasant characters lingers on.[79]

Conclusion

The powerful figure of Mordred thus becomes an archetype for other literary traitors. However, they do not share the disturbingly sexual side of his treachery and, because their characterization is not nuanced but unambiguously wicked, they do not partake of his ambivalence. Aspects of Mordred's character, provided by a large range of writers over four centuries, often suggest a figure more complex than an out-and-out villain. He may contain some qualities more worthy of a hero than an anti-hero; and his actions may spring from murky origins for which he is not altogether responsible. The early narrative shift which makes him a nephew rather than a cousin is an important one. It suggests a familiar tragic theme, that the fall of a great man is caused not by an exterior power but by what Chaucer called 'the ny sly', deception very close to home. A nephew, especially a sister's son, is closer than a cousin, and is a potential heir to a childless uncle, replacing the son that uncle never had, but also able to replace uncle on the throne and in the bed. There is a parallel situation in the story of Tristan, Mark and Iseut, which probably influenced the developing Arthurian narrative. Tristan is usually more sympathetically portrayed than Mordred, because the potion he unknowingly drinks partly removes his responsibility for adultery. Mordred seems the blacker character because he *chooses* to betray his uncle and to love his wife. Yet from Wace onwards there is a counter-movement amongst some Arthurian writers to diminish Mordred's responsibility by suggesting that others – starting with Guinevere – share culpability, and this movement reaches its climax in those texts which double the element of incest. Product of an incestuous union, Mordred is swayed towards repeating the same sin; we deplore his action but understand its origins, and our understanding entails a modicum of sympathy for a character in so many other respects the very personification of an anti-hero.

---

[78] *The Romance of Sir Beues of Hamtoun*, ed. Eugen Kölbing, EETS ES 46, 48, 65 (London, 1885–94), lines 4045, 4082.

[79] Jennifer Fellows comments on this passage: 'if [the] author had any specific purpose in so naming his villain, it may be sought in the attitude of distrust towards Cornwall and its inhabitants that can probably be assumed to have existed in the late fifteenth century': n. to line 3173 on Syr Bryane of Cornewayle, in '*Sir Beves of Hampton*: Study and Edition', 5 vols, unpublished doctoral thesis (Cambridge, 1980).

6
Merlin

Gareth Griffith

For modern audiences, Merlin has had an enduring appeal as the wizard at the court of King Arthur. In the Middle Ages, his fame was if anything even greater, but his supporting role alongside Arthur was only one part of it, and neither the first nor necessarily the most important part at that. Merlin was a figure of fascination in his own right, someone to whom medieval writers returned for a variety of reasons, over centuries of retelling and reinterpretation. This process might be likened to a great river, rising from several springs, and ultimately flowing out in many different streams, as the stories of Merlin and of Arthur spread across Europe and down centuries. It is obviously beyond the scope of the present essay to examine in detail all of the medieval texts in which Merlin appears, but the main course of this 'river' is easy enough to trace. From scattered sources in Welsh myth and the ninth-century *Historia Brittonum*, it is first recognisable in Geoffrey of Monmouth's *Historia Regum Britanniae* (hereafter *Historia*) and passes from there into the literary chronicles that were its direct descendants, such as Wace's *Roman de Brut* and Laȝamon's *Brut*.[1] It swelled significantly when Robert de Boron wrote his *Merlin* in the thirteenth century,[2] a text so popular that it served, directly or indirectly, as the basis for many of the most important subsequent retellings, including the stories of Merlin in the

[1] Nennius, *British History and the Welsh Annals*, ed. and trans. John Morris (London, 1980); *Geoffrey of Monmouth: The History of the Kings of Britain*, ed. Michael D. Reeve, trans. Neil Wright (Woodbridge, 2007); *Wace's Roman de Brut: A History of the British: Text and Translation*, ed. Judith Weiss (Exeter, 2002); Laȝamon, *Brut*, ed. G.L. Brook and R.F. Leslie, EETS OS 250, 277 (London, 1963, 1978).

[2] Robert's only surviving poems are a complete *Joseph of Arimathea*, which greatly embellished the Grail legend found in Chrétien de Troyes's *Le Conte du Graal*, and the first 508 lines of his *Merlin*. However, a prose version of both of these exists, in which the *Merlin* is completed, and in two manuscripts they are joined by a third prose romance, *Perceval*. The authorship of this trilogy, and their precise relation to Robert's surviving poems, is still a matter of debate which cannot be settled here. I shall refer to Robert as the author of the three prose romances throughout this essay, but purely for reasons of concision. All quotations from Robert de Boron are from *Merlin: Roman du XIIIe siècle*, ed. Alexandre Micha (Geneva, 1980). Translations are from *Merlin and the Grail: Joseph of Arimathea, Merlin, Perceval: the Trilogy of Arthurian Romances attributed to Robert de Boron*, trans. Nigel Bryant (Cambridge, 2001).

French Vulgate romances (*Lestoire de Merlin*, the *Suite de Merlin*, and scattered references in other sections of the cycle), and in English the verse romance *Arthour and Merlin*, the anonymous English prose *Merlin*, the fifteenth-century *Merlin* of Henry Lovelich, and Malory's *Morte Darthur*.[3] In what follows, I shall focus on the *Historia* and Robert's *Merlin*, since these are the texts that between them established the pattern of Merlin's character, although I shall have cause to examine details from some of the other major texts mentioned above.

To see Merlin in his medieval guises, we must first dispense with the word 'wizard', which is at any rate not recorded in English before the fifteenth century. This word became more current in the sixteenth century, but it referred as much to a sage as to a magician, and not always with approval.[4] In the *Historia*, the noun generally used to describe Merlin is *uates* ('prophet', pp. 170–71; and p. 187). This accurately describes Merlin's key role in this text, something that Geoffrey emphasized by incorporating his substantial earlier work, the *Prophetiae Merlini*, into the *Historia*. At one point, a more startling judgement is expressed by witnesses to one of Merlin's wonders: 'Ammirabantur etiam cuncti qui astabant tantam in eo sapientiam, existimantes numen esse in illo' ('All the bystanders too were filled with wonder at his wisdom, thinking he was inspired', pp. 140–41). 'Inspired' hints at the potentially strong meaning of *numen*, which in medieval Latin has senses related to divinity or divine power.[5] One might almost translate 'and they concluded that the power of God was in him'. At first sight, this seems like strong approbation of Merlin's character, crediting him with being a conduit for God himself. Yet this is only the opinion of figures within the narrative, not the authorial verdict. As such, it is still open to question and qualification in the light of what will follow.

Robert's *Merlin* has a subtly different understanding of Merlin's character, placing emphasis on his wisdom (he is a 'saige home', p. 104, and 'le plus sage home dou monde', p. 120), but also adding a new and ambiguous dimension to the description of Merlin by calling him a 'devin' (as at p. 106). This word can simply mean a theologian (a 'divine'), but it is etymologically linked to the verb 'deviner', which can mean 'to teach', or alternatively 'to mislead'; to 'devinance', the science of divination; and to 'devinaille', sorcery.[6] Linguistically, Robert's Merlin hovers on the borders between sacred and sinful powers, a reflection of his troubling ancestry and make-up, as we shall see.

---

[3] *The Vulgate Version of the Arthurian Romances*, 7 vols, ed. H. Oskar Sommer (Washington, D.C., 1908–16) and *Lancelot-Grail: The Old French Arthurian Vulgate and Post-Vulgate in Translation*, 5 vols, ed. Norris J. Lacy et al. (New York, 1993); *Of Arthour and of Merlin*, ed. O.D. Macrae-Gibson, 2 vols EETS OS 268, 279 (London, 1973, 1979); *Merlin, or the Early History of King Arthur*, 4 vols, ed. Henry B. Wheatley, EETS OS 10, 21, 36, 112 (London, 1899); Henry Lovelich, *Merlin: a Middle-English Metrical Version of a French Romance*, 3 vols, ed. Ernst A. Kock, EETS ES 93, 112, 185 (London, 1904, 1913, 1932); Thomas Malory, *The Works of Sir Thomas Malory*, 3 vols, ed. Eugène Vinaver, 3rd edn rev. P.J.C. Field (Oxford, 1990).
[4] *OED*, s.v. 'wizard'.
[5] *Lexicon Latinitatis medii aevi*, ed. Albert Blaise, CCCM (Turnhout, 1975), s.v. *numen*.
[6] See A. Tobler and Erhard Lommatzsch, *Altfranzösiches Wörterbuch* (Wiesbaden, 1915–74), s.v. 'devin', and especially A.J. Greimas, *Dictionnaire de l'ancien français jusqu'au milieu du XIVe siècle*, 2nd edn (Paris, 1976), s.v. 'devin', 'deviner', 'devinance' and 'devinaille'.

The Vulgate uses less ambiguous words to refer to Merlin, but problematizes them by placing contrasting judgements on Merlin's character in close proximity. A good example can be found in an early passage from the *Lancelot* where, much as in passages of the *Historia* already mentioned, Merlin is confirmed as 'le prophete as englois', before we are told that 'tout lapeloient lor saint prophete. Et tout la menue gent lapeloient lor dieu' ('everyone called him a holy prophet and the ordinary people all called him their god').[7] If there is room for doubt as to how far the potentially idolatrous view of 'la menue' is to be accepted, then the fact that Merlin is declared a 'saint prophete' by *everyone* would seem to make this passage unequivocal in its assessment of his gifts (even though it also acknowledges that their origins, as we shall see, are demonic). However, only a few paragraphs later, we are told that 'il ne fu onques baptisies' ('the boy was never baptised').[8] This is an uncompromising judgement on Merlin: ever since Augustine, it had been clear to medieval theology that 'the child [...] must be baptized urgently, and certainly before he dies, in order to avoid eternal banishment from the vision of God'.[9] To say that Merlin is unbaptised is to number him amongst the damned, to place him as far as possible from being 'holy', the word used of him only a few sentences earlier.

How did one figure come to encompass so many roles, and to provoke such widely differing opinions and moral judgements? To answer that question, we must explore how the figure of Merlin, which fascinated so many in the Middle Ages, was created, and which earlier figures contributed to his makeup.

Geoffrey's *Historia* is the first full-blown account of Merlin, but Geoffrey did not write in a total vacuum, and the fragmentary remains of the traditions on which he must have drawn include clues to how the figure of Merlin emerged. In Welsh traditions, Geoffrey would have found the figure of Myrddin, whose name he would Latinize to 'Merlinus', a poet and possible nobleman, who was on the losing side at the battle of Arfderydd in 575, with remarkable results:

> In the course of the battle he lost his reason. He fled to the Wood of Celyddon (Caledonia), and there he lived for half a century [...] In this frenzied condition Myrddin acquired the gift of prophecy.[10]

This legend was already known by 930, and it extends through to Welsh poems from the twelfth century which claim to be both prophetic and written by Myrddin. (They postdate the *Historia*, but their archaic diction suggests that they may have been composed much earlier).[11] It is not hard to see why the combination of

---

[7] Sommer, vol. 3, p. 19; Lacy, vol. 2, p. 11.
[8] Sommer, vol. 3, p. 21; Lacy, vol. 2, p. 12.
[9] Peter Cramer, *Baptism and Change in the Early Middle Ages, c. 200–c. 1150* (Cambridge, 1993), p. 125. Thomas Aquinas (*Summa Theologiae*, III, LXVIII, 2: '*utrum sine baptismo aliquis possit salvari*') did argue that it was possible to be saved without baptism, but only if the individual concerned wished to be baptised but could not be: the *Lancelot* offers no hint that this is the case with Merlin.
[10] Thomas Parry, *A History of Welsh Literature*, trans. H. Idris Bell (Oxford, 1955), p. 27. The literatures of some other European cultures mention figures who undergo a similar crisis, but Myrddin seems to have been the one known to Geoffrey.
[11] Stephen Knight, *Merlin: Knowledge and Power Through the Ages* (Ithaca, 2009), pp. 5–6.

characteristics in this one figure was attractive to Geoffrey the fabulist (as his later *Vita Merlini* shows). Myrddin is at once fighter, poet, hermit and prophet – a sort of 'Renaissance man' centuries before the Renaissance. As a warrior-prince, Myrddin would surely appeal to a chronicler's interest in political life and succession through victory in battle; as a poet he is perhaps kin to Geoffrey the writer and teller of tales; and as hermit and prophet he can be a detached figure, even from within the narrative of history, commenting and interpreting, helping to shape a series of events into a story with meaning and direction – just as a historian might do. Merlin could therefore perform a number of useful narrative functions for Geoffrey, and in doing so he could also act as a kind of surrogate author from within the text. These are roles which he would be called upon to play again and again as his career developed.

Merlin's unusual status is made clear not only during his life, but even before it begins. He enters the narrative of Geoffrey's *Historia* as one of two boys fighting at the gates of Kaermerdin (Carmarthen).[12] The other boy, Dinabutius, taunts him that whilst he (Dinabutius) is descended from royalty on both sides, 'your identity is unknown since you have no father' ('de te autem nescitur quis sis, cum patrem non habeas', pp. 136–37). This catches the ears of messengers from King Vortigern who are nearby, resting in their search for just such a fatherless child. Their investigations allow us to learn more about who Merlin is, and especially about how he was conceived. Geoffrey gives only sketchy details of this: we are told that his mother was a nun, and that she was daughter of the king of Demetia (the southern kingdom of Wales). His father is initially said to be unknown, but it is soon revealed that he is an incubus. This marks Geoffrey's first serious divergence from Nennius's *Historia Brittonum*, which is his source here. In that text, the near-victim is called Ambrosius, and his fatherlessness is given a more prosaic explanation: in spite of his mother's protests of virginity, Ambrosius explains that his father is 'one of the consuls of the Roman people' ('Unus [...] de consulibus romanicae gentis'). This Ambrosius seems later to become chief amongst the kings of Britain ('rex magnus inter omnes reges Brittainnicae gentis').[13] Geoffrey changes the genesis of his prophet, removing him from a purely political context to an avowedly supernatural one, but in fact he will continue to inhabit both, acting as bridge between the two worlds and yoking them uneasily together.

The whole episode of the discovery of Merlin is clearly entertaining in its own right, not least for presenting the audience with a seeming impossibility (how can a boy be born without a father?) and then producing a more or less plausible explanation of it: the pleasure of a whodunit in miniature. More importantly, this brief narrative also shows Merlin in many different lights, and the very profusion of these overlapping identities is characteristic of the figure who will emerge not only in the rest of the *Historia* but in the texts that drew inspiration from it. Merlin is a mystery, sought by the king's men and found by chance; he is a potential victim (the king has been told that the fatherless boy's blood is all that can prevent a new castle from being supernaturally torn down every night); his ancestry manages to combine royalty, piety and supernatural evil; he is the counsellor to the king, whose word

---

[12] The episode is in chapters 106–108 in the *Historia* (Thorpe, pp. 166–69).
[13] Nennius, ed. and trans. Morris, p. 72 (trans. p. 30) and p. 74.

comes to have the force of a command even amongst royalty; yet he is also a very human young boy, fighting as boys did (and still do) over their fathers.

The abrupt introduction of 'Maugantius' to tell the king that incubal conceptions are not unheard of serves only to provide authenticating precedent for Merlin's conception, and thus to make it more plausible – it does nothing to make it less strange. Thus from the point where Merlin first enters Geoffrey's narrative (and through Geoffrey the narrative of the rest of the Middle Ages and beyond), he is already torn between heaven and hell, offspring of the union between a demon and a nun, a birth paralleled by other demonic progeny, but also distantly echoing, perhaps parodying, that of Christ. This last parallel seems reinforced by the tantalising (and ultimately unfulfilled) prospect of Merlin's murder as a sacrifice, and the focus on the importance that his blood will have after his death.

Geoffrey's account of Merlin's conception and birth is typical of his style: he provides details that appear to authenticate the narrative, yet leaves so many questions unanswered. In doing so, he invited later writers to elaborate on his tales, to fill in the gaps that he has created. It was not long before the invitation was taken up, and it was the early thirteenth-century French poet Robert de Boron who ensured both the development of Merlin and his continued popularity. The trilogy of prose romances linked to Robert's name sees Merlin take on an even greater significance, and marked the beginning of him as a romance figure proper. In Robert's *Merlin*, the visit of the incubus comes as the climax of a protracted spiritual battle between the Devil and a family consisting of father, mother, son and three daughters. The parents and son are killed, and the elder two daughters tricked into sexual activity that leaves them either dead or disgraced. A hermit teaches the third daughter how to protect herself from the sexual attentions of demons by blessing every door and window before she sleeps. This works for a time, but the Devil prompts the middle sister to attack her with a mob, forcing the youngest sister to lock herself in her room, where she falls down exhausted and sleeps without remembering to bless the doors and windows. The Devil duly lies with her, and Merlin is conceived.

It is significant that the expansion of this episode intensifies the demonic interaction with what will be Merlin's family. His mother is no longer a nun, although her moral integrity is stressed: she alone of the sisters has not been a willing partner in sexual activity. Yet this very fact makes it plain that in this account Merlin's successful conception is a victory for evil over good. As if to make this clearer, Robert begins the *Merlin* with a debate between the demons about how to respond to the Harrowing of Hell (pp. 18–23). They seek a means of counter-attack and retaliation, of regaining ('ravoir', p. 21) what has been taken from them by Christ, and decide to create a man who will be their spokesperson in the world of human beings, a counterpart to Christian prophets whom they blame (along with Christ himself) for their defeat. In Robert's account, this is not only *how* Merlin begins, but *why*: he is brought into existence as a servant of the devils, their riposte to the work of Christ, and their attempt to reverse it. Merlin is intended to deceive those he speaks to and bring about their damnation, acting as an exact opposite to Christ. A text which deliberately frames Merlin in these terms from the beginning can never entirely banish the suspicions it creates, now matter how much it later insists on Merlin's religious and moral conformity.

In the Vulgate Cycle, *Lestoire de Merlin* follows this account closely, but Merlin's conception is briefly retold in the first part of the *Lancelot*, and this version has important differences. Here, Merlin's mother is still deceived (she thinks the demon she finds in her bed is a man) but she does consent to the intercourse. This means that Merlin is no longer conceived by rape but by adultery, and in the context of a romance which will celebrate unmarried (sexual) love, this might seem to represent a softening of some of the unpalatable aspects of Merlin's conception, even while it retains the essential element of his demonic origin. Yet a comment soon after in the authorial voice leaves us in no doubt about the opinion of him that we are expected to hold: 'Il fu de la nature son peire decheuans & desloiaus & sot quanques cuers pooit sauoir de toute peruerse science' ('He was of the same nature as his father, deceptive and disloyal, and he possessed all the false and perverted knowledge that an individual could have').[14] This judgement is not based on any new information about who Merlin is: all of the things he is accused of here could be inferred from his demonic parentage, perhaps under the influence of biblical texts such as John 8, 44, 'cum loquitur mendacium ex propriis loquitur quia mendax est et pater eius' ('When he [the Devil] speaketh a lie, he speaketh of his own: for he is a liar, and the father thereof').[15] The difference here is that rather than seeking to excuse or counteract the influence of his demonic origins, as Robert does, the writer of the *Lancelot* chooses to emphasize them, perhaps in order to make sure that the heroic focus in this romance remains on its eponymous figure. In doing so, he reveals the extent to which Merlin's character is always flexible, always subject to the interpretative pressure placed upon it by writer and audience at any given moment.

It was not only in his conception that Merlin had the disturbing potential to unite moral opposites in himself, but also in his subsequent behaviour. Nowhere was this more evident than in his practice of magic, something with which the dominant trends of medieval thought had an uneasy relationship throughout the period.[16] As a term, 'magic' is fluid and frequently defies attempts to map modern categories of natural and supernatural onto medieval thinking. It also encompasses a wide range of practices, some of which were condemned by most medieval lawmakers and theologians, whereas others were tolerated or actively encouraged. The main differential between these attitudes was the perceived source of the power used to create the magical act in question. If the power was believed to be a property lying within the objects concerned, then this was a legitimate action, and found in the most orthodox of environments:

---

[14] Sommer, vol. 3, p. 21, Lacy, vol. 2, p. 12.
[15] Biblical quotations are from *Biblia Sacra Iuxta Vulgata Versionem*, ed. R. Weber et al., 4th edn (Stuttgart, 1969) and *The Holy Bible: Douay Version* (London, 1956).
[16] There is a large literature on this subject. The best guides are Valerie I.J. Flint, *The Rise of Magic in Early Medieval Europe* (Oxford, 1991); Richard Kieckhefer, *Magic in the Middle Ages* (Cambridge, 1990); Jeffrey Burton Russell, *Witchcraft in the Middle Ages* (Ithaca, 1972); and, with specific reference to Arthurian literature, Corinne Saunders, 'Religion and Magic', in *The Cambridge Companion to the Arthurian Legend* (Cambridge, 2009), ed. Elizabeth Archibald and Ad Putter (Cambridge, 2009), pp. 201–17.

The early medieval monks would not have thought of themselves as dabbling in the magical arts. Without scruples, however, they would use mandrake for its mysterious curative powers, and they might also use charms to drive away the 'elves' that were causing sickness.[17]

There are two sorts of magic at work here: the use of plants, which was largely seen as a legitimate, and charms, which were much more open to debate, depending upon which supernatural powers were invoked and to what ends. This is where the truly unacceptable (to medieval orthodoxy) forms of magic began, with the invocation and manipulation of demonic powers.[18]

Merlin performs various magical acts, and it is by no means always easy to determine how he does so, and therefore what an appropriate reaction would be. Take for example Merlin's ability to shapeshift. In Robert's *Merlin*, this facility is used in a decidedly mischievous way, as when he appears successively as a woodcutter; 'an ugly, deformed herdsman' ('un home molt lait et molt hidos qui ces bestes gardoit');[19] two distinct handsome, well-dressed men; an old, white-haired man; and a serving boy in the employ of Uther's beloved. Rationalist explanations suggesting the use of disguises fail to account for the completeness of each change, and the speed with which it is accomplished. For any medieval audience, these rapid and unexplained changes of appearance would have been obvious examples of some form of magical activity. Geoffrey, in the *Historia*, makes it clear that Merlin is able to give Uther the appearance of Gorlois (and Ulfin the appearance of Jordan, and himself the appearance of Britaelis) by the use of drugs ('medicaminis', p. 187), although he does not specify which drugs, or how they are used. Robert follows Geoffrey here in giving this particular transformation a pharmacological/medical cause, adding the detail that it is achieved by rubbing a herb on the face and hands, a practice which a medieval audience would recognize as associated with magic.[20] Yet he introduces this episode with more original shapechanging by Merlin, seemingly simply for Merlin's own amusement and the puzzlement of Uther and his messenger. Robert does not provide any hint at all of how these transformations are achieved, and, although an audience is certainly free to assume that they too are the result of the application of herbs, that is by no means an inevitable conclusion from the narrative. Moreover, from Augustine onwards shapeshifting had been understood as a demonic illusion, since only God can truly make and remake natural forms.[21] In changing his form, Merlin is using powers inherited from his evil father, in mockery of the activity of God, and with no pressing need to do so. Shapeshifting is therefore part of the darker side of Merlin's character, when seen from the perspective of medieval orthodoxy.

At other times, Merlin uses his powers in an altogether more practical way, such as when he arranges for the transportation of Stonehenge from Ireland to Wiltshire.

---

17 Kieckhefer, p. 58.
18 For a brief but illuminating survey of medieval thinking regarding the place of demons in the natural world, see C.S. Lewis, *The Discarded Image* (Cambridge, 1964), pp. 117–38.
19 Micha, p. 128, trans. Bryant, p. 79.
20 Russell, p. 216.
21 See examples in Russell, pp. 56–57, 76–77, 135.

But exactly how does he manage this? Robert gives scant information, simply stating that 'Lors fist Merlins par force d'art apporter d'Irlande les pierres' ('Then, by magic, Merlin brought the stones from Ireland'),[22] leaving it unclear exactly what 'force d'art' is involved. The same phrase is used in the Vulgate *Lestoire de Merlin*), and its implications are perhaps primarily magical, but they do not necessarily exclude a more mechanical solution. This ambiguity is even more pronounced in Geoffrey's account, where several kinds of 'magic' are hinted at. Merlin explains that the stones themselves have intrinsic magical properties ('Mistici sunt lapides et ad diuersa medicamenta salubres'), but considerable emphasis is also laid on his purely mechanical genius, and Bishop Tremorinus recommends him for the task as much for his pragmatic as for his prophetic abilities:

> non existimo alterum esse in regno tuo cui sit clarius ingenium siue in futuris dicendis siue in operationibus machinandis.
>
> I do not think there is anyone in your kingdom more distinguished in foretelling the future or in feats of engineering. (pp. 170–71)

Yet when he comes to describe the moving of the stones itself, Geoffrey characteristically gives nothing away:

> Merlinus in risum suasque machinationes confecit. Denique, cum quaeque necessaria apposuisset, leuius quam credi potest lapides deposuit.
>
> Merlin laughed [...] As soon as everything was ready, he took down the stones with incredible ease. (pp. 174–75)

We are left wondering exactly what these 'machinaciones' are: they could be truly supernatural apparatus, but it seems more likely that they are simply examples of cutting-edge technology, beyond the knowledge of the contemporary 'artifices lignorum et lapidum' ('the carpenters and stonemasons', p. 171) who failed to move the stones. This casts Merlin as a great engineer as well as magician, soothsayer and prophet (there is no indication here that Merlin has used his prophetic knowledge to access technologies of the future). This combination of abilities illustrates how science and magic were not so sharply differentiated in medieval culture, as in the modern world, and also Merlin's overwhelming omnicompetence in these overlapping disciplines.

As well as a magician (someone who has privileged knowledge which enables him to manipulate the natural world in some way), Merlin is also a prophet, someone who has privileged knowledge of past, present and future events. This ability was also hotly contested in the centuries when the Merlin of romance developed and flourished. The *possibility* of prophecy was never seriously questioned, because of its prominence in the Bible. The debate was instead focused on such questions as what prophecy was and could be; whether it still happened and to whom; and what possible causes it might have.

---

[22] Micha, p. 180, trans. Bryant, p. 91.

These controversies bloomed in the two hundred years or so from the publication of the *Historia*, not least in the university schools that were coming into being in the thirteenth century. Thomas Aquinas devoted four *quæstiones* of the *Summa Theologiæ* to the nature, cause, manner, and divisions of prophecy (II–II, CLXXI–CLXXIV). In particular, he dealt with the question of whether prophecy could have a demonic origin (CLXXII, 5, '*utrum aliqua prophetia sit a dæmonibus*'), and, having concluded that it can, he considered whether demonic prophecy could ever be truthful (CLXXII, 6, '*utrum prophetæ dæmonum aliquando prædicant uerum*'). This proved to be a more tricky point, but Aquinas was able to cite Bede, Augustine and Pseudo-Chrysostom, as well as the example of Balaam from the book of Numbers, to argue that:

> sicut se habet bonum in rebus, ita verum in cognitione. Impossibile est autem inveniri aliquid in rebus quod totaliter bono privetur. Unde etiam impossibile est esse aliquam cognitionem quæ totaliter sit falsa absque admixtione alicuius veritatis.
>
> Goodness has the same relation to realities as truth has to knowledge. Now it is impossible to find in creatures anything which is wholly destitute of good. So too is it impossible for some knowledge to be wholly false to the exclusion of every particle of truth.[23]

The implication of Aquinas's argument was that, even if what a man (or woman) prophesied was true, or partly true, it did not follow that he or she was a true prophet: his or her prophecy could still be demonic rather than divine in origin. Moreover, Aquinas had already argued that even a divine gift of prophecy did not require or imply goodness ('bonitas') in the recipient ('prophetia potest esse sine bonitate morum').[24]

Such arguments, expressed in these forms by Aquinas in the 1260s and 1270s, but founded on an understanding of divine and demonic prophecy going back at least to Augustine,[25] had implications for Merlin's prophetic gift. Simply to declare that Merlin was a prophet, and that his prophecies could sometimes be shown to come true, was not enough to establish that he was a 'good' figure, morally admirable or divinely inspired. If that question was not to be left open, then more information had to be supplied about the source of Merlin's gift. Robert de Boron proposes an ingenious solution to this issue, granting Merlin prophetic gifts that are both demonic and divine in origin. Since the Devil is his father, Merlin cannot help but inherit some powers from him: 'si ot et dut avoir le pooir et l'enging dou deable, com cil qui l'avoit conceu' ('he had the power and the intelligence of the devil – he was bound to, being conceived by him').[26] Yet while God (in Robert's presentation of him) is scrupulous to allow the Devil his 'rights', he manages to outmanoeuvre him by adding a gift of his own:

---

[23] *Summa Theologiæ*, vol. 45, trans. Roland Potter (London, 1970), qu. 172, art. 4, '*utrum bonitas morum requiratur ad prophetiam*'.
[24] CLXXII, 4, '*utrum bonitas morum requiratur ad prophetiam*'.
[25] See for example *De Civitate Dei*, 10.32, for Augustine's distinctions between natural prediction, demonic prophecy, and divine prophecy (*The City of God Against the Pagans*, ed. and trans. R.W. Dyson (Cambridge, 1998), pp. 442–48).
[26] Micha, p. 49; trans. Bryant, p. 54.

Par cestes raisons sot cist les choses faites, dites et alees, car il les a et tient de l'enemi; et le surplus qu'il set des choses qui sont a avenir volt Nostre Sires qu'il seust contre les autres choses qu'il savoit por endroit de la soue partie: si se tenra a laquele il veura, car se il volt, il puet randre as deables lor droit et a Nostre Seingnor le suen: car plus n'a deables en lui formet que le cors, et Nostre Sire met en touz les cors son esperit et por veir et por oïr et por entendre, a chascun selonc ce que il li preste memoire. Et il a a cestui plus doné que a autre por ce que graindre mestiers li estoit, si savra or bien au quiel il se devra tenir.

And so it was that the child inherited knowledge of things past from the Enemy, and, in addition, knowledge of things to come was bequeathed him by God. It was up to him which way he inclined. If he wished, he could answer the claims both of Our Lord and of the devils; for a demon had made his body, but Our Lord had given him the spirit to hear and understand. Indeed, he had given more to him that to other men because he would certainly be needing it. It remained to be seen which way the child would lean. (Micha, pp. 50–51; p. 55)

Robert repeatedly stresses here the fact that Merlin is the product of two conflicting forces, and that as a result supernatural powers of both good and evil are present in him, and available to him. The audience is left to anticipate a narrative in which he will have to choose between them, a choice that will determine what they are to make of his character. At the same time, the phrase 'il puet randre as deables lor droit *et* a Nostre Seingnor le suen' (my emphasis) is ambiguous: it might simply emphasize Merlin's equal freedom to choose to serve either God or the Devil, but the use of 'et' suggests that Merlin can serve both concurrently. It leaves open the possibility that the union of opposites that marked Merlin's conception and birth will also mark the rest of his life. In the event, Robert works hard to exclude that possibility, but the fact that he has to do so only underlines its threatening presence.

In fact, at least some of Merlin's uses of his prophetic gifts suggest a character more cruel than otherwise. In the prose *Merlin*, Robert de Boron introduces two episodes between Merlin's discovery by the messengers from Vortigern, and his arrival at court. In the first of these, Merlin sees a man about to travel on pilgrimage, who has bought a new pair of shoes and some spare leather to repair them. Merlin's reaction to this sight is unusual: he laughs ('rist'). When the messengers ask why, he explains that the mans is 'going to die before he even reaches home' ('sera morz ainz que il soit en sa meson').[27] Laughing at someone else's impending death, even if only because it makes his preparations for the future ironic, is black humour indeed, and it is by no means certain that an audience can share it, any more than the messengers do. Similarly, a few lines later Merlin is laughing again, this time at the funeral of a young boy. This time, he is amused by the fact that the child's mother conceived him not after sleeping with her husband (who is weeping in the procession), but with the priest who is now, dry-eyed, leading the cortège to the burial. Again, this seems like a strange subject for amusement, and there is nothing in the surrounding prose to

---

[27] Micha, p 103; trans. Bryant, p. 107.

suggest a tone of irony, satire, or *memento mori* humour. Merlin is proving his extraordinary powers, but also revealing his attitudes.

Yet perhaps this should be taken as polemical, a determined use of Merlin's somewhat detached social and moral position in order to place human suffering in an eternal context. On this reading, Merlin is harnessed to Robert's recurring emphasis on sound theological doctrine throughout *Merlin* and *Joseph of Arimathea*. In the introduction to his translation of Robert's works, Nigel Bryant draws attention to Robert's insistent orthodoxy, especially his repeated iterations of the doctrine of the Trinity, and suggests that this may have been at least partly a reaction against the perceived dangers of Cathar teaching in early thirteenth-century France.[28] Whatever truth there may be in this explanation (which is certainly plausible), it is undeniable that Robert tries hard to reassure his audience that Merlin is a character of moral rectitude. He repeatedly makes Uther and Pendragon swear on holy relics. He even declares to Uther 'the Enemy have lost me: I will never [God willing] work on their behalf' ('m'ont perdu li enemi, que je, se Deu plaist, n'en vendrai ja a lor volenté').[29] Nevertheless the qualifying phrase 'se Deu plaist' simultaneously adds both a pious touch and an equivocal note of doubt, and Merlin's subsequent actions serve to increase rather than allay such misgivings.

There is, for example, at least an irony, if not an outright contradiction, between the attitudes taken by this text towards the various episodes of extra-marital sex within it. Robert takes the trouble to elaborate on Merlin's conception, underscoring the importance of chastity through the counter-examples of his mother's elder sisters and their ruin through sexual incontinence, and noting that this adultery itself is prompted by a demon. Moreover, several of the episodes that Robert invents in order to demonstrate and prove Merlin's supernatural knowledge are concerned with the exposure (and implicit condemnation) of adulterous sexual relations, including the one that led to the conception of the man judging Merlin's mother for adultery. Yet Robert also retains the later episode from Geoffrey's *Historia* dealing with the conception of Arthur, who is begotten by Utherpendragon on Igerne – another man's wife who is tricked into sleeping with him. And in this case, it is Merlin himself who actually makes such a deception possible. There is of course nothing unique about a medieval text endorsing adulterous passion, but it is striking when it comes in the same text that has earlier gone to such lengths to illustrate the dangers of illicit sexual activity. The conceptions of both Merlin and Arthur in each case involve a woman who believes she is being chaste (Igerne consents to intercourse, but believes it is with her husband), but who is tricked by a male figure. The rape of Merlin's mother is to some extent redeemed by God's granting Merlin the power to resist his demonic origins and turn his powers against the evil purpose from which he derived them. There is, however, no parallel intervention in the case of Uther and Igerne, and thus scant justification for Merlin's connivance at a similar act of deception and what is, in effect, rape. Merlin himself acknowledges that he is culpable, and later declares to Uther regarding this act 'je ne me sui mie aquitez dou pechié que j'ai' ('I am not yet absolved of my sin', p. 247; my translation).

---

[28] Bryant, p. 6.
[29] Micha, p. 183; trans. Bryant, p. 92.

The measures that Merlin proposes as penance for this sin are curious to say the least. He asks Uther to give him the child who will be born as a result of the liaison with Igerne, and subsequently has him raised by an impoverished local knight (incidentally forcing the knight to have his own child reared by another, anonymous couple). Of course, this child is Arthur, who will eventually succeed Uther and reign as a model king, and thus the implication might be that in ensuring this Merlin has atoned for his sin. Yet nothing in Robert's text suggests that Merlin's intervention and adoption of the child are strictly necessary for him to become king. Indeed, if he had been born and raised as a child of Uther, he might even have ascended to the throne with less opposition, since the main reason given for the barons' objection to his rule is Arthur's apparently lowly birth. The audience may assume that Merlin knows best (and it will certainly enjoy the added twists to the story generated by his intervention), but this is surely a dangerous assumption given the morality of the conduct for which he is already seeking to atone. Once again, Merlin's prophetic gift seems insufficient to justify his behaviour, or completely to reassure us of his moral worth.

One of the reasons why the sources of prophecy were of interest to theologians such as Aquinas was the challenge that prophets posed to the existing power structures of Church and State. A prophet laid claim to knowledge directly from God, bypassing temporal and ecclesiastical authorities, and therefore threatening those authorities by doing so. In this context, Merlin can be seen as a device by which medieval writers could arrogate prophetic authority and power to themselves, but in a comparatively safe way. As their titles suggest, the *Prophetiæ Merlini* do not overtly claim prophetic status for Geoffrey of Monmouth himself, but for Merlin, someone now long dead and beyond the reach of any living temporal or ecclesiastical powers. Yet prophecies put into the mouth of Merlin could be used as a commentary on contemporary issues, as when John of Cornwall expounded on Merlinic prophecies derived from Geoffrey and elsewhere, producing a largely original poem with prose commentary clearly relating the prophecies to the Anarchy under King Stephen.[30] In such ways, Merlin could be used in prophesy and chronicle to comment on the politics of the present, but to do so from the safe-haven of the distant past, bypassing any of the dangers faced by contemporary individuals claiming to be prophets.[31]

However, within the romance tradition, Merlin is often not so much a critic of and threat to the prevailing political order, but rather co-opted into its service. This is clear from the beginning: Merlin first uses his prophetic gifts in the *Historia* to aid rather than oppose Vortigern, who is a usurper, but nevertheless the established king. He continues to advise and aid, in fact almost to control, the kings who succeed Vortigern: Aurelius Ambrosius and Utherpendragon in the *Historia*, Pendragon and Uther in Robert's *Merlin*. Nevertheless, Merlin's relation to the king and kingdom he so often helps is somewhat anomalous. Indeed, just as his nature is poised between the divine and the demonic, so he is also positioned on the periphery of the court,

---

[30] See A.G. Rigg, *A History of Anglo-Latin Literature 1066–1422* (Cambridge, 1992), p. 47.
[31] On this see further Ad Putter, 'Gerald of Wales and the Prophet Merlin', *Anglo-Norman Studies* 31 (2008), pp. 90–103.

neither opposed to it nor fully a part of it. His is an independent power, reliant not on political or military might, but on his prophetic and magical knowledge. Stephen Knight sees this opposition as crucial to the character and continued appeal of Merlin:

> Whether it is based on bard versus lord, magician versus monarch, scientist versus capitalist, academic versus politician, the conflict between knowledge and power is inherent to organized species, and the many formations of Myrddin-Merlin and his story have represented the many versions of this conflict.[32]

This is only part of the truth, however, for whilst Merlin preserves a mischievous independence that allows him to disappear from the text until narrative function requires him again, he is also deeply invested in the fortunes of the court and usually works to further the interests of the king. Moreover, his knowledge *confers* power, in many ways greater than any other present in the world of the text. Indeed, Merlin repeatedly mirrors the supreme power of the author (or, as has been noted above, the historian), interpreting the events of the past and telling the events of the future. This role is foregrounded by Robert, who repeatedly sends Merlin away to inform Blaise (his mother's former confessor) of recent events so that he can write them down for posterity: in effect, Merlin is authoring *Merlin*.[33] As such, he has power over his own representation – perhaps the ultimate power in a textual realm.

Besides the problems of morality, theology, and personality that went with the figure of Merlin, he was also a mixed blessing to writers in terms of plot and structure. The granting of supernatural powers to a character in a story can potentially create such an imbalance that it removes tension. If Arthur has a magician on his side, he could easily become effectively invulnerable, and thus the risk and uncertainty necessary for the creation of an engaging story would be removed. To be sure, an unfair advantage in itself would not be an insuperable problem for the narrator of a medieval romance. The heroes of romance are frequently given magical advantages over their enemies, without any sense that this reduces or compromises their chivalry or heroism. Thus Yvain in Chrétien de Troyes's *Chevalier au lion* is given a ring which will preserve him from all harm; the eponymous hero of *Sir Launfal* has a similar gift from his lady, Triamour, and also the services of an invisible squire (Gyfré), who can replace his master's helmet or shield when it is lost in the joust. Yet Merlin's all-encompassing knowledge is so powerful a narrative tool that he could easily overwhelm not only the other characters, but the very process of telling a story itself. There can be no tension or audience-engagement in the unfolding of events if they are always known in advance.

For these reasons, the narratives of Merlin usually find a way to sideline him and finally remove him from the narrative action. Geoffrey's *Historia* simply ceases to mention him after he has made the transformations necessary for Arthur's conception, except for one odd reference almost at the end: 'Nolebat enim Deus

---

[32] Knight, p. 4.
[33] See, for example, pp. 138–39, 163, 190, 235.

Britones in insula Britannie diutius regnare antequam tempus illud uenisset quod Merlinus Arturo prophetauerat' ('God did not wish the Britons to rule in Britain any more, until the moment should come which Merlin had prophesied to Arthur' (205.5–7; 282). The clause 'antequam tempus illud uenisset quod Merlinus Arturo prophetauerat' is, as Lewis Thorpe points out, a 'curious' one, since 'Merlin never met Arthur', at least not in the *Historia*.[34] Yet such was Merlin's powerful attraction for the writers of medieval romance that from Robert de Boron onwards his biography was extended to make him guide and confidant to Arthur, as he had been to Vortigern and Uther, and it would not be at all surprising if this tradition had influenced scribes in their copying of the *Historia*. In any case, it seems appropriate for a figure as mysterious and unpredictable as Merlin that he should not so much exit Geoffrey's text, as fade out of it.

Robert invents an exit which is even more enigmatic. Having returned once again, at the end of the *Merlin*, to Northumberland, in order to inform Blaise of the latest developments in the story, Merlin is absent for most of the *Perceval*, returning only to remind the eponymous hero of his quest and the vows he has made, and to inform Arthur that the quest is complete. These are further examples of his function as a quasi-author, not simply in controlling events but in making others aware of them. Yet such examples are kept to a minimum, not only so that Merlin's sudden re-appearance is all the more dramatic, but also to allow Perceval to be truly tested in his *aventure*, without undue assistance from Merlin's potentially dubious powers. His final reappearance is at the very end of the *Perceval*, where he announces that it is Christ's will for him not to appear any more in the world. Nevertheless, he will not die until the world itself does, after which he will live in eternal joy. This supernatural longevity gives Merlin a suitable otherworldliness, and also leaves the door open for him to make future appearances and pronouncements: it makes him a live force, still speaking, still prophesying, still capable of guiding events in the here and now. Yet Robert also needs to explain Merlin's absence from the contemporary world of himself and his audience, and so he says that Merlin will continue to live in the wilderness of Northumbria by Blaise's house, in a dwelling place that will be called his *esplumoir*. As Nigel Bryant notes, this is probably a neologism of Robert's, with connotations of transformation and renewal, but in its link to the verb *esplumer* it also suggests the act of removing feathers, perhaps suggesting that Merlin has been 'plucked out' of the narrative.[35] From then on Merlin was (so Robert assures us) never seen again, but the transformative implications of the *esplumoir* leave the possibility open that he is still present, merely unrecognized, just as he so often has been throughout Robert's narratives.

Yet it was the Vulgate cycle that popularized the most enigmatic and powerful of all the exit-strategies used for Merlin. This seems to have originated in the *Lancelot*, was later elaborated in *Lestoire de Merlin* and the Post-Vulgate *Suite de Merlin*, and became well-known in the post-medieval period through its use by Malory in his

---

[34] Thorpe, p. 282.
[35] Bryant, p. 172. See Tobler-Lommatzsch, s.v. 'esplumer'.

Morte Darthur.³⁶ The core idea is that Merlin becomes infatuated with a woman (variously called Ninniane, Viviane, and Nenive) and at her request teaches her the spells necessary to entrap a man, only for her to use them against him and imprison him in a cave or under a stone. Significantly, this marks Merlin's first (and only) personal engagement with sexuality since his own birth, unless one counts his collusion with Uther in the deception of Igerne. In its earliest form, this defeat is not only humiliating for Merlin, but also intended to be final, 'for never again did anyone see or hear of him or have news to tell of him' ('Car onques puis par nului ne fu seus ne par nul home veus qui noueles en seust dire').³⁷ As such, it shows romantic and sexual love as Merlin's fatal weakness, and (given the *Lancelot*'s damning portrayal of Merlin more generally) it is pointed in its ironic suggestion that for all his knowledge, he was unable to bridle desire with reason. If being half-demon is not enough to damn Merlin, then the *Lancelot* seems determined to add a new charge against him that will be unequivocal.

If such was the intention, it failed, for subsequent recastings of the episode increasingly removed aspects that placed Merlin in an unfavourable light. In particular, *Lestoire de Merlin* makes him considerably more sympathetic, almost tragic, firstly by making it clear that he knows what will happen and accepts his fate for the sake of love, and secondly by changing the lady's character. Now, she loves Merlin – after he has told her what she wants to know, 'she was very happy and loved him more' ('la damoisele moult grant ioie & plus lama')³⁸ – and repeatedly returns to spend time with him in his prison. Even more importantly, Merlin is not lost to the narrative, reappearing a few pages later to speak to Sir Gawainet. This is only a partial erosion of the prison's power over him, however, for he laments 'after you leave here, I'll never speak to you or to anyone else but my lady' ('quant vous departires de chi iamais ne parlerai a vous ne a autre que a mamie').³⁹ Malory's version grants Merlin both more and less freedom. As in the *Lancelot* and the *Suite de Merlin*, Merlin is deceived by a woman who does not love him and locked away seemingly forever: 'she wrought so there for hym that he come never oute for all the craufte he coude do, and so she departed and leffte Merlyon'.⁴⁰ Yet later on in the *Morte*, near the beginning of 'The Book of Sir Tristram de Lyones', Malory mentions in passing 'Than this meanewhyle Merlyon had delyverede kynge Melyodas oute of preson [...]'.⁴¹ One hesitates to say that this is a deliberate 'liberation' of Merlin, given that Malory is notorious for continuity-errors. Nevertheless, it is notable that there are five further references in the *Morte* to Merlin's actions, all of them admittedly retrospective, so that whilst Merlin may physically be captive, he continues in a sense to roam through the text. His imprisonment has been effectively effaced and drained of its meaning: it happens, but only partially eliminates his presence. Merlin, it appears, still has some tricks up his sleeve, even if they are only narratological ones.

---

36 Sommer, vol. 3, p. 21 and vol. 2, pp. 451–52; Gaston Paris and Jacob Ulrich, eds, *Merlin: Roman en prose de XIIIe siècle*, 8 vols (Paris, 1886), vol. 2, pp. 191–99; Vinaver, vol. 1, p. 126.
37 Sommer, vol. 3, p. 21; Lacy, vol. 2, p. 6.
38 Sommer, vol. 2, p. 452; Lacy, vol. 1, p. 416.
39 Sommer, vol. 2, p. 461; Lacy, vol. 1, p. 421.
40 Vinaver, vol. 1, p. 126.
41 Vinaver, vol. 2, p. 372.

From before birth to death (if that occurs at all) and seemingly beyond, Merlin is perennially open to representation and reinterpretation. In every aspect of his character, he is finely poised between good and evil, heavenly and demonic powers, usefulness and danger. If this makes him hard to summarize, it also helps to explain his enduring fascination for medieval writers, since he can readily be drawn to whatever moral, theological or political position a writer wishes. Yet the darker aspects of his powers and his ancestry continually threaten to overwhelm both him and the stories in which he features, and attempts to remove him from the narrative are not always entirely successful. Merlin exerted (and still exerts) great cultural influence as the counsellor and advisor to King Arthur, but his own domain is much greater and more unruly than that of any king, and all the richer for that.

7
Gawain

Kate McClune

Malory's Gawain

The killing of Lamorak de Galys 'by treson' (2:716) is a defining moment in Sir Thomas Malory's portrayal of the perpetrators of the slaying, Sir Gawain of Orkney and his brothers Aggravayne, Gaheris, and Mordred.[1] The murder (as it is repeatedly defined by Malory's other knights, see 2:688, 691, 698–99) takes place 'off-screen', and its description is twice relayed to the audience in varying detail. First, Palomides informs Lamorak's brother, Percival de Galys, that the Orkney brothers 'slewe hym [Lamorak] felounsly' (2:688), and subsequently he describes to Tristram, Dinadan, and Gareth, the fifth Orkney brother, the full particulars of the brutal, and (it would appear) cowardly, murder of Lamorak. Palomides' relation does not reflect well upon the nephews of King Arthur. Lamorak, we are told, was 'sette uppon...in a pryvy place' (2:699) by the combined might of four of the five Orkney brethren. First, they kill his horse, then, on foot, they fight him – four against one – 'bothe byfore hym and behynde hym' (2:699) for over three hours, until eventually he is stabbed in the back by Mordred, the youngest of the brothers, and his body is hacked to pieces.[2] Towards the end of the *Morte*, after Lancelot has killed Gareth, Gawain challenges him. During their exchange, it is abundantly obvious that even Gawain knows that the killing of Lamorak is viewed as a shameful event by his peers. Lancelot, in defending himself for accidentally slaying Gareth in the mêlée surrounding Guinevere's rescue, tells Gawain that 'may hit never be seyde on me and opynly preved that ever I be forecaste of treson slew no goode knyght as ye, my lord sir Gawayne, have done'. Gawain's immediate recognition of the unspecified event to which Lancelot refers as the murder of Lamorak, 'that thou menyst by sir Lamorak' (3:1190), and his failure to excuse or defend himself, indicate that he too seems to be aware that this was not an honourable killing.

Lamorak's violent death is the culmination of an inter-familial feud that claims many victims, not least of whom is his lover Morgawse, decapitated by her son

---

[1] All quotations from the *Morte Darthur* are from *The Works of Sir Thomas Malory*, ed. Eugène Vinaver, rev. P.J.C. Field, 3 vols (Oxford, 1990), henceforth *Works*, with references to volume- and page-number.
[2] 'Sir Mordrede gaff hym his dethis wounde behynde hym at his bakke, and all to-hewe hym' (2:699). For further discussion of Malory's description of the killing, and the changes made to the source, see Vinaver, *Works*, 3:1513.

Gaheris while she is in bed with Lamorak. Morgawse is, moreover, Arthur's half-sister (and erstwhile lover), the matriarch of the Orkney clan, and the widowed queen of King Lot of Orkney and Lothian, whose death in battle at the hands of Lamorak's father Pellinore de Galys is the incident that initially inspires the bloody vendetta. The Orkneys and the de Galys are not the only families who seem to be at war in Malory's text,[3] and in general Malory's presentation of such family feuds has its genesis ultimately in the various source texts, but the conflict between the de Galys and the Orkneys is of particular note. It highlights the fissures in the Round Table fellowship (the knights involved are all members of Arthur's fictive brotherhood) and – more pertinently for this essay – Malory's depiction has contributed substantially to the paradoxical reputation of one of the most enduringly popular and well known of Arthur's knights, Sir Gawain of Orkney.[4]

Malory's depiction of Gawain is not prevailingly negative:[5] it is, after all, Gawain who attempts to dissuade his brothers Aggravayne and Mordred from revealing

---

[3] There are many examples of family vengeance: Balin kills the Lady of the Lake because, he says, 'she was causer that my modir was brente' (1:66), an act that leads to his expulsion from Arthur's court; the green knight who fights Sir Gareth declares to him that 'thou shalt dye for sleyng of my brothir!' (1:305), and Dalan accuses Sir Dynadan of being the knight who 'slewe my fadir', and vows 'thou shalt dye therefore!' (2:614–15). For further discussion of Balin's revenge, see Carolyne Larrington, 'Sibling Relations in Malory's *Morte Darthur*', *Arthurian Literature 28: Blood, Sex, Malory: essays on the 'Morte Darthur'*, ed. David Clark and Kate McClune (Cambridge, 2011), 57–74. On bloodfeud more generally in Malory's *Morte*, see in the same collection Sally Mapstone, 'Malory and the Scots', pp. 107–20, and Kate McClune, '"The vengeaunce of my brethirne": blood ties in Malory's *Morte Darthur*', pp. 89–106.

[4] Gawain is the central character in numerous medieval romances in a variety of European languages, and his sometimes contradictory characterisation is the subject of much critical discussion: see especially Keith Busby, *Gauvain in Old French Literature* (Amsterdam, 1980) and *Gawain: A Casebook*, eds Raymond H. Thompson and Keith Busby (New York, 2006), in which see B.J. Whiting, 'Gawain: His Reputation, His Courtesy, and His Appearance in Chaucer's *Squire's Tale*', pp. 45–94; Phillip C. Boardman, 'Middle English Arthurian Romance: The Repetition and Reputation of Gawain', pp. 255–72; Beverly Kennedy, 'Gawain and Heroic Knighthood in Malory', pp. 287–296; Raymond H. Thompson, 'Gawain in Post-Medieval English Literature', pp. 297–317. See also Lena Petrovic, 'Gawain: Transformations of an Archetype', *Linguistics and Literature* 2 (2000), 129–50; Thomas Hahn, 'Gawain and popular chivalric romance in Britain', in *The Cambridge Companion to Medieval Romance*, ed. Roberta L. Krueger (Cambridge, 2000), pp. 218–34; Margaret Robson, 'Local hero: Gawain and the Politics of Arthurianism', *Arthurian Literature* 23, ed. Keith Busby with Roger Dalrymple (Cambridge, 2006), 81–94; Lori J. Walters, 'More Bread from Stone: Gauvain as a Figure of Plenitude in the French, Dutch, and English Traditions', *Arthurian Literature 24: The European Dimensions of Arthurian Literature*, ed. Bart Besamusca and Frank Brandsma (Cambridge, 2007), 15–32; Cory J. Rushton, 'Gawain as Lover in Middle English Literature', in *The Erotic in the Literature of Medieval Britain*, ed. Amanda Hopkins and Cory Rushton (Cambridge, 2007), pp. 27–37; Roger Dalrymple, 'Sir Gawain in Middle English Romance', in *A Companion to Arthurian Literature*, ed. Helen Fulton (Oxford, 2009), pp. 265–77.

[5] Whiting points to Malory's ambivalence towards the knight: his Gawain is 'sometimes good and sometimes bad' (p. 48), a feature that is in part attributable to the varied sources that Malory uses and their correspondingly diverse portrayals of Gawain. For a useful discussion of Gawain's portrayal in the French prose romances, see Fanni Bogdanow, 'The character of Gauvain in the thirteenth-century prose romances', *Medium Ævum* 27 (1958), 154–161. In my article, 'Malory, the Orkneys, and the Sinclairs', *Nottingham Medieval Studies* 54 (2010), 167–85, I suggest that another factor influencing Malory's presentation of Gawain is his familiarity with Gawain's nationality. On Gawain's Scottishness, see Mapstone; Cory J. Rushton, '"Of an uncouthe stede": The Scottish Knight in Middle English Arthurian Romances', in *The Scots and Medieval Arthurian Legend*, ed. Rhiannon Purdie and Nicola Royan (Cambridge, 2005), pp.

Lancelot's and Guenevere's adulterous relationship to Arthur (3:1161–13) – but he nevertheless emphasises, certainly more so than his English sources,[6] Gawain's more questionable qualities: his mercilessness, his anger, his implacable thirst for vengeance if he believes that his family has been slighted. It is Gawain who, at a young age, vows vengeance upon Pellinore and all his blood for the death of Lot; it is Gawain who, after promising Pelleas that he will aid him in his pursuit of Lady Ettarde, sleeps with her himself (1:167–71);[7] it is Gawain, explicitly, whose ethical code is rejected by his brother Gareth, identified as 'the beste knyght of all the brethirne' (2:696) in favour of that of Lancelot; it is Gawain who is told by the hermit Naciens that he will never attain the Grail because he is 'an untrew knyght and a grete murtherar' (2:948); and finally, notoriously, it is Gawain who refuses to be accorded with Lancelot, and who carries Arthur with him in his unceasing and destructive quest for revenge for the killing of his unarmed brother, the same Gareth who earlier repudiated Gawain and chose Lancelot.

A reader familiar with Gawain only through Malory's rendering might be forgiven for thinking that he, rather than Mordred, is the archetypal problem-knight. His acts of valour seem to be secondary to his acts of anger, and the parameters of his knightly career are framed in his youth by a desire to avenge his father, and later in life, by a desire to avenge his brother. In between, he gains notoriety, and inadvertently partly inspires the creation of the Pentecostal Oath,[8] when he refuses to grant mercy to a defeated knight, a refusal that ends with his accidental killing of the knight's lady. Much of Malory's narrative is naturally indebted to his French and English sources, but as has been argued elsewhere,[9] he consciously embellishes and expands upon his sources' depictions of Gawain, particularly in episodes that deal with the subject of family pride and bloodfeud. Malory's treatment of Gawain is more equivocal than in many of the other English and Scots texts that engage with him. The aforementioned slaying of the lady, for example, is also present in Malory's main source, the post-Vulgate *Suite de Merlin*, but only in Malory is Gawain's refusal to grant mercy to his adversary explicitly associated with a perceived deficiency in knightly honour. The twice-repeated assertion, which Malory adds to the source

---

109–19; Martin B. Shichtman, 'Sir Gawain in Scotland: A Hometown Boy Made Good', in *King Arthur through the Ages*, eds Valerie M. Lagorio and Mildred Leake Day (New York, 1990), pp. 234–47.

[6] A comparison of Malory's treatment of Gawain's vengeance and that presented in the Middle English Stanzaic *Le Morte Arthure* and the Old French *Mort Artu* is contained in McClune, '"The vengeaunce of my brethirne"'.

[7] The Pelleas and Ettarde episode seems to play off Gawain's reputation as an exemplary figure of courtesy – hence one might expect him to aid his fellow knight – and a knight who enjoys success with the opposite sex.

[8] The Pentecostal Oath comes at the end of the episode in which Gawain has accidentally killed a lady. As punishment, he is forced to return to court with her corpse; her head 'was hanged aboute hys necke, and the hole body of hir before hym on hys horse mane' (1:108). Upon his return to Camelot, he is sentenced by the queen and her ladies to 'be with all ladyes and to fyght for hir quarels; and ever that he sholde be curteyse, and never to refuse mercy…' (1:108). Key portions of the Pentecostal Oath seem to speak to Gawain's punishment, including the portion that requires knights to 'gyff mercy unto hym that askith mercy… and allwayes to do ladyes, damesels, and jantilwomen and wydowes [socour:] strengthe hem in hir ryghtes…' (1:120).

[9] See further Thompson and Busby, p. 17, and McClune, '"The vengeaunce of my brethirne"'.

account,[10] that a 'knyght without mercy ys withoute worship' (1:106; 107), suggests that even at this comparatively early stage in the *Morte*, Malory is sensitive to the creative potential that results from the notoriously conflicting literary representations of Gawain. The decision to present 'his' Gawain as a flawed individual whose preoccupation with his family and its reputation becomes damaging, is a conscious choice, and it moves the character away from the idealised individual of *Sir Gawain and the Green Knight* and closer to the scoundrel depicted in two of Malory's French sources, the *Queste del Saint Graal* (c. 1225–1230) and the prose *Tristan* and its derivatives (dating from the 1230s onward).

Gawain before Malory

'More than that of any other knight of the Round Table, the reputation of Gawain, King Arthur's favourite nephew, has fluctuated through the extremes of heroism and villainy',[11] write the editors of the most comprehensive recent collection of essays on Gawain's literary development. The statement (and the wealth of material that examines Gawain) highlights the critical fascination with Gawain's shifting reputation, and the modern interest arguably reflects a similar concern in medieval accounts. General qualities identified with Gawain include his amatory success and his valour: he is the 'standard of courtesy'.[12] But he acquires more problematic connotations in the French prose romances, and different texts augment or downplay these features in various ways.

Reputation is, for Gawain, crucial, and its importance is manifest on two levels. As a character whose literary existence is not confined to a single work, he has an extra-textual reputation that means his presence inspires certain expectations on the part of an audience that is presumed to recognise him. Gawain's character traits range from the noble to the troubling; readers should therefore be wary of assuming consistency or coherence in the various European chronicle and romance depictions of the man – as Bogdanow notes, in Malory alone Gawain 'is found in two entirely different roles'.[13] Nevertheless, the very existence of such traits provides authors with features that can be deployed or exploited in order to emphasise a particular theme.[14] Secondly, Gawain's fame and reputation are features that loom large *within* many of the texts in which he appears. Suppositions based on his fame are often made by his fictional peers: his reputation alluded to directly, or implicitly evoked. The sheer range of different ways in which Gawain is characterized raises important questions about the way in which we read medieval characters whose literary existence is not confined to a single text. This paper examines the importance of Gawain's reputation. It considers the shaping of his extra-literary fame, and analyses how this often plays a role in developing his literary appearances. It also discusses how his character is portrayed, or explicitly commented on, within literary works, and

---

[10] *Works*, 3:1328–29.
[11] Thompson and Busby, 'Introduction', p. 1.
[12] Boardman, p. 257.
[13] Bogdanow, p. 154.
[14] Hahn notes that the treatment of Gawain in Middle English romances depends less on a 'novelistic sense of "character", dependent upon a unique and consistent personality', and more upon the ability of the character Gawain to 'play a *role*; [to] routinely facilitate…extravagant adventures' (Hahn, 'Gawain and popular chivalric romance', p. 223).

suggests that every 'new' textual version of Gawain carries with it inevitable associations stemming from his previous literary incarnations. Such associations need not always be explicitly addressed or highlighted in the text; nevertheless, a short examination of the Gawains presented in medieval chronicle and romance suggests the extent to which such hangovers from his earlier literary appearances continue to contribute to his textual relevance over the centuries.

Particularly by the time of Malory's *Morte* and the fifteenth-century Scots romances, *Lancelot of the Laik* and *Golagros and Gawane*, he is a figure with diverse associations that allow authors subtly to manipulate audience expectations of his behaviour. Not least among these associations is his supposed nationality as a Scot, which has a binary impact on British (as opposed to mainland European) delineations of his character, and results in his largely positive depiction in Scots chronicles and romances which were circulating at around the same time as Malory's rather more enigmatic portrayal. This essay is not intended to be a comprehensive survey of every literary treatment of Gawain. To begin with, I present a (necessarily selective) summary of Gawain's pre-Malory history that highlights some of his longstanding and prominent characteristics.[15] I move on to a consideration of how self-conciousness of reputation is presented in *Le Chevalier à l'épée* (ca. 1190–1210) and *Sir Gawain and the Green Knight* (c. 1375–1400). My brief assessment of the alliterative *Awntyrs off Arthure* (ca. 1410–20?) and *The Wedding of Sir Gawain and Dame Ragnelle* (ca. 1450) examines Gawain's presentation in relation to that of his king, and considers the extent to which nationality appears to affect his depiction. The concluding analysis of the Older Scots chronicle and romance accounts builds upon the significance of Gawain's reputed regional affiliations, and proposes that, while in *Golagros* Gawain is the 'flour' of chivalry, he is nevertheless presented as a character who is able to ignore the image he presents to others.

Before Malory's portrayal of him as a loyal nephew, and a threat to the Round Table's stability, Gawain was already a well-established presence in European chronicle and romance.[16] Originally, he was particularly famed for his bravery in battle. Hahn notes that tales from the Welsh *Mabinogion* and 'scattered allusions from other Celtic works' imply that he was 'well-established in oral narratives as the nephew, companion, and defender of the great king';[17] while the unusual detail that his strength is at its peak before noon, and wanes as the sun sets (mentioned in the Stanzaic *Morte Arthure*, lines 2802–807, and in Malory (3:1216–18), where it is a 'gyffte that an holy man had gyvyn hym'), might indicate that such presentations

---

[15] For more discussion of the developing character of Gawain prior to Malory's depiction, see Richard J. Moll, *Before Malory: Reading Arthur in later Medieval England* (Toronto, 2003), esp. pp. 102, 221.

[16] While Gawain's role in the demise of the Round Table fellowship is often associated with his desire to be avenged upon Lancelot, it is also notable that he plays a key part in its physical disintegration in the 'Sankgreal' episode. He vows never to return to the court until he sees the grail 'more opynly than hit hath bene shewed here' (2:866). The other Round Table notables 'made such avowes as sir Gawayne hathe made', and Arthur accuses Gawain of having 'berauffte' him of his fellowship, and states his certainty that 'they all shall never mete more togydir in thys worlde' (2:866).

[17] Hahn, p. 218.

descend from oral tales of a solar deity.[18] He is one of the figures represented in the stone sculpture over the doorway of Modena Cathedral (pre-1130),[19] and is praised in William of Malmesbury's *Gesta Regum Anglorum* (ca. 1125),[20] where the discovery of his tomb is described and he is said to be particularly renowned for his valour. Geoffrey of Monmouth's *Historia Regum Britanniae* (ca. 1138) presents a more expansive description.[21] Here Gawain is the son of Lot, duke of Lothian, and his wife Anna (Arthur's sister), and is the brother of the usurper Mordred. He remains loyal to Arthur, and fights well in the battle against Lucius the Roman Emperor.[22] He is finally killed by the army of Chelricus the Saxon, one of Mordred's supporters.[23] Wace's Anglo-Norman *Le Roman de Brut* (ca. 1155) reiterates Gawain's role as one of Arthur's most courageous and loyal warriors, but his ardent vocal support for romantic pursuits introduces a characteristic that is more familiar to modern audiences. When messengers from Rome arrive and challenge Arthur to a battle, Cador, earl of Cornwall, argues that peace is troublesome 'kar oisdive atrait malvaistied/ E maint hume ad aperecied' ('because idleness attracts weakness and makes many a man lazy', lines 10741–42).[24] Gawain speaks out in praise of peace in his response:

> Mult sunt bones les gaberies
> E bones sunt les drueries.
> Pur amistié e pur amies
> Funt chevaliers chevaleries'

Jokes are excellent and so are love affairs. It's for love and their beloved that knights do knightly deeds (Wace, *Brut*, lines 10769–72)

The same episode in Laʒamon's *Brut* (ca. 1290–1310) removes the focus on amatory adventure: '...god is grið and god is frið þe freoliche þer haldeð wið [...] for grið makeð godne mon gode workes wurchen/ for alle monnen bið þa bet þat lond bið þa murgre' ('peace and quiet are good if one maintains them willingly [...] for peace allows a good man to do good deeds whereby all men are the better and the land the happier', lines 12455, 12457–58).[25] Laʒamon describes Gawain as 'þe alre

---

[18] For further discussion of this feature, see R.M. Lumiansky, 'Gawain's Miraculous Strength', *Études anglaises* 10 (1957), 97–108, and *Works*, p. 1645.
[19] For photographic reproductions of the carvings, see Muriel Whitaker, *The Legends of King Arthur in Art* (Cambridge, 1990).
[20] For the full text see *Gesta Regum Anglorum*, ed. and trans. R.A.B. Mynors, completed by R.M. Thomson and M. Winterbottom, 2 vols (Oxford, 1998–99).
[21] See *Geoffrey of Monmouth: The History of the Kings of Britain*, ed. Michael D. Reeve, trans. Neil Wright (Woodbridge, 2007).
[22] Reeve and Wright, pp. 228–29, 244–45. Dalrymple identifies the episode in which Gawain is provoked to anger by the jibes of Caius Quintilianus, the nephew of Lucius, and beheads him (Reeve and Wright, pp. 228–29) as instating 'a tradition of ascribing to the hero an impetuous nature' (Dalrymple, p. 267).
[23] Reeve and Wright, pp. 250–51.
[24] For more detailed discussion, see Walters, p. 20. For the text of Wace, see *Wace's 'Roman de Brut': A History of the British: Text and Translation*, ed. Judith Weiss (Exeter, 1999), pp. 270–71.
[25] The Otho Manuscript has: 'for god his griþ god his friþ þat freoliche hit holdeþ wiþ/ and Godd seolf hit maked þorh his god cunde' (lines 12455–56) with no equivalent to Caligula's lines 12457–58. See *Laʒamon: Brut*, ed. G.L. Brook and R.F. Leslie, EETS OS 250, 277 (London, 1963, 1978). All quotations are from the Caligula manuscript. Translations are taken from *Laʒamon's Brut*, ed./trans. W.R.J. Barron and S.C. Weinberg (Harlow, 1995)

treoweste gume þe tuhte to þan hirede' ('the most loyal man of all who came to court', line 12720) and he is said by Arthur to be 'monne me leofest' ('dearest of men to me', line 11974), although, in his avowal to 'awræke' ('avenge', line 14085) the adulterous betrayal suffered by his uncle, we see indications of the family pride and thirst for revenge that prove so damaging in Malory's version.

Gawain's Reputation

Certain of Gawain's defining characteristics, including bravery, and unswerving loyalty to Arthur, are established early in his literary career. However, the speech ascribed to him in Wace suggests some of the less militaristic features that are also associated with him, namely his prowess as a lover and his courtesy. The twelfth-century romances of Chrétien de Troyes also emphasise these aspects of Gawain's character.[26] Hahn notes that in the years between Chrétien's romances up until around 1250, in a series of ten Old French romances Gawain 'habitually exemplifies a distinctive model of masculinity', whose exemplary performance in tournaments and battle serves to iterate his attractiveness to 'a long sequence of women'. He suggests that Gawain's famed dedication to fighting, and corresponding lack of time for a 'settled union'[27] plays its part in the tendency to associate his name with a thirteenth-century anti-matrimonial satire, 'On Not Taking a Wife',[28] although one wonders if this is also in part attributable to his increasingly depicted predilection for amatory adventure: one recent critical account refers to Gawain as a 'prominent medieval philanderer [with a] reputation for numerous love affairs', and likens him to a medieval James Bond.[29]

Literary Gawain is a man with a prestigious reputation, but he has his weak points. His name is invoked by Chaucer in his *Squire's Tale* as the paragon of courtesy, a brief allusion that surely depends for its effectiveness upon the audience's familiarity with that aspect of Gawain's fame.[30] In addition, however, to this extrinsic literary celebrity that surrounds his depiction in texts, it is perhaps even more significant that Gawain's self-consciousness of his public image (and by extension, the public image of his family) plays a prominent role in certain romances. This apparent self-awareness is often exploited for subtle humour, arguably so in the works of Chrétien. In his *Erec et Enide* (c. 1165), Gawain is the best of all knights (lines 1691–92), but in *Yvain* (c. 1179–80), Gawain's reputation as an inveterate lover is evoked in his romance with Lunete, while he poses a threat to matrimonial stability in the speech that persuades the newly-wed Yvain to renege upon his responsibility to protect Laudine's fountain, and return to a life of questing and chivalric adventure. He tells Yvain that his wife will soon cease to love him if he curtails his displays of bravery, and, moreover, that such behaviour will have a detrimental effect on his reputation

---

[26] Thompson and Busby note that Chrétien's Gawain is 'hardly recognizable as the same character from Geoffrey and Wace' (Thompson and Busby, p. 5).
[27] Hahn, p. 220.
[28] For the text of this, see A.G. Rigg, *Gawain on Marriage: The Textual Tradition of the 'De coniuge non ducenda' with Critical Edition and Translation* (Toronto, 1986).
[29] Rushton, 'Gawain as Lover', pp. 27–28.
[30] See Whiting, pp. 49, 87, for further discussion of Gawain's reputation.

(lines 2484–2538).[31] Gawain states that while he would not himself be capable of following his own advice to leave a beautiful woman alone, that should certainly not dissuade Yvain. This apparent acknowledgement of his amatory reputation as something of a philanderer is underscored by the playing-out of his relationship with Lunete, to whom he vows loyalty:

> Ne me cangiés ja pour nului,
> Së amender ne vous quidiés.
> Je sui vostres, et vous soiés
> D'ore en avant ma damoisele!

Do not trade me for another unless you think you can do better. I am yours and you will be, from this day forth, my fair damsel! (Chrétien de Troyes, *Yvain*, lines 2436–39)

As Rushton points out, his promise to be at her command is shown to be an empty one during her time of need, at which he does not appear to champion her.[32]

Le chevalier à l'épée similarly appears to use Gawain's reputation for comic effect – in fact, it opens by focusing on Gawain's apparent sense of his own celebrity. He travels into a forest on a beautiful summer's day and, lulled into a reverie by the sun and the birdsong, he happily reminisces about an adventure that he once experienced: 'que il entra en un pensé/ D'une aventure qu'il savoit,/ Qui avenue li estoit' ('…he fell into a reverie about an adventure that he called to mind that had happened to him', lines 54–56).[33] His memories prove so absorbing that he loses track of time, darkness falls, and he is still in the forest. Luckily, however, he comes across another knight, who offers him accommodation in his castle. Gawain's self-consciousness of his reputation is once again indicated when the knight travels ahead, supposedly to prepare the lodgings, and Gawain encounters a group of shepherds who warn him that he faces death if he proceeds. Gawain tells them he will never abandon his route because 's'il fust seü en son païs/ Que il l'eüst por tant lessié,/ A toz jorz li fust reprochié ('If it had become known in his country that he had hesitated for such a thing, he would have been reproached to the end of his days', lines 200–203). After dinner, his host sends Gawain to bed with his beautiful daughter; but above the bed is a sword that will strike anyone who makes love to the daughter. Once again, Gawain's self-image is emphasised. He worries about the potential for humiliation if it is revealed to his peers that he has lain naked with the damsel and failed to take his pleasure (lines 575–89). Thus emboldened, he makes advances, and is wounded by the magic sword. However, the cut is so minor that he is identified as the best knight, and is rewarded with marriage to the daughter, but in

---

[31] For the full text, see *Chrétien de Troyes: Romans* (Paris, 1994), text of *Yvain* edited by D.F. Hult, pp. 705–936; translations from *Chrétien de Troyes: Arthurian Romances*, ed. and trans. William W. Kibler (London, 2004), pp. 295–380.

[32] See Rushton, 'Gawain as Lover', p. 29.

[33] For the Old French text of the poem, see *Two Old French Gawain Romances*, ed. R.C. Johnston and D.D.R. Owen (Edinburgh, 1972), pp. 30–60. The manuscript dates to the late thirteenth or early fourteenth century, while the poem itself, which the editors note is heavily influenced by Chrétien, is dated to some time between the late twelfth century and the early thirteenth (pp. 1–2). For the translation, see *From Cuchulainn to Gawain: Sources and analogues of* Sir Gawain and the Green Knight, ed. and trans. Elisabeth Brewer (Cambridge, 1973), pp. 59–74. All quotations and translations are from these editions.

the second half of the tale, his new wife leaves him for another man, and worse still, attempts to take her greyhounds with her. This inspires a misogynistic diatribe from Gawain, in which the loyalty of women is disparagingly compared to the more reliable fidelity of dogs. In the final lines of the tale, Gawain returns to his own land and relates the events to his friends. His retelling of the events in which he is the hero, is significant: much of his earlier behaviour has been explicitly governed by his presumptions about what his fellows will expect of him, and in turning his experience into a 'text' for their entertainment, he reinstates and corroborates their perceived expectations of his behaviour. While the text relies for its effect upon its implied audience's familiarity with certain stereotypical features of Gawain, such as his martial and his amatory prowess, Gawain too is shown to be *au fait* with these elements of his reputation. He takes pleasure in thinking about it, and he expresses concern about how it might be read by his peers.

Le chevalier à l'épée contains a number of recognisable parallels to the Middle English romance, *Sir Gawain and the Green Knight*, including the emphasis upon the importance of reputation.[34] When the Green Knight enters Arthur's court, he casts aspersions on the reputed bravery of the inhabitants of Camelot, crying out:

> What, is þis Arþures hous…
> Þat al þe rous rennes of þurȝ ryalmes so mony?
> Where is now your sourquydrye and your conquestes,
> Your gryndellayk and your greme, and your grete wordes?
> Now is þe reuel and þe renoun of þe Rounde Table
> Ouerwalt wyth a worde of on wyȝes speche,
> For al dares for drede withoute dynt schewed!
>
> (*SGGK*, lines 309–15)[35]

His scornful laughter at the apparent misrepresentation of Camelot as the home of bravery sets the scene for a romance in which reputation is everything – Gawain's reputation for courtesy,[36] his customary role as brave warrior and noble lover, and the conflict between these roles and his representation in the poem as a Christian knight with a special devotion to the mother of God.[37] There is a further layer to the significance of fame in this poem, because, as with Arthur's court, it is evident that Gawain too has a widespread reputation within the fictional framework. When he arrives at Hautdesert, the inhabitants of Bertilak's castle have heard of him and his reputation. 'Now', they say, 'schal we semlych se sleȝtez of þewez/ And þe teccheles termes of talkyng noble' (lines 916–17). The presence of this celebrity in their castle is exciting, and their hope that they will gain education in the matter of love-talking

---

[34] See Johnston and Owen, pp. 159–208.
[35] For the full text, see *Sir Gawain and the Green Knight*, eds J.R.R. Tolkien and E.V. Gordon, revised by Norman Davis (Oxford, 1967).
[36] Carolyne Larrington notes the importance of Gawain's extra-textual reputation when she asserts that the poem 'relies for much of its literary effect on its audience's knowledge of French Arthurian tradition': see Larrington, 'English Chivalry and *Sir Gawain and the Green Knight*', in Fulton, pp. 252–64, 252.
[37] Larrington argues that the poem engages with Gawain's conflicting depictions in English chronicle and French romance: the brave Gawain of the New Year's feast represents the former, while his experiences in Bertilak's castle are more akin to the adventures he faces in the French tradition (Larrington, 'English Chivalry', pp. 257–58).

and courtesy reveals much about their perceptions of Gawain. It is this element of his character that is alluded to by Bertilak's wife when she attempts to seduce him, and it is in these scenes that we witness the more problematic ramifications of Gawain's literary reputation. In not requesting a kiss from her, he fails to live up to his reputed courtesy, and she questions his identity:

> So god as Gawayn gaynly is halden,
> And cortaysye is closed so clene in hymseluen,
> Couth not ly3tly haf lenged so long wyth a lady,
> Bot he had craued a cosse, bi his courtaysye,
> Bi sum towch of summe tryfle at sum talez ende.
> (*SGGK*, lines 1297–1301)

In *Sir Gawain and the Green Knight*, Gawain is not only trapped by the expectations of those who have heard of him. His sense of self-worth ensures that he puts additional pressure upon himself to live up to those expectations. En route to his meeting with the Green Knight, his guide advises him to flee certain death, and swears to keep his secret (lines 2091–2159). Significantly, the guide's promise not to reveal the putative flight to anyone highlights the centrality of public image, and Gawain's response indicates that he too is concerned with the perceptions of others: if he runs, he would be a 'kny3t kowarde' and could 'not be excused'. At this point in the narrative, of course, he has already accepted the girdle, and failed to exchange it with his host: he seems to make an implicit distinction between this kind of concealed self-preservation, and the more public kind that is offered by his guide.

Sir Gawain and the Green Knight plays upon the multiple connotations that are elicited by the protagonist's pre-history in French and English tradition, and in comparison with this, Malory's portrayal of a more threatening Gawain is relatively unusual.[38] *Sir Gawain and the Green Knight* indicates that audiences were very likely to have been familiar with this other, idealised, literary Gawain.[39] In some of these tales, Gawain's reputation for bravery and courtesy is accentuated by contrasting it with the corresponding lack of such qualities in his regal uncle Arthur.[40] In *Dame Ragnelle* (c. 1450),[41] for example, Arthur orders his men to wait while he alone stalks a hart, the impetuosity of which decision is quickly realised when he is challenged by a knight of 'greatt myghte' (line 52), Sir Gromer Somer Joure, who accuses the king of having wrongfully confiscated his lands and given them to Gawain. Arthur, in his response does not engage with his accusation about the land, but rather pleads with Gromer to let him go, offering him what he most desires in return.[42] Gromer demands that Arthur show him 'whate wemen love best in feld and town' (line 91),

---

[38] Dalrymple (p. 267) identifies 'three dominant interpretations' of Gawain in Middle English: heroic; dark and ambivalent; idealised and exemplary. The second group consists only of Malory's *Morte Darthur*, the Stanzaic *Le Morte Arthur*, and *Ywain and Gawain* (a Middle English translation of Chrétien's *Yvain*).

[39] *Sir Gawain: Eleven Romances and Tales*, ed. Thomas Hahn (Kalamazoo, MI, 1995). Note that Gawain is also a key secondary character in various other romances, including the Stanzaic and Alliterative *Morte Arthure* and *Lancelot of the Laik*.

[40] For more on the ambiguous presentation of Arthur in certain Middle English romances, see Boardman, pp. 256–57.

[41] For the text of the poem, see Hahn, *Sir Gawain: Eleven Romances and Tales*.

[42] See Robson, pp. 87–88 for further discussion of Arthur's 'craven' behaviour.

and further orders Arthur not to reveal the details of their meeting to anyone. Arthur's vow to maintain secrecy is quickly broken, however, when he divulges what has happened to Gawain. The rather ambivalent treatment of Arthur and his repeated lack of good judgement in this romance draws attention by contrast to Gawain's selfless behaviour in helping his king, even to the extent of marrying the hideous Dame Ragnelle.

The Awntyrs off Arthur, which predates *Ragnelle* by perhaps as much as four decades, presents a similar scene.[43] Once more, Arthur is accused, this time by Sir Galeron, of having won his land wrongfully, and of having unjustly gifted it to Gawain: 'thou has wonen hem in werre with a wrange wile/ And geven hem to Sir Gawayn' (lines 421–22). But while Arthur's acumen is found wanting, no such criticism can be levelled at Gawain; even his opponent Sir Galeron recognises his superlative courage, saying 'I wende never wee in this world had ben half so wight' (line 639), and formally resigns his claim to the disputed territory. Arthur then rewards Gawain with more lands, on the condition that he 'graunte him [Galeron] his londe' (line 676). Margaret Robson has suggested that 'the regional poems of the north-west midlands are deeply politicized'[44] in their tacit commentary on the deficiencies of King Arthur and their focus on marginal territory at the edges of Arthur's power. Both *Ragnelle* and *Awntyrs* feature the uncharted Inglewood forest and both exalt Gawain, who is 'a genuine alternative to the nation-building figure of King Arthur'.[45] This necessarily depends upon recognition of another aspect of Gawain's traditional reputation; his nationality as a Scots knight traditionally associated with borders, with Orkney and Lothian.

The Scottish Gawain

The importance of Gawain's national affiliation, and the impact that this has upon his portrayal, both in English and Scots texts, should not be underestimated. Rushton, Mapstone and I have all argued that it affects his depiction by Malory;[46] and it is no coincidence that his depiction in Scots texts is generally adulatory. Such descriptions of Gawain in Scotland have sometimes been read purely in the context of his generally exemplary reputation rather than as connected to his nationality: 'even the Scottish chronicles exempt Gawain from the criticism that they level at Arthur in their warning against English imperialism'.[47] But there is more to the portrayal than this: chroniclers like John of Fordun and Andrew Wyntoun recognised Gawain's Scottishness, and this influences their depiction. In his *Chronica gentis Scotorum* (1385), John of Fordun uses Geoffrey of Monmouth's account of Arthur's birth to demonstrate that either Mordred or his younger brother Gawain is the true heir to the throne, but that Arthur, despite his illegitimacy, takes the crown because

---

[43] For the text, see Hahn, *Sir Gawain: Eleven Romances and Tales*, and *The Awntyrs off Arthure at the Terne Wathelyn: An Edition based on Bodleian Library MS Douce 324*, ed. Ralph Hanna (New York, 1974).
[44] Robson, p. 93.
[45] Robson, p. 86.
[46] For further discussion, see Rushton, '"Of an uncouthe stede"'; and the essays by McClune and Mapstone in *Arthurian Literature 28: Blood, Sex, Malory*.
[47] Thompson and Busby, p. 4.

of their comparative youth.[48] Subsequent accounts become more vitriolic in their reading of Arthur's usurping behaviour, so that in 'The Cronycle of Scotland in a part' contained in the Dalhousie Manuscript,[49] Arthur is described as 'spurius' [illegitimate] and a 'huris sone'.[50] The positive portrayal of Gawain, sometimes though not always at the expense of Arthur,[51] is further iterated in the two Scots Arthurian romances in which he is of central importance: *Lancelot of the Laik* (ca. 1460–79) and *Golagros and Gawane* (ca. 1475–1508).[52] Both are based on French sources, and both authors make changes that engage with Arthur's inadequacy, and which highlight Gawain's role as the epitome of perfect knighthood.

The incomplete text of *Lancelot of the Laik* survives in one manuscript, and is based on an episode from the thirteenth-century non-cyclic prose *Lancelot* that deals with the affair of Lancelot and Guinevere, and the conflict between Arthur and Galiot (Galehaut).[53] The poet evidently knows the source well; an extended *occupatio* (lines 198–315) refers to elements of the original that are not treated in the romance, and as Archibald points out, he 'clearly assumes that his readers both know and care a good deal about the Arthurian world'.[54] *Lancelot* often attracts interest because of the extended political discourse of Book II, an addition to the source, in which Amytans advises Arthur on the importance of good kingship.[55] But while the effect of this addition is to raise tacit questions about Arthur's kingship, and his need for guidance, it is the presentation of Gawain that is of note here. Although Lancelot is the professed focus of the poem, in Book I, Gawain's bravery is alluded to repeatedly: he

---

[48] For Fordun's account, see *The Historians of Scotland*, ed. W. Skene, trans. Felix J.H. Skene, 10 vols (Edinburgh: William Patterson, 1871–72), 4:101–103.

[49] National Archives of Scotland, ref. GD/45/31/1.

[50] Other versions of the chronicle also appear in the Asloan Manuscript, where it is entitled 'The Scottis Originale' (see *The Asloan Manuscript*, ed. W.A. Craigie, STS NS 14, 16 (Edinburgh, 1923, 1925), vol. 1, pp. 185–96 for *The Scottis Originale*, pp. 189–92 on Arthur) and in British Library MS Royal 17. D. 20. For the Dalhousie text see *The Bannatyne Miscellany*, ed. W. Scott, D. Laing, and T. Thomson, 3 vols (Edinburgh, 1855; repr. New York, 1973), 3:27–60. For a discussion of the Scots chronicle portrayal of Arthur, see Nicola Royan, 'The Fine Art of Faint Praise in Older Scots Historiography', in Purdie and Royan, pp. 43–54. For more detailed discussion of the depiction of Arthur and Gawain in these texts, see McClune, '"The vengeaunce of my brethirne"'.

[51] See Flora Alexander, 'Late Medieval Scottish Attitudes to the Figure of King Arthur: A Reassessment', *Anglia* 93 (1975), 17–34.

[52] *Lancelot* survives in a unique manuscript, while the earliest witness to *Golagros* is in the Chepman and Myllar print of 1508 (Edinburgh, National Library of Scotland, 19.2.16). Evidently, there was enough interest in both texts for one to be copied and the other to be printed in the late fifteenth/early sixteenth centuries. 'The book of Sir Gawain', which is presumably a reference to Pinkerton's 1792 publication of *Golagros*, is referred to by one of the central characters in James Hogg's 1822 work *The Three Perils of Man: War, Women, and Witchcraft*, ed. Douglas Gifford (Edinburgh, 1989), pp. 131, 476.

[53] Cambridge, University Library MS Kk.1.5. For discussion of the manuscript and its contents, see Elizabeth Archibald, '*Lancelot of the Laik*: Sources, Genre, Reception', in Purdie and Royan, pp. 71–82, 79, and Emily Wingfield, 'The Manuscript and Print Contexts of Older Scots Romance', unpublished doctoral thesis (Oxford, 2010), pp. 131–70. For the text of the poem, see Alan Lupack, ed., *Lancelot of the Laik and Sir Tristrem* (Kalamazoo, MI, 1994), pp. 12–112.

[54] Archibald, p. 71.

[55] For a detailed analysis of the Scottish preoccupation with just rule and a discussion of *Lancelot*, see Joanna Martin, *Kingship and Love in Scottish Poetry 1424–1540* (Aldershot, 2007), esp. pp. 41–60.

is the 'flour of chevelry' (line 782), a brave leader on the battlefield, and Arthur's trusted counsellor (lines 2571–72).

Gawain's reputation for bravery is again foregrounded in *Golagros*, loosely based on two sources: the 'First Continuation' of Chrétien de Troyes' *Perceval* and the *Awntyrs*.[56] The changes made by the poet to the French source present an Arthur with a deteriorating reputation, while certain potentially problematic elements of Gawain's depiction are removed. Gawain's reputation for amatory adventure evidently conflicts with the poet's intended presentation of his local hero,[57] so that the Scots text excises a digression that treats one of Gawain's love affairs, presumably because this kind of vulnerability to fleshly desire undermines what is intended to be a wholly positive depiction of the native knight.[58] Gawain's favourable portrayal thus contrasts with that of Arthur who, in the Scots poem, is aggressive and greedy for power. In the French, Arthur has set out to rescue his imprisoned knight, Girflet le filz Do, and reinstate the honour of the Round Table, but in *Golagros*, he is instead 'engaged in an honourable journey to Holy Land, [and] gets dishonourably distracted by a desire to conquer lands he happens to pass along the way'.[59] Most damning for Arthur is the expression of his desire for sovereignty: upon discovering that Golagros (Le Riche Souldoier in the French) professes allegiance to no man, he vows that Golagros 'sall at my aganecumyng/ Mak homag and oblissing –/ I mak myne avow!' (lines 271–73), regardless of the potentially bloody consequences (lines 296–99).

The rashness of Arthur's decision is underscored by the expanded advisory material in *Golagros*, in which the character of Spynagros (Bran de Liz in the French) chides him for his pride. After a conflict in which many good knights are wounded or injured, it is left to Gawain, as in *Dame Ragnelle* and the *Awntyrs*, to provide the solution in his single combat with Golagros. Whereas in the French text Gawain feigns defeat as a face-saving device in order to accommodate the happiness of Le Riche Souldoier's 'unusually highlystrung' lover,[60] who will die of shame if she sees him defeated, in the Scots poem, Golagros asks him to behave as though 'I had wonnyn þe of were' (line 1100) because he wants to ask his men whether they would prefer to have him as their lord, defeated but living, or see him dead and be subject to 'sum berne þat myght be your beild?' (line 1187). Golagros's men, of course, prefer that he remains 'our gouernour' (line 1193), and the poem concludes with Golagros swearing loyalty to Arthur (notably, he gives 'vourschipfull Wawane' the

---

[56] See Rhiannon Purdie, 'The Search for Scottishness in *Golagros and Gawane*', in Purdie and Royan, pp. 95–107, at pp. 97–100. Purdie presents a nuanced discussion of the supposed 'Scottishness' of the poem, pointing out that many elements often identified as characteristically Scots can in fact also be identified in English Arthurian texts. She concludes, however, that the poet's creation of the advisory figure of Spynagros and its 'new thematic focus on the nature of sovereignty' (p. 101) represent distinctively Scottish preoccupations. For the text of the poem, see *The Knightly Tale of Golagros and Gawane*, ed. Ralph Hanna, STS 5th ser. 7 (2008). Hanna discusses the poem's relationship to the *Awntyrs* at pp. xxxiv–xxxviii.
[57] The Scots poet generally streamlines the amatory context of his source: he also cuts the description of Le Riche Souldoier's love affair. See Hanna, *Golagros and Gawane*, pp. xxxii–xxxiii.
[58] Purdie, p. 98.
[59] Purdie, p. 97.
[60] Hanna, *Golagros and Gawane*, pp. xxxiii; Purdie, p. 98.

credit for having achieved Arthur's victory), and Arthur in turn releases Golagros from his short-lived allegiance (lines 1357–65).

Purdie sees *Golagros* as offering 'an optimistic resolution of the problem of Arthur's pride' because of its emphasis on the 'king's reformability, rather than his infallibility';[61] but while the poem's conclusion rehabilitates Arthur, the real hero is Gawain. Here, we see a new development in the treatment of his reputation: while the generally positive portrayal of his chivalry perhaps speaks to his native associations with Scotland, Gawain himself seems less concerned with public perceptions of him than he is in some of the other poems under discussion here. Although he is the rightful champion, he is persuaded to place his trust in Golagros' honour, and pretend that he has been publicly overcome. What such a defeat might mean for Gawain, were it real, is hinted at in the reaction of Arthur and his men:

> 'The flour of knighthede is caught throu his cruelte!
> Now is þe Round Tabil rebutit, richest of rent,
> Quhen wourschipfull Wawane, þe wit of our were,
> Is led to ane presoune.
> Now failyeis gude fortoune.'
> The king cumly with croune
> Grat mony salt tere… (*Golagros and Gawane*, lines 1138–42)

The Gawain of *Golagros* is not only victorious in battle, and (by omission) exempt from the temptations of the flesh. By agreeing to Golagros' counterfeit success, he appears to move away from his consciousness of public image. Although he has to consider this image carefully (lines 1104–14), he ultimately places his trust in Golagros's 'gentrice' (line 1114), and implicitly recognises that there are more important things than simply his martial reputation as a fighter.

Conclusion

While the courage of the Gawain presented in *Lancelot* and *Golagros* conjures forth characteristics that are outlined in the chronicles, he is clearly not, in these incarnations, the 'same' Gawain presented by Laȝamon and Wace. Nor is he the generally promising, but perhaps somewhat overly self-conscious, figure of *Le Chevalier à l'épée* or *Sir Gawain and the Green Knight*. Neither, however, is he the vengeful killer of Malory's 'Sir Tristram', or the grieving brother of his 'Morte Arthur Saunz Guerdon'. In the latter texts, Gawain's concern with reputation is presented as potentially damaging, to humorous effect in the verse romances, but with more sinister undertones in Malory, where it is translated into a desire to ensure that no discernible slight suffered by his family is ignored. What these texts have in common, however, is authorial reliance on the 'Gawain-effect', and the corresponding audience assumptions when his name is invoked. Rushton's likening of Gawain the philanderer to James Bond could perhaps be extended:[62] like James Bond, the name of Gawain carries with it a wealth of connotations.

---

[61] Purdie, pp. 102–103.
[62] Rushton, 'Gawain as Lover', pp. 27–28.

8
Gamelyn

Nancy Mason Bradbury

Gamelyn finds a place among this volume's potential anti-heroes because his behaviour has so often struck readers as gratuitously violent. In his influential study *Chivalry and Violence in Medieval Europe*, Richard W. Kaeuper cites *The Tale of Gamelyn* to illustrate the propensity of lay elites to claim the right to violence as a 'defining privilege... in any matter touching their prickly sense of honour'. He writes that Gamelyn recovers 'right and honour by violently overwhelming the meeting of a corrupt royal court, has hanged the sheriff and jurors, and will shortly hang the king's justice, after cleaving his cheekbone and breaking his arm'.[1] Jean E. Jost's characterization in *Violence in Medieval Courtly Literature* marks the extreme pole of negative response to Gamelyn as hero: the tale asks us to accept, and even admire, his 'brutality' and 'hard-hearted vengeance'; he partakes of his villainous brother's 'crassness and cruelty'; 'he becomes inured to violence; his anger and aggression become more gratuitous, part of his ordinary behavior'; his response to mistreatment is 'brutally unchivalric'; he seems 'to know no other path of resolution but violence'.[2] Enough has doubtless been said to justify an inquiry into Gamelyn's heroism in a volume meant to step back from authorial praise of romance heroes to re-examine their often morally ambiguous deeds.

Gamelyn is indeed a knight, and he does indeed break spines, limbs, and cheekbones throughout the tale. But, despite the words *Chivalry* in Kaeuper's title and *Courtly Literature* in the title of the volume that contains Jost's essay, I question whether Gamelyn's exuberant sprees of bone-cracking are best understood under the rubric of chivalry, medieval romance's key justification for knightly violence. As many scholars have noted, the most relevant context for the tale, and thus for the protagonist's violence, is provided by tales of Robin Hood and other greenwood outlaws.[3] To place *Gamelyn* among outlaw tales is by no means to eliminate the problem of its violence, however. Maurice Keen calls *The Tale of Gamelyn* 'quite easily

---

[1] Richard W. Kaeuper, *Chivalry and Violence in Medieval Europe* (Oxford, 1999), p. 8.
[2] Jean E. Jost, 'Why is Middle English Romance So Violent? The Literary and Aesthetic Purposes of Violence', in *Violence in Medieval Courtly Literature: A Casebook*, ed. Albrecht Classen (New York, 2004), pp. 248, 249, 250.
[3] *Gamelyn*'s relation to other outlaw tales has long been recognized; Francis James Child stated that it 'clearly belongs to the cycle of Robin Hood' in his first, 8-volume ballad collection of 1857–59, *English and Scottish Ballads*. I quote Child from the 4-volume reprint (Boston, MA, 1885–86), vol. 3, p. xxv. Maurice Keen includes the tale in his pioneering survey, *The Outlaws of Medieval Legend*, rev. edn. (London, 1977). I explore its oral-traditional roots in *Writing Aloud: Storytelling in Late Medieval England* (Urbana, IL, 1998), pp. 23–64.

the most ferocious of the outlaw legends', and in a richly contextualized study of *Gamelyn* among fictional and historical outlaws, John Scattergood remarks on the teller's 'heartlessly sardonic relish' and 'ferocious humour', as well as on Gamelyn's 'aptitude for violence'.[4] Knightly violence has been studied more carefully than the non-chivalric (and in places mock-chivalric) violence of the outlaw tales, which circulated widely outside the circles of lay elite patronage that produced the majority of surviving Middle English romances. As a number of scholars have argued, differences in audience and modes of transmission help to account for the outlaw ballads' different ethical orientation and distinctive handling of violence.[5] With special attention to the weapons wielded, I examine five key conflicts in *The Tale of Gamelyn*: a domestic quarrel, a nearly fatal wrestling contest, the riotous occupation of a badly run household that bears some similarities to the folk ritual of charivari, a clerical banquet that erupts into a brawl, and the notorious inquest at which Gamelyn and his men hang the justice and jurors out to dry like washing on a line. Stepping back from overt authorial praise of the hero, but not from the tale's language, imagery, deep logic, or imagined world, I will argue that Gamelyn's fictional violence is undeniable but not gratuitous; he is not the anti-hero of a chivalric romance, but rather the genuine hero of a vehemently anti-clerical, mildly anti-chivalric, and deeply anti-authoritarian popular tale.

Relatively few works of literature survive from the late Middle Ages to help illuminate the perspective on violence taken by those with little investment in pleasing wealthy or powerful patrons and little interest in reflecting on contradictions among chivalric ideals. Although the great majority of people in medieval England had no personal stake in chivalry, their storytelling was much less likely to survive than fictions underwritten by elite patrons, a circumstance that makes the copying of *Gamelyn* into manuscripts of *The Canterbury Tales* all the more fortunate.[6] As Scattergood points out, the *Tale of Gamlyn* is a 'precious text' because 'it preserves intact and unmodified certain attitudes and assumptions, characteristic of a provincial

---

[4] Keen, p. 89; John Scattergood, '*The Tale of Gamelyn*: The Noble Robber as Provincial Hero', in *Readings in Medieval English Romance*, ed. Carol M. Meale (Cambridge, 1994), pp. 159–94, at p. 176 and p. 164.

[5] In their introduction to the tale, Knight and Ohlgren refer to *Gamelyn*'s 'rugged sense of equity' and to 'a strong fictional and ideological structure of ethics at the heart of the poem' (*Robin Hood and Other Outlaw Tales*, ed. Stephen Knight and Thomas Ohlgren, 2nd edn (Kalamazoo MI, 2000), p. 189). In the same vein, Richard Firth Green points out that the ritual violence of the outlaw tales 'is contained by a set of clearly recognized rules' and operates in open resistance to the perceived violence and injustice of the state and its system of enforcement and punishment: 'Violence in the Early Robin Hood Poems', in '*A Great Effusion of Blood': Interpreting Medieval Violence*, ed. Mark D. Meyerson, Daniel Thiery, and Oren Falk (Toronto, 2004), pp. 268–86, at p. 268. Underlying such readings of the outlaw tales is the concept of the 'social bandit' forwarded by Eric J. Hobsbawm, *Bandits*, rev. ed. (New York, 1981).

[6] *The Tale of Gamelyn* survives in twenty-five manuscripts of *The Canterbury Tales*, pressed into use to substitute for, or to supplement, the apparently fragmentary Cook's Tale. No persuasive evidence has been offered for an authorial, rather than a scribal, role in the tale's inclusion in texts of Chaucer's work. It does not occur in the authoritative a-group of manuscripts that forms the basis for modern editions of the *Tales*. See *The Tale of Gamelyn*, ed. Walter W. Skeat (Oxford, 1884); Aage Brusendorff, *The Chaucer Tradition* (London, 1925), pp. 72–73; Charles A. Owen, Jr., 'The Alternative Reading of *The Canterbury Tales*: Chaucer's Text and the Early Manuscripts', *PMLA* 97 (1982), 237–50; *The Riverside Chaucer*, ed. Larry Benson et al. (Boston, MA, 1987), pp. 1118–21.

culture and a gentry class which... felt itself to be threatened by encroachments against its traditional privileges and local ways, which it intended to preserve by any means that were necessary'.[7] Like the tales of Robin Hood, *Gamelyn* possesses only an 'anti-authoritative textual tradition'.[8] A stowaway in *The Canterbury Tales*, it survives in 'fugitive' form in a cultural monument to which it has no known legitimate connection.

Its survival in writing only as a spurious Canterbury Tale, its relative brevity (898 long lines), and its highly repetitive, conventional style, suggest that *Gamelyn* was in oral circulation, very likely recited from memory with limited improvisation, just as tales of Robin Hood were apparently in wide circulation as recited 'rymes' by 1377, but survive in writing only in mid-fifteenth- and sixteenth-century texts.[9] The tale's most recent editors follow earlier scholars in opting for a mid-fourteenth-century date,[10] but no written texts survive before the early fifteenth century. As with its date, the tale offers few internal clues to its regional origins. Mainly on linguistic grounds, Skeat suggested the area of Lincolnshire; Kaeuper and Scattergood offer corroborating support for a location in the northeast or north-central midlands.[11] In terms of social location, Gamelyn's father is identified as a knight a dozen times in the poem's first 65 lines; his heir is called a 'lord' in line 608; and the father's great concern is the division of his lands, both purchased and inherited from his own father (lines 57–62). Indeed, a perceived injustice in the conveyance of the father's property initiates the poem's violence, and the exceptionally detailed knowledge of property law revealed by its author has long been noted.[12] However, unlike a number of the 'Matter of England' romances with which it is often classed, *Gamelyn* does not glorify a great and recognizable baronial family, as do 'ancestral romances' such as *Guy of Warwick* or *Bevis of Hampton*. Nor does it explore challenges to the authority and legitimacy of a legendary monarch, as do *King Horn*, *Havelok*, and *Athelston*.[13] Rather, it depicts a family drawn from 'the amorphous social level of minor landowners, lesser knights and retainers – those who might at most hobnob with the prior of a nearby religious house and know the sheriff, but whose horizons are essentially local'.[14] Gamelyn's father is 'Sire John of Boundes', an otherwise unknown designation; its apparent denotation, 'of the boundaries' or 'of the borders',[15] suits Sir John's position at the very margins of medieval elite society.

---

[7] '*Tale of Gamelyn*', p. 190.
[8] These are the words of Stephen Knight, ed., *Robin Hood: An Anthology of Scholarship and Criticism* (Cambridge, 1999), p. xv; 'fugitive' in the next sentence is also Knight's word, quoted from the same page.
[9] The reference to 'rymes' of Robyn Hood in lines V.394–96 of the *Piers Plowman* B-text criticizes an allegorical figure's unfamiliarity with the words of simplest devotional text when he 'knows' (*kan*) lively secular tales.
[10] Knight and Ohlgren, eds, *Robin Hood and Other Outlaw Tales*, p. 185.
[11] Skeat, ed., *Tale of Gamelyn*, p. xvi. Richard W. Kaeuper, 'An Historian's Reading of *The Tale of Gamelyn*', *Medium Aevum* 52 (1983), 51–62; Scattergood, pp. 163 (n. 12) and pp. 170–74.
[12] Edgar F. Shannon, Jr., 'Mediaeval Law in *The Tale of Gamelyn*', *Speculum* 26 (1951), 458–64; Kaeuper, 'Historian's Reading'.
[13] See Susan Crane, *Insular Romance: Politics, Faith, and Culture in Anglo-Norman and Middle English Literature* (Berkeley, CA, 1986).
[14] Kaeuper, 'Historian's Reading', 52–53.
[15] Except where noted, I cite *The Tale of Gamelyn* by line number from Knight and Ohlgren, pp. 184–226; the Petworth MS of *The Canterbury Tales* serves as a base text for their edition. While Knight and Ohlgren use only blank space to mark the break in the middle of each line, I use

The first of the five episodes of violence I propose to examine, the domestic quarrel, erupts when Gamelyn reaches maturity and protests that his oldest brother has defied their father's wishes by depriving him of his rightful inheritance. At the beginning of the tale, some local knights charged with carrying out the dying father's instructions override his directive that his three sons share equally in his estate and choose instead to split it between Gamelyn's two older brothers. They exclude Gamelyn until such time as his brothers might find him worthy of sharing in their father's property (lines 41–48), a likelihood their father has already dismissed with the mordant proverb, 'Seelde ye seen eny hier/ helpen his brother' (40). The choice of a two-way division may represent a compromise between the father's wish for three-way partition and the preference of the knights to hold the estate together under the impetus of primogeniture.[16] The tale stresses that Gamelyn is much younger than his two brothers, and another possibility is that the knights charged with conveying the property are reluctant to assign property to a young child in a setting as lawless as the one imagined by this tale. Whatever their reasoning, their two-way division leads to conflict when Gamelyn realizes that what he considers his property has been wholly neglected by the oldest brother, John, for sixteen years: the lands unsown, the oaks felled, the deer stolen, the house unroofed. When the oldest brother emphasizes Gamelyn's menial status in the household by asking whether dinner is ready, Gamelyn replies, 'Thow schalt go bake thi self/ I wil not be thi coke!' (92). After more hostile exchanges, the brother orders his men to 'beteth this boye/ and reveth hym his witte,// And lat him lerne another tyme/ to answere me bette' (111–12), using staves (118) as their means of instruction.

Barbara A. Hanawalt cautions that modern scholars may apply the term *violence* too easily and anachronistically to physical castigation and correction in a medieval domestic setting, writing that 'Medieval Europeans favored physical correction as a valuable tool in educating students, novices, and apprentices, in training servants, and in castigating wives and children.'[17] But the brother's furious order that his men use sticks to beat Gamelyn senseless (111) in return for replying in kind to insults makes it obvious that Gamelyn is the recipient, not the agent, of the tale's first act of excessive violence. The teller emphasizes John's cowardliness, not his dignity as *pater familias* and disciplinarian. He dares not approach Gamelyn himself (109), and when he sees the fight going against his men, he flees to a loft and shuts the door securely (126–27). The tale has been singled out for its unusually faithful historicity, and, according to Hanawalt, domestic quarrels among brothers account for the majority of cases of familial violence heard in medieval manorial courts.[18] Although Gamelyn's zest in returning blows is not to be denied, the episode foregrounds a

---

one virgule (/) to mark the mid-line breaks and two to mark line breaks in shorter quotations. My own preference would be to see *Gamelyn* printed in short line quatrains, as are the Robin Hood ballads. For the gloss on the name 'Boundes', see p. 220 (n. to line 3) in Knight and Ohlgren's edition.

[16] Knight and Ohlgren, eds., *Robin Hood and Other Outlaw Tales*, p. 220 (nn. to lines 14 and 45).

[17] Barbara A. Hanawalt, 'Violence in the Domestic Milieu of Late Medieval England', in *Violence in Medieval Society*, ed. Richard W. Kaeuper (Woodbridge, 2000), pp. 197–214, at p. 199.

[18] For the tale's historicity, see Shannon; Kaeuper, 'Historian's Reading'; and Scattergood. For domestic quarrels among brothers, see Hanawalt, 'Violence in the Domestic Milieu', pp. 198–99.

contemporary social problem, undue violence in the name of discipline within the older brother's household, and Gamelyn is its recipient, not the aggressor.

Throughout the tale, the conflicts in which Gamelyn engages are emphatically non-chivalric, none more so than this first scene in which he defends himself with a wooden pestle against the staves wielded by his brother's men. 'Knighthood', Kaeuper writes, '... existed to use its shining armour and sharp-edged weaponry in acts of showy and bloody violence'; warning against a romanticized view of chivalry, he urges that we 'take care not to be blinded by the light reflected off shining armour'.[19] Gamelyn apparently inherited 'armes' from his father (98), but they have gone the way of his oaks, steeds, deer, and other property, long since lost, stolen, or destroyed by his oldest brother's neglect. No fear of our being blinded by light reflected from arms in the utterly unromanticized *Tale of Gamelyn* – blunt wooden implements take the place of sharp weapons and glittering armour;[20] and nothing shines but the night moon (235). Despite the tale's notorious violence, bloodshed too is nearly absent. In contrast to those chivalric romances in which heroes fight up to their ankles in blood drawn by sharp-edged weapons, the only reference I find to shedding blood in *Gamelyn* is an injunction against it: 'drowe of hem no blode' (518) is part of a rough jest about reverently sparing the tonsures of clerics while breaking their arms and legs.

Gamelyn's pestle sets the tone for the conflicts and weaponry to follow, and it is worth exploring its implications in some detail. We should picture a substantial implement: it was found leaning against a wall (122), and the early to mid-fourteenth century Luttrell Psalter shows a man grinding food with a very stout pestle taller than he is.[21] Gamelyn spots this improvised weapon just as his brother's men close in with their staves; thus the teller underscores the defensive nature of his hero's blows in this early scene. The culinary associations of the weapon reflect ironically on his brother's arrogant treatment of Gamelyn as though he were his cook, and the scene's parodic overtones emerge more clearly when Gamelyn invites his brother to 'play/ at the bokelere' (136), that is, engage in an absurd fencing match with a man wielding a long wooden pestle in place of a sword. By having Gamelyn invite his brother to bake himself as well as menacing him with a cook's implement, the teller gives his protagonist an aptly ironic response to the brother's condescending treatment of him as a menial. As in the early Robin Hood ballads, a mocking, humorous response serves to parry arrogant condescension; such humour was doubtless an important aspect of the appeal of these tales to broad audiences that extended well beyond the patronage circles whose interests helped to shape chivalric romances.

Kitchen implements as mock-knightly weapons turn up in other telling contexts in late medieval and early modern literature. In *The Canterbury Tales*, Chaucer's Host ridicules the Cook's unchivalric horsemanship by evoking another culinary tool: 'This was a fair chyvachee of a cook!/ Allas, he nadde holde hym by his ladell' (IX.50–

---

[19] *Chivalry and Violence*, p. 2.
[20] Noting that beatings with sticks and staves (in contrast to swords and lances) echo throughout petitions against injustice sent to the Crown in this period, Kaeuper describes the tale's violence as in important ways 'peculiar to xiv-century England' and 'characteristic of one particular (if broad) social stratum,' the 'minor landowners, lesser knights and retainers' mentioned above. 'Historian's Reading', pp. 52–53.
[21] Janet Backhouse, *Medieval Rural Life in the Luttrell Psalter* (Toronto, 2000), pp. 12–13.

51).²² In the overtly carnivalesque fifteenth-century *Tournament of Tottenham*, a group of peasants engage in mock-knightly combat using a variety of arms and armour highly unlikely to blind anyone with their reflected light. One goes into battle 'armed at the full' with a 'dough trough' and a *pele* (122–24), a baker's peel, the long, flat wooden paddle used for removing bread from wood-burning ovens.²³ The peasant participants in this tournament are described as 'gadelings with ther long staves' (28); *gadlynge* is an insult also applied to Gamelyn by his oldest brother, one that Gamelyn interprets as class-based (102, 104, 107), and 'long staves' are of course a staple of our tale's action. Understanding the target of such carnivalesque parody is always complex; in the words of Peter Stallybrass, carnivalesque meaning is 'never a simple given', but 'is made and remade in the contested domain of social practices'.²⁴ Stallybrass writes that, unlike the power of an earlier feudal aristocracy, the ascendent position of late medieval and early modern elites 'depended upon deference even more than upon military strength' (p. 305). This reliance on deference creates the vulnerability to ridicule that gives the mocking inversions of the carnivalesque their power. In laughing at fencing with a pestle in *Gamelyn* or entering a tournament armed with a dough trough and peel in the *Tournament of Tottenham*, an ordinary listener or reader may have been more amused by the travesty of high knightly dignity than by the lack of chivalric sophistication revealed by the combatants' blunt wooden weapons, though carnivalesque humour is itself sharp-edged and can almost always cut in more than one direction.

One further dimension of the literary use of implements from the food trade as mock-knightly weapons reveals itself in a later carnivalesque text, Francis Beaumont's early seventeenth-century play, *The Knight of the Burning Pestle*. There a romance-reading 'grocer errant' reminiscent of Don Quixote vows that 'in remembrance of my former trade, upon my shield shall be portrayed a burning pestle' (I.266–67).²⁵ In addition to its mock-chivalric resonance, the phallic implications of the pestle are often close to the play's verbal surface, as when the grocer-knight vows never to forsake his beloved Susan, a cobbler's maid in Milk Street, 'whilst life and pestle last' (IV.100). The emphasis laid on Gamelyn's weapon suggests that some of the same implications may be operative in our tale as well: 'Gamelyn with his pestel/ made hem al agast' (128); his brother John will not approach Gamelyn 'while that pestel is in thine honde' (138); John is 'sore aferd/ of the pestelle' (152). Such jesting would suit the tale's assertively masculine sense of humour, but if this emphasis on the hero's virility is jesting, it serves a serious purpose as well: Gamelyn's new manhood,

---

²² All citations from *The Canterbury Tales* are from *The Riverside Chaucer*.
²³ For the tale's carnivalesque nature, see Carol M. Meale, 'Romance and its Anti-Type? The *Turnament of Totenham*, the Carnivalesque, and Popular Culture', in *Middle English Poetry: Texts and Traditions, Essays in Honour of Derek Pearsall*, ed. A.J. Minnis (York, 2001), pp. 102–27. I cite the *Tournament* from *Middle English Verse Romances*, ed. Donald B. Sands (New York, 1966), pp. 313–22.
²⁴ '"Drunk with the Cup of Liberty": Robin Hood, the Carnivalesque, and the Rhetoric of Violence in Early Modern England', in *Robin Hood: An Anthology of Scholarship and Criticism*, ed. Stephen Knight (Cambridge, 1999), pp. 297–327, quotation at p. 298. Mikhail Bakhtin, *Rabelais and His World*, trans. Hélène Iswolsky (Bloomington, Indiana, 1984). For adaptation of Bakhtin's ideas to a firmer historical basis, especially as regards the medieval period, see Aron Gurevich, *Medieval Popular Culture: Problems of Belief and Perception*, trans. Janos M. Bak and Paul A. Hollingsworth (Cambridge, 1988).
²⁵ Ed. Sheldon P. Zitner (Manchester, 1984).

signalled by his stroking of his beard in line 82, reveals a dangerous new force capable of beating his assailants 'right sone on an hepe' (124). John's lying explanation for this first outbreak of utterly unchivalric violence is that having his men attack a single unarmed youth with sticks was only a 'fondinge' or test meant to determine whether the lad is 'stronge/ and art so yenge' (147–48). In addition to carnivalesque mockery of knightly warfare, the scene with the pestle also serves the simpler function of laying the blame for the excessive violence within the household quite squarely on the shoulders of the oldest brother.

Having established his adult position within the household by defending himself from his brother's men, Gamelyn's next act is to assert his adult identity in public by entering a wrestling match at a country fair (270) for the traditional prizes of 'a ramme and a ringe' (172). Here the only weapons are strong arms, and wrestling for a ram at a country fair is either non-chivalric, or, as in the case of Chaucer's Sir Thopas (VII.740–41), mock-chivalric. As in the household quarrel, the most disturbing violence in the wrestling match is not initiated or inflicted by Gamelyn, but by his antagonist, this time the fair's champion wrestler. Shown contending only with inexperienced young wrestlers, the champion functions as an extra-familial equivalent of Gamelyn's excessively violent and bullying oldest brother. Just as John taunted Gamelyn as a *gadlynge* (102, 104) so the champion taunts him as a 'grete fool' (222) and a 'moche shrewe' (230). Once again Gamelyn demonstrates a strategy for resisting humiliation by an opponent in a position of more power: instead of denying the champion's taunt, he re-appropriates it. Told that he was a 'moche shrewe' as a child, he responds, 'Now I am older wexe/ thou shalt finde me a more!' (232).

The wrestling episode is highly compressed, and the reader must piece together its implications. In a line that has caused some readers trouble, a distressed father laments bitterly that the champion 'hath sclayn my two sones/ but if God hem borowe' (204). The most straightforward interpretation is that the champion has hurt the sons badly, and they will die of their injuries unless God 'borowes' them or saves their lives. In suggesting that his sons will die 'but if God hem borowe', the franklin may, however, mean more specifically that in the absence of a human to *borowe*, or stand in for them, they will need to rely on God because they are somehow rule- or honour-bound to face this champion again.[26] Given their condition, without divine intervention another encounter might indeed be fatal. The franklin vows to reward handsomely the man who will defeat the champion, and Gamelyn agrees to try. After receiving several 'turns' or holds, he throws the champion once, breaking three of his ribs (244–45). Earlier the franklin lamented and bitterly wrung his hands out of grief and fear for his sons (197–98), but when the champion concedes to Gamelyn, the franklin blesses Gamelyn heartily and banters cheerfully with the defeated champion; his gratitude and good cheer seem to imply that his sons are restored to him (275–78). The scene is more comprehensible if Gamelyn has not simply avenged their mistreatment but saved them further injury or death by serving as their *borowe*. At any rate, the 'two gentile men' who officiate over the wrestling are eager to end the match now that night has fallen and the fair is over (267–70); they or others who

---

[26] As an example of resort to a divine 'borowe' when a human one is lacking, in *A Gest of Robyn Hode*, Robin turns down God but accepts the Virgin as the 'borowe' for a loan when a knight says that he has no friend to stand surety for him (lines 245–64). I take the franklin to mean that no human 'borowe' exists to step in for his sons, and thus only God can help them.

'wardeynes were/ of that wrastelinge' simply give Gamelyn his prizes (279–80), and no one expresses any concern about the injuries inflicted by the champion on the franklin's two sons.

Whether the potentially lethal violence of wrestling matches in the outlaw tales reflects historical reality or adds color to fictional narrative, in a wrestling episode in *A Gest of Robyn Hode*, another life is endangered: 'There was a yoman in that place,/ And best worthy was he,/And for he was ferre and frembde bested,/ Slayne he shulde haue be'.[27] The episode in *A Gest* is even more compressed than the one in *Gamelyn*, but it implies that the yeoman is in peril of his life on account of the valuable prizes he has won (if indeed this is the meaning of 'best worthy was he'),[28] another instance of the violently lawless society imagined as the backdrop against which these outlaw tales take place. In *Gamelyn*, it is not the tale's protagonist who initiates domestic beatings or transforms a sporting event into a near-slaughter.

The third and fourth scenes to be considered here are two contrasting banquets, one that begins and one that ends in violence. The first begins when Gamelyn returns from his success at the fair to his brother's house, accompanied by a 'grete route' against whom John orders that the house be secured (283–84). The narrative pays close attention to the material mechanisms of exclusion: the porter has gone to the gate and 'lokked it fast' (286); when Gamelyn finds it 'shette faste/ with a stronge pynne' (290), he 'smote the wikett with his foote/ and breke awaie the pyne' (296). Both the gate and its porter are emblems of restriction, and Gamelyn 'breaks' the latter just as he does the former: he 'girt him in the nek/ that the boon to-brake' and then slung him by the arm into a well (302–304). The porter dispensed with, Gamelyn 'yede to the gate/ and lete it up wide;// He lete inne alle/ that gone wolde or ride' (309–10). From Gamelyn's point of view, the arrivals are 'good menys sones' (292), a 'faire company' (308); to those within who have witnessed Gamelyn's treatment of gate and porter, they obviously appear more ominous. Both the transgression of boundaries and the replacement of fasting by feasting are among the most familiar of carnivalesque images,[29] and they usher in a reversal of an existing hierarchy: Gamelyn welcomes his companions with the announcement that 'we wil be maisters here/ and axe no man leve' (312). They break out the wine and begin an uproarious seven-day banquet. No one menaces John directly, but the treatment of his gate and his porter are enough to warn him not to intervene. His own violence has now come home to him, and just as he hid earlier while Gamelyn trounced his men with the pestle, so he hides himself again 'in a litel torret' and 'dorst no worde speke' (327–28).

Without approving the fictional calculus that puts no more value on the porter than on the gate, it is worth noting a resemblance between this visitation and that raucous instrument of folk justice and social regulation, the charivari, in medieval and early modern England 'a quasi-legal means of correcting "domestic crimes"'.[30] Natalie Zemon Davis describes the 'boisterous mixture of playfulness and cruelty'

---

[27] Knight and Ohlgren, eds., *Robin Hood and Other Outlaw Tales*, lines 549–52.
[28] This is the interpretation of William H. Clawson, *The Gest of Robin Hood* (Toronto, 1909), p. 47.
[29] For a convenient summary of carnivalesque rhetorical practices that includes replacement of fast by feast and transgression of spatial boundaries, see Stallybrass, p. 298.
[30] Stallybrass, p. 302.

that characterizes such efforts, a phrase that also applies well to the fictional scene in question.[31] We are not told what motivates the boisterous visit by these men; they simply appear with Gamelyn (283) and their first priority appears to have been celebratory carousing. However, the complicity of these local men in a forcible entry and occupation of the brother's house and in Gamelyn's inversion of his brother's authority as 'maister' also suggests communal disapproval of the domestic situation within. Their interim host is determined to 'spende largely' what his brother has hoarded (322). Often wryly, the outlaw tales insist that their heroes practice reciprocity, not theft,[32] and here, as ironic justification for depleting his brother's larder, Gamelyn informs him that the expenses of this banquet were paid in advance by the sixteen years of income the brother earned from sowing Gamelyn's inherited lands and breeding his animals (353–60), a sardonic reference to the brother's complete neglect of same (83–87).

Gamelyn's banquet abounds in carnivalesque images of open-handedness and free access, with the gate thrown wide to admit all and the brother's larder too thrown open to feasting; by contrast, the transition to his brother's mean-spirited banquet begins in lines 367–74 with images of bondage and restraint. Pretending that he swore an oath to bind Gamelyn 'honde and fote' after the assault on his porter (372), John asks Gamelyn to allow him to do so in fact, lest he be forsworn. The young man's overly trusting nature here can strike the modern reader as doltish, but within the tale's value system, it is the brother, a 'fals knyght' (349, 361, 379), 'a party fals' (388) guilty of *gile* (367) and *lesingges* (381), who is at fault for deceptively misusing that foundation stone of the old legal system, the obligation to keep one's pledged word.[33] Images of bondage and incarceration abound in this section of the tale: John 'sente efter fetters/ to fetter hym fast' (380), Gamelyn stands 'bounden' to a post in the hall (383), standing there 'ybounde stronge' (393), he appeals to the spencer, Adam, to 'lese me out of bonde' (397), and he will eventually appeal to his brother's clerical guests to release him 'out of prisoun' (438).

To avoid incurring John's wrath by freeing Gamelyn himself, Adam concocts a plan by which Gamelyn will pretend that he is still unwillingly bound and appeal for release to the 'abbotes and priours' and 'other men of holy chirch' (431–32) who will attend the brother's Sunday banquet. If these monastics will 'borowe' Gamelyn 'out of prisoun' (437, 438), the problem is solved; if not, says Adam, 'Thow shalt have a good staf/ and I wil have another,//And Cristes curs haf that on/ that failleth that other' (441–42). As each clerical guest arrives, the brother reports 'al the harme and the shame' that he can tell about Gamelyn (462), whom they see bound in the middle

---

[31] 'Charivari, Honor, and Community in Seventeenth-Century Lyon and Geneva', in *Rite, Drama, Festival, Spectacle*, ed. John J. MacAloon (Philadelphia, 1984), pp. 42–57, at p. 42.

[32] Joseph Falaky Nagy's comment on the Robin Hood ballads captures the tone of this incident in *Gamelyn* as well: 'Rarely in the ballads do Robin or his men commit an outright act of theft; the taking of goods is often described, albeit whimsically, as the collecting of a debt, or a matter of indirect reciprocity', 'The Paradoxes of Robin Hood', *Folklore* 91 (1980), 198–210, at p. 205.

[33] In *A Crisis of Truth: Literature and Law in Ricardian England* (Philadelphia, 1999), Richard Firth Green explores the importance of keeping one's pledges in the personal, oath-based culture of early medieval England. He comments on Gamelyn's willingness to be bound in this scene as an indication that he 'understands at once the obligation under which such an oath puts his brother' (p. 196).

of the hall where they will feast. Earlier, when he understood that he had been tricked, Gamelyn swore that, had he known of his brother's duplicity, he would have dealt out 'strokes' before he allowed himself to be 'bounde' (390). Now, either these clerics will release Gamelyn 'out of bendes' or feel his 'good strokes/ right on her lendes' (453–54). Bonds or blows: as critics of its violence rightly observe, the tale frames these as the only alternatives, and the obdurate clerics who refuse to unbind Gamelyn are battered accordingly. The one positive social relation that brightens this dark banquet is the loyal fellowship sworn by Adam to Gamelyn: 'And Cristes curs haf that on/ that failleth that other' (442). Although the poet openly acknowledges Adam's 'hope of avauncement' (414), the voluntary bond he and Gamelyn form, called a 'forward' and a 'covenaunt' (407, 410), represents a positive alternative to the older brother's 'trecherye' (344).

Whatever moral judgments we make on the tale's stick-enforced sprees of vigilante justice, they give us valuable insight into a late medieval worldview much harder to recover than that of the clerics who receive these fictional blows. In sermons, penitential manuals, and other writings, medieval clerics have left ample commentary on the disorderly behavior of the laity, but insights into how the late medieval clergy appeared to ordinary people are rarer. In *Gamelyn* and the Robin Hood tales, the monastics who feast while others fast meet with robbery, blows, and rallying cries such as that of Adam and Gamelyn:

> 'Cursed mote he worth/ both flesshe and blood,
> That ever doth priour/ or abbot eny good!' (487–88)

Just as Gamelyn's earlier offer to use a pestle to teach his brother 'a play/ at the bokelere' (136) parodied a characteristically knightly pastime, here another wooden weapon, an 'oken spire', parodies the rituals of the clergy. Gamelyn uses his oaken rod as an aspergillum to 'spreyeth holy watere' – that is, blows – on the heads of the feasting clerics (499). Adam insists that the banquet guests also be 'assoilled' (512), while Gamelyn 'made orders/ of monke and frere' (529), in both cases of course with blows. Behind these rough jests lies the rankling late medieval grievance that monastics and mendicants feast in defiance of their rule while ordinary people in need of a meal look hungrily on, as Gamelyn does at this hard-hearted banquet. As part of the tale's fantasy of accomplishing clerical reform by wielding stout wooden sticks, the clerics themselves are made to state the lesson they have been taught: rather than banqueting, 'Us had be bet at home/ with water and breed' (528).

Immoderate feasting is a familiar accusation against the clergy in this period; a subtler source of resentment is implied by an interesting and little-noted moment at the brother's banquet when the *lewe* (here, probably, 'lay') men of John's household stand aside and offer no resistance while Gamelyn and Adam rain blows on the fictional 'men of holy chirche':

> Ther was no lewe man/ that in the halle stode,
> That wolde do Gamelyn/ enything but goode,
> But stoden bisides/ and lete hem both wirche,
> For thei had no rewthe/ of men of holy chirche;
> Abbot or priour,/ monk or chanoun. (501–505)

By standing aside to let Gamelyn and Adam 'work', the brother's retainers express silent affiliation with them against the clerics. The *forward* or *covenaunt* between Gamelyn and Adam, the riotous but perhaps also purposeful behavior of the local men who occupy the brother's house for a week, the tacit assent of the brother's retainers who hold with Gamelyn and Adam against the clerics – behind the carnivalesque exaggerations of the protagonist's ready head-bashing lies a more realistic desire for positive social bonds that would allow ordinary men to join together and uphold the interests of their own groups. In theory, the bonds of chivalry hold knights together; the bonds of communal life under a rule – whether it is observed or flouted – allow monastics to make common cause in pursuit of their interests. In the tale's aggrieved representation of provincial domestic and social life, the bonds all too readily available to the hero and his allies are fetters.

Historical outlaws of the fourteenth century also sought voluntary association by means of a *forward* or *covenaunt* such as binds Gamelyn and Adam.[34] An instance with particularly intriguing parallels to the *Tale of Gamelyn* involves 80 Yorkshiremen from Cottingham and its environs who dress in 'one livery of a single company' and are accused of having 'beat, wounded and ill-treated' a man 'so that his life was despaired of, in breach of the king's peace'. Part of the evidence against them is a 'certain rhyme [*rima*] in English' they are said to have composed and recited in various public places. The *coram rege* plea that records the incident and the poem or song dwells less upon the near-murder than upon the threat posed by the 'covin' these 'malefactors' form 'by corrupt allegiance and confederacy'.[35] Their alleged rhyme asserts that friars and other orders 'maintain' one another and uphold their mutual interests:

> Among this frers it is so
> And other ordres many mo
> > Whether [th]ei slepe or wake;
>
> And [y]et wil ilkan hel vp other
> And meynteyn him als his brother
> > Bothe in wronge and righte.

Therefore, the rhyme continues, the Yorkshire men too have formed a brotherhood of mutual aid, pledging to 'meynteyn owre negheboure/ with al oure myghte' and vowing that 'Who so dose vs any wrang… myght als wele… do again vs alle.' A *Gest of Robyn Hode* also likens an outlaw fellowship to an order of friars when Robin refers to 'our ordre' (787), and the sheriff, after sleeping on the ground one night, calls it 'harder order' than 'any ankir or frere' (789–90). The expression by the historical Yorkshiremen of a desire for advantageous associations such as friars enjoy helps us

---

[34] See Green, *A Crisis of Truth*, cap. 5, for a wealth of historical examples.
[35] *Select Cases in the Court of the King's Bench Under Richard II, Henry IV, and Henry V,* Vol. VII, ed. G.O. Sayles (London, 1971), pp. 83–85. After a list of accused individual participants, the record continues, 'simul cum aliis malefactoribus ad numerum quateruiginti malefactorum de eorum couina, quorum nomina ignorantur, per sex annos vltimo elapsos vestiti fuerunt in vna liberata de vnica secta per falsam alliganciam et confederacionem', pp. 83–84. Carolyn P. Collette and Harold Garrett-Goodyear reproduce this record in *The Later Middle Ages: A Sourcebook* (New York, 2011), with a comment on the consternation it reveals about voluntary associations among the lower ranks of medieval society (pp. 131–34); Green relates it to the alternate system of justice recognizable in the outlaw ballads, *A Crisis of Truth*, pp. 189–90.

to see what ideas contemporary audiences may have warmed to in *Gamelyn* and the outlaw ballads.

The clerical banquet ends climactically with Gamelyn using his staff to break his oppressive brother's spine, an injury apparently healed by the doctor summoned in line 610, at least to the extent that John regains mobility, but one that continues to mark him in a way that elicits Gamelyn's later insult 'broke bak' (716), in response to the news that his brother has had him outlawed. Throughout the scene, where a modern reader sees vengeance, the poet in his partisanship stresses reciprocity: Gamelyn puts his brother in the same fetters 'theras he sat arst' (534) and invites him to sit and cool his body 'as I did myn' (536). Between this dark clerical banquet and the fifth and final scene of violence to be examined here intervene two instructive glimpses of brighter possible worlds in which social relations might be healthier and less violent. The first is the interval Gamelyn and Adam spend in the greenwood as outlaws; the second is the unexpected entry into the tale of chivalric idealism in the person of Gamelyn's as-yet unmentioned middle brother, Sir Ote.

The portion of the tale we have examined so far represents a lawless world in which the best bet for a young man menaced by his brother seems to be to grab a stick, not to send for the sheriff. When at the close of the second banquet the law finally does arrive, Gamelyn and Adam assume that the sheriff and his men are already their foes and have sworn to seize them (578–80); they imagine no inquiry into possible justifications for the violence they have committed. More blows ensue with stout wooden weapons – this time Gamelyn grabs a 'cartstaf' (the shaft of a cart) and Adam 'another grete staff' (586–87) – thus enabling their escape to the greenwood. In the words of one of the tale's many terse and pragmatic maxims, 'Better is us ther loos/ than in town y-bounde'; in another, 'He moste needes walk in woode/ that may not walke in towne'.[36]

Although its residents are wary of strangers, in the greenwood the sparring is verbal only, and no sticks are raised there, no blows exchanged. As in other outlaw tales, the greenwood offers 'a kind of alternative commonwealth and morality';[37] it is more justly administered, offers more fellowship, and thus is much less violent than the town. The woods themselves are less romanticized in *Gamelyn* than in the surviving fifteenth- and sixteenth-century ballads of Robin Hood, and Adam longs to return to his duties as spencer, rather than walk in the 'wilde wode/ my clothes to tere' (617). Still, the greenwood is effectively ruled by a trusted royal figure, a 'king of outlawes', a 'king/ with his croune' (664, 666). The circle in which the outlaws sit at meals, 'compas aboute' (624), suggests King Arthur's egalitarian round table. When the outlaws relieve Gamelyn and Adam of their heretofore unmentioned bows and arrows (643), Gamelyn explains the benign and survival-oriented function of these quintessential weapons of the English common man: 'Sire, we walk not here/ no

---

[36] I quote these two proverbs from Skeat's text (based on Harley 7334), lines 606 and 672, because their alliteration, rhythm, and parallelism seem to me more in keeping with the mnemonic qualities of proverbial expressions than the versions in Knight and Ohlgren's edition, lines 602 and 667. See Bartlett Jere Whiting with Helen Wescott Whiting, *Proverbs, Sentences, and Proverbial Phrases from English Writings Mainly before 1500* (Cambridge, MA, 1968), W558, W559, and cf. M384.

[37] Quoted from Douglas Gray's essential 1984 article, 'The Robin Hood Poems', reprinted in Knight, *Robin Hood: An Anthology*, pp. 3–37, quotation at p. 18.

harme to doo,// But yif we mete a deer/ to shete therto,/ As men that bene hungry/ and mow no mete fynde' (668–69). In direct contrast to Gamelyn's brother John and his feasting clerical friends, the master outlaw immediately has 'reuthe' on Gamelyn's hunger (672).

The outlaws have their own orderly hierarchy, and the king makes Gamelyn his second in command: 'maister/ under hym over hem alle' (682). While Robin Hood and his men can live on in the 'alternative commonwealth' of the greenwood, in *Gamelyn*, it can serve only as a way station, a means by which wanted men can step temporarily out of the violent social world of the tale. News soon comes to the outlaw king that he has been pardoned, and Gamelyn peacefully succeeds him. At the same time that Gamelyn is crowned king of this imaginary just kingdom, his brother is appointed sheriff of the unjust local world outside the forest. As sheriff, John has Gamelyn formally outlawed or declared 'wolfeshede' (696); his neighbors are thus theoretically encouraged to kill him at sight as they would a wolf. His peaceful interval in the greenwood reminds the audience once again that Gamelyn is not an aggressor who seeks out violent confrontation. However, the period of relative peace ends, and Gamelyn must go back to protect his dependents from his brother's mistreatment (695–700). As he shifts mentally back into the violent world outside the greenwood, he regrets that before he was outlawed and while he had the opportunity, he was so slack as to break only his brother's back and not his neck (707–708).

Violent as it is, the poem's social world as we have seen it so far has given us hardly a hint of the chivalric violence characteristic of most medieval romance. The tale's eschewing of knightly weapons in favour of the pestle, strong arm, 'oken spir', 'cartstaf', and other 'good staves,' has been amply demonstrated. Chivalry does, however, make two successive appearances in the poem, and before we move to the final scene, it will be useful to see what attitude is taken toward it. First, the crowned king of the greenwood outlaws reveals himself both *hende* (here, 'knightly' or 'courtly') and *of gentil blood* (658) by his graciousness in feeding Adam and Gamelyn; his royal role is in obvious parallel to the tale's idea of a just and benevolent king who appears briefly at the end to pardon Gamelyn. Despite their outlaw status, the outlaw king's followers are men of *pris* (768). Under Gamelyn's brief reign, loyalty and community hold sway among ordinary men, and only one order is subject to robbery:

> There was no man/ that for him ferde the wors,
> But abbots and priours,/ monk and chanoun;
> On hem left he nought/ whan he myghte hem nome. (776–78)

In the outlaw tales, the implication that the greenwood kingdom is held together by a loyalty and fellowship that surpasses that of the actual monarchy is sometimes made overt, as when the legitimate king expresses his admiration for the unqualified loyalty Robin inspires from his men in 'Robin Hood and the Monk' (345–50) and *A Gest of Robyn Hode* (1559–64). Despite the tale's earlier parodic treatment of knightly combat, chivalric ideals such as loyalty to one's king are not themselves valued negatively in *Gamelyn*; they are simply more in evidence in the utopian outlaw kingdom than in the tale's ordinary social world.

Chivalry also appears closer to home in the person of the idealistic, generous, yet strangely ineffectual and passive character of Gamelyn's middle brother, Sir Ote, unmentioned since the partition of the estate in the opening lines. Ote is the first of the brothers to be called 'Sir'; not since the initial mention of Gamelyn's father by his full title, 'Sire John of Boundes', has a member of the family been so designated. While in the works of fourteenth-century court poets such as Chaucer and Froissart prefixing 'Sir' to the first name of a knight appears to be a déclassé usage (Chaucer reserves it for Sir Thopas),[38] in popular romance it is straightforwardly honorific and no slight is meant to Sir Launfal, Sir Orfeo, or Sir Guy. In *Gamelyn*, it helps to call attention to the middle brother's distinctively chivalric nature. Sir Ote is introduced as 'Als good an knyght and hende' (724) as walks the land, and 'Sire Ote the hende' (751) represents a knightly idealism nearly absent from the world outside the greenwood. Because he believes that his younger brother is in the right and the best of the three (733), he agrees to risk his own life by standing surety for Gamelyn's release from the prison to which John, now sheriff, sentences him. The pragmatic proverbial wisdom that runs through the outlaw tales advises that one take the best of one's opportunities while acknowledging that the best is often far from ideal: 'It may no better be' is a repeated counsel to fatalistic resignation. When John reports that Gamelyn is to be imprisoned, Ote reverses the usual formula. 'Better it shal be' (739), he resolves, as he offers himself as Gamelyn's surety. Ote is generous and idealistic, and even the king who appears at the tale's end 'loved wel Sir Ote' (886), but as the tale's most direct representative of chivalry, Ote is notably ineffectual. For most of his brief appearance in the tale, he remains 'fetred ful fast' (805, cf. 808, 810) and 'bonde so sore' (814), presumably by the same corrupt forces that repeatedly bind Gamelyn. Ote would have been hanged in his brother's stead had Gamelyn not arrived in time to rescue him by means of a last and most deadly spree of violence. As represented by Sir Ote, chivalric idealism is admirable, generous, and loyal, but in a violently lawless society, such idealism is fettered and ineffectual. The results of Ote's generous and law-abiding intervention offer yet another figurative justification for the tale's insistence that in a restrictive and unjust social milieu, one has only two choices, fetters or blows.

The reciprocity that governs the tale's carnivalesque finale represents its most important justification for Gamelyn's violence. The oldest brother, now sheriff, who has fettered first Gamelyn and then Ote is fettered himself along with the justice he bribed to condemn them (855). Those who were bribed to hang Ote in Gamelyn's stead before Gamelyn was tried are themselves hanged, and left to swing in the wind ('To weyven with the ropes/ and the winde drye', line 876). For modern readers what stands out is the death count – twelve jurors, the justice, and the sheriff all hanged – and this violence seems the more disruptive for being committed against the supposed guardians of the king's peace. The fettering of a noble but passive Sir Ote suggests the ineffectuality of chivalry as a means of regulating the lawlessness of local society, and the repeated image of a fettered 'justice' demonstrates symbolically that the legal system too fails in this capacity (855, 862).

Gamelyn and his oldest brother vow to be avenged on one another (719, 820), but with a marked difference between them. Gamelyn at least aspires to justice, vowing that 'We wil slee the giltif/ and lat the other go.... Of hem that bene giltif/ I wil ben awreke' (818–20). He rebukes the justice directly for corrupt judgments: 'domes/ of

---

[38] For references, see the note to line 717 of *Sir Thopas* in *The Riverside Chaucer*, p. 918.

the worst assise' (866). Overturning the corrupt legal hierarchy, he assumes the role in which the justice bribed by his brother has failed:

> 'Lat no skape at the door/ take, yonge men, yeme;
> For I wil be justice this day/ domes to deme.
> God spede me this day/ at my newe werk!
> Adam, com with me/ for thou shalt be my clerk'. (821–24)

This important act of appropriation and substitution is imagined in highly concrete terms:

> Than seide Gamelyn/ to the justise,
> 'Now is thi power don,/ the most nedes rise;
> Thow hast yeven domes/ that bene evel dight,
> I will sitten in thi sete/ and dressen hem aright.' (841–44)

The tale begins with the knights who fail to 'dress' (15, 18, 36), that is, 'dipose' or 'divide', the lands of John of Boundes in a way that is legal and that the three brothers and the local community can live with, and now, very near the end, Gamelyn states his intention to 'dressen' the corrupt justice's 'domes' that are 'evel dight' – he will 'redispose' or reverse them, presumably, but also 'redress' in the sense of righting them, now that the unjust justice has lost his seat and his power.

The hanging of the justice and jurors is the harshest and most disturbing of the five violent scenes examined here. The model for its particular form of violence is also the easiest to identify. Hanging is clearly not a chivalric form of combat – no shining armour, no sharp, bloody weapons – nor does it bear any relation to the bone-cracking with blunt sticks practiced by Gamelyn and the tale's ordinary men. It is of course the increasingly centralized authority of the state that hangs its enemies, who are fortunate if they are only hanged and not also dragged, disembowelled, or dismembered. The multiple hangings that provide the climax to *The Tale of Gamelyn* give us a view from below of the official mechanisms of correction and punishment. That these hangings should represent the cruelest and most shocking violence of all is surely an irony not lost on the teller and his implied audience. What most disturbs the modern reader, I think, is that like the fight with the pestle or the blows that spare clerical tonsures while breaking their limbs, the poet's representation of these hangings is carnivalesque. It includes the element of parodic laughter that Bakhtin thought of as the very essence of popular resistance to the authoritarian aspects of medieval society, which relied upon 'violence, prohibitions, limitations and always contain an element of fear and of intimidation'.[39] Modern readers of *Gamelyn* feel no particular anxiety about being unjustly hanged and thus are excluded from the scene's carnivalesque laughter; to us these darkly comic hangings thus can seem incongruous, if not sadistic. As Green observes, the scene's humour 'may be a bit strong for the modern palate, but it does convey vividly the sense of outraged custom'; that is, it

---

[39] *Rabelais*, p. 90. Medieval European culture was made up of many conflicting currents and forces, not just two, one 'official' and one 'unofficial', as Bakhtin often seems to imply. What seems most useful to me here is not his binary division, but his insight into the role of laughter as a powerful defensive weapon against authoritarian strategies of intimidation. I am also indebted to the discussions of carnivalesque laughter in the outlaw ballads found in Stallybrass, and Green, 'Violence'.

conveys the strong sense among ordinary people that a new centralized bureaucracy is usurping older, more communal forms of law enforcement.[40]

Throughout the tale, behind and in sympathy with Gamelyn are little noted but significant numbers of local men: the franklin at the wrestling match, Adam the spencer, the men who accompany Gamelyn home from the fair, the 'laymen' within John's household who silently hold with Gamelyn against the crowd of monks and canons, and finally in the courtroom the 'yonge men of pris' from the greenwood who assure Gamelyn that they will 'stonde with the/ while that we may dure' (827). In the end, these men all 'maden pees' with the king whose peace they have been accused of disturbing, and the king in his turn is given the final statement of the values for which Gamelyn stands. The king makes him 'cheef justice/ of his free forest' (888), an act that has understandably been described as making the poacher the gamekeeper,[41] but also one that ties into a language and image system deeply engrained within the tale. Gamelyn is no longer a fugitive from injustice in the forest or greenwood; his new, legitimate appointment represents the possibility that the justice and freedom formerly found only in the forest can extend to the larger society as well.

It is not inaccurate, in my view, but also not sufficient, to call Gamelyn a 'social bandit' in the sense made famous by Eric Hobsbawm: one of those individuals criminalized by authorities but 'considered by their people as heroes, as champions, avengers, fighters for justice'.[42] Unlike the Robin Hood of the early ballads, Gamelyn is only a 'bandit' at all for part of the tale. His greenwood, like Robin's, is a well run utopian space that contrasts favorably with the unjust society around it, but in *Gamelyn* it serves only as a temporary way-station where men wait out the time until they receive royal pardons, as does every greenwood outlaw from the shadowy 'king' whom Gamelyn succeeds to the hero himself and all the men he inherits from his predecessor. For the poet, outlaws in the greenwood are only one example of the various groups of ordinary men who stand in the background throughout the tale, men whose interests are not looked after by the clergy, nor by the attenuated chivalric order represented by Ote, and least of all by the corrupted legal system represented by a 'justice' and jury who have been bribed by the sheriff. When Gamelyn is finally free of the tale's many fetters, one assumes that he need no longer deal out blows to escape them. He assures the men who have kept faith with him that they will find him a 'trusty maister' (830). One senses that in these words the whole tale has arrived at its goal: exposing the clergy as heartless and self-indulgent, bypassing an idealistic but ineffectual chivalric order, and installing 'trusty' domestic and local authorities who understand and respond to the longing for a just community unspoken but deeply felt by the 'good menys sones' (292) of the tale, men of the ordinary stamp, who stand staunchly and often silently present throughout the tale, and who doubtless had their counterparts among its most appreciative contemporary listeners and readers.

---

[40] *A Crisis of Truth*, p. 197.
[41] Scattergood, '*The Tale of Gamelyn*', p. 168.
[42] Hobsbawm, p. 17.

9

Ralph the Collier

AD PUTTER

The Tale of Ralph the Collier has come down to us in a single copy, a book printed by Robert Lekpreuik at St Andrews in 1572.[1] Its story runs as follows. One day, as King Charles (i.e. Charlemagne) and his knights are on their way to Paris, they are surprised by a terrible storm, and Charles is separated from his companions. Fearing for his life, he is relieved to meet a collier (i.e. a charcoal burner) who does not recognize him as the king but who agrees to take him into his home. Charles is well looked after, but roughly treated by his host when he does not do as he is told. When Ralph asks his guest for his name, Charles calls himself Wymond of the Wardrobe, one of the Queen's chamber servants. Before returning to the court in Paris, 'Wymond' invites the collier to meet him at court the next day with a load of charcoal to sell. Ralph duly leaves for Paris to find 'Wymond'. In anticipation of his arrival, Charles sends Roland out into the countryside with orders to bring back any traveller he meets. However, the only person Roland encounters is a collier, who is most uncooperative when ordered to come along, insisting that it is his duty to meet Wymond, not the the king. When it transpires that Ralph is in any case on his way to the king's court to meet Wymond, the standoff between the two is momentarily resolved, though they arrange to fight a duel in the same place the next day. When Ralph eventually turns up at court, he is surprised to discover that the man he knew as 'Wymond' is none other than King Charles. Although Charles's knights think the collier should be hanged for his impudence, the king decides to knight him. The following day Ralph has a chance to earn his spurs when he returns to the spot to fight Roland. However, unbeknownst to Ralph, the opponent he meets there is not Roland but the Saracen Magog. Ralph manages to hold his own against his giant opponent, who finally converts to Christianity and joins Roland and Ralph as knights in Charles's service.

Although the printed edition is late, *Ralph the Collier* is undoubtedly a medieval romance. By the end of the fifteenth century Ralph had evidently become a famous literary hero in Scotland, for he is mentioned *en passant* by both Gavin Douglas and

---

[1] The early print is available in a facsimile edition by W. Beattie, *The Taill of Rauf Coilyear: Printed by Robert Lekpreuik at St. Andrews in 1572: A Facsimile of the Only Known Copy* (Edinburgh, 1966). My citations are from the edition by Sidney Herrtage, *The Taill of Rauf Coilyear with the Fragments of Roland and Vernagu and Otuel*, EETS ES 39 (London, 1882), though I have modernized spelling, punctuation, and the use of upper and lower case. More substantive alterations are discussed below.

William Dunbar. Dunbar's reference to 'Raf Coilyear' is the earlier (ca. 1500) and the more interesting of the two:

> Quhone servit is all uther man,
> Gentill and sempill, of everie clan,
> Rauf Coilyearis kynd and Johnne the Reif,
> No thing I gett nor conqueis [*acquire*] can
> Exces of thocht dois me mischief.
>
> ('Schir, yit remember as befoir', lines 31–35)[2]

Ralph the Collier, like the hero of the analogous tale of *John the Reeve* (to which we shall return later), is here commemorated as the archetypal upstart at court. That low-born men of Ralph's ilk should get their reward while Dunbar gets nothing is an injustice so gross that it can only exacerbate Dunbar's painful 'excess of thought'.

The 'thought' that Ralph inspired in Dunbar is also the starting point of my essay: by what right should a gruff collier, who is just minding his own business at the start of the story, end up as Charles's knight, as 'Schir Rauf' (line 963) and 'Marshall of France' (line 965)? The easy answer – too easy in the case *Ralph the Collier* – is that the knighting of the churl is simply something that always happens in these kinds of stories. Certainly, the motif is part and parcel of the traditional and widely disseminated story that lies behind *Ralph the Collier*, the story of the king in disguise.[3] In Middle English this story type is represented by at least three earlier medieval tales: *King Edward and the Hermit* and *King Edward and the Shepherd* (both incomplete),[4] and last but not least *John the Reeve*, extant in the seventeenth-century Percy Folio but datable on internal grounds to c. 1450.[5] According to Rhiannon Purdie, *John the Reeve* is most likely to have been a source for *Ralph*.[6] In all three stories the king is entertained by a rustic host who treats him to a sumptuous supper consisting of the king's own game, illegally poached. The host only recognizes that his guest is the king when he turns up at court, where he is lavishly wined and dined and knighted by the king.[7] The social elevation of the hero in stories of this type tells us that the hero has been a good sport and marks the end of the story.

The situation in *Ralph the Collier* is more complicated, however, because its story is rather different. The most conspicuous difference is that it does not end with the

---

[2] Ed. Priscilla Bawcutt, *William Dunbar: Selected Poems* (London, 1996), pp. 287–90.

[3] For a discussion of this story type, see Rachel Snell, 'The Undercover King: *Rauf Coilyear* and its English analogues', in *Medieval Insular Romance: Translation and Innovation*, ed. Judith Weiss, Jennifer Fellows, and Morgan Dickson (Cambridge, 2000), pp. 133–54. See also H.M. Smyser, 'The Taill of Rauf Coilyear and Its Sources', *Harvard Studies and Notes in Philology and Literature* 14 (1932), 135–50.

[4] References are to the following editions: *King Edward and the Shepherd*, ed. Walter Hoyt French and Charles Brockway Hale, *Middle English Metrical Romances*, 2 vols (New York, 1964), 2:947–85; *King Edward and the Hermit*, in *Codex Ashmole 61: A Compilation of Popular Middle English Verse*, ed. George Shuffleton, TEAMS (Kalamazoo MI, 2008), pp. 401–13.

[5] Ed. John Hales and Frederick J. Furnivall, *Bishop Percy's Folio Manuscript: Ballads and Romances*, 3 vols (London, 1867–68), 2: 550–94.

[6] Rhiannon Purdie, 'Medieval Romance in Scotland', in *A Companion to Medieval Scottish Poetry*, ed. Priscilla Bawcutt and Janet Hadley Williams (Cambridge, 2006), pp. 165–77, at p. 172.

[7] Because *Edward and the Hermit* and *Edward and the Shepherd* are incomplete, the knighting of the hero is missing from both, but the presence of this motif in later ballad versions of the story, such as *King Edward the Fourth and a Tanner of Tamworth* (ed. H.C. Sargent and G.L. Kittredge, *English and Scottish Popular Ballads* (London, 1904), no. 273), suggests it was archetypal.

knighting of the hero. In *Ralph* the hero still has unsettled business with Roland and is thus given the opportunity to prove himself worthy of the knighthood bestowed upon him. This additional story line, initiated by Roland's encounter with Ralph and ending in the latter's fight with the Saracen, has demonstrable parallels in other Charlemagne romances,[8] but it is far from obvious why the poet intertwined it with a king-in-disguise story. The two story lines (king-meets-commoner and Christian-meets-Saracen) are from very different traditions, they presuppose different protagonists – a churl in the former, a knight in the latter – and it is very tempting to conclude that they are 'only loosely' connected, as Alan Lupack believes.[9] In my view, the poet has gone out of his way to link the two story lines by introducing a unifying theme and a corresponding plot motif – the theme of loyalty and the motif of making and keeping promises – and by creating a protagonist who combines churlishness with knightly instincts. The Scottish poet was evidently not content with the traditional story of a peasant who is gratuitously made a knight: his various elaborations of the story all serve to create a hero who *deserves* to be a knight – a hero who, before he becomes a knight, behaves in some striking ways as if he were one already. My argument focuses on the two most important manifestations of Ralph's 'churlish chivalry': his generous hospitality and his commitment to promises and covenants.

Hospitality

The theme of hospitality is foregrounded by the poet's choice of Christmas as the seasonal setting for his poem.[10] This setting is prominent from the start, acting as a catalyst for the plot, which is set in motion when Charles and his barons head off to Paris 'befoir the Yule tide' (4) in order to celebrate Christmas at home.[11] From then on, the coming of Yuletide repeatedly impinges on the consciousness of characters. For example, when 'Wymond' apologizes to his host for being unable to stay any longer, he explains that, as a domestic servant, he cannot afford to go missing at Christmas time:

> 'Sa mot I thrive', said the King, 'me war laith to byde:
> Is not the morne Yule day, formest [*first*] of the yeir?
> Ane man that office suld beir be tyme at this tyde,
> He will be found in his fault that wantis, forouten weir.'
>
> (*Ralph the Collier*, lines 287–90)

---

[8] See Herrtage, ed., *Rauf*, p. vii.
[9] Alan Lupack, ed., *Three Middle English Charlemagne Romances: The Sultan of Babylon, The Siege of Milan, and The Tale of Ralph the Collier*, TEAMS (Kamazoo MI, 1990), p. 162. Lupack's subsequent attempt to find unity in 'the theme of recognition or awareness – on the political, religious, and social levels that must combine to make one a good knight, or, we might say, a good person' (p. 63) is bound to fail. The development of moral character which he thinks he has found in *Ralph* simply is not there.
[10] For further discussion of the Christmas setting in *Ralph the Collier*, see Roseanna Cross, *Time Past Well Remembered: The Handling of Time in Some Middle English and Old French Texts* (Saarbrücken, 2009), pp. 81–98.
[11] The statement by F.J. Amours in his introduction to *Ralph The Collier* (in *Scottish Alliterative Poems in Riming Stanzas*, STS 27, 38 (Edinburgh, 1891–97)) that the king gets lost as he 'goes out hunting with his court' (p. xxxvi) may be true of the analogues but has no basis in the present poem.

According to Church regulations, laymen were expected to rest on Christmas Day, except for kitchen and chamber staff, without whose labour there would be no vacation for the rest of the household.[12]

When on Christmas morning Charlemagne sends Roland on a mission to bring back any wayfarers, the Christmas season and its conventions are again evoked. Roland is surprised and more than a little dismayed to be sent away, though he is noble enough not to show it:

> Schir Rolland had greit ferly, and in hart kest
> Quhat that suld betakin, that the King tald:
> Upon solempnit Yule day, quhen ilk man suld rest,
> That him behovit neidlinges to watche on the wald,
> Quhen his God to serve he suld have him drest.
> And syne, with ane blyith cheir, buskit that bald.
>
> (*Ralph the Collier*, lines 404–409)

Christmas Day, so Roland reflects, is not a time when a knight should be out of doors; amongst other things, he should be in church to attend high mass (as Charles and his knights do: see lines 575–76). Moreover, the layman's obligation to rest makes the mission with which he has been charged seem pointless, for who in their right mind would be travelling on Christmas Day? When he returns from his mission, Roland tells the king it is hardly surprising that no-one was stirring:

> 'Thair wald na douchtie [*no worthy man*] this day for iornay be dicht.
> Fairand over the feildis full few thair I fand;
> Saif anerly ane man that semblit in my sicht
> Thair was no leid on lyfe lent in this land.'
>
> (*Ralph the Collier*, lines 590–93)[13]

'This day', the first day of Christmas, no-one is about – apart from a lone countryman and a knight grudgingly obeying orders.

The Christmas season is so thickly woven into the fabric of *Ralph* that it may come as a surprise to learn that it is the poet's innovation. In all the analogues the story unfolds in spring or summer.[14] However, though the Christmas season separates *Ralph* from other king-and-commoner stories, it brings the tale closer to various Middle English chivalric romances that similarly (and again often in contrast to their sources and analogues) set their adventures at Christmas time. The most notable example is, of course, *Sir Gawain and the Green Knight*, which also makes Christmas central to the plot; by contrast, its closest analogue, the Old French *Livre*

---

[12] For discussion of these regulations and their relevance to Middle English romance, see Ad Putter, 'In Search of Lost Time: Missing Days in *Sir Cleges* and *Sir Gawain and the Green Knight*', in *Time in the Medieval World*, ed. Chris Humphrey and W.M. Ormrod (York, 2001), pp. 119–136, at p. 133.

[13] The sense of 'jornay' at line 588 may be 'jousting, battle' (cf. line 799) rather than 'travel': both were forbidden on holy days.

[14] This is explicit in *King Edward and the Shepherd* ('In a morning of May', line 15) and *King Edward the Fourth and a Tanner of Tamworth* ('In summer time, when leeves grew green', line 1) and implicit in *John the Reeve*, where night 'came att the last' after 'eueninge late' (lines 25–28) and *King Edward and the Hermit*, where the king gets lost pursuing a male adult deer – a type of hunt forbidden in the closed season (September 14–June 24).

de Caradoc, places the Beheading Game 'au moys de May'.¹⁵ The choice of season in both *Sir Gawain* and *Ralph the Collier* serves, amongst other things, to give meaning and consequence to the hospitality scenes in these romances: *bon hostel* (conviviality, comfort, warmth, food and drink) obviously matters more when the weather outside is inhospitable; and it mattered still more at this period, because the liturgical occasion, the birth of the redeemer, made good cheer a moral as well as a social obligation. (There is nothing frivolous about the injunction in numerous Middle English carols to make merry.)

The importance of the theme of hospitality in *Ralph* is further underlined by the conclusion of the romance, which ends with the foundation of a 'fair place' for all those in need of lodging:

> Syne [Ralph] foundit ane fair place quhair he met the King,
> Ever mair perpetually,
> In the name of Sanct July,
> That all that wantis harbery,
> Suld haue gestning [*lodging*].   (*Ralph the Collier*, lines 971–75)

'Sanct July' is Saint Julian, the patron saint of all who seek and give hospitality.

The episode where the poet of *Ralph* is able to celebrate generous 'harbery' most fully is Ralph's lavish reception of Charlemagne. This episode is full of surprises, both on its own terms and in comparison with its analogues. In the medieval analogues (with the exception of *The King and the Shepherd*), the king is initially served the kind of food you would expect from a churl: bread and cheese in *King Edward and the Hermit* (lines 228–30), thin ale, bean bread and salted meat in *John the Reeve* (lines 387–97). Only when the king offers to pay handsomely does the host produce fresh meat; and since this meat has been illegally poached, it is offered by the host on condition of strict secrecy, for the king's officers would be after him if they knew he was breaking Forest Law. The indebtedness of *Ralph the Collier* to these earlier stories becomes very apparent when Ralph boasts that the venison he has served up has been poached from under the noses of the king's 'forestaris' (line 197). But also noticeable is the selfless generosity of the hero in *Ralph*. The collier treats his guest to the best food he has to offer from the start and without expectation of reward. Indeed, when Charles offers to pay before leaving, Ralph waves away the offer with disdain:

> 'Call furth the gude wyfe, lat pay hir or we ryde,
> For the worthie harberie that I have fundin heir.'
> 'Lat be, God forbid,' the Coilyear said,
> 'And thow of Charlis company,
> Chief king of chevalry,

---

¹⁵ The relevant episode from the *Livre de Caradoc*, in the version closest to that known to the *Gawain* poet, has been edited by Larry D. Benson in his *Art and Tradition in 'Sir Gawain and the Green Knight'* (New Brunswick NJ, 1965), pp. 249–56 (see p. 250 for the May season). Other examples of chivalric 'Christmas romances' are *Sir Perceval of Gales* (based on the *Conte du Graal*, which opens in spring); *Amis and Amiloun* (based on an Anglo-Norman source which leaves the setting unspecified); *Sir Cleges* (a Christmas romance with no known source); and the *Alliterative Morte Arthure* which opens with a Christmas banquet (in lieu of the Whitsuntide Feast that features in the chronicle tradition).

> That for ane nichtis harbery,
> Pay suld be laid.' (*Ralph the Collier*, lines 293–99)

Coming from someone who ekes out a living selling charcoal, such high-mindedness may seem out of character, but Ralph knows how to behave chivalrously.

This sense of *noblesse oblige* explains why the collier's reception of 'Wymond' unfolds in so many ways 'by the book', as if Ralph were a noble *vavasour* rather than a collier.[16] First of all, his house looks more like a manor than a peasant cottage. Ralph says politely that it is far beneath the dignity of his guest, but he also lets slip that it is his 'awin house, maist [*biggest*] in this land' (line 68). And so it appears: the poet describes it as a fine building ('burelie bigging', line 190),[17] with a 'hall' (line 154) where supper is served, a 'byre' (line 111) for the animals, a 'stabill' (line 166) for the horses, and a number of bedrooms, including a dedicated guestroom. Douglas Gray asks just the right question here: is this a 'cottage… or would-be manor house'?[18]

There is a similar blend of the churlish and the courtly in the way husband and wife relate to each other. He is 'Rauf' and she is 'Gill'. He is short-tempered and bosses her about; she is sensible and knows better than to disobey. Even so, he addresses her as 'Dame' (an address fondly echoed by the poet at line 102: 'To the dure went our dame') – and she him as 'Schir'.

This 'Sir' and his 'Dame' know how to welcome a guest, and a comparison with the courtly rituals of hospitality as found in the *Gawain* poems is surprisingly relevant.[19] First of all, the guest's horse must be stabled. In Castle Hautdesert servants come forward to relieve Gawain of his horse ('And sythen stabeled his stede stif men innoghe': *Sir Gawain and the Green Knight*, line 823), while in Ralph's 'would-be manor house':

> Twa cant knaifis of his awin haistelie he bad:
> 'The ane of you my capill ta,
> The uther his corsour alswa;
> To the stabill swyith ye ga.'
> Than was the King glaid. (*Ralph the Collier*, lines 114–18)

Were it not for the fact that Ralph's horse is a 'capill' (a cart-horse) rather than a 'corsour', we could be in a courtly romance.

Next the guest will want to warm up in front of a blazing fire, so Charles is directed 'To ane bricht byrnand fyre, as the Carll bad' (line 132), just as in *Sir Gawain* 'A chayer byfore the chemné, ther charcole brenned,/ Watz grayþed for Sir Gawan' (lines 875–76). Then it is supper time. In polite society hands are washed – 'Þe wye wesch at his wylle, and went to his mete' (*Sir Gawain*, line 887) – and fastidious readers can rest assured that in *Ralph*, too, 'thay had weschin' both before and after

---

[16] For a discussion of the conventions of hospitality as they apply in courtly romances see Matilda Tomaryn Bruckner, *Narrative Invention in Twelfth-Century French Romance: The Convention of Hospitality* (Lexington, 1980), and Ad Putter, 'The Convention of Hospitality', in *Sir Gawain and the Green Knight and French Arthurian Romance* (Oxford, 1995), pp. 51–99.

[17] The word means 'excellent, noble', or possibly 'massive' (see *MED* s.v. 'borli(ch)'; the gloss 'rough, rustic' offered by Herrtage is erroneous.

[18] Douglas Gray, *Later Medieval English Literature* (Oxford, 2008), p. 517.

[19] All references to the *Gawain*-poet are to the edition by Malcolm Andrew and Roland Waldron, *Poems of the 'Pearl' Manuscript*, revised fifth edition (Exeter, 2007). I have modernized thorns and yoghs.

supper (lines 145, 217). Because there are only three diners, a seating plan should not have to come into it, but Ralph sets great store by decorum. As the honoured guest, Charles is invited to sit in the seat of honour with Gill on one side and Ralph on the other:

> Quhen thay were servit and set to the suppar,
> Gyll and the gentill king, Charlis of micht,
> Syne on the tother side sat the Coilyear.
> Thus war thay marschellit but mair [*without further ado*], and matchit
> that nicht.
> (*Ralph the Collier*, lines 181–84)

In the households of the great, the marshal was the court official who supervised the seating arrangements. The guests at the Wedding Feast in *Cleanness*, for instance, are 'ful mannerly with marschal mad for-to sitte' (*Cleanness*, line 91). Ralph is not grand enough to have an actual marshal on duty, but the diners are nevertheless 'marshellit' with the protocol it was his duty to observe.

The meal itself is also reminiscent of the courtly tradition. The first dish is boar's meat, 'braun of ane bair', accompanied by the 'worthiest wyne' (lines 187–88); more meat dishes follow; then 'enteris their dayteis, on deis dicht dayntelie;/ Within that worthy wane/ Forsuith wantit thay nane' (lines 191–93). The 'deis' is the high table, where 'dainties' (i.e. delicacies) are elegantly arranged; the alliterative collocation of *dais* and *dainty* must have been familiar to the poet from descriptions of great feasts, like Belshazzar's Feast in *Cleanness*, with its 'dukez on dece with daintyes served' (*Cleanness*, line 38). The excellent wine that Ralph serves with every course marks him out as an un-miserly gentleman, for while wine was the common drink for the higher aristocracy it remained a luxury for gentry and knightly families (in the lower echelons ale was the norm).[20] The inclusion of 'vennysoun' is a pointed reminder that some of the meat has been poached, but, while this is the main point in the analogues *John the Reeve*, *The King and the Hermit* and *The King and the Shepherd*, it is incidental in *Ralph*, where the general effect is one of opulence and culinary refinement. To pick out just one detail, the animals that receive particular attention from the poet are not the poached deer, but the 'capounis' that Gill is instructed to 'knap doun' in the byre (line 111) and which then appear 'in plentie' on Ralph's dinner table (line 209). These are not the free-range hens we prize today but castrated cockerels which in baronial households were kept in pens and fed on oats.[21] Again comparison can usefully be made with *Cleanness*, where the great lord who organizes the wedding banquet speaks proudly of 'my polyle þat is penne-fed' (*Cleanness*, line 57).

The ebb and flow of polite conversation are also reminiscent of the *Gawain*-poet. Protocol demanded that a visitor should not be asked his name or business until after dinner. This principle is enshrined in various medieval courtesy books, including the thirteenth-century Anglo-Norman *Petit traitise de nurture*:

---

[20] See Chris Woolgar, *The Great Household in Late Medieval England* (New Haven, 1999), p. 102, and Noriko Matsui, 'Realistic Detail in Poetry of the Alliterative Revival', unpublished doctoral dissertation (Bristol, 2010), p. 93.
[21] See Margaret Labarge, *A Baronial Household of the Thirteenth Century* (London, 1965), p. 77.

> Estrange ne devez aresoner
> Au commencement del manger,
> Ne trop de novels lui demandez
> K'il n'ert de manger desturbez.
> Aprés manger, si vous volez,
> Aventure et novels demandez.   (*Petit Traitise de Nurture*, lines 133–38)[22]

'You should not talk too much with a stranger at the beginning of a meal. And do not ask him too many questions, for you will keep him from his dinner. If you like, you can ask after dinner what has been happening and what the news is.'

This point of etiquette explains why in *Sir Gawain and the Green Knight* no-one asks Gawain for his name until the end of the supper, and even then only tactfully and indirectly:

> Þenne watz spyed and spured vpon spare wyse,
> Bi preué poyntez of þat prynce, put to hymseluen,
> Þat he beknew cortaysly of þe court þat he were...
>
> (*Sir Gawain*, lines 901–903)

The Carl is also too well brought up to ask any personal questions until the correct moment has come:

> Quhen they had maid thame at eise, the Coilyear tald
> Mony sindrie taillis efter suppair.
> Ane bricht byrnand fyre was byrnand full bald;
> The King held gude countenance, and company bair,
> And ever to his asking ane answer he yald;
> Quhill [*until*] at the last he began to frane [*inquire*] farther mair,
> 'In faith, friend, I wald wit, tell gif ye wald,
> Quhaur is thy maistt wynning?' said the Coilyear.
> 'Out of weir', said the King, I waynd [*desisted*] it never to tell'
> With my lady the Queen
> In office maist I have bene...'   (*Ralph the Collier*, lines 222–32)

Ralph shows good manners by refraining from questions 'efter suppair'. As in *Sir Gawain* the first question is exploratory; more searching questions (including: what's your name?) follow only after the guest has shown himself willing to answer questions of a personal nature.

Finally, there are the bedroom rituals to consider. Again *Sir Gawain and the Green Knight* provides a model: the guest is escorted to a 'chambre' (line 850), a private bedroom, where he sleeps in a well-appointed bed, 'under covertour ful clene, cortyned aboute' (line 1181). Gawain's own chamberlain dresses him when he leaves early in the morning on New Year's Day. The courtesies extended to Charles are similar:

> To ane preuie chalmer beliue thay him led,

---

[22] Ed. Rosamund H. Parsons, 'Anglo-Norman Books of Courtesy and Nurture', *PMLA* 44 (1929), 383–455.

> Quahair ane burely bed was wrocht in that wane,
> Closet with courtinges and cumly cled.
>
> (*Ralph the Collier*, lines 265–67)

No chamberlain is available to dress Charles in the morning, the poet notes (lines 273–74), but it is found worthy of remark that he does enjoy the services of a little page ('pavyot', line 278), who brings him his horse.

But what about the Carl's habit of putting the king in his place – with a smart wallop if necessary? Does this not show that Ralph is, after all, a rough customer? I think the answer is both 'yes' and 'no'. While Ralph is certainly quick to correct his guest, his reprimands are always aimed at social blunders committed by the king. Charles gets his first ticking-off when he thanks Ralph for his hospitality before he has even received it. Ralph retorts that expressions of gratitude would be more appropriate on departing:

> 'To-morne, on the morning, quhen thow sall on leip,
> Pryse at the parting, how that thow dois…'
>
> (*Ralph the Collier*, lines 85–86)

As Nancy Mason Bradbury has noted, Ralph has a habit of speaking in proverbs, and she forcefully argues that these proverbs associate his discourse with peasant speech as represented in other medieval texts.[23] However, Ralph is not always down-to-earth, and on this particular occasion his proverb gives expression to a point of etiquette popularized by the one of the earliest medieval courtesy books, the *Facetus cum nihil utilius*, which schoolboys in the period read as a supplement to Cato's *Distichs*:

> Noctem mane, diem cubiturus vespere laudes,
> hospitibus tuis, dum discendis, dato laudes.
>
> (*Facetus cum nihil utilius*, no. 78)[24]

> 'Praise the night in the morning, and praise the day when you go to sleep in the evening, and thank your hosts when you depart.'

Not surprisingly, then, Charles accepts that Ralph's criticism is fully justified: 'in gud fay,/ Schir, it is suith that ye say' (88–89).

In the two tiffs that follow, Ralph also has right on his side. When Ralph and the king go into the hall to eat, Ralph, 'as ressoun had bene' (line 119), gives precedence to his guest, but 'Wymond' waits on the doorstep and beckons Ralph to go in first (lines 120–21). If a king did this, it would be considered polite, for a king's primacy is so unquestionable that the gesture could only ever be taken as a symbolic renunciation of his social superiority. But Charles is supposed to be Wymond, not himself, and by declining Ralph's deference and substituting his own he is implicitly claiming a right to condescend. Since Ralph is the host and the boss in his own house, this is obviously bad manners. As an old French proverb has it: 'charbonnier

---

[23] Nancy Mason Bradbury, 'Representations of Peasant Speech: Some Literary and Social Contexts for *The Taill of Rauf Coilyear*', in *Medieval Romance, Medieval Contexts*, ed. Rhiannon Purdie and Michael Cichon (Cambridge, 2011), pp. 19–33.
[24] Ed. Carl Schroeder, *Der deutsche Facetus* (Berlin, 1911).

est maître chez soi' ('even the charcoal-burner is master in his own home').[25] Once again, then, Charles has infringed a rule of etiquette of which medieval society was very conscious. As the *Petite traitise de nurture* (lines 163–64) stipulates: 'Ton hoste en sa meson/ Contredire n'est pas reson' ('It is not right to contradict your host in his own home'). Ralph's miffed response to Charles's gesture is thus perfectly understandable: 'He said, "thow art uncourtes, that sall I warrand"' (line 121). When Charles subsequently commits the same *faux-pas* twice, by refusing to sit down before the collier himself is seated, Ralph loses his temper and thumps the king so hard that he ends up flat on the floor. It does not need saying that this is *not* the way to treat a guest; but what does need saying is that Ralph becomes churlish because he wants to give, not accept, courtesy, and feels that his courtesy should in courtesy be accepted, not declined: 'Schir, thow art unskillful [*unreasonable*], and that sall I warrand;/ Thow byrd [*should*] to have nurtour anuech, and thow hes nane' (lines 161–62).

The paradoxical character of Ralph, the chivalrous churl, is thus reflected in the contradiction that his roughness is the outward manifestation of a burning sense of propriety which compels him (in Ralph's own words) to 'ken [= teach] kingis courtasie' (line 722). Charles is fortunately big enough to appreciate this when, against the advice of his knights, he chooses to honour Ralph for being at once hard-hitting and courteous:

> Him semes ane stalwart man, and stout in strykyng,
> That carll for his courtaisie salbe maid knicht.
> (*Ralph the Collier*, lines 748–49)

In giving Charles a justification for his decision, the poet shows that the knighting of the hero is a matter of merit rather than an inert literary convention: Ralph has both the doughtiness and the courtesy proper to a knight and so gets what he has deserved.

Loyalty

Ralph demonstrates his chivalric potential not only in his generous hospitality but also in the 'mekle lawtie' (line 511) by which he lives his life. Both virtues, generosity and good faith, had a special association with knighthood in the medieval period. In *Sir Gawain and the Green Knight*, 'larges' and 'lewté' are linked as the two virtues that 'longez to knyghtez' (line 2381), and both *Sir Gawain* and *Rauf* give their heroes the opportunity to prove their *lewté* in circumstances where their commitment to promises and agreements (*covenauntes*) comes under strain.

Ralph's lively interest in the hero's word of honour becomes immediately apparent if we compare its story with that of its probable source, *John the Reeve*. John the Reeve is summoned to court by a messenger sent to him by the queen, who is very curious to see the fellow (lines 574–80). In *Ralph*, on the other hand, 'Wymond' invites him to visit him at court, and Ralph solemnly pledges his troth that he will do so: 'In faith', said the Coilyear,/ 'Traist weill I salbe thair' (lines 309–10). After his guest's departure, Ralph, having 'greit thocht on the cunnand [= covenant] he had maid'

---

[25] For the proverb and its history see Amours, *Scottish Alliterative Poems*, p. xxxix.

(line 321), prepares to set off to Paris.[26] Going to court with a cargo of charcoal is hardly a chivalrous quest, but the conventions of chivalric romance clearly colour the poet's description of Ralph's departure. As in the chivalric romances, the hero's resolve is tested by the voice of common sense ('don't go there'!),[27] embodied in this instance by dame Gill, who warns her husband that he might get into trouble at court (as he would have done if Charles's knights had had their way). Naturally, the hero's role in such circumstances is to persist, and so Ralph, again giving 'great thocht quhat he had undertane' (line 366), dismisses his wife's concerns:

> 'Yea, Dame, have nane dreid of my lyfe to day;
> Lat me wirk as I will, the weird is mine awin ...
> ... That I have hecht [*promised*] I sall hald, happin as it may,
> Quhiddir sa it gang to greif or to gawin [*gain*].'
>
> (*Ralph the Collier*, lines 378–82)

A man of honour must take the adventure, come what may. To my ears at least, this is not the down-to-earth discourse of the peasant but the high-minded ethos of chivalry. To find a match for it we need look no further than *Sir Gawain*, where the hero similarly shrugs off the guide's apparently well-intended concern for his welfare because his word of honour comes before his own safety (lines 2118–39).

If, following Ralph's example, we pay close attention to covenants, the problem of how and why the two plot lines connect becomes easier to deal with. Before Ralph has had a chance to arrive at court, Charles charges Roland with a mission to bring anyone he meets on the moor back to him without delay:

> Quhat sumever that he be
> Bring him *haistely* to me,
> *Befoire none* that I him se
> In this hall the day.
>
> (*Ralph the Collier*, lines 400–403; italics mine)

When Roland meets Ralph, who refuses to come back with him, the two nearly come to blows, but battle is deferred until the following day when, by another accident of mistaken identity, Ralph ends up fighting not Roland, but the Saracen Magog. In order to connect these developments with the plot-line of the 'king-in-disguise' story, the poet uses the motif of promises and the theme of truthfulness. The first thing to notice is that Roland is chosen by Charles as his most loyal knight: 'Ane man he traistit in, maist atour [*above*] all uther thing' (line 393). Although Roland does not really want to be outdoors on Christmas day, he obeys and rides out, fully intending 'his hechtis for to hald' (line 411). Roland, then, has a covenant to keep, just as does Ralph, who has promised to meet Wymond at court. The confrontation between Roland and Ralph thus becomes a test of the depth of each man's commitment to a promise – Roland's promise to Charles, and Ralph's to Wymond – and the exchanges between the two are phrased in such as way as to reveal these stakes. Roland, for

---

[26] Rhiannon Purdie has remarked upon this difference between *Ralph* and *John the Reeve* in 'Medieval Romance in Scotland', p. 166.

[27] For a study of this romance convention see T.A. Shippey, 'The Uses of Chivalry: *Erec and Gawain*', *MLR* 66 (1971), 241–50.

example, tries to persuade Ralph that the latter's covenant with Wymond must take second place to Roland's covenant with the king:

> 'Sa thrive I', said Rolland, 'it is mine intent
> That nouther to Wymond nor Will
> Thow sald hald nor hecht till
> Quhill I have brocht the to fulfil
> The kingis commandment.' (*Ralph the Collier*, lines 451–55)

But even though this argument is backed up by Roland's intimidating physique and weaponry, Ralph refuses to give way. *His* business is with Wymond of the queen's chamber: 'thair I undertuke to be, Into Paris pardie/ Withouten delay'; Ralph's obstinacy is thus not just a matter of churlish recalcitrance (as Roland sees it), but a reflection of his single-minded devotion to his word of honour.

The resulting stalemate is only resolved when Roland learns that Ralph is in any case on his way to court – which means that Roland can return peacefully to Charles's court to await his arrival:

> 'Me tharth [*I need*] have nane noy of myne errand,
> For me think thow will be thair efter, as thow tellis,
> Bot gif [*unless*] I fand the forrow now to keip my cunnand.'[28]
> 'Schir Knicht', said the Coilyear, thow trowis me never ellis,
> Bot gif sum suddand let [*hindrance*] put it out of delay;
> For that I hecht of my will,
> And na main threit me thair till,
> That I am haldin to fulfill,
> And sall do quhill I may.'
>
> 'Yea, sen thow will be their, thy cunnandis to new,
> I neid nane airar myne errand nor none of the day.'[29]
> 'Be thow traist', said the Coilyear, 'man, as I am trew,
> I will not haist me ane fute faster on the way ...'
>
> (*Ralph the Collier*, lines 538–550)

The passage begins with Roland expressing relief that he can make light work of his errand. Instead of trying to coerce the churl by force of arms, which would be a lot of trouble ('noy'), he can return to court, since Ralph, who is due to meet Wymond in the king's castle, will turn up eventually ('efter'). To this Ralph replies that Roland can trust him to be unchanged in his commitment to his word; barring some unforeseen circumstance, he will get to court later that day in his own time. He will not be made to hurry.

---

[28] The meaning of this line is unclear. F.J. Amours (followed by W.H. Browne, ed., *The Taill of Rauf Coilyear* (Baltimore, 1903)) glossed 'But since I have found you, (go) forward now to keep my promise (to the king).' Sidney Herrtage confessed he could not understand line 540, while the most recent editor, Alan Lupack, thinks the line is corrupt. Perhaps the sense is: 'Unless I now find you willing ("forward") to fulfil my covenant', i.e. unless you have now changed your mind and are now willing to obey the king's order.

[29] The general sense of this line must be 'I don't need to fulfil my errand any earlier than noon of the day', but the construction is suspect.

A man who takes his promises seriously is also careful not to promise more than he can deliver,[30] and Ralph's cautious exit clause ('Bot gif sum suddand let put it out of delay') marks him out as a scrupulously honest man. Roland, by contrast, is less single-minded about executing his commission to the letter. For even though it is clear that Ralph, burdened with carthorse and coal, is not going to get to Paris in a hurry (and arrives *after* noon),[31] Roland is happy to accept this arrangement, and rushes back to rejoin the Christmas party. Someone more scrupulous than Roland about covenants would have remembered that the king had explicitly asked Roland to *bring back* any wayfarer *hastily* to the king *before noon*. This explains why the king is displeased when Roland, his most trusted knight, confesses over Christmas dinner (after noontime) that he has not heeded the king's precise orders (lines 599–603). His hopes of leading the husbandman before Charles at all now depend on whether Ralph will keep *his* promises by coming to court. Chastened by the king's anger, Roland leaves the dinner table and goes to the castle entrance 'to se gif the Coilyearis lawtie was leill' (line 604). Fortunately for him, Ralph does not disappoint. The churl has kept his promise, and has out-knighted a knight in 'lawtie'.[32]

The final episode of the tale, Ralph's duel with Magog, is again connected with the preceding plot by means of a promise. Before Ralph and Roland go their separate ways, Ralph plights his troth that he will return to the same spot on the following morning, to fight Roland, and Roland alone – if his health permits, he scrupulously adds. The wording of promises matters, and Ralph recalls the precise terms of the agreement later on, when he is dismayed to see the Saracen (whom he mistakes for Roland) accompanied by a huge army. Comically and characteristically, his first thought is not fear for his own safety but disappointment that Roland has 'broken conditioun' (line 847) by not coming alone, as he had promised: 'Thairto I tuik thy hand, as thou was trew knicht' (line 849).

The ritual handclasp which Ralph remembers (cf. line 567: 'and thairto my hand') gives the covenant between Roland and Charles a solemn formality, and on the morning of their appointed meeting, Ralph thinks immediately of his promise:

> Upon the morne airly, Schir Rauf wald not rest,
> Bot in ryall array he reddyit him to ryde:
> 'For to hald that I have hecht, I hope it be the best.
> To yone busteous beirne that boistit me to byde.
> Among the galyart gromis I am bot ane gest.
> I will the ganandest gait [*most convenient way*] to that gay glyde;
> Sall never Lord lauch on loft, quhill my lyfe may lest,
> That I for liddernes suld leif, and leuand beside.

---

[30] Compare Gawain's carefully worded pledge to the Green Knight (*Sir Gawain and the Green Knight*, lines 402–403) that he will do his best to find his dwelling (but can promise nothing more).

[31] The passing of time is measured with care: Ralph and Roland meet a little after 'midmorne' (line 417). Leaving Ralph to make his own, slow way, to Paris, Roland rides back as fast as he can, and arrives in time to see Charles and his knights coming out of church where they have attended 'hie mes'. He changes attire and joins them for dinner in the hall 'at none' (line 579). Ralph arrives some time later.

[32] I do not think it is the case that Roland and Ralph emerge from their 'contest of "courtesy" and "lawtie"' with '[h]onours even', as Douglas Gray argues, *Later Medieval English Literature*, p. 519.

> It war ane graceles gude that I were cummin to,
> Gif that the king hard on hicht
> That he had maid ane carll knight
> Amang thir weryouris wicht,
> And docht [*was able*] nocht to do.' (*Ralph the Collier*, lines 781–793)

In this scene Ralph has become a knight, and so he can express his sense of obligation as something proper to his newly acquired status; but, of course, the promise he seeks to honour was one he made when he was still a churl, and the similarities between this scene and his earlier departure from home (compare lines 783–84 with 363–64 and line 785 with 382) confirm that Ralph is fundamentally unchanged. He is and always was a man of his word.

Conclusion

Ralph's chivalric credentials are evident from his scrupulousness as a host and a promiser. Of course, this does not mean that our collier is a model knight. Brusque and short-tempered, Ralph is a very rough diamond, and there is much truth in Nancy Mason Bradbury's argument that Ralph's complaints about high-handed royal officials and his predilection for proverbs recall the tradition of peasant discourse as stylized in medieval proverb collections, political complaints, and dialogues like *Solomon and Marcolf*. However, the poet of *Ralph* did not seek to typecast his hero as the archetypal peasant. Ralph's ideals of truthfulness are high-minded and have nothing to do with practical common sense. Moreover, he upholds and insists on the finest traditions of hospitality as codified in medieval courtesy books and in courtly romances such as *Sir Gawain and the Green Knight*. In short, he is seen to demonstrate in many of his actions that 'larges and lewté that longez to knyghtez'.

Our hero is therefore neither peasant nor knight but an irresistible blend of both. By a perplexing 'performative contradiction' (the philosophers' term for self-contradictions such as saying 'yes' while shaking your head), Ralph actually manages to behave chivalrously *and* churlishly at one and the same time, as when he slaps Charles to teach him good manners, or is stubbornly uncooperative to Roland because he has given his word of honour to 'Wymond'. Ralph's churlishness seems, on these and other occasions, to be inseparable from, even expressive of, his chivalry. To really appreciate *Ralph* we must enter into the poet's presentation of the hero as simultaneously churl and knight. The poet's attempt to create a synthesis of the two explains why he combined the story of the king and the commoner with that of the knight and the Saracen. The two story lines are carefully connected, as I have argued, by the leitmotif of promises and loyalty, but of course what ultimately links the two is a mongrel hero who is equally at home in both environments, in tales of churls and tales of chivalry.

10

The Anti-heroic Heart*

STEPHANIE VIERECK GIBBS KAMATH

Triumphs achieved, tasks accomplished, challenges mastered: such are the conclusions expected for a hero's quest. What kind of quest ends with the hero hospitalized after being clubbed down by a fat, rude, rebellious hunchback clad in worn-out rusty armour? And why would a medieval nobleman want to claim such a story as his own? These questions face the readers of a unique French work known as the *Livre du Cuer d'Amours Espris* (*Book of the Love-smitten Heart*), written by René, the duke of Anjou, during the last half of the fifteenth century. The *Livre du Cuer* is both a testament to the enduring legacy of the great heroic narratives of the Middle Ages and a radical reinterpretation of their meaning. René borrows the form of Arthurian romance to tell a story about his experience of being in love, transforming romance into allegory, a narrative with multiple levels of meaning. In a simple sense, acknowledging the combination of forms explains the ending of the work and its author's aim in writing it. The hero of this work is *Cuer* (Heart), the author's own heart personified in the form of a knight, and the repulsive opponent responsible for his downfall is *Reffus* (Refusal); René has quashed the triumphant ending typical of heroic narrative in order to depict himself figuratively as a desperate lover. Yet René's combination of forms deserves more attention than this simple explanation suggests. René's Heart is undoubtedly envisioned as a hero in terms of the attributes and adventures assigned to him, but Heart might also be considered an anti-heroic figure, in the sense that Heart's story challenges the expectations of heroic narrative. We expect heroes to be distinguished from anti-heroes by their ethical virtue, cultural identity, and ultimate success in combat, but the models René claims for Heart and for his failure blur these distinctions; we expect the stories of heroes to be drawn from history and characterized by a focus on action but the *Livre du Cuer* adopts the style and structure of such stories to convey immediate, internal experience, forcing us to reconsider the question of what a hero meant to medieval readers.

René's *Livre du Cuer* blends together features from two differing but interrelated types of narrative popular in the later Middle Ages, the heroic romance and the love vision or allegory. Love visions convey the experience of idealized erotic passion in a manner different from heroic romance, which typically chronicles events and often

---

* This paper reflects the beneficial feedback of the editor and anonymous reviewers of the volume, my colleague Alex Mueller, and my treasured non-specialist readers, John and Valerie Gibbs.

cites the authority of histories.¹ Usually written from a first-person perspective, love visions invite interpretation as allegories through being marked as distant from quotidian reality in a number of ways, narrating symbolic interactions between personifications and identifying the narrative as a dream or other form of special revelation. The interaction of personifications within visions often resembles or alludes to the martial or chivalric encounters found in romance, however, and the elaboration or even addition of attention to the erotic passions of heroic characters is also an important characteristic of romance, at times expressed through interpolating the literary devices of personifications or dreams.² René greatly extends the interrelation of these types of narratives, particularly in the long central section of the *Livre de Cuer*, which begins with the arming of the personification Heart and describes his quest for the equally symbolic lady, Sweet Mercy. Heart's quest follows the structure of romance; he serves a powerful lord (Love), drinks from a marvellous fountain (of Fortune), crosses a perilous bridge (across the River of Tears), encounters a hostile dwarf (Jealousy) and a wise hermit (the host of Hope), endures harsh imprisonment (by Sadness and Melancholy), journeys across the sea (to Love's Isle), and engages in jousting (with Worry and with Anger).³ Even Heart's final request to return to a hospital kept by a prioress and a nurse in religious garb (the Hospital of Love governed by Pity and Courtesy) would not be out of keeping with other heroic narratives, if this holy end were not preceded by a final failure to vanquish his foes.⁴

The style in which Heart's adventures are recounted also resembles heroic romance. This section is written in prose, more typical of chronicles and romances in the fifteenth century than of visionary literature, although inset verses represent speeches, songs, and inscriptions and could recall a much earlier tradition of heroic narratives that incorporate differing verse forms, famously exemplified by *Aucassin et Nicolette*. The prose narrative replicates the interlaced style typical of Arthurian romance from the turn of the thirteenth century, threading accounts of Heart's quest between the related doings of such characters as the lord Honour and the ladies

---

[1] The modern association of the English word 'romance' with love as well as with the story of a hero reflects the taste for both heroes and *eros* as subjects in French literature from around the turn of the twelfth century, when the French term *roman* referred more broadly to literature produced in or translated into the romance languages (Latin, the speech of the Romans, and its derivatives, such as French). For a useful general introduction to romance as a category, see Barbara Fuchs, *Romance* (New York, 2004).

[2] Armand Strubel's seminal study describes how both love visions and quests, as well as animal fables, can invite allegorical reading; see *La Rose, Renart et le Graal: la littérature allégorique en France au XIIIe siècle* (Geneva, 1989).

[3] Jousting as an active practice of chivalry was a subject of particular interest to René, as we know from surviving copies of his treatise on setting up a tournament properly, the *Traicte de la Forme de Devis d'un Tournoi*, composed ca. 1460. See René d'Anjou, *Le Livre des tournois du Roi René: de la Bibliothèque nationale (ms. français 2695)*, ed. François Avril (Paris, 2003).

[4] The religious implications of Heart's narrative are fascinating but exceed what this essay can cover, especially as René also wrote a late fifteenth-century allegory in which the narrator's heart is removed and crucified, the *Mortifiement de Vaine Plaisance*; see René d'Anjou, *Le mortifiement de vaine plaisance de René d'Anjou, étude du texte et des manuscrits à peintures*, ed. Frédéric Lyna (Paris, 1926). A recent comparative study of the salvific implications of René's heart imagery can be found in Virginie Minet-Mahy, 'L'iconographie du cœur et de la croix dans le *Mortifiement* de René d'Anjou et les *Douze Dames de Rhétorique* de George Chastelain: Un dialogue avec Jean Gerson', *Le Moyen Age* 113 (2007), 569–590.

Hope and Pity. In doing so, the narrative frequently employs common phrases suggesting a distanced perspective, 'as the story says' or 'as the author says', rather than claiming direct knowledge of events. Indeed, the description of Heart's arming at the start of his adventures is explicitly likened to the 'ancient' stories of the conquests of the greatest Arthurian knights:

> As once many romances had been made and recounted for everlasting memory of noble deeds and prowess, of great conquests and wartime courage, of astonishing events and most awesome dangers which were concluded, carried out, and accomplished to win the Holy Grail by the courageous and bold knights Lancelot, Gawain, Galahad, Tristan, Palomides, and other knights as well, peers of the Round Table in King Arthur's time, as ancient histories tell of from beginning to end, so similarly to better grant you the means to understand my present work, which tells of the quest for most Sweet Mercy by the love-smitten Heart, I will follow the plan of the book of the quest for the Holy Grail, telling how and with what arms Desire armed the Heart.[5]

Readers are reminded of this comparison of Heart's arming with Arthurian romances by the description of Heart's visit to the Hospital of Love while pursuing his quest. Here, Heart beholds a multitude of coats of arms hung upon the gate of the adjoining cemetery, symbolizing the conquest of their bearers by the god of Love. The arms are those of Arthurian knights as well as more ancient rulers and noble members of the French court, including René himself.[6] Inset verses are described as present beneath each of the coats of arms. These short verse sections, generally around fifteen lines, open with first-person identification by name and, after listing notable deeds, recount submission to the ultimate conqueror, Love. When Heart's armour fails to save him from wounds inflicted by Love's rebellious servant, Refusal, Heart asks Lady Pity to let him spend his last days in the Hospital of Love. This final request links Heart's identity not just with René but with all those named in this armorial series, echoing Heart's comparison to Arthurian knights when his arming is described, and we will discuss the consequences of these parallels for our understanding not only of Heart's adventures but also of heroic identity.

We must first acknowledge, however, that Heart's adventures do not comprise the whole of the *Livre du Cuer*. René's work begins with a prose letter asking his nephew, John of Bourbon, for his advice, describing the text that follows as a parable for René's personal affliction. Verses then describe a vision of the mythic god of Love

---

[5] Rene d'Anjou, *Livre du Cuer d'Amours Espris* (*Book of the Love-smitten Heart*), ed. and trans. Stephanie Viereck Gibbs [Kamath] and Kathryn Karczewska (New York, 2001), 3.1–11. Subsequent citations of this translation by section and line number are provided in the text; the French text is drawn from the facing page edition.

[6] The list differs slightly in early manuscripts. The best known manuscript describes a series of 28 coats of arms: Julius Caesar, Augustus Caesar, Nero, Marcus Aurelius, David, Charles VII, Theseus, Aeneas, Achilles, Hercules, Paris, Troilus, Diomedes, Demonphoön, Lancelot, Tristan, Ponthus, Arthur of Brittany, Louis of Orléans, Jean of Berry, Louis of Bourbon, Philip of Burgundy, Charles of Bourbon, René of Anjou, Charles of Anjou, Gaston of Foix, Louis of Luxembourg, Pierre of Brézé. Another early manuscript adds Charles of Orléans and Louis of France and replaces Pierre of Brézé with Louis of Beauvau. Florence Bouchet provides an edition detailing the variant versions; see René d'Anjou, *Le Livre du Cœur d'amour épris*, ed. and trans. Florence Bouchet (Paris, 2003).

seizing the heart of the poet, who is identified with René by context. At this point the text begins its prose description of Heart's quest, ending with Heart's failure. Afterwards, verses resume, in which the anguished poet calls a servant of his chamber to whom he declares his heart is lost; the servant examines his lord's body but sees no wound, and the ashamed poet declares he will say no more. René then concludes his prose letter, which asserts again that the text represents René's own situation, requests a remedy against torment by Love, and finally wishes that John may attain the desire of his own heart. The perspectives established by the surrounding letter to a kinsman and by the visionary verses depicting physically close relations of courtiers work in concert with the peopling of the central narrative with embodied ideas to collapse the apparent distance of medieval readers from the reading matter of romance. Despite the detached, interlaced prose style of the central narrative and the naming of models who certainly appeared in medieval histories, as René applies the style and structure of romance to the allegorical representation of his inner self, Heart, and concludes by extending heart imagery to his dedicatee, the 'action' described becomes a record of thought and emotion that encourages reflective self-examination. Gloria Cigman has argued that one defining characteristic of the heroic narrative is the absence of an interior life for the hero: 'only a being with neither the emotions nor the introspection that comprise the inner self can be a hero'.[7] Yet the *Livre du Cuer* claims this style of narrative as usable for the purpose of self-description by casting the inner self and emotions as its characters. In doing so, René opens the possibility of doubt about how distant any heroic narrative is from its audience. Are all of these tales of 'long ago and far away' in truth readable as explorations of what lies within, right now? The framing of the heroic narrative in René's *Livre du Cuer* works against a simple reading of the claim made when Heart is armed; encircled by the letter and the poetic vision, Heart's story suggests that we do not read about heroes in order to perpetuate memory of ancient victories but rather to perceive ourselves anew.[8]

As the 'past' of heroic narrative here becomes readable as a framework for understanding the present, cultural divisions also appear to collapse. Geraldine Heng's *Empire of Magic* recently posited an origin for medieval romance in the desire to fantasize about western cultural identity by 'othering' the east, but René's fifteenth-century text already prods readers to perceive the seemingly exotic elements of romance as a pretext for re-introducing contemplation of what is familiar.[9] Like

---

[7] Gloria Cigman, 'The Medieval Self as Anti-Hero', in *Heroes and Heroines in Medieval English Literature, A Festschrift presented to André Crépin on the occasion of his sixty-fifth birthday*, ed. Leo Carruthers (Cambridge, 1994), pp. 161–170, at p. 167.

[8] The interests of self-representation may in truth not be separable from the reading or writing of history, even when history appears in far more straightforward guise than it is in René's text; Gabrielle Spiegel has advocated recognition of this relationship, most recently in *The Past as Text: the Theory and Practice of Medieval Historiography* (Baltimore, 1997).

[9] Geraldine Heng, *Empire of Magic: Medieval Romance and the Politics of Cultural Fantasy* (New York, 2003). The claim that René directs the imagination inward is not a denial that actual encounters served this fantasy; the most beautifully illuminated early manuscript of the *Livre du Cuer* depicts the god of Love wearing a tunic decorated on the fringe with Arabic lettering that recognizably reproduces the name of a fifteenth-century Mamluk prince. See Franz Unterkircher, 'Le cœur enluminé' in *Le Cœur d'Amour Épris: reproduction intégrale en fac-similé des miniatures du Codex Vindobonensis 2597 de la Bibliothèque nationale de Vienne*, ed. Marie-Thérèse Gousset, Daniel Poirion, and Franz Unterkircher (Paris, 1981), pp. 81–108, at p. 95.

many a romance hero, Heart must undertake an overseas journey to carry out his mission; his linguistic confusion as he journeys to the isle ruled by Love exemplifies how the depiction of this 'other' realm is recognizable as not very 'other' after all. Heart enjoys a fish dinner en route but queries the strange name of the fish, *validire*, which he discovers is known as a *maquereau*, mackerel, in France (137.1–11, 138.1–12). Here, *maquereau* acts as a pun, since the word is not only the name of a fish but also slang for a panderer, even in contemporary French speech, and *validire*, masquerading here as the foreign speech of distant shores, is an abbreviated form of the French command 'va lui dire' (go talk to her/him) that refers to a messenger; both words designate the sort of go-between useful when arranging to meet a desired person. What purports to be the hero's discovery of strange tongues and cuisines is in truth a guide to the intimate mechanisms of French courtly society.

As René's work lays claim to romance as a vehicle for personal and cultural self-reflection, it is worth taking a closer look at the passages that establish the most dramatic connections between the heroes of romance and René's Heart. As noted above, readers are particularly encouraged to envision Heart according to the model of romance by the explicit comparison with Arthurian knights at the start of Heart's adventures and by the series of arms attributed to named individuals in the passage describing the Hospital of Love, designated as Heart's last resting place when his adventures end. Yet the named comparisons in these passages also reframe the perception of the romance hero according to the vision of the heart, diverging significantly from the way we might expect the hero to look. Although the romance-style structure of the *Livre du Cuer*, like the structure of armour itself, seems fitted to advance militaristic aims, armour's heraldic symbolism turns out to be more valuable here than its function in combat. The seemingly external decoration that makes armour a form of identification plays an integral part in conveying the text's allegorical meaning. Heart's extensively described arming does not ensure him success in his quest and it is impossible for readers to miss this point, as the encircling frames and the central narrative foreshadow this ending early and often. For example, just after recounting how Desire places a halberd named 'pleasure' upon Heart and promises him protection thereby, the narrative declares 'it was not so, for since then oftentimes the Heart was wounded [...] neither protection nor shield availed him that was not damaged' (3.16–19). Rather than this failure of arms differentiating Heart from the Arthurian knights to whose stories his arming is compared, not only Heart but also his Arthurian predecessors are envisioned as conquered in combat within the *Livre du Cuer*. Two Arthurian heroes named at the moment of Heart's arming are also named as the owners of arms hung up in submission at the Hospital of Love, 'un-shielded' in this fashion.

According to the verses that Heart sees under the coats of arms for Lancelot and for Tristan, the conclusion of both of these heroes' stories is their conquest by Love rather than the 'great conquests [...] accomplished to win the Holy Grail' to which the initial comparison had alluded; looking back, it seems no coincidence that neither of these named heroes fully achieves the grail quest in the romances. This alteration in focus from victory to loss is particularly interesting in the case of Lancelot since the text emphasizes his affiliation with René. In addition to Lancelot's name appearing first in the list of Arthurian knights at the opening of Heart's adventures and within the longer armorial series, the core of René's lands, the Anjou valley, is identified as the location of the 'lake' by which Lancelot grew up (275.42).[10] Yet even as it brings this hero closer to René, the *Livre du Cuer* places primary emphasis on the element of Lancelot's story that seems at first glance the least heroic: Lancelot's yielding to passion, described as wounding and defeat.[11] Although the verses under Lancelot's arms initially recount Lancelot's successes in battle, they end with him acknowledging that Love's powerful arrow, striking him through Guenievere, forced him to yield as it drove him 'from prowess to reflection' (180.12), a transformation highlighted in the French text by alliteration on these words ['de proesse a pensee'].

The *Livre du Cuer* challenges our expectations of heroic narrative not only in the pensive culmination of Lancelot's representation but also by the choice of those represented alongside Lancelot. Although Lancelot is the first Arthurian hero named, the list begins with Julius Caesar and concludes with living members of the French court. Like the multiple frameworks presented for the work as a whole, these arms span temporal distance and blur cultural differences. The text claims there are more arms on display than Heart can read and specifically mentions that some arms can be identified by shape as 'Moorish and German ones' (187.2) and that the ancient verses on the wall are written 'in Greek letters, in Moorish letters, in German, Latin, English, Spanish, Lombard, French, Hungarian, Bohemian' as well as unidentified 'other languages' (187.6–8).[12] The list of the particular arms studied by Heart does not include those of Palomides, the Saracen convert of Arthurian legend, or any verses in letters identified as 'Moorish'; nonetheless, like the laudatory mention of Palomides at the start of Heart's adventures, the references to multiple forms and tongues open the possibility that this list could extend beyond the immediate bounds of Christendom and the cultures most commonly claimed as past precedents. More specific distinctions between heroes and anti-heroes drawn according to historic battle-lines are also blurred by the inclusion of the arms of famed opponents among those that are described and by their placement side by side. The series pairs Aeneas and Achilles as well as Troilus and Diomedes, rewriting the narratives of these Greek and Trojan enemies to mirror one another in acknowledging Love as their conqueror.[13] The verses presented for Aeneas and Achilles both claim renown for

---

[10] The episode containing this claim is not found in all manuscripts; it may have been the work of a member of René's circle rather than René's, but it does resemble similar comparisons attested more widely, such as the comparison of the Castle of Love to René's castle of Saumer (236.20–21).

[11] The naming of Guenievere and commemoration of Lancelot's love here stands in direct contrast to the epitaph given for Lancelot in romances such as *La mort le roi artu*. See Emma Campbell, 'Commemoration in *La Mort le Roi Artu*', *Arthurian Literature* 27 (2010), 1–17.

[12] In addition, illegible 'Hebrew letters' are described as appearing under the arms described for King David (160.6–7); René's introduction of his own arms asserts his exceedingly tenuous claim to be 'king of Jerusalem' among other powers (198.1).

[13] The *Livre du Cuer*'s focus on armorial description is reminiscent of the *ekphrasis*, or effort to convey visual artistry through poetic skills, dedicated to the armour of heroes in classical epics, which already memorably associates Homer's Achilles and Virgil's Aeneas. On the possibility for negative as well as positive interpretation of classical and medieval English heraldic ekphrasis, see Alex Mueller, 'The Historiography of the Dragon: Heraldic Violence in the Alliterative *Morte*', *Studies in the Age of Chaucer* 32 (2010), 295–324, especially p. 310, note 38. The fact that the shield of Achilles is described as hung 'much higher than any of the others' could reflect recognition as a literary precedent (167.4–5); Heart himself seems to react with wonder that these arms should appear above those of 'emperors or kings' (167.5). In relation to the subject explored in this volume's first essay, we should also note that

these men and also make specific mention of their travel to the site of the Hospital of Love. René's *Livre du Cuer* does not conceal the rivalry of Diomedes and Troilus in love as well as war yet gives particular emphasis to the resemblance of the two not only in the sets of verses that mention, in each case, the name of the lady Brisiada, but also through the visual similarities and spatial juxtaposition of their arms; the shield of Diomedes is described as 'another made of silver', recalling the first feature attributed to the shield of Troilus, and it is hung so that it is 'facing' that of Troilus (175.2). The question of Lancelot's heroism posed in this text is not readily resolved by the consideration of the armorial depictions surrounding his.

There are certainly medieval precedents for René's commemoration of Arthurian heroes in conjunction with figures from classical and more contemporary medieval histories, but close comparison tends to make the series in the *Livre du Cuer* seem more rather than less unusual. The cross-European tradition of the nine worthies, for example, set Arthur himself in a thematic group of nine heroes selected as exemplary; the number itself stood as a symbol of excellence and the group was usually divided into triads representing the pagan, Jewish, and Christian cultures recognized as powerful in medieval world history. From around 1300, with variation, the group of nine finds representation in romances and chronicles and provided heraldic decoration for medieval halls.[14] At least two of those who appear in René's list were typically members of this group (Julius Caesar, King David). Yet although conjoining the names of Caesar and David as models suggests a resemblance to the tradition of the worthies, other names René included upset the idea that the *Livre du Cuer* series could exemplify ethical virtue. Nero, for example, although declared to be 'the most treacherous and cruel emperor' (156.2), also evidently serves as a model for Heart's form of heroism; his arms are described as almost identical to those of Augustus and his narrative of surrender as Love's prisoner matches the others.

Even comparison with a source cited in the *Livre du Cuer* reveals a significant difference in the pattern of heroism established by the presentation of arms in this passage. Heart is instructed to consider the work of a young clerk of Troyes, recognizable as Achilles Caulier, as a guide to the Hospital of Love. Caulier's poem, *L'Hospital d'Amours (The Hospital of Love)*, was written as a response to Alain Chartier's *Belle Dame Sans Mercy (Beautiful Lady Without Mercy)*, which relates the death of a lover who fails to persuade his lady to grant him her love.[15] In Caulier's poem, another lover who has been rejected by his lady dreams of visiting a hospital ruled by Love, where he beholds a burial place for the noble dead who loved loyally. Tombstone epitaphs for the legendary heroes Tristan and Lancelot and the medieval courtier and poet, John, seneschal of Hainault, are recounted as appearing near a magnificent tomb enclosing both Alain Chartier and the lover from his *Belle Dame* poem. The remains of those excommunicated by Love for deserting or refusing lovers, by

---

Turnus, the later opponent of Aeneas, is not included in this series. Yet the sword that killed Turnus is described as a precious relic that sits on the altar in the hospital's chapel, alongside such items as a crystal bowl filled with the water that drowned Leander and the cup from which Ghismonda drank poison (223.16–18).

[14] See J. Favier, *Un rêve de chevalerie: Les Neuf Preux* (Langeais, 2003).

[15] See Achilles Caulier, *L'Hôpital d'Amour* in *Le cycle de 'La belle dame sans mercy': une anthologie poétique du XVe siècle (BNF MS FR. 1131)*, ed. and trans. David F. Hult and Joan E. McRae (Paris, 2003).

contrast, are seen thrown into a murky pit. Jason, Aeneas, and Briseida are recognizable here along with the merciless beautiful lady of Chartier's poem, also named 'the cruel woman', a reference to the title of another poem Caulier wrote envisioning this character on trial in the court of Love. Situating Chartier and the lover denied mercy beside Lancelot, and picturing the female literary character penned by Chartier and Caulier as sharing a pit with Aeneas, Caulier's poem set René an example of an allegorical reclassification of heroic narratives according to the priorities of love visions.

Although René reproduces much of Caulier's allegorical landscape, he shows more interest in distinguishing the heroes by the kind of power they resign than by their treatment of individual women. Magnificent tombs for Chartier and other love vision poets are described in the *Livre du Cuer* but these tombs appear within the gates of the cemetery, set apart from the armorial series on the gate, and only the pressure exerted by Lady Courtesy manages to draw Heart's attention away from the arms of aristocratic warriors to the tombs of poets (207.1–7). Aeneas is not relegated to the pit – in René's account, none of the bodies in the pit are recognizable – instead, Aeneas is celebrated through armorial display. The names of multiple ladies appear as instruments of Love's power over Aeneas just as in the immediately preceding narrative of Theseus; the shields above these two verse sections are described explicitly as being 'of similar fashion' (165.1–2) although the wear and discoloration ascribed to the arms of Theseus may correspond to the duality of erotic pursuit being more evident in his verses.[16] The verses ascribed to René himself do not bother to assign any specific identity to the female instruments of Love's power over him, instead generally citing both shepherdesses and town dwellers, Italian and French, as forces inciting him to yield his arms (198.1–16).[17] The pattern of the arms on the wall of Love's Cemetery thus reaffirms the importance of class and gender as defining characteristics of the hero even as it suggests that the noble male experience of love constitutes a kind of heroic identity that supersedes the particulars of any affair and the accompanying ethical questions concerning the behaviour the passion promotes and the 'hero' exemplifies.

Not only the ladies that the *Livre du Cuer* lists as the objects of quests, including the Heart's never attained and mostly silent Sweet Mercy, but also the particular victories and kingdoms of those named seem to be mere variant details in contrast to the shared loss of self-mastery that concludes the narrative of each. From the standpoint of the *Livre du Cuer*, heroic narrative is not about the acquisition of power and control but about its loss. Here, the loss of power to the force of love is the essential identifying act of a hero. The idea resonates with certain strands of the medieval ideology of nobility. After all, the line Geoffrey Chaucer uses most frequently in his poetry advertises that 'Pity renneth sone in gentil herte'; even when

---

[16] The verses for Aeneas name Creusa and Lavinia, entirely omitting Dido, the basis of Caulier's characterization of Aeneas as a deserter; the verses for Theseus do name the deserted Ariadne as well as Phedra. For more detailed study of precedent for René's presentation of Aeneas, see Jean-Claude Mühlethaler, 'De la disparition de Didon dans le *Roman du Cuers d'amours espris*: René d'Anjou entre Boccace et Pétrarque ou la difficile récupération d'Enée en France au XVe siècle', in *Pour acquerir honneur et pris: Mélanges de moyen français offerts à Giuseppe Di Stefano*, ed. Maria Colombo Timelli and Claudio Galderisi (Montreal, 2004), pp. 467–482.

[17] On the differing versions of these verses in manuscripts, see *Le Livre du Cœur d'amour épris*, ed. Bouchet, p. 344, footnote 1.

the line's meaning is undermined by its context, the association remains of noble hearts and a susceptibility to emotion.[18] But instead of the hero being empowered by erotic devotion to achieve victory in combat or to reign magnanimously, a scenario played out in many romances, engagement with *eros* is dramatized in the *Livre du Cuer* as the ultimate combat itself, a struggle which the warrior can neither refuse nor win. René replaces the image of the hero as universally triumphant with his extended vision of the hero as universally subject to love. (Of course, René's vision concomitantly demands that those forced to yield to love already have considerable power to resign.) This shift could be called anti-heroic in the sense that, as we have seen, it upsets the notion of the hero as a victor of distinctive ethical and cultural significance, breaking down distinctions between historical opponents as heroes and anti-heroes.

If we turn to examine not how this textual perspective is anti-heroic but rather what looks anti-heroic from the perspective of this text, we discover another way of thinking about the question of what a hero meant to medieval readers. If heroism is defined as conquest by love, then the forces that work against heroism are those that could enable resistance to passion. We noted the nature of Refusal as an exceedingly unattractive ultimate victor over Heart at the start of this essay, but Refusal is not the only or even the most worrisome challenger to heroism as defined by submission to Love.[19] The *Livre du Cuer* indirectly recognizes the potential obstacles posed by reason, epicurean self-love, and old age, weaving their representation into a passage that suggests the actions of Refusal in truth work in concert with Love's power over Heart. The personification of Honour, as he relays to Heart permission from Love to undertake his quest, enjoins Heart not to kill Refusal, a limitation both Heart and his companion Desire recognize as damaging to their quest. Love makes the decision that Refusal must not die in a council from which Heart is excluded and of which readers are given only a summary. The selectively omniscient narrative voice relates parts of the story that frequently lie beyond Heart's perception; for example, it recounts Honour and Desire's speech encouraging those who seek to rescue Heart from the prison of Sadness. In the case of Love's council, however, the narrative instead elaborates on what Heart sees while the council takes place, a series of tapestries in the hall that offer, like the cemetery wall behind the Hospital of Love, a pictorial forecast of Heart's experience. The series of verses on the ten panels of tapestry conclude with one spoken in the voice of Reason, protesting about being

---

[18] For more discussion of 'Chaucer's favorite line', see the textual notes for Chaucer's *Knight's Tale* l. 1761 in *The Riverside Chaucer*, ed. Larry Benson, 3rd edn (Boston, 1987), p. 834. Love's relationship to nobility is of course complicated by the notion of nobility as a quality of birth as well as of virtue. The often cited twelfth-century Latin treatise on love by Andreas Capellanus, most likely produced in the same the court setting as the romances of Chrétien de Troyes, extols love as a noble activity both by claiming love can engender virtue regardless of birth and by specifically excluding peasants from love's influence. New insight into this inherently contradictory text can be found in Kathleen Andersen-Wyman, *Andreas Capellanus on Love? Desire, Seduction, and Subversion in a Twelfth-Century Latin Text* (New York, 2007).

[19] The manuscripts of the *Livre du Cuer* witness a number of different names being considered for this character; *Reffus* (Refusal) and *Discort* (Discord) variably replace the name *Dangier*, which was in the process of changing its meaning, initially indicating dominion or the power to withhold or to harm, later conveying the sense of risk or peril ('danger') once associated with such power. See Florence Bouchet, 'Principes d'édition et de traduction' in René d'Anjou, *Le Livre du Cœur d'amour épris*, ed. Bouchet, pp. 64–79, at 67–68.

shut out of sight and excluded by Love and his company (259.1–11). After summarizing the unreasonable outcome of Love's council and Heart's equally unreasonable response of acceptance, the narrative again envisions where these decisions will lead through describing a set of tapestries, this time belonging to the character of Venus, showing the trapping and misery of many hearts. At this point, a speaker identified as 'Roger Good Times' declares that, as he has seen no heart receives mercy, he plans to withdraw his heart and place it where it will be forgotten; immediately following these verses are another set attributed to a voice named only as 'the Old Man' who acclaims Roger as wise (271, 272). Old, forgotten, barred from sight, worn-out, the characteristic adjectives describing those Love does not entirely dominate are far less inviting than the gorgeous, fascinating, public display of the arms of those Love conquers. The story of Heart challenges us to read carefully, as it not only suggests that the loss of self-mastery to love is the essential component of heroic identity but also questions whether it is rational, prudent, or enjoyable to be a hero on such terms.

René of Anjou was not alone in the project of dreaming up an allegorical hero with a claim to contemporary political representation, even if his project took a unique form. Emperor Maximilian I was the subject and patron of the multiple early sixteenth-century chivalric allegories, *Freydal*, *Weisskunig*, and *Theuerdank*.[20] Edmund Spenser would famously characterize his late sixteenth-century *Faerie Queene* as an endeavour to shadow forth Elizabeth of England. René's ascription of a heroic character to Heart, however, represents a special challenge as a reinvention of heroic narrative. The true subject of medieval romance, as represented in René's book, is not, after all, a singular and solitary hero, nor is it the hero's triumphant subjection of opposing forces or even the glorious worth of the object that may be won through such triumph. Instead, Heart's narrative invites meditation on the emotional vulnerability that seems to constitute the identity shared by René and all the male aristocrats he cared to associate with romance heroes. Rather than instructing readers to remember the power of ancient warriors or foreign realms, the *Livre de Cuer* reveals such instruction to be coded directives for introspection. In crafting such a peculiar heroic narrative to represent himself and his world, René asks his readers not for simple acclamation but for interpretation. Here is a tale chock full of armour, adventure, and famous names of history and legend that celebrates the discomfiture of heroes, making defeat the rationale for a commonalty that persists across the divisions drawn elsewhere according to battle-lines, ethical virtue, language community, the span of history, even the poles of life and death. In a certain sense, the heroic narrative of the *Livre du Cuer* also depends upon the triumph of a *villain*, if we return to the original sense of the word, deriving from the same Latin roots as *village*, meaning a country laborer of low birth, attached to manor or villa as a servant. Low birth is only one of the many repulsive attributes repeatedly ascribed to the victor Refusal. Has the assignment of leading roles to love vision personifications destroyed the coherence of heroic romance? Or has this intermixture of genres merely made more visible a kind of instability inherent in any definition of the

---

[20] For more information and gorgeous reproduction of the last, the only completed work, see Stephan Füssel, *The Theuerdank of 1517: Emperor Maximilian and the Media of his Day*, 2 vols (Cologne, 2003).

medieval hero? Certainly, as the essays of this volume suggest, heroic narrative is rarely the simple matter it might seem.

The *Livre du Cuer* questions the meaning of the hero not only through framing this figure in the realm of allegory, but also by insisting on the hero's relation to actual lived experience. René advanced the resemblance between literature and life through his evident concern with the disposition of his physical as well as symbolic heart. In a role similar to that René's *Livre du Cuer* ascribes to Lady Pity, René's widow Joan of Laval ensured that René's heart found a requested resting place apart from his body after death: René's last testament desired his body to be buried in Angers, his heart specifically and separately in the chapel of Saint Bernard, and, as he died in Aix-in-Provence, Joan had to circumvent local opposition to the movement of his remains.[21] In a certain sense, the life of René of Anjou as well as his characterization of his Heart could be read as the story of a magnificent loser. His love of noble display, in literature as well as in tournament and in theatre, won him lasting remembrance as *le bon roi René* (the good king René).[22] But his military losses were more numerous than his successes and, like the character Heart, René found the will of his own lord perhaps the greatest threat to his power. The control of Anjou passed into the possession of the rapacious French crown before René's own death, and the title of the duchy soon after. Perhaps René would have thought it fitting if the history and stories of his life, like his account of Lancelot's story in the *Livre du Cuer*, disconcert our notion of the medieval hero and turns our attention 'from prowess to reflection'.

---

[21] More information on the memorials René planned for himself in the context of his compositions can be found in two classic essays by Daniel Poirion: 'L'allégorie dans le *Livre du Cuer d'Amours espris*, de René d'Anjou', *Travaux de linguistique et de literature* 9 (1971), 51–64 at pp. 63–64, and 'Le cœur du René d'Anjou' (B3), *Les Angevins de la literature, Colloque d'Angers, 14–16 décembre 1978* (Angers, 1979), pp. 48–62, at pp. 48–49.

[22] See N. Coulet, Alice Planche, and F. Robin, *Le roi René: Le prince, le mécène, l'écrivain, le mythe* (Aix-en-Provence, 1982).

Part II
Character-Types

11

Crusaders

ROBERT ALLEN ROUSE

Sometime between March and November 1481, William Caxton printed *Godfrey de Bouillon or the Siege and Conquest of Jerusalem*. Published some 190 years after the fall of Acre and the destruction of the last crusader state in the Levant, this text highlights the enduring attraction of crusade narratives – and of the crusader heroes contained within them – for late-fifteenth-century English society.[1] As the first English translation of the First Crusade portions of William of Tyre's *Historia rerum in partibus transmarinis gestarum*, the production of the text has been interpreted as the product of Caxton's canny awareness of the reading tastes of the English book-buying public.[2] At the heart of the marketability of *Godfrey* as a text – and of Godfrey as a hero – lies his reputation as the European crusading hero *par excellence*. Despite the existence of other more specifically English crusader-narratives, such as that of Richard the Lionheart, Godfrey's appeal as a universal exemplar of a hero of unified Christendom seems to have won out. Celebrated in chronicle accounts and the legendary *Chanson d'Antioche* and the *Chanson de Jerusalem*, and elevated to the ranks of the nine worthies, Godfrey represents the epitome of a heroic model that takes on many forms in the literature and culture of medieval Europe. The late-medieval renown of Godfrey is emblematic of the long-held appeal of crusading figures in the medieval popular mind. From the late eleventh-century *Chanson de Roland* through to Caxton's *Godfrey*, we find a dizzying array of heroic crusaders brought to life within chronicle, romance and other forms of medieval narrative. Faced with this range of possible heroic figures, Caxton's decision to print *Godfrey* rather than a romance of one of the English crusade-heroes demands consideration. I would suggest that at least part of the explanation for the selection of *Godfrey* instead of insular crusade-text lies in the way in which crusade heroes were represented in England during the later Middle Ages.

While Caxton's *Godfrey* recalls the glories of the successful First Crusade for the late fifteenth-century reader, not all English crusade-romance was so adulatory in its

---

[1] I use the term 'Crusader' with a full awareness of its anachronistic nature: the participants of the crusades considered themselves to be *peregrini* (pilgrims), and it was not until the late twelfth century that the term *crucesignati* was used. For a discussion of this see Michael Markowski, '*Crucesignatus*: its Origins and Early Usage', *Journal of Medieval History* 10 (1984), 157–65, at p. 158.

[2] Christopher Tyerman, *England and the Crusades: 1095–1588* (Chicago, 1998), p. 305.

depiction of crusaders. The corpus of crusade-romances produced in England in the century following the end of the crusades – the fall of Acre in 1291 – are of a more critical mood, forming part of what Christopher Tyerman has coined 'recovery literature'.[3] Tyerman describes this textual effusion as a 'mountain of written advice thrown up in the two centuries after 1291 consistently associating the recovery of the Holy Land or the defence of the church with personal redemption, honour and the resolution of Europe's internal political, social and religious problems'.[4] Contributing to the inward turn of this post-crusade *Zeitgeist*, crusade-romances provided a vehicle for the expression of the frustrated desire for crusade in the fourteenth century, and as such they dwell not only on the heroic and salvational aspects of crusade, but also on the pitfalls and failures of the enterprise. While abortive attempts to resurrect the crusades as a practical project were not infrequent during this period – in England as well as in other parts of Europe – literary fantasies were the only form in which any such endeavour came to successful fruition.

Geraldine Heng has argued that the rise of romance in Western European literary culture is concomitant with the period of the crusades, romance acting as a vehicle for the recounting and the glorifying of crusading heroes, both real and imaginary.[5] Within England we find circulating Anglo-Norman narratives such as *Gui de Warewic*, *Boeve de Hamtoune*, and insular versions of the Charlemagne cycle, including of course the *Chanson de Roland*. Similarly, the end of the crusades engendered its own characteristic body of romance. Post-1291 we find such Middle English narratives as *Richard Coer de Lyon*, *Guy of Warwick*, *Bevis of Hampton*, *Sir Gowther*, and *Sir Isumbras* – amongst others – which stand testament to the fevered production of crusade fantasies in post-crusade medieval England. There is also good reason to include English reworkings of the Charlemagne romances such as *The Sultan of Babylon* and the *Siege of Milan* as part of this body of 'recovery' romance, as these narratives present an ideological archaeology of crusading zeal, extending the conflict with the Muslim East back into the European past.[6] My interest here is in how these romances mediate both the continued desire for crusade *and* the impact of the loss of Acre and the legacy of failure that this event embodied. In addressing the romances of the fourteenth century, we should consider this cultural mood in terms of both the production and the reception of romance, acknowledging the contextual and contemporal specificity of those romances that are translated and expanded from Anglo-Norman and French antecedents.

In *Richard Coer de Lyon* we find narrated a particularly English view of the Third Crusade.[7] The powerful image of the cannibal King Richard has provided fecund ground for critical engagement in recent years. The romance, existing in two main variants (A and B), tells the story of Richard's journey to the Holy Land by way of

---

[3] Tyerman, *God's War: a New History of the Crusades* (London, 2006), p. 827.
[4] Tyerman, *God's War*, p. 827.
[5] Geraldine Heng, *Empire of Magic: Medieval Romance and the Politics of Cultural Fantasy* (New York, 2003), p. 6.
[6] Robert Warm, 'Identity, Narrative and Participation: Defining a Context for the Middle English Charlemagne Romances', in *Tradition and Transformation in Medieval Romance*, ed. Rosalind Field (Cambridge, 1999), pp. 87–100.
[7] *Richard Coer de Lyon. Der Mittelenglische Versroman* Richard Löwenherz, ed. Karl Brunner (Vienna, 1913).

Sicily and Cyprus, eventually arriving at Acre where he proceeds to break the seven-year-old siege. The romance is marked by a palpable sense of national spirit, with the virtuous Englishness of Richard and his men contrasted against both the Saracens and – importantly – the perfidy of his erstwhile allies, especially the French King Phillip.[8] The romance even goes so far as assigning the blame for the loss of *Surri* – in the romance literally referring to those lands lost prior to the Third Crusade, but with obvious wider connotations of territorial loss in the post-1291 era – to the ineptitude of the French nobility. Despite the romance casting an accusatory gaze upon the French, much of the recent critical work on it has focussed on one strange and disturbing episode: the cannibalistic consumption of the Saracen dead by King Richard himself. This story, which appears in different forms in the various surviving versions of the romance, can be summarized thus: Richard, having fallen ill upon his arrival at the siege of Acre, yearns for pork as a curative. His men, finding that no pork is available to serve to their king, hit upon an ingenious solution, cooking, carving and serving up the body of a recently-deceased Saracen. The meal restores the king to boisterous health, after which he throws himself back into battle with the Saracens. On his return from the battle, Richard demands to be brought the head of the beast upon which he feasted, as he wishes to restore his energies once more. This provokes no small consternation in the royal kitchen, but eventually the king is presented with the grinning head of the black Saracen. Richard's response is one of high amusement: he enthuses once more as to the nutritious qualities of the meal, and states that never again will the crusaders go hungry while on campaign in the Holy Land, not while there is such a plentiful supply of meat on offer.[9]

Heng, in a reading of the romance in terms of the fraught medieval discourses of race and nation, interprets this episode as a nationalistic joke that acts as a metaphor for the romance's 'aggressive territorial ambitions, the consumption and discipline of alien communities, and the nascent, overarching impulse toward the formation of the medieval nation'.[10] Nicola McDonald likewise reads the episode as participating in the poetics of identity formation, arguing that 'Richard's consumption of the Saracen, constructed as both an alimentary necessity and an act of sacral devotion, provides the romance audience with a convenient focus for its own fantasies of religious supremacy, political dominion, nationalism and a good meal.'[11] Both Heng and McDonald emphasize the way in which this crusade narrative works to construct identities, both Christian and English, by reading this episode of the ingestion of the racial and religious *other* as working to rearticulate and reinforce notions of Christian English superiority. However, prioritizing such a reading of the episode necessarily minimizes the more problematic aspects of an English king engaging in cannibalism. Heather Blurton, contextualizing Richard's dietary ingenuity against the wider history

[8] For a detailed discussion see Geraldine Barnes, *Counsel and Strategy in Middle English Romance* (Cambridge, 1993), pp. 108–11.
[9] A more extensive plot summary can be found in Geraldine Heng, 'The Romance of England: *Richard Coer de Lyon*, Saracens, Jews, and the Politics of Race and Nation', in *The Postcolonial Middle Ages*, ed. Jeffery Jerome Cohen (New York, 2001), pp. 135–71, at p. 136.
[10] Heng, 'The Romance of England', p. 137.
[11] Nicola McDonald, 'Eating People and the Alimentary Logic of Richard Cœur de Lion', in *Pulp Fictions of Medieval England: Essays in Popular Romance*, ed. Nicola McDonald (Manchester, 2004), pp. 124–50, at p. 143.

of cannibalism in medieval literature, notes that cannibalism is more typically associated with the Saracens, by way of the monstrous races tradition.[12] As a common literary and historiographical technique of *othering*, the casting of the body of the Saracen as cannibalistic makes it 'ethically monstrous in order to legitimate violence against it'.[13] When this trope is transferred to the body of the English King Richard, perversely transforming the vice into a virtue, a contradiction between the text's nationalistic *othering* of the French – as treacherous, as inept – and the representation of the English themselves becomes clear. Alan Ambrisco wryly observes that '[t]he English are cannibalistic and barbaric; the French, to their deep discredit, are neither'.[14] While this text may work, as McDonald and Heng rightly suggest, to articulate a developing sense of English identity, it does so at the cost of unified Christian – and crusader – unity. Blurton concludes her analysis by posing that such a reading 'suggests that the English have replaced the Muslim threat, and that, on the international scene, the English are the new ones to watch'.[15] The implications of Blurton's reading of Richard's cannibalism are damning when read as a retrospective critique of the crusading period: the French and the English did not work together, pointing towards the commonly-held belief that the loss of the Holy Land was due primarily to Christian infighting and disunity. *Richard Coer de Lyon* is a romance that maps the Anglo-French animosity of the fourteenth century back onto the period of the crusades, presenting Richard's cannibalism as a trope that dismembers and consumes not just the literal body of the Saracen, but more importantly denotes the cannibalistic autophagy of Christendom itself as it was riven by competing and contradictory national interests.[16]

While *Richard Coer de Lyon* celebrates an historical English crusader-king, more characteristic of English post-crusade romance are the narratives of such pseudo-historical romances as *Guy of Warwick*.[17] Representative of a developing mode of pious or penitential romance, this narrative presents a model of chivalric behaviour that merges the superlative knighthood of earlier romance with the Christian discipline of the ideal crusading knight. Guy of Warwick first appears in the early thirteenth-century Anglo-Norman *Gui de Warewic*.[18] Guy, a romance hero who transcends the romance genre, appears as the legendary forebear of the powerful earls of Warwick and – in some later texts – even replaces Godfrey as one of the nine worthies.[19] Read as a 'recovery literature' romance, the Middle English *Guy of Warwick* can be seen to provide a critique of the practice of western chivalry, a model

---

[12] Heather Blurton, *Cannibalism in High Medieval English Literature* (New York, 2007), p. 108.
[13] Blurton, p. 114.
[14] Alan Ambrisco, 'Cannibalism and Cultural Encounters in *Richard Coeur de Lion*', *Journal of Medieval and Early Modern Studies* 29.3 (1999), 501–28, at p. 518.
[15] Blurton p. 131.
[16] Tyerman, *God's War*, pp. 906–11.
[17] For the purposes of this essay I will refer to *The Romance of Guy of Warwick, Edited from the Auchinleck MS. in the Advocates' Library, Edinburgh and from MS. 107 in Caius College, Cambridge*, ed. J. Zupitza EETS ES 42, 49, 59 (1883, 1887, 1891; repr. in 1 vol., Oxford, 1966).
[18] *Gui de Warewic*, ed. Alfred Ewert (Paris, 1932).
[19] Siân Echard, 'Of Dragons and Saracens: Guy and Bevis in Early Print Illustration', in *Guy of Warwick: Icon and Ancestor*, ed. Alison Wiggins and Rosalind Field (Cambridge, 2007), pp. 154–68, at p. 164.

of potential reform, and a cautionary commentary upon the territorial goals of crusading activity. These concerns can be seen in three key narrative episodes: Guy's defence of Constantinople (lines 2801–4490); his epiphany as to his motivations for chivalric endeavour (st. 21:1–34:12); and the story of the earl of Durras (st. 50:1–54:12). These three textual moments all share a concern with the legitimate deployment of violence, a common issue in criticism of both chivalric and crusade activity.

The legitimate use of violence is a central concern of much chivalric literature. The ideal knight must discipline both the body and his actions, deploying violence in a controlled and directed manner. If he does not, he becomes that which he abhors: the monstrous figure of indiscipline, the emblematic giant of romance.[20] Violence, of course, is near ubiquitous in romance: '[f]or the Middle Ages and its vernacular cultures, violence is every bit as pervasive a topos as love. Like courtly love, violence tends to be stipulated as a self-evident feature of medieval culture.'[21] For secular romance heroes, the governance of violence is primarily a matter of chivalric honour and courtesy, with communal codes such as the Arthurian Pentecost oath providing chivalric norms regarding to whom and in what manner violence was appropriate. These codes of chivalric behaviour differ across texts and contexts, but maintain an investment in what has been termed the chivalric economy of shame.[22]

Violence is an even more fraught concept when considered within the context of crusade. While crusades are by their very nature an expression of violence, they were also deemed to be a Christian pilgrimage, and as such come into conflict with important Christian tenets opposing violence. This contradiction had been the subject of much debate ever since Christianity was adopted by Constantine in 312 and the Edict of Milan declared the following year. Now a state religion in all but name, Christianity had to both permit and eventually legitimate violence done in its name. Such issues led to the development – over time – of the Christian concept of the Just War. Frederick Russell, in *The Just War in the Middle Ages*, '[c]harts a progressive movement among theologians and legalists to build a theoretical base for the concept of the "just war", a movement that gains momentum with St. Augustine and Gratian and culminates in the work of St. Thomas Aquinas'.[23] This concept was employed during the crusade period to justify both the plenary indulgences promising salvation to those who fell on crusade, and the formation of the militant religious orders such as the Knights Templar, the Hospitallers, and others. Bernard of Clairvaux writes that '[w]hen he strikes he does service to Christ… Surely, if he kills an evil-doer, he is not a man-killer, but, if I may so put it, an evil-killer.'[24]

---

[20] On the use of the giant as the antithesis of the chivalric knight, see Jeffrey Jerome Cohen, *On Giants: Sex, Monsters, and the Middle Ages* (Minneapolis, 1999).

[21] Siegfried R. Christoph, 'Violence Stylized', in *Violence in Medieval Courtly Literature: A Casebook*, ed. Albrecht Classen (London, 2004), pp. 115–25, at p. 115.

[22] Elizabeth Archibald, 'Beginnings: *The Tale of King Arthur* and *The Tale of King Arthur and the Emperor Lucius*', in *A Companion to Malory*, ed. Elizabeth Archibald and A.S.G. Edwards (Cambridge, 1996), pp. 133–52, at p. 81.

[23] Nancy B. Block, 'Violence in *La Queste del Saint Graal* and *La Morte le roi Artu* (Yale 229)', in *Violence in Medieval Courtly Literature*, pp. 151–67, at p. 156.

[24] *In Praise of the New Knighthood: A Treatise on the Knights Templar and the Holy Places of Jerusalem*, trans. M. Conrad Greenia (Kalamazoo, MI, 2000), p. 39.

Violence, then, was to be understood in relation to its victims. Violence deployed upon evil–doers, such as Saracens and other non-Christians, was seen as legitimate in the eyes of God, and thus of the Church. This attitude towards violence was not only predicated upon a theological context, but also upon the pragmatics of Christian-Pagan interaction, as can be seen from the following passage from Jean de Joinville's *Life of Saint Louis*. Joinville, King Louis IX's companion on the Seventh Crusade (1248–54), relates a story that Louis once told of a meeting of Christian clergy and Jews at the monastery at Cluny. First to speak in this meeting was an aged knight, who asked the most learned Rabbi amongst the Jews whether he believed that the Virgin Mary was the Mother of God? The Jew denied this, and the knight's response was to attack the Rabbi with his crutch, sorely wounding him and putting the Jews to flight:

> The abbot went up to the knight and told him he had acted most unwisely. The knight retorted that the abbot had been guilty of even greater folly in calling people together for such a conference, because there were many good Christians there who, before such a discussion ended, would have gone away with doubts about their own religion through not fully understanding the Jews. 'So I tell you,' said the king, 'that no one, unless he is an expert theologian, should venture to argue with these people. But a layman, whenever he hears the Christian religion abused, should not attempt to defend its tenets, except with his sword, and that he should thrust into the scoundrel's belly, as far as it will enter.'[25]

While this violent anecdote may seem like an expression of the fragility of Christian faith, it makes the point that the suitability of discourse with the religious *other* must be understood within the context of audience. A learned theologian – such as the abbot – may safely debate with the heathen and unorthodox, but a knight or other layman puts their faith at risk in doing so, and should instead respond with violent opposition. One might reasonably extend this not only to direct spoken interaction, but also to the audience of texts. Such a muscular approach to the defense of Christianity allies itself well with the romance enjoyment of violence, providing an underpinning for the deployment of violence against the Saracen body within English crusade romance. While violence lies at the heart of performance of crusade-heroism, the English crusade romances of the fourteenth century express the common 'recovery literature' concern with the legitimate deployment of this violence. Not only are chivalric heroes admonished to fight against the Saracens rather than amongst themselves, but they are also cautioned as to the correct motivations and circumstances that should lie behind such conflict.

So how does the discourse on the legitimate use of violence manifest itself in *Guy of Warwick*? The first two narrative moments – the defence of Constantinople and Guy's epiphany – have been discussed in length elsewhere, but for the purposes of my argument here it is important to note the way in which they provide a

---

[25] Jean de Joinville, 'The Life of Saint Louis', in *Chronicles of the Crusades*, trans. M.R.B. Shaw (London, 1963), p. 175.

commentary upon the legitimate use of chivalric violence in the text.[26] Guy's defence of Constantinople operates in the narrative as the apex of the development of his secular reputation as Europe's superlative knight.[27] Imbedded in this episode, however, are a number of subversive – if not outright condemnatory – readings. If one examines the events that lead up to Guy's journey to Constantinople, one is struck by the fact that it is not a love of Christ, or even of his fellow Christians, that motivates Guy to fight the Saracens. Rather, it is the complaints of a group of displaced merchants who complain that their – and by extension Western Europe's – access to luxury Eastern commodities has been interdicted by the Saracen threat. Guy can be read in this passage as being motivated by either Western mercantile interest, or by a desire for secular chivalric reputation, as indicated by the comments of his companion Herhaud, who wryly notes that 'y graunt it be/ Miche worþschipe it worþ to þe' (lines 2855–56).[28] As a critique of crusading practice this may seem somewhat slight, but when the suggestive nature of Guy's motivations for his 'crusade' against the Saracens at Constantinople is contextualized in terms of the events of the Fourth Crusade, a critical reading becomes more evident. While the choice of Constantinople as the site of Guy's confrontation with the Saracen is one that is geographically appropriate, it is one that is historically problematic, given the legacy of the sack of the city in 1204 during the Fourth Crusade. Rebecca Wilcox has argued that Guy's defence of Constantinople, and more importantly his refusal to marry Ernis's daughter Clarice, is emblematic of a narrative that seeks to elide the historical memory of the conquest and sack of Constantinople by the Western crusaders during the Fourth Crusade.[29] In contrast, however, Geraldine Heng views such romance refiguring of crusade history not as acts of elision, but rather as narratives that emphasize the discourse of empire and conquest that is implicit within crusade.[30] However, in a reading of *Guy of Warwick* in the context of 'recovery literature', a third possible interpretation arises: that the narrative episode is reflecting critically upon Guy's *motivations* for crusade. Carol Heffernan provides a revealing context for the episode in her comments on the mercantile motivation for the historical conquest in 1204. She writes that

> [b]efore the conquest of Constantinople in 1204, the Byzantine Emperor, Manuel Comnenus, ordered the arrest and imprisonment of Venetians in the empire and the confiscation of their property on March 12, 1171. It is frequently maintained that capitalistic greed and a desire for revenge led Venetians to take the cross on the Fourth Crusade that led to the 1204 conquest of Constantinople. Scholars have long argued that the events of 1171 explain the conquest of Constantinople.[31]

---

[26] For a discussion of these episodes see Robert Allen Rouse, 'An Exemplary Life: Guy of Warwick as Medieval Culture Hero', in *Guy of Warwick: Icon and Ancestor*, pp. 94–109.
[27] Rouse, p. 101.
[28] Rouse, p. 99.
[29] Rebecca Wilcox, 'Romancing the East: Greeks and Saracens in *Guy of Warwick*', in McDonald, *Pulp Fictions*, pp. 217–40, at p. 222.
[30] Heng, *Empire of Magic*, pp. 153–54.
[31] Carol F. Heffernan, *The Orient in Chaucer and Medieval Romance* (Cambridge, 2003), p. 21.

Such criticism of the Fourth Crusade is not restricted to modern historians, with the Venetian misdirection of the crusade being a common point of contention in contemporary accounts such as Geoffrey de Villehardouin's *Chronicle*.[32]

Such a reading of implied criticism of a secular motivation for conflict with the Saracens is supported internally in the case of *Guy of Warwick* by the episode in which Guy receives an epiphany about his past life and deeds. Soon after having married Felice, the love interest of the first half of the romance, Guy undergoes an epiphany that alters the course of the romance. Late one summer's evening, walking upon the battlements of a tower in Warwick castle, Guy is taken aback by the vastness of the heavens. Falling into a reverie, he reflects upon the life that he has led thus far, and upon his motivations in carrying out his chivalric deeds. Turning his thoughts to Christ, Guy realizes that 'For Iesu loue, our saueour,/ Neuer no dede he gode./ Mani man he hadde slayn wiþ wrong' (st. 21:8–10). Guy's revelation – that he has performed deeds of arms solely for earthly motivations – can be read here as a critique of his chivalric career to date, including the prominent episode of 'crusading' against the Saracens at Constantinople. Guy recognizes that his motivation has been misdirected, and it is this realization that acts as the catalyst for his transformation from secular chivalric hero into an *exemplum* of the *miles Christi*. His former secular motivation is transformed into his love for Christ: 'For his loue ichil now wende/ Barfot to mi liues ende,/ Mine sinnes for to bete' (st. 26:4–6).

Following this moment Guy embarks on a pilgrimage, which like that of the *peregrini* of the First Crusade is characterized by regular bloody conflict with the Saracens. While the majority of the second narrative movement presents the audience with a legitimate deployment of violence against the enemies of Christ, even here the romance does not avoid admonitory commentary upon crusading practice. After setting out on his new path, Guy travels first to Jerusalem and Bethlehem, before eventually arriving in Antioch, where he encounters Jonas, the Christian earl of Durras. Here Jonas tells Guy a long tale of misfortune, which has resulted in him being sent to search for Guy, so that the latter can champion the Saracen king Triamour in a judicial combat. Jonas narrates how he and his sons bravely defended Jerusalem from a Saracen attack: 'Ich & mi sones, wiþouten lesing,/ Out of þat lond we driuen þe king,/ And his men yaf dedli wounde' (st. 51:7–9). Then, however, they made the mistake of following the Saracens back into their own lands, where the population rises in support of their king: 'Þan dede we wel-gret foly:/ We suwed him wiþ maistrie/ Into his owhen lond./ Into Alisaundre þai fleye owy:/ Þe cuntre ros vp wiþ a cri,/ To help her king anhond' (st. 52:1–6). This episode suggests that Jonas and his sons have over-stepped the legitimate bounds of crusade in turning their warfare from a defensive action into an offensive one. The legitimate deployment of crusade violence here seems directed towards a defence of Jerusalem, as opposed to the 'wel-gret foly' of invading the Saracen's 'owhen lond' of Alexandria. Read against the context of the later crusades – often, like the ill-fated Seventh Crusade, directed against Alexandria in an attempt to break the economic stranglehold of the Mamluk rulers of Egypt – this episode contains an explicit criticism about the geographical

---

[32] Geoffrey de Villehardouin, '*Chronicle of the Fourth Crusade*', in *Chronicles of the Crusades*, trans. Shaw.

focus of crusade. To seek to conquer or defend Jerusalem is a legitimate aim of crusade; to invade Alexandria is not.

While Guy's narrative contains a certain degree of corrective commentary, he is far from embodying the figure of the fallen knight, but rather stands as one who redirects himself towards the martial service of God after coming to a self-realization of his motivational misdirection. In contrast to the rather mild chastising of the Guy romance, later Middle English crusade romance takes on a more self-evidently penitential quality, casting the life of the crusading knight as a primarily redemptive practice. In the late fourteenth-century romance of *Sir Gowther*, we find a clear embodiment of the difference between legitimate and misdirected violence.[33] The story of Gowther, born the prodigal son of a devil,[34] is one that narrates a clear distinction between legitimate and illegitimate violence. Engendered upon his mother by an incubus in the seeming form of her husband, Gowther slays wet-nurses as a child and once he comes of age becomes the terrifying embodiment of medieval fears of unrestrained hyper-masculine knightly power: raping nuns and maidens, slaying monks and burning churches. At the very nadir of his reputation, the young Gowther is confronted by an elderly earl, who accuses him of being 'sum fendys son' (line 209).[35] Enraged by the accusation, Gowther confronts his mother and extracts from her the fearful truth of his lineage: 'In owre orcharde apon a day/ A fende gat the thare,/ As lyke my lorde as he myght be,/ Undurneyth a cheston tre' (lines 230–33). Faced with this damning revelation, Gowther cries to God for mercy, and heads forthwith towards Rome to seek penance and absolution for his violent deeds.

The penance that is placed upon Gowther by the Pope is one that degrades him to the level of an animal, a suitable commentary on the nature of the violence that he has performed:

> Wherser thu travellys, be northe or soth
> Thu eyt no meyt bot that thu revus of howndus mothe
> Cum thy body within;
> Ne no worde speke for evyll ne gud,
> Or thu reyde tokyn have fro God,
> That forgyfyn is thi syn. (*Sir Gowther*, lines 295–300)

Mute and reduced performatively to the status of a dog, Gowther leaves Rome and travels to 'anodur far cuntré' (line 308) where he finds a place as a court fool in the castle of an emperor. While the Pope has explicitly stated that his redemption shall be earned through his abjection as a man-dog, the narrative soon presents Gowther with another tried and trusted method of salvation for a knight: armed conflict with the Saracen *other*. Soon after Gowther arrives at this court, the emperor receives a messenger from the sultan demanding his mute daughter in marriage, at pain of war

---

[33] While *Sir Gowther* is preserved in two late fifteenth-century manuscripts (British Library Royal MS 17.B.43 and National Library of Scotland MS Advocates 19.3.19), the composition of the romance has been dated to c. 1400 by Alcuin Blamires ('The Twin Demons of Aristocratic Society in *Sir Gowther*', in McDonald, *Pulp Fictions*, pp. 45–63, at p. 45).

[34] On the significance of this motif, see Neil Cartlidge's chapter, below, cap. 14.

[35] *Sir Gowther*, in *The Middle English Breton Lays*, ed. Anne Laskaya and Eve Salisbury (Kalamazoo, MI, 1995).

if he declines. Refusing to marry his daughter to a 'hethon hownde' (line 392), the emperor prepares for battle. This situation now presents Gowther with a heaven-sent opportunity to expedite his redemption. Praying to God for arms and armour, Gowther is divinely supplied with arms and a steed, and proceeds to fight anonymously against the Saracens – for three days in succession – ultimately slaying the sultan in single combat and receiving his hard-won 'tokyn [...] fro God' (line 299), in the form of the miraculous healing of the emperor's daughter's mutism.

Violence is the sinful manifestation of Gowther's devilish nature, but violence also acts as the means of his redemption. The message of the romance is that violence directed against the legitimate body of the Saracen *other* is the true goal of the Christian knight, leading to both earthly and heavenly reward. Read in the light of Tyerman's notion of 'recovery literature', *Sir Gowther* may be understood as a call for chivalric violence to be redirected outside of Christendom, once again critiquing the internal dissent that was commonly held to be the cause of the loss of the Holy Land. Both *Guy of Warwick* and *Sir Gowther* present their audiences with protagonists in need of correction. Legitimate chivalric violence – directed against the Saracen in the right time and place – becomes a penitential salve for their past misdeeds, linking internal salvation with external crusade.

The loss of Acre in 1291 had a profound impact on the culture and literature of Western Europe. As the culminating moment of some two centuries of military failure, the loss proved a deep wound to the collective Christian imagination. Gone were the great hopes of the early years of the crusading period and Christendom was left to face the undeniable fact that the Islamic foe had triumphed, depriving the West of both political control and spiritual access to the geographical heart of the Christian faith. Jerusalem, so medieval notions of geography held, was the centre of the world, the prime stage of biblical history and the arena of Christian salvation. What had the West done to deserve this defeat? Why had their God abandoned them? Such questions became a communal preoccupation during the decades following the fall of Acre, with meditations on the West's need for penitence finding expression in a wide range of historiographical and literary forms. In that fourteenth-century bestseller *The Travels of Sir John Mandeville* we find an expansive account of the reasons that were thought to underlie the failure of the crusades. Mandeville, narrating his time in Egypt, recounts a conversation with his employer, the sultan. After describing the sinful state of Christendom – the general lack of piety, the infighting amongst Christian Princes and the unreformed state of the clergy – the sultan goes on to identify the cancer at the heart of Christendom:

> Certainly it is because of your sinfulness that you have lost all this land which we now hold and keep. Because of your evil living and your sin and not because of our strength God has given it into our hands. And we well know that when you serve your God properly and serve Him with good works, no man shall be able to stand against you. We know too by our prophecies that the Christians shall recover this land again in the time to come, when you

serve your God well and devoutly. But as long as you live as you do in wickedness and sin, we have no fear of you; for your God will not help you.[36]

Mandeville, which occupies an important place in Tyerman's body of 'recovery literature', voices the lack that lies at the heart of the penitential mood of the crusade romances discussed above. In a similar mode to penitential romances such as *Guy of Warwick* and *Sir Gowther*, *Mandeville* calls for internal reform, cohesion, and a refocusing of Christian martial endeavour outwards towards the true goal of Crusade. Both chastising and hopeful, *Mandeville* and the romances highlight both the problem and the solution to the problem, pointing towards a prophesied future victory over the Saracen foes.

Caxton, seeking in the late fifteenth century a crusade hero who was the unequivocal embodiment of crusade heroism, seems to have found the English romances lacking in such an exemplar. While versions of *Guy of Warwick* were printed during the sixteenth-century, Caxton turned first to a less problematic crusade hero in the form of Godfrey. Godfrey's story is the story of the First Crusade, a crusade that was unambiguously a success, leading to the capture of Jerusalem and the establishment of the crusader states of Outremer. From the perspective of post-1291 Christendom, the history of the crusades was a slow and violent decline from this early high point, characterized by the fragmentation of Christian unity and the loss of the original motivation and zeal of the early crusaders. This was, of course, largely a fiction – the motivations of the participants of the First Crusade were as varied as those of later crusaders – but the fiction was a useful one to explain the decline in the fortunes of the crusading enterprise. The depictions of the problematic heroes of *Richard Coer de Lyon*, *Guy of Warwick* and *Sir Gowther* participate in the articulation of this cultural fiction and of the ongoing cultural trauma of the loss of the Holy Land.

---

[36] *The Travels of Sir John Mandeville*, trans. C.W.R.D. Moseley (London, 1983), p. 108.

12

Saracens[*]

Siobhain Bly Calkin

Although scholars often disagree about what defines a medieval romance, most agree that romances share a concern with heroic exemplarity, be it chivalric, religious, or moral. Yin Liu, for example, writes:

> these texts are about exemplarity. The protagonist [...] is unfailingly described as the best knight of the world, or the most beautiful woman; the knight's personal armor is always the best ever made, his horse the strongest, his battles the most spectacular; the protagonist's hardships are inevitably the worst ever suffered.[1]

This emphasis on exemplarity, however, may blind readers to the complexity of the characterization of some romance protagonists and their antagonists. Sometimes the heroes of medieval romance are not nearly as admirable as the textual celebration of their victories implies, and sometimes the hero's enemies are not nearly as vile as their discomfiture implies. Indeed, the antagonists in many romances are depicted in ways that call into question the exemplarity of the heroes who fight them. This essay explores the extent to which Saracen knights in Middle English romances cast a critical light on the Christian heroes they encounter, and what such criticism might imply about the nature of the heroic behaviour depicted.[2] Admittedly, many of the

---

[*] Portions of this essay were first presented at the annual meeting of the Canadian Society of Medievalists, Carleton University, Ottawa, May 23–26, 2009. I thank my colleagues there for their discussion and suggestions. Research for this article was funded by a grant from the Social Sciences and Humanities Research Council of Canada.

[1] Yin Liu, 'Middle English Romance as Prototype Genre', *Chaucer Review* 40 (2006), 335–53, p. 347. For other comments on romance and exemplarity, see Dieter Mehl, *The Middle English Romances of the Thirteenth and Fourteenth Centuries* (London, 1968), pp. 253–54; Susan Crane Dannenbaum, 'Guy of Warwick and the Question of Exemplary Romance', *Genre* 17 (1984), 351–374, p. 368; Andrea Hopkins, *The Sinful Knights: A Study of Middle English Penitential Romance* (Oxford, 1990), pp. 2, 7, 31.

[2] No essay could discuss Saracens in all the European romance traditions. Since this is an English-language collection of essays, I have focussed on English-language romances. Because of space constraints and the collection's focus, this essay discusses only Saracen knights, as opposed to Saracen women. For discussion of the fascinating roles played by Saracen women in medieval romances, and their interactions with heroes, see Jacqueline De Weever, *Sheba's Daughters: Whitening and Demonizing the Saracen Woman in Medieval French Epic* (New York, 1998); Geraldine Heng, *Empire of Magic: Medieval Romance and the Politics of Cultural Fantasy* (New York, 2003), pp. 181–237; Siobhain Bly Calkin, *Saracens and the Making of English Identity: The Auchinleck Manuscript* (New York, 2005), pp. 61–95.

Saracen warriors who appear in romance do serve simply as occasions for the demonstration of Christian martial prowess. However, some play much more substantive narrative roles. These Saracens tend to fall into two broad categories: those who convert to Christianity and those who refuse to do so. Saracen knights of both types can appear as admirable opponents of Christian heroes, while those who convert often become exemplary Christian protagonists in their own right, sometimes switching from one role to the other in the same romance. As such mobile characters, Saracens indicate how ideas of Christian heroism may be challenged in a variety of thought-provoking ways by medieval romance redactors.

Convert Heroes

Among the best-known Saracen knights of medieval romance are those who become the heroes of their own narratives. Otuel and Ferumbras, for example, are the defeated antagonists of Christian heroes who, as Saracens, demonstrate admirable martial prowess before converting and becoming eponymous romance heroes. They appear first in French *chansons de geste*, which were later translated into English. In Middle English, Otuel is the focus of *Otuel a Kniȝt (OK)*, *Þe Romance of Duke Rowlande and of Sir Ottuell of Spayne (DRSO)*, and *Otuel and Roland (OR)*,[3] while Ferumbras's story is retold in *Sir Ferumbras (SF)*, *Firumbras (F)*, and *The Sowdone of Babylone (SB)*.[4] Since both these characters become Christian heroes, it may seem odd to suggest that they offer any critique of the Christian chivalric society with which they interact. However, there are moments when each hero does just that.

In Otuel's tale, the Saracen convert participates in two incidents that cast a disparaging light on Charlemagne and other Matter of France heroes. The first incident occurs when Otuel arrives at Charlemagne's court as a messenger from the Saracen king Garsie. In all versions of the text either Charlemagne or Roland or both assure Otuel that he may speak without being attacked, and forbid the French knights from harming the Saracen. For example, in *Otuel a Kniȝt*, Charlemagne says:

> Ich for bede oppon alle þing,
> Þat noman be so wood,
> For to don hym oþer þan good.
> A kinges messager for he is,

---

[3] *Otuel a Kniȝt* is found in the Auchinleck Manuscript (Edinburgh, National Library of Scotland MS 19.2.1), which dates to the 1330s. *Þe Romance of Duke Rowlande and of Sir Ottuell of Spayne* is found in the London Thornton Manuscript (London, BL MS Additional 31042), dated to the mid-1400s, and *Otuel and Roland* in the Fillingham Manuscript (London, BL MS Additional 37492), dated to the second half of the 1400s. Dates for the Auchinleck manuscript are taken from *The Auchinleck Manuscript*, ed. David Burnley and Alison Wiggins (Edinburgh, 2003), http://digital.nls.uk/auchinleck/editorial/history.html, Version 1.1, accessed October 25, 2010. Dates for the Thornton and Fillingham manuscripts are taken from Gisela Guddat-Figge, *Catalogue of Manuscripts Containing Middle English Romances* (Munich, 1976), pp. 159, 168.

[4] *Sir Ferumbras* is found in Oxford, Bodleian Library MS Ashmole 33, which has been dated to the late fourteenth century. *Firumbras* is found in the Fillingham Manuscript (London, BL MS Additional 37492), dated to the second half of the 1400s; and *The Sowdone of Babylone* is found in Princeton, Princeton University Library MS Garrett 140, dated to the mid-1400s. The manuscript dates given here are taken from Guddat-Figge, pp. 245, 159, 301.

He ne schal habbe non harm, i-wis.   (*OK*, lines 140–44).[5]

Despite this assurance, however, in two versions of the romance Otuel is attacked by a French knight and forced to defend himself by killing his assailant (*OK* lines 163–66; *DRSO* lines 164–68). The inefficacy of the prohibition points to traditional problems within Charlemagne's court, namely the king's inability to maintain discipline and the willingness of some of his knights to behave reprehensibly. The incident suggests that, as honourable and courteous as Charlemagne and Roland are, the larger court to which they belong does not share their sense of honour, and instead actively invalidates their assurances of safe conduct. In *Duke Rowlande and Sir Otuell*, Roland makes this point explicit when he rebukes the knight who moves to attack Otuel:

> 'Now gud sir Estut, let it be,
>   He es a Messangere:
> He es Ensurede to myn Eme & mee.
> For-thi, gud sir, par charyte,
>   thyn hert þat þou wolde stere.'
> Bot ȝit þe knyghte ne wolde noghte spare.   (*DRSO*, lines 158–63)[6]

Roland's words make clear the affront to honour involved in any attack on the Saracen, while Estut's refusal to desist indicates how little such concerns matter to some Christian knights. The incident as a whole suggests that knights must rein in their desire to fight in certain situations, but may well refuse to do so. This point is made again later in the text when Roland himself is criticized for advancing too impetuously against the enemy.

After Otuel has been converted, he, the Peers and the rest of Charlemagne's army position themselves to attack the Saracen hordes. Roland, Oliver and Ogier ride out to seek battle before the larger engagement is to take place. In one version they enter the Saracen camp 'Wil charles in his bed lay' (*OK*, line 702), while in another they steal away' '[f]ull prevaly' to seek '[a]wnters' while the rest of the company is dining (*DRSO*, lines 757–68). In so doing, they behave in a manner Geoffroi de Charny identifies as problematic. He describes warriors who 'when they are in action, [...] do not consider the benefit or advantage for their friends or the harm done to their enemies, but, without, giving or taking advice, they spur forward in a disorderly way and perform personally many feats of arms'.[7] Although such men, he states, 'cannot

---

[5]   Quotations from *Otuel a Kniȝt* are taken from *The Taill of Rauf Coilyear, with the Fragments of Roland and Vernagu and Otuel*, ed. S. Herrtage, EETS ES 39 (1882; repr. Oxford, 1969), pp. 65–119.
[6]   Quotations from *Þe Romance of Duke Rowlande and of Sir Otuell of Spayne* are taken from *The Sege off Melayne and The Romance of Duke Rowlande and Sir Otuell of Spayne*, ed. S. Herrtage, EETS ES 35 (1880; repr. Eastbourne, 2002), pp. 53–104. For a rich discussion of this romance's heightened concern with chivalry, see Diane Speed, 'Chivalric Perspectives in the Middle English Otuel Romances,' in *Medieval Cultural Studies: Essays in Honour of Stephen Knight*, ed. R. Evans, H. Fulton, and D. Matthews (Cardiff, 2006), pp. 213–24. Here, among other incidents, she discusses Estut's attack and the rash sortie (see below) that I also discuss, albeit with different emphases.
[7]   Geoffroi de Charny, *The Book of Chivalry of Geoffroi de Charny*, ed. and trans. Richard W. Kaeuper and Elspeth Kennedy (Philadelphia, 1996), p. 151. The French reads: 'quant il sont sur les besoignes faire, il n'y regardent profit, ne avantage pour leurs amis, ne a la grant

be reproached in relation to the honor earned through bravery', he adds that 'as for being worthy in the truest sense, it would be possible to do better'.[8] This seems to be the same judgement expressed by various romance redactors in this episode. Although it is clear from their actions that Roland, Oliver and Ogier are doughty knights, all versions of the Middle English romance include some condemnation of these actions, voiced by the text's Saracen convert.

These condemnations take slightly different forms and, when assembled together, provide a rich sense of why the three Peers' behaviour is problematic. In *Otuel a Kniȝt*, Otuel states that the knights 'Beþ went for envie of me,/ To loke wher þei miȝten spede,/ To don any douȝti deede' (lines 1020–22). His comment suggests that a sense of competitiveness permeates Charlemagne's forces, and that this competitiveness ranks above any concern for Charlemagne's larger war in knights' decisions about what courses of action to pursue. In *Duke Rowlande and Sir Otuell*, after Otuel has rescued Roland and Oliver from Saracen forces that far outnumber them, he rebukes them, saying 'Wene ȝe for ȝoure chevalrye,/ For ȝoure boste and ȝoure folye,/ Þat þe Saraȝenes will late ȝow one?' (*DRSO*, lines 1048–50). Otuel here implies that the Christian heroes place too much faith in their renown to keep them safe, and reminds them that 'boste' and 'folye' will not deter the enemy. Finally, in *Otuel and Roland*, the Saracen convert condemns Roland for pride and strategic ineptitude:

> ...Roulond, for thy pryde,
> Thy lyfe þu wylt for-lete!
> What! wenes tou and Olyvere alone
> To sle þe sarsyns everchone,
> And thus to grounde hem bete?
>
> Nay, þouȝ þou and y & Olyver,
> Hadde ben þere al in fer
> Aȝeyns þe hethyn lawe, –
> And ek charlys, the conqueror,
> Thouȝ he Brouȝt alle hys power, –
> Ȝyt schuld they be nouȝt alle slawe.   (*OR*, lines 1056–66)[9]

Otuel's words suggest that Roland and his companions have no realistic battle plan, and that their behaviour only highlights the deadly foolishness of their pride as well as the limits of their abilities. Taken together, Otuel's judgements of the Peers' behaviour condemn it as prideful glory-seeking that takes into account neither the enemy's fighting abilities nor Charlemagne's plans. The Otuel tales clearly consider such knightly over-eagerness for combat problematic; not only is it depicted twice in these romances, but it also becomes the occasion for direct criticism of three of the

---

grevance de leurs ennemis, mais sanz conseil donner ne prendre fierent des esperons et a po d'arroy, et font d'armes assez de leur main' (p. 150).

[8] The French reads: 'mais contre l'onnour de hardiesce ne leur peut l'en rienz reprouver... l'en les doit bien appeller preux, combien que, quant a estre preus a droit, l'en y pourroit encores miex faire' (p. 150).

[9] Quotations from *Otuel and Roland* are taken from *Firumbras and Otuel and Roland*, ed. M.I. O'Sullivan, EETS OS 198 (1935; repr. New York, 1971), pp. 59–146.

Matter of France's most famous Christian heroes. These romances, however, are not alone in according this behaviour flaw significant attention. Many historical chronicles do so as well. Ambroise's *Estoire de la Guerre Sainte*, for example, recounts the high costs of knightly impetuosity during the Third Crusade. Ambroise notes that in one battle 'All was lost because of two [Christian knights] who could not hold back from charging', and he laments:

> God! What loss, what misfortune, what sorrow and what suffering came to the army at this time, when so many Saracens would have died had sin not interfered with the attack that had been planned. If only they had carried out the plan of attack, which everyone agreed upon and which had already been decided.[10]

Ambroise, like the fictional Otuel, indicates the problems caused by Christian heroes' heedless over-eagerness for battle and overweening pride in their abilities.

If Otuel identifies behavioural problems among Charlemagne's knights, Ferumbras actually serves as a corrective to bad behaviour in this group. In *Firumbras*, Charlemagne fears that Roland and Oliver, who have been sent on a message to the Saracen leader, have been either overcome or killed. Charlemagne swears that if they have been overcome:

> y ne schal suffre in fraunce, no bellys ryng
> In Chyrch ne in chapel, no prest mas to synge,
> Ne in none oþer plas halywater to spryng,
> No non bokes, godys name worchipyng.
> The vygours and þe autar, þat in holy chyrche be3th found,
> I schal hem adoun falle and bete to þe grounde.
> Be my dussepers overcom, to god a 3yfte y 3eve,
> Ne schal I never worschyp god, whyles þat y leve.
>
> (*F*, lines 1115–22)[11]

It is, perhaps surprisingly, the Saracen convert who becomes the voice of faith arguing against despair, and who tells Charlemagne:

> 'Syr, let be þese wordes, for þey be nou3t slayn.
> Pray we for hem to god þat sytteth in mageste,

---

[10] Ambroise, *The History of the Holy War/ Ambroise's Estoire de la guerre sainte*, ed. M. Ailes and M. Barber, trans. M. Ailes, 2 vols (Woodbridge, 2003), 2:119. The French reads:

> Mais par deus homes les perdirent
> Qui pas de poindre ne se tindrent...

and:

> Deus! quel perte, quel mescheance
> E quel doel e quel mesestance,
> Avint en l'ost a cel termine,
> Ou tant [...] ont gent sarazine
> Se pechié n'eüst destorbiee
> La pointe qui fud devisee!
> En dementers qu'il devisoient
> Cele pointe ou tuit s'acordoient,
> E avoient ja esgardé.

See 1:103–104, lines 6413–15 and 6395–403.

[11] Quotations from *Firumbras* are taken from *Firumbras and Otuel and Roland*, pp. 3–58.

As he ys ful of mercy, on hem he have pyte!
And sche þat fayled never, hevene quene marye,
Sche be here governour & schylde hem fro vylonye!'

(*F*, lines 1124–28)

Ferumbras here reminds Charlemagne of what a Christian should do in a situation like this, namely pray for assistance. He also, since Charlemagne heeds his words, prevents the French king from behaving just like the Saracen king he opposes in this text, who frequently beats and renounces his gods. The convert becomes the preserver of the difference between Christian and Saracen, and the voice of right Christian behaviour when that is menaced by the words of the Christian leader.

In another Ferumbras text, the Saracen convert again serves as a corrective to flaws in the Christian army, although this time in martial rather than religious matters. *The Sowdone of Babylone* narrates an incident in which Charlemagne pushes ahead with some of his knights in a battle to take a bridge whose control is essential for the rescue of Roland and other Peers from their captivity in Saracen lands. In the mêlée, Charlemagne is trapped on the bridge. Ganelon, perceiving this, claims 'the kinge is dede [...]/ Let us hye to Fraunce warde!/ For I wele be crownede kinge' (lines 2973–76).[12] The French turn away, abandoning Charlemagne. Ferumbras rides up with his retainers, and asks Ganelon what has happened. Upon being told that Charles is trapped, Ferumbras upbraids the Frenchman, saying:

God gyf the an yvel falle!
Turne agayne, thou traytoure!
And helpe to reskowe thy lorde.
And ye, sires, alle for your honour!   (*SB*, lines 2990–93)

Ferumbras here becomes the lone loyal retainer among the French forces. Admittedly, his behaviour serves mainly to cast Ganelon, already a reviled traitor in the Charlemagne tradition, in a critical light. However, the fact that no one except the convert advocates troth to one's overlord suggests that this particular lack of 'honour' extends to most of the French Christian camp.

The nameless sultan of Damascus in *The King of Tars* is another Saracen convert who exposes weaknesses among Christians. In his case, it is Christian military weakness that is revealed. In the opening battles of this text, the Sultan and his forces kill 'þritti þousend [...] kniʒtes of Cristen lawe' (lines 211–212).[13] The Saracen onslaught is so fierce that the Christian king of Tars is forced to give his daughter to the Sultan as his wife. After conversion, the Sultan achieves what the king of Tars could not: the Christianization or destruction of Saracens. Within the Sultan's own realm:

þo þat Mahoun wald forsake
Cristen men he lete hem make [...]

---

[12] Quotations of *The Sowdone of Babylone* are taken from *The Romaunce of The Sowdone of Babylone and of Ferumbras his Sone who conquerede Rome*, ed. E. Hausknecht, EETS ES 38 (1881; repr. Oxford, 2002).

[13] Quotations from this romance are taken from *The King of Tars, ed. from the Auchinleck MS, Advocates 19.2.1*, ed. Judith Perryman (Heidelberg, 1980), pp. 73–106.

> & he þat dede nouȝt bi his rede,
> Anon he dede strike of his hed.   (*King of Tars*, lines 1051–54)

When five Saracen kings subsequently attack the convert and his forces, the Sultan and his father-in-law defeat them as well. The Auchinleck manuscript expands the narrative of this victory in thirty-four lines not found elsewhere,[14] enumerating the conquest thus:

> þritti þousende þer wer take
> Of Sarra[ȝ]ins boþe blo & blac, [...]
> & he þat wald his lay forsake
> Cristen m[a]n he lete him make [...]
> & þai þat wald be christned nouȝt [...]
> Cristen men, wiþouten wene,
> Striken of her hevedes al bidene...   (*King of Tars*, lines 1225–35)

This version explicitly parallels the 30,000 Christian deaths recounted earlier with 30,000 Saracen conversions or killings at the end of the text, thereby signalling the Sultan's military effectiveness on both sides of the religious divide. Admittedly, the Sultan's father-in-law and his forces assist the Sultan and his men with the final battles. Nevertheless, the fact remains that it is Saracen military prowess that definitively triumphs in the end, as in the beginning, indicating the desirability, and perhaps the necessity, of the Sultan's conversion if Christians are ever to win power in the Saracen world. The historical pertinence of such a suggestion seems immediately apparent when one considers, as Perryman notes, that 'the basis of [this] romance is a historical incident from the late thirteenth-century crusades'.[15] The late thirteenth century was, of course, the period during which the Crusader kingdoms definitively fell to Muslim powers after a series of Christian military defeats and failures culminating in the Fall of Acre in 1291.[16]

Otuel, Ferumbras, and the sultan of Damascus all offer pointed critiques of Christian warriors as their stories unfold. Interactions between these Saracens and Christians become occasions for the demonstration of Christian heroes' lack of discipline, over-competitiveness, weak faith, and military failure. In this way, Saracen converts call into question the exemplarity of characters like Roland, Charlemagne, and Oliver, as well as the military abilities of Christian king-crusaders like the king of Tars. The Saracen converts in these texts, however, are themselves Christian heroes by virtue of their conversion; thus they do in some ways reinforce ideas of heroic exemplarity. Their critiques of Christian heroes can be read as the justifiable critiques of comrades made by the character designated best knight of all in his particular romance. These Saracens do draw problematic Christian weaknesses to the audience's attention, but their conversion and narrative role mean that they do not radically challenge what Neil Cartlidge (in the Introduction to this volume) calls romances' 'insistent celebration' of heroes' triumphs. To find characters who might

---

[14] The other versions are found in Oxford, Bodleian Library MS English Poetry a.1 and London, BL MS Additional 22283.
[15] Perryman, *King of Tars*, p. 42.
[16] See Christopher Tyerman, *God's War: A New History of the Crusades* (Cambridge, MA, 2006), pp. 715–822 regarding the military losses affecting the Crusader kingdoms in the 1200s.

offer such a challenge, it is necessary to consider Saracens who do not convert, and are therefore debarred from becoming the heroes of a Christian romance. These characters offer more subtle, and perhaps more devastating, critiques of the models of Christian heroism found in the romances in which they appear.

Noble Non-Converts

One Saracen who refuses to convert is King Clarel, who appears in all three Middle English Otuel romances. He participates in a battle against three French Peers in which he is captured and then freed, and he later challenges the newly converted Otuel to single combat. Clarel is a particularly interesting character because he is a noble non-convert. Nobility of appearance and prowess have a long history of association with Saracen warriors, dating back to depictions of specific Saracens in twelfth-century crusading chronicles and the *Chanson de Roland*.[17] As Marianne Ailes notes, noble traits became increasingly associated with Saracens who convert,[18] but they also appear in some Saracens who do not convert. Clarel's nobility is made clear in all versions of the Middle English romance. He is a doughty warrior who urges his companions to attack the Christian Peers, unhorses Roland, and then fights valiantly on after his fellow Saracens have been killed. In one version, Clarel's battle against Otuel prompts Roland to say:

> ne sey y never her by-fore
> suche two men of my3tys
> [...] none dou3tyer,
> ne suche othyr to kny3tys.   (*OR*, lines 1417–21)

Clarel is also described as 'faire and avenante/ With a full Manly Semblande' (*DRSO* lines 790–91). He both looks noble and acts nobly, and these details are important because they enable him to demonstrate the occasionally wavering exemplarity of his Christian opponents. He is not some monstrous Saracen who can be dismissed as wholly Other to the Christian world with which he interacts. Rather, he is a noble warrior who earns Christian respect in the texts in which he appears, and whose opinions and behaviours cannot therefore be easily ignored, even if they are not the focus of readerly attention.

In one text, Clarel's capture by Ogier, Roland and Oliver becomes the occasion for a discussion of how knights should treat their prisoners. Ogier asks Roland and Oliver, 'Lordinges, what is nou 3oure red,/ Wole we smiten of his hed?' (*OK*, lines 849–50). Roland vehemently opposes this course of action, as does Oliver who adds that more may be gained from showing mercy (*OK*, lines 857–58). It is Ogier himself, however, who finally condemns his idea as dishonourable, saying 'Hit where sschame to ous, iwis,/ To sslen a man þat 3olden him is' (*OK*, lines 861–62). Ogier's final judgement accords with the other two versions of the tale, in which no Peer even suggests killing the Saracen prisoner. Killing prisoners is an act explicitly condemned in some treatises of knightly behaviour, as when Christine de Pizan writes 'it is

---

[17] Marianne Ailes, 'Chivalry and Conversion: The Chivalrous Saracen in the Old French Epics *Fierabras* and *Otinel*', *Al-Masaq* 9 (1997), 1–21, pp. 1–6.
[18] Ailes, 'Chivalry and Conversion', pp. 7–12, 14–18.

against right and gentility to slay the one who gives himself up'.[19] In *Otuel a Kniȝt*, Clarel's capture becomes the occasion for Christian voicing of a course of action that, even if ultimately abandoned, does mitigate the exemplarity of one of the Peers. The fact that other versions of the tale do not include Ogier's first, less-than-ideal, response would seem to support this suggestion. Certainly Clarel himself, by contrast, manifests a wholly admirable treatment of captives. When he later captures Ogier, he in two versions cuts down a fellow Saracen who attempts to kill the Christian (*DRSO*, lines 949–54; *OR*, lines 977–88), and in all versions sends Ogier under safe guard to his lemman's house, with instructions that the captive be well treated.

Clarel also suggests that the romance's eponymous hero falls short of ideal knightly behaviour. In all Middle English versions of *Otuel*, Clarel challenges the new convert to a single combat characterized as a contest of religions. Two versions, however, use the combat to reflect upon the ways in which Otuel's conversion constitutes earthly treason. In *Otuel a Kniȝt*, Clarel responds to Otuel's announcement of his apostasy by saying:

> So wrecheliche havestou do.
> ȝit i rede þou turne þi mood,
> & leef on mahoun, ore þou art wod,
> & ich wole pese, ȝef þou wilt,
> þat þou havest garsie a-gult.   (*OK*, lines 1158–62)

Clarel's words remind the audience and Otuel that the convert's change of faith means he has abandoned and wronged his overlord. In *Duke Rowlande and Sir Otuell*, Clarel makes the problematic earthly aspects of Otuel's conversion even more apparent, saying:

> ...allas,
> Now is this a wikkede case,
>   & þou so noble a knyghte.
> Whi duelles þou there amonges thi fase?
> Foully there thou wichede was,
>   & whi es this dede thus dighte?
>
> I rede þat þou converte the in hye,
> & then sall saughtyll with thyn Eme sir Garcy,
>   & forsake not thy lawe.'   (*DRSO*, lines 1147–55)

Clarel's words cast Otuel's act as battlefield treachery, while his description of Garsie as 'Eme' makes the convert's betrayal one of both overlord and kinsman. This Clarel

---

[19] Christine de Pizan, *The Book of Deeds of Arms and of Chivalry*, ed. C.C. Willard, trans. S. Willard (University Park, 1999), p. 169. See Richard W. Kaeuper, *Chivalry and Violence in Medieval Europe* (Oxford, 1999), pp. 169–70 regarding the improved treatment of prisoners with the rise of chivalry. See also Richard Barber, *The Knight and Chivalry*, rev. edn (Woodbridge, 1995), pp. 241–44, esp. p. 241, where he writes, 'From the mid-eleventh century onwards, it was extremely rare for captives of any standing to be killed, partly because of the very lucrative systems of ransom. Ransoms were a question of business rather than chivalry, but they, in a sense, made chivalry on the battlefield possible by reducing the likelihood that a knight would be killed.'

makes earthly treachery the focus of his reproach, referring only in the last line to religious apostasy.

Clarel's outlook here is decidedly Saracen, and can be easily discounted as the product of a non-believer's religious error and misguided loyalties. Otuel, in fact, consciously works to indicate this by characterizing the battle as about religion alone. He affirms his right to fight Clarel by stating in *Otuel a Kni3t* that Clarel 'wolde habbe maked me…/ To habbe reneied my lay' (lines 1259–60), in *Duke Rowlande and Sir Otuell* that Clarel 'sett þe lawes of Cristyantee/ Nott at a pillynge of a tree' (lines 1264–65), and in *Otuel and Roland* that Clarel 'sayde that oure god [w]as nou3t worth a tord,/ And that he wold prove with dynt of swerd' (lines 1322–23). Otuel steadfastly refuses to address the issue of treason in his characterizations of his conflict with Clarel, and his view that this is a religious conflict ultimately dominates on the field of battle and in the audience's mind. Clarel, however, repeatedly makes the battle one about earthly lordship. He reviles Charlemagne, Otuel's new overlord, pointing out the king's age, foolhardiness, weakness, lack of energy, and lack of martial prowess (*OK*, lines 1225–30; *DRSO*, lines 1250–57; *OR*, lines 1265–82). Both characters are right; in a Saracen-Christian conflict, as Norman Daniel has pointed out, change of religion is change of allegiance.[20] In romances, however, it is always the Christian hero's perception, and the religious change of allegiance, that win out. Clarel's repeated charges of treachery are ultimately silenced when Otuel kills him. However, the Saracen's assertions signal some problematic aspects of Otuel's behaviour and hold the convert accountable for a manifest lack of loyalty to earthly overlord and kinsman, even if that treachery is ultimately made right by the religious correctness of conversion to Christianity.

Clarel serves as an example of both the hero's noble opponent and his non-Christian critic. Other unconverted Saracens also demonstrate nobility while offering more indirect critiques of the Christian heroes with whom they interact. The Saracen king Triamour in the *Guy of Warwick* romances is one such character. This king appears in the three complete Middle English versions of the romance, namely those found in the Auchinleck manuscript (of the 1330s); Cambridge, Gonville and Caius College, MS 107/176, dated to the 1470s; and Cambridge, University Library MS Ff. 2. 38, dated to the late 1400s or early 1500s.[21] In all versions, King Triamour is the occasion for the first battle Guy undertakes after he has abandoned his pregnant wife and earthly lordship to go on pilgrimage in atonement for the fact that heretofore he has not fought for God. Guy's first battle as a pilgrim is a trial by combat necessitated by the fact that Triamour's son, Fabour, kills the son of Triamour's overlord in an exchange of blows following a chess match. Triamour is required to find a champion to fight the Sultan's ferocious giant to determine whether Triamour and his son are ultimately guilty of the death of the Sultan's son. Triamour finds no Saracens to help him, and turns to a Christian captive of his, Earl Jonas, for advice on Christian champions brave enough to undertake this battle. Jonas suggests either Guy or his companion Herhaud, and Triamour sets Jonas free to find one of these

---

[20] Norman Daniel, *Heroes and Saracens: An Interpretation of the Chansons de Geste* (Edinburgh, 1984), pp. 179, 192, 211.

[21] Dates and list taken from Alison Wiggins, 'The Manuscripts and Texts of the Middle English *Guy of Warwick*', in *Guy of Warwick: Icon and Ancestor*, ed. A. Wiggins and R. Field (Cambridge, 2007), pp. 61–80.

champions with the understanding that should Jonas succeed, he and his fifteen sons will be freed, while if he fails, he and his sons will be slain. The disguised Guy comes upon Jonas outside Antioch and agrees to undertake the battle. Guy wins, Jonas and his sons are freed, and Triamour attempts to retain Guy by offering him a portion of his kingdom.

Triamour proves, like Clarel, to be an admirable character. Although he and Guy differ religiously, Guy's claims of Mahoun's worthlessness prompt Triamour not to attack him, but instead to offer him a fitting reward for his possible success in battle. In all versions Triamour promises to release Christian captives in his realm, as well as to ensure safe passage for Christians traveling through his lands. The reader is clearly guided to perceive the praiseworthiness of this action, for Guy himself in all versions calls it a fair gift (Auchinleck, 88/11; Caius, line 8072; CUL, line 7880).[22] The Saracen's generosity is stressed in other ways, too. Not only does he offer Guy wealth, rich clothes, armour and food, but also a good portion of his kingdom, with no concomitant insistence that Guy change his religion. Triamour is also true to his word; he releases Jonas and his fifteen sons as promised. The Saracen thus manifests ideal largesse and troth. As Geoffroi de Charny writes in his guide to knightly behaviour, 'the more you have given, the more you should give', and 'if you are wise, you will only do good and ought not to excuse yourself from being a man of worth and loyal, as it is the greatest and most supreme good there is'.[23] Triamour, like Clarel, clearly falls into the literary tradition of admirable Saracen characters, despite his religiously antagonistic views. Unlike Clarel, however, Triamour does not directly criticize Guy. Instead, events involving Triamour cast a critical light on the Christian hero of this romance.

In *Guy of Warwick*, the critique of Guy is effected by narrative structure and the depictions of Triamour, the Saracen Sultan, and Jonas. The Triamour episode occurs immediately after Guy has left Felice, having informed her that she will bear a son, that she should entrust the boy to Guy's steadfast companion, Herhaud, to raise, and that she should pass Guy's sword on to their son. The abandonment of lady and offspring, the dynastic trappings of knightly success, are part of the religious life Guy has chosen, and for which he is so revered. There is clearly a tension, however, between Guy's pilgrimage and the dynastic concerns that occupy many romances. Andrea Hopkins, in her book *Sinful Knights*, suggests that Guy reconciles these tensions, and affirms his ultimate support of knightly values, by 'express[ing] his concern on several occasions that his would-be benefactors should instead of rewarding him protect and advance his son Reinbrun', and by emphasizing his son's future knightly career.[24] I am not sure, however, that Guy is as successful as Hopkins

---

[22] Quotations of the Caius and Auchinleck manuscript versions are taken from *The Romance of Guy of Warwick, Edited from the Auchinleck MS. in the Advocates' Library, Edinburgh and from MS. 107 in Caius College, Cambridge*, ed. J. Zupitza, EETS ES 42, 49, 59 (1883, 1887, 1891; repr. in 1 vol., Oxford, 1966). Quotations of the Cambridge University Library (CUL) version are taken from *The Romance of Guy of Warwick, The Second or 15th-century Version*, ed. J. Zupitza, EETS ES 25–26 (1875–76; repr. in 1 vol., Oxford, 1966).

[23] Geoffroi de Charny, *The Book of Chivalry*, pp. 131, 135. The French reads: 'quant plus avrez donné, donnez encores plus' (p. 130), and 'Quar se vous estes sages, vous ne ferez fors bien et ne vous devez excuser de estre preudoms et loyaux, car c'est le plus grant bien et le plus souverain qui soit' (p. 134).

[24] Hopkins, pp. 78–79.

perceives him to be in managing his duties as father. His absence from England means, ultimately, that he is not there to prevent his son's abduction and sale to a Saracen ruler in Africa. This event is depicted immediately following the Triamour episode in the Caius and Cambridge University Library versions of the romance. The Triamour episode is thus framed, in two of the three Middle English texts, by narratives recounting Guy's abandonment of his son and that son's subsequent vulnerability to violence.

The positioning of the Reinbrun material in the Guy romances suggests, as Hopkins notes, that it proved problematic for some Middle English romancers.[25] The Cambridge University Library version intersperses this material throughout Guy's story and finishes the romance by recounting Reinbrun's knightly successes after Guy's death. The Auchinleck version, however, excises the Reinbrun material and makes it the subject of a separate romance. The Caius manuscript ends with the deaths of Guy and Felice and leaves Reinbrun in limbo at a Saracen king's court, neglecting to narrate his eventual escape. Hopkins sees these variations as evidence of some Middle English redactors' discomfort with a version of Guy's story in which the final focus is the knightly endeavor of Guy's son rather than the pious death of the contrite pilgrim-knight.[26] I would suggest, however, that the Reinbrun material is problematic because it hints at less-than-ideal behaviour as a father on Guy's part.

The Triamour episode provides some support for such a reading. Positioned between incidents involving Guy's son, the episode itself draws attention to father-son relationships. Jonas, Triamour, and the Saracen Sultan evince a lively concern for the fate of their sons that is matched only by paternal absence and silence on Guy's part. When Guy meets Jonas, Jonas identifies himself as an earl with fifteen sons. In all versions, his words emphasize at length his relationship with his sons and concern for them. For example, in the Caius version he states:

> Erle Ionas some tyme I hyght,
> I had sonnes full fyftene,
> And bold men and kene.
> I wene there was never man levande,
> Syth crystendome was brought in hand,
> That had so many sonnes wyght:
> Everych was a man att all ryght.
> All they be take fro me a-weye:
> Allas that ever I sye thys daye.   (Caius, lines 7614–22)[27]

In all texts, it is the promise of his sons' release that impels Jonas on his quest for Guy, and it is the thought of their deaths that most upsets him when he believes he must return to Triamour unsuccessful. He states:

> Of my selfe yeve I nought,
> But of my sonnes is all my thought;
> For they be knyghtis bold and wyght,

---

[25] Hopkins, p. 79. The following overview of the various manuscript versions draws substantially on Hopkins's summary.
[26] Hopkins, pp. 78–79.
[27] Cf. Auchinleck 49/1–12 and CUL, lines 7432–40.

> And well assayd in meny a fyght.
> Yf they myght leve and old men bee,
> They myght much helpe crystiante.   (Caius, lines 7875–80)[28]

These two substantial speeches indicate the affective ties of fatherhood and the military benefits noble Christian sons bring to Christendom as a whole.

Jonas's account of his sons and his efforts to free them frames a tale of two Saracen fathers and their engagements with their respective sons. After the deadly chess game, Triamour's son runs to his father for assistance in navigating the perilous consequences of his act, and the two flee to safety. Triamour later handles the legal process of trial by battle for his son, seeks, with Jonas's aid, the assistance of a hero against the Sultan's monstrous champion, and arranges matters to save his son and himself. His activities suggest the vital role of paternal guidance and assistance in a young nobleman's life. The activities of the Sultan also indicate a lively sense of affection and paternal responsibility:

> When that wyste that fell sowdan
> That sadoyne, hys sonne, was slayne,
> He was sory, that grete syre,
> And he was full of tene and ire.
> He beryed hys son Richelye,
> And thought to avenge hym in hye.   (Caius, lines 7733–38)[29]

The Sultan's keen sense of loss is communicated clearly, as well as his desire to seek redress for the death of his son and heir. Both he and Triamour present portraits of fathers involved in their sons' lives and concerned with their sons' fates.

The first episode following Guy's decision to become a pilgrim thus centers on fathers and sons. Paternal responsibilities and worries form the backdrop for the spectacular fight between Guy and the Saracen giant Amoraunt. The martial details of this battle admittedly dominate the romance episode. The whole event, however, occurs because of Triamour's involvement in his son's life, the Sultan's sense that the death of his son is a crime meriting fierce punishment, and Jonas's desire to free his sons from captivity. In contrast, the Christian hero of this battle never refers to his own fatherhood, and appears patently unconcerned with events in his son's life, including his very birth. Guy, unlike the other characters in this episode, evinces a distinctly anti-social, or at least anti-paternal aspect. Even if one must assume that dynastic concerns in Guy's case are rightfully trumped by religious penitence, as the romance as a whole implies, one can read this particular encounter between Christian hero and Saracen world as suggesting, in some of its details, a less-than-ideal aspect of the romance hero.

Another encounter between Christian hero and Saracen world, in another romance, also critiques the hero's anti-social tendencies. One of the most infamous episodes in the Richard Coer de Lion romances is the crusading hero's cannibalism

---

[28] Cf. Auchinleck 72/1–12 and CUL, lines 7691–96.

[29] Cf. Auchinleck 60/1–6 and CUL, lines 7551–56. Interestingly, in the versions that recount this episode between accounts of Guy's son (Caius and CUL), the Sultan's sorrow is described, as well as his desire to bury his son 'richelye', details which emphasize paternal grief. In Auchinleck, which moves the Reinbrun material to its own separate text, only the Sultan's desire for vengeance is mentioned.

of his defeated Saracen opponents. Richard eats his first Saracen unwittingly, when his retainers seek to satisfy their ill king's desire for pork during a siege by providing him with a carefully cooked 'Sarezyn ȝonge and ffat' (line 3088).[30] He later orders that a feast of labeled Saracen heads be served up to messengers from the Saracen Sultan Saladin. As Geraldine Heng argues, these cannibalistic episodes in the Richard romances are presented as a joke and as a testament to English ferocity.[31] The English retainers who feed Richard his first Saracen laugh at his appreciation of the dish (line 3114) while Richard himself also laughs when he discovers what he has done (line 3215). The Saracens present at the second cannibalistic episode, however, emphasize the troubling aspects of Richard's behaviour. While Richard feasts on his Saracen head, none of Saladin's messengers ' . . . wolde hys mese neyȝe,/ Ne þeroff eeten on morsel' (lines 3476–77). They watch Richard eat and 'wenden he hadde be wood' (line 3482), and they are unable to eat a thing when Richard finally removes the heads and provides a regular feast (lines 3507, 3634–39). The Saracen messengers manifest the incomprehension, horror and revulsion considered appropriate to human cannibalism in the Middle Ages,[32] and thereby condemn Richard and his act, or at least indicate the potentially troubling aspects of this heroic behaviour.

The Saracens in the cannibalism episode do more than signal the monstrosity of Richard's breaking of a taboo, however. They also describe the event in terms that reveal the human and social costs of Richard's behaviour. When the Saracen nobles discover that Richard has captured a number of their sons and heirs, they urge Saladin to:

> ...make acord
> Wiþ Kyng Richard, þat is so stoute,
> Ffor to delyvere oure chyldren oute,
> Þat þey ne be hongyd, ne to drawe.
> Off tresore Kyng R. wole be fawe;
> Þat oure chyldren may come hom hayl,
> Charges mules and hors, be our counsayl,
> Off brende gold, and of bawdekyn,
> Ffor oure heyres to make ffyn. (*Richard Coer de Lion*, lines 3366–74)

Three times in nine lines the nobles articulate their affective and dynastic ties to Richard's captives, referring to them as 'oure chyldren' and 'oure heyres' and thereby emphasizing the familial and social ties that structure the Saracen community. Richard responds to the eventual embassy by ordering the slaughter and culinary preparation of the prisoners, decreeing that their names should be fastened around their heads, what each man 'hyȝte, and off what kyn born(e)' (line 3433). Richard's words signal that he knows full well the social and affective blow his cannibal feast

---

[30] Quotations from *Richard Coer de Lion* are taken from *Der mittelenglische Versroman über Richard Löwenherz*, ed. K. Brunner (Vienna, 1913), pp. 81–452, and are referred to by line number. The base text for this edition is Cambridge, Gonville and Caius College MS 175/96, which Brunner dates to the fifteenth century, as does Guddat-Figge, p. 82.

[31] See Heng, pp. 63–113, for a discussion of the Richard romances, especially pp. 63–78 regarding the cannibalism episodes. See pp. 21–35 for a discussion of historical crusader cannibalism.

[32] See Heng, pp. 21–35, on the historical attitudes towards cannibalism in medieval western culture, especially pp. 21–30 on the revulsion it occasioned.

will achieve, and the Saracen retelling of the event emphasizes this cannibalization of heirs. The spokesman messenger tells Saladin that the Saracen head set before him was that of 'þe Sawdones sone off Damaske' (line 3592), and then lists the other heads as belonging to the sons of various Saracen kings (lines 3597–603). He concludes by stating that 'Ffor sorwe þoo we gan to syke./ Us þouȝte oure herte barst ryȝt insunder' (lines 3604–605). The woe the Saracens articulate signals an emotional attachment to family and a concern for dynastic succession that are noticeably, and problematically, absent from Richard's life story.

Although the romance begins by emphasizing the need for dynastic succession, describing 'How Kyng Rychard was gete and bore' (line 36), the achievement of dynasty proves somewhat problematic in the Christian realm of England. Richard's father 'wolde no wyff' (line 45), and marries only when urged to do so by his barons. When he does marry, he chooses a queen of questionable background, from 'Antyoche' (line 164), who cannot abide the elevation of the Host at Mass and, when forced to stay for that portion of Mass, rises out through the roof and is never seen again, suggesting a devilish heritage for the Lion Heart (lines 185–240). Richard's own parentage is thus somewhat problematic, but his father did at least produce an heir. Richard himself does not, and the romance ends by relating how 'Kyng R. reynyd here/ No more but ten ȝere/ Syþþe he was schot, allas' (lines 7205–207). The kingdom thus passes to Richard's brother John, whose treachery is recounted at various points in the romance, and who is blamed for Richard's inability to stay and complete his conquest of Saladin's realm (lines 6533–86). The familial disunity displayed by the Christian hero and his brother stands in direct contrast to the unity displayed by Saracens and their families. Saladin's heirs, his sons, fight bravely for their father in battle against Richard (lines 4857–64, 7119–37). Richard's heir, on the other hand, ultimately thwarts the Christian hero's attempts to conquer the Holy Land. This is not to say that the Saracens are depicted as more admirable than the Christians; they are not. One of Saladin's sons fights with envenomed weapons (7135), and the romance depicts Richard's slaughter of Saladin's heirs, as well as of countless other Saracens (including the ones he eats), as behaviour that makes Richard a great warrior. The Saracen response to cannibalism, however, and the Saracen displays of familial affection and concern for patrilineal succession, point to problematic aspects of Richard's achievements as king and hero.

Conclusion

Saracen warriors in medieval romances offer some surprisingly cogent critiques of their Christian antagonists. Sometimes these critiques appear in the words and acts of Saracens who become the Christian heroes of their own romances. Otuel, Ferumbras, and the sultan of Damascus, both before and after conversion, signal problems in the Christian ranks they join. Their criticisms are somewhat mitigated, however, by a romance's tendency to celebrate its hero as superior to his peers. This romance tendency does not mean that the converts' points about Christian competitiveness, overweening pride, treachery, and military weakness are to be ignored. It simply means that these critiques are less surprising because they are the observations of a knight characterized in his text as the best in the world. More surprising, and perhaps more disturbing, are the critiques of Christian heroes that can be discerned from consideration of Saracens who do not convert. Clarel indicates some wavering of Christian heroic exemplarity in the treatment of prisoners and the loyalty owed to overlord and kin, while the episode involving Triamour in *Guy of Warwick* suggests ideals of paternal concern and protection not manifested by the romance's hero. Saracen nobles in *Richard Coer de Lion* draw attention to similar issues, highlighting the lack of familial unity and generational succession in Richard's world as well as signalling the disturbing aspects of extending his battlefield ferocity to the dining table. Consideration of noble non-converts indicates that Saracen characters who might seem to be mere opportunities for the demonstration of Christian martial prowess actually offer intriguing perspectives on the hero's heroism. Even if in the end these non-converts participate in events that predominantly celebrate the romance's hero, they draw the audience's attention to the social costs and potential destructiveness of that hero's 'exemplary' behaviour.

13

Ungallant Knights

JAMES WADE

Than the Kynge stablysshed all the knyghtes and gaff them rychesse and londys – and charged them [...] allwayes to do ladyes, damesels, and jantilwomen and wydowes [socour], strengthe hem in hir ryghtes, and never to enforce them, uppon payne of dethe. (Sir Thomas Malory, *Le Morte Darthur*)[1]

Brothir, the Kynge oure Sovereyne Lorde woll that [...] ye schall sustene wydowes in ther right at every tyme they wol requere yow, and maydenys in ther virginité, and helpe hem and socoure hem with yowre good that for lak of good they be not mysgovernyd. ('How Knyghtis of the Bath Shulde Be Made')[2]

Malory's famous Round Table oath, which Arthur and his knights are said to have sworn every Pentecost, gives special emphasis to the appropriate treatment of women. As Neil Cartlidge has recently noted, one might assume that insistence on such behaviour would be self-evident, regardless of one's aristocratic status. But as Cartlidge also notes, it is remarkable just how often romance heroes fail to live up to these basic standards.[3] Eugène Vinaver calls this passage the 'most complete and authentic record of Malory's conception of chivalry', and judging from its correspondences with the oath of the Order of the Bath, recorded in about 1461 by Sir John Astley, Malory's conception of chivalry owes much to contemporary chivalric practices.[4] Undoubtedly, though, in that interchange of chivalric art and chivalric life that typified aristocratic activities in the later Middle Ages, these practices were themselves inspired by romance ideals.[5] Such ideals, however, were

---

[1] Sir Thomas Malory, *Le Morte Darthur*, ed. Stephen H.A. Shepherd (New York, 2004), p. 77 (III.15).
[2] From Harold Arthur, Viscount Dillon, 'On a MS. Collection of Ordinances of Chivalry of the fifteenth century, belonging to Lord Hastings', *Archaeologia* 57 (1900), 29–70, at pp. 67–68. The manuscript is now New York, Pierpont Morgan Library MS 775.
[3] Neil Cartlidge, 'The Fairies in the Fountain: Promiscuous Liaisons', in *The Exploitations of Medieval Romance*, ed. Laura Ashe, Ivana Djordjević and Judith Weiss (Cambridge, 2010), pp. 15–27, at pp. 25–26.
[4] The oath does not occur in Malory's surviving sources. See *The Works of Sir Thomas Malory*, ed. Eugène Vinaver, revised by P.J.C. Field, 3rd edn, 3 vols (Oxford, 1990), 3:1335, n. 120.
[5] The Order of the Bath was founded along the same lines as the Order of the Garter, which was established in 1348 by Edward III in emulation of Arthur's Round Table. The Order of

not always realized in practice. Malory's own life records, in which he is accused (among other things) of raping the same woman twice, provide an extreme example of how the contradictions of ordinary life allow for a knight to fully understand and valorize chivalric standards, and yet not always live up to them. Indeed, whether guilty or not, one might wonder with what sense of irony he penned 'never to enforce them', a prescription Caxton omits since it must have seemed, as Vinaver says, 'singularly incongruous in an Arthurian context'; that is, out of place because too far removed from the norms of idealized courteous behaviour.[6] In the epilogue to his translation of Ramón Llull's *Order of Chivalry* (1484) Caxton notes that 'curtosye and gentylnesse' are two of the fundamental principles of knighthood, and indeed that they are to be found exemplified in romance.[7] In the following year Caxton would complete his edition of the *Morte Darthur* with these standards fresh in his mind, and he would do so, as he says in his preface, so that 'noble men may see and lerne the noble actes of chyvalrye'.[8] This Round Table oath is the closest the *Morte Darthur* comes to a chivalric manual, but on the whole what Llull does didactically, Malory does by example.

As in real life, however, the examples of romance heroes are not always clear-cut. If Malory himself was a bundle of contradictions, so too is his best knight, Lancelot; and for different reasons so is Gawain, Malory's version of the traditionally best English knight, whose early antics lead Arthur to institute the yearly oath in the first place. This chapter will focus on the examples given by 'heroes' of this sort, ungallant knights who would not live up to the standards of such a chivalric oath, Arthurian or otherwise, fictional or real. To be gallant (from OF 'galant', ppl. of 'galer', 'to make merry') is to be both physically fashionable and fashionable to society; in short, it is to have good manners. Even in romance, though, nobility of appearance and nobility of birth do not assure nobility of behaviour. As one wise woman puts it to a particularly ungallant knight, he who does 'shame and vileynye' is not noble, even if he comes from a 'gentil hous'. While knights in romance may represent the best humanity had to offer, even the Wife of Bath recognises that 'highe parage' does not always equate to 'gentil dedes', and that manners maketh man.[9] With very few exceptions, medieval romance is insistent on its heroes being nobly born, but at the same time it is much less interested in insisting that they behave as though they are. It is this tension between the knight and the man, between the ideal and the real, which drives much of romance's human interest.

the Bath had been instituted by 1399, when it is mentioned in connection with the coronation of Henry IV. On chivalric orders and chivalric anthologies, or 'great books', see Shepherd, *Le Morte Darthur*, p. 780, n. 1; also, Maurice Keen, *Chivalry* (New Haven, 1984), esp. pp. 179–99; Richard Barber, 'Malory's *Morte Darthur* and Court Culture under Edward IV', *Arthurian Literature* 12, ed. James P. Carley and Felicity Riddy (Cambridge, 1993), 133–55, at pp. 147–49; Karen Cherewatuk, 'Sir Thomas Malory's "Grete booke"', in *The Social and Literary Contexts of Malory's 'Morte Darthur'*, ed. D. Thomas Hanks Jr. and Jessica G. Brogdon (Cambridge, 2000), pp. 42–67.

[6] Vinaver, *Works*, 3:1335, n. 120. On Malory's eventful life, see P.J.C. Field, *The Life and Times of Sir Thomas Malory* (Cambridge, 1993).

[7] *The Order of Chivalry*, trans. William Caxton, ed. F.S. Ellis (London, 1893), p. 99; also in N.F. Blake, *Caxton's Own Prose* (London, 1973), p. 126.

[8] *Le Morte Darthur*, p. 817.

[9] Geoffrey Chaucer, *The Riverside Chaucer*, ed. Larry D. Benson, 3rd edn (Oxford, 1987), p. 120 (III.1146–58).

The various dangers of erotic temptation and inappropriate behaviour toward women consistently emerge as major narrative and thematic threads in romance, from twelfth-century texts like the *Erec et Enide* of Chrétien de Troyes, through fourteenth-century texts such as *Sir Gawain and the Green Knight*, to black-letter prints like *Arthur of Little Britain*. A survey of these trends in a broad generic context, however, may not be the most useful way of imagining how these texts were actually read in practice. Instead, in this chapter I want to focus on the kinds of multi-genre textual networks witnessed in miscellany collections. This manuscript context should allow for localized discussions of the exemplary potential of those badly behaved knights, and of how the propensity for late medieval audiences to 'read for the moral' might have been affected by the interactions of proximal texts.[10] Narrative authority was not strictly the preserve of clerical writings in the later Middle Ages, as Larry Scanlon argues, though I would not go so far as to suggest that romances were being read simply as exempla, or that erring heroes should be fitted to the *de casibus* tradition writ large. As Melissa Furrow argues, exemplarity was not so much a generic category as a reading strategy: reared on sermon exempla and the fifteenth-century popularity of Chaucer and his followers, audiences 'expected what they read to be exemplary in some way'.[11] It is to this expectation that Caxton caters in his preface to the *Morte Darthur*, even though readings of Malory's best knights – Lancelot, Gawain, Tristram, Lamerok – might not always be considered improving. While the aristocracy of the fifteenth century was living out its appropriations of romance through their own tournaments and chivalric Orders, a growing reading public was encountering these same texts in both cheap prints and in the household miscellanies that were becoming increasingly popular sources of family instruction and entertainment.

What follows is a study of two fifteenth-century manuscripts containing romances that prominently feature ill-behaved heroes. In Oxford, Bodleian Library MS Ashmole 61 appears the dubious and at times wayward behaviour of Gyngeleyne, the protagonist of *Lybeaus Desconus*, and in Cambridge, University Library MS Ff.5.48, the strange conduct of the eponymous hero of *Thomas of Erceldoune*. What I hope to show is that the manuscript contexts of these romances can have a significant effect on how they might have been read for the moral, or rather on how early audiences might have used these miscellaneous combinations of texts to calibrate their understanding of the moral implications of particular romance heroes.

Oxford, Bodleian Library MS Ashmole 61

This paper manuscript compiled in about 1500 is the work of a single scribe, the 'Rate' who signs his name at the conclusion of 19 of the manuscript's 43 texts. The identity of this scribe has not been confirmed, but a good hypothesis is that he was an amateur from Leicestershire collecting texts for use in his own household – in

---

[10] I borrow the phrase from J. Allan Mitchell, *Ethics and Exemplary Narrative in Chaucer and Gower* (Cambridge, 2004), esp. pp. 8–21.

[11] See Larry Scanlon, *Narrative, Authority, and Power: The Medieval Exemplum and the Chaucerian Tradition* (Cambridge, 1994), esp. pp. 13–17; Melissa Furrow, *Expectations of Romance: The Reception of a Genre in Medieval England* (Cambridge, 2009), p. 11; Mitchell, pp. 14–15.

many ways a Robert Thornton of the Midlands.[12] How Rate managed to collect the copy-texts is uncertain, as is whether he made any conscious decisions in ordering the contents of his book. It is certainly possible to detect patterns or at least clusters of patterning in the existing order, but one could just as well see this as a case of 'correlation without causation'.[13] To whatever extent it was planned, at least, the Table of Contents drawn up in Rate's hand is a good reason (among others) to believe that the existing order of texts must have been set at a very early date.[14] This hodgepodge accumulation of texts is typical of the household books of the period, designed to cater to the diverse needs of what were often very large lay households.[15] Interspersed amid saints' lives, exempla, fabliaux, lyrics and didactic texts are five romances, four of them in the fully Anglicized tail-rhyme form – *Sir Isumbras* (item 5), *The Erle of Tolous* (item 19), *Lybeaus Desconus* (item 20) and *Sir Cleges* (item 24); the other, *Sir Orfeo* (item 39), in four-stress couplets.[16] Following *The Erle of Tolous* and *Lybeaus Desconus* is *Sir Corneus* (item 21), an Arthurian burlesque also composed in tail-rhyme, the form itself suggestive of its romance associations. Thus if these three texts together do not constitute an intentional clustering, it is at least an interesting coincidence, though readers were under no compulsion to read straight through.[17] As

---

[12] A good discussion of the manuscript and the scribe can be found in George Shuffelton's introduction to his edition, *Codex Ashmole 61: A Compilation of Popular Middle English Verse* (Kalamazoo, 2008), pp. 1–16; and also in his companion article, 'Is There a Minstrel in the House?: Domestic Entertainment in Late Medieval England', *Philological Quarterly* 87 (2008), 51–76. See too *Ten Fifteenth-Century Comic Poems*, ed. Melissa M. Furrow (New York, 1985), pp. 237–40. Much of the best work on this manuscript has been done by Lynne S. Blanchfield. See '"An Idiosyncratic Scribe": A Study of the Practice and Purpose of Rate, the Scribe of Bodleian Library MS Ashmole 61', unpublished doctoral dissertation (University of Wales, Aberystwyth, 1991); 'The Romances of Ashmole 61: An Idiosyncratic Scribe', in *Romance in Medieval England*, ed. Maldwyn Mills, Jennifer Fellows and Carol M. Meale (Cambridge, 1991), pp. 65–87; 'Rate Revisited: The Compilation of Narrative Works in MS Ashmole 61', in *Romance Reading on the Book: Essays in Medieval Narrative presented to Maldwyn Mills*, ed. Jennifer Fellows, Rosalind Field, Gillian Rogers and Judith Weiss (Cardiff, 1996), pp. 208–20.

[13] Blanchfield observes that 'it is possible to perceive thematic groupings of texts, even though these sequences are usually "interrupted" by a text of contrasting character, as if Rate tried to vary the tone even while pursuing particular interests'. But even this strategy, she notes, would have been subject to the availability of exemplars. She does, however, conclude that 'the manuscript was compiled sequentially, rather than as a series of main texts interspersed with filler items within single gatherings or booklets' ('Rate Revisited', p. 211). For the different methods of compiling miscellanies see Julia Boffey and John Thompson, 'Anthologies and Miscellanies: Production and Choice of Texts', in *Book Production and Publishing in Britain, 1375–1475*, ed. Jeremy Griffiths and Derek Pearsall (Cambridge, 1989), pp. 290–97, 298–99.

[14] See Shuffelton, *Codex Ashmole 61*, pp. 6–8.

[15] Suggestive of a network of exemplar circulation, Ashmole 61 shares a number of its texts with other similar household books: six with CUL MS Ff.5.48, six with CUL MS Ff.2.38, four with London, BL MS Cotton Caligula A.2 (including *Lybeaus Desconus*), and two with the 'Heege' manuscript, Edinburgh, National Library of Scotland MS Advocates, 19.3.1. Boffey and Thompson first coined the term 'household miscellany' in 'Anthologies and Miscellanies', pp. 279–315, at p. 294; also, Julia Boffey, 'Bodleian Library, MS Arch. Selden. B. 24 and Definitions of the Household Book', in *The English Medieval Book: Studies in Memory of Jeremy Griffiths*, ed. A.S.G. Edwards, V. Gillespie and R. Hanna (London, 2000), pp. 125–34.

[16] On tail-rhyme generally, and particularly on the form having a home in the North and Central/East Midlands, see Rhiannon Purdie, *Anglicising Romance: Tail-Rhyme and Genre in Medieval English Literature* (Cambridge, 2008), esp. pp. 144–49.

[17] Shuffelton considers the juxtaposition of the latter two 'one of Rate's more inspired choices' (*Codex Ashmole 61*, p. 473).

Nicola McDonald has said in reference to another household book, 'the freedom to "turne over the leef" was not the prerogative of Chaucer's readers alone'.[18]

For our purposes, though, the grouping of *The Erle of Tolous*, *Lybeaus Desconus* and *Sir Corneus* raises some interesting questions about the display of appropriate chivalric behaviour. *The Erle of Tolous*, in many ways, is an exercise in the proper constraint of erotic desires.[19] When the Earl falls in love with the suitably named Beulybon (i.e. 'belle et bonne'), the wife of the emperor, he manages to arrange a meeting with her in – significantly – a church. Though apparently mutually smitten (she gives him a ring), Beulybon only allows the Earl a brief, and fully clothed, personal display:

> Thrys sche turned hyre abowte
> Betwen the erles that were stoute,
> For that lorde schuld here se.
>
> (*The Erle of Tolous*, lines 346–48; fol. 30br)[20]

Followed by a rhetorical *effectio* describing her beauty, this presentation is perhaps the protagonists' most morally dubious encounter. The Earl prays 'Lord God [...] that sche non husband hade' (lines 364, 367; fol. 30bv), but when he receives the ring, he admits: 'That any love be us between,/ This may be owre tokenyng' (lines 404–405; fol. 30bv). This theme of sexual fidelity is cleverly integrated into the narrative's main conflict. When the Emperor is away, his two stewards attempt to seduce her, but, when she refuses, they accuse her of infidelity with a duped (and quickly murdered) page. With Beulybon scheduled for execution, the Earl returns to fight a judicial combat on her behalf, but first he needs assurances of her innocence. Just before her execution he meets the abbot, Beulybon's confessor:

> The Erle seyd, 'So have I blys,
> Me thinke of hyr dole it is,
> Trew if that sche be.'
> The abot seyd, 'be Seynt Paule,
> For hyr I durste ley my saule
> That never gylty was sche.

---

[18] Nicola McDonald, 'A York Primer and Its Alphabet: Reading Women in a Lay Household', in *The Oxford Handbook of Medieval Literature in English*, ed. Elaine Treharne and Greg Walker (Oxford, 2010), pp. 181–99, at p. 195. For readers dipping in and out the number of possible combinations of texts in Ashmole 61 is truly astronomical. Factorial 43 (expressed mathematically as 43!) represents the total number of possible ways all of the manuscript's texts could be read in sequence. That number is $6.04152631 \times 10^{52}$, or 60,415,263 billion billion billion billion billion. Clearly no reader would run out of new ways of reading texts next to each other. (Thanks to Sebastian Ahnert for help with the maths.)

[19] *The Erle of Tolous* survives in three other manuscripts, two of which being large fifteenth-century miscellanies: Lincoln, Cathedral Library MS 91 (the Lincoln Thornton manuscript), CUL MS Ff.2.38 and Oxford, Bodleian Library MS Ashmole 45. For an excellent study of Ashmole 45, a presentation text with a distinctive frontispiece, see Carol M. Meale, '"Prenes: engre": an early sixteenth-century presentation copy of *The Erle of Tolous*', in *Romance Reading on the Book: Essays in Medieval Narrative presented to Maldwyn Mills*, pp. 221–36.

[20] For all references to Ashmole 61, I quote from Shuffelton's edition, though I will also give MS folio references after the line numbers. In the Lincoln Thornton and Ff.2.38, Beulybon only turns twice. One might also compare this initial meeting with the highly eroticized first encounter in *Sir Launfal* (lines 277–312), another Middle English Breton lay. See *The Middle English Breton Lays*, ed. Anne Laskaya and Eve Salisbury (Kalamazoo, 2001), pp. 201–62, at pp. 217–18.

> Syche werkys sche never wrought,
> Nother in dede ne in thought,
> Save a ryng so fre
> To the Erle of Tolous sche gafe with wyn,
> In es of hym and for no syn;
> In schryft thus told sche.'
>
> (*The Erle of Tolous*, lines 1017–28; fol. 36v)

The Earl then admits to the Abbot that he is the Earl of Tolous:

> 'Syr', he seyd, 'withowte lesyng,
> I ame he sche gafe the ryng;
> Hold consell, for the rode.'
>
> (*The Erle of Tolous*, lines 1035–37; fol. 36v)

With which we might compare:

> 'Y am he that sche gaf the rynge
> For to be oure tokenynge.
> Now heyle hyt, for the rode.'
>
> (*The Erle of Tolous*, CUL Ff.2.38; fol. 69vb)[21]

Here it should be noted that the Lincoln Thornton accords with Ashmole 61, and Ashmole 45 with Ff.2.38.[22] What the Lincoln Thornton and Ashmole 61 are trying to avoid, it seems, is the recollection of lines 404–405 (quoted above), in which the ring is signalled as a 'tokenynge' of their love – these two texts, presumably, trying to downplay the possibility that this ring-giving was in fact a 'sin', that it was given for love rather than for the 'ease' of the Earl.

This attention to Beulybon's sexual fidelity is given even further emphasis when the Earl, playing fast and loose with the sacrament of confession, dresses up like a hermit and shrives her himself: 'He freyned of hir full wytterly' (line 1062; fol. 37r), the mock-confession begins. It is a largely repetitive scene, in that the romance has already established Beulybon's innocence, but part of its dramatic irony is that the examination interrogates the Earl's behaviour as much as hers. When the narrator says 'Sche was withouten gylte' (line 1064; fol. 37r), the romance also seems to be working hard to balance extra-marital love with marital chastity.[23] Of course Beulybon and the Earl end up together after the Emperor dies of natural causes (very soon after), but throughout their pseudo-courtship the bar of appropriate sexual behaviour has been set very high indeed. If a fifteenth-century audience was reading for the moral, they would have found the purity of confession sacrificed for the purity of even an unhappy marriage, the integrity of one sacrament compromised for

---

[21] For a facsimile edition see *Cambridge University Library MS Ff.2.38*, ed. P.R. Robinson (London, 1979).

[22] For a parallel edition of the texts from Ff.2.38 and Ashmole 45, see *The Erle of Tolous: Eine Paralleledition mit Einleitung und Glossar*, ed. Friedrich Hülsmann (Essen, 1987). For a facsimile of the Lincoln Thornton, see *The Thornton Manuscript (Lincoln Cathedral MS. 91)*, ed. D.S. Brewer and A.E.B. Owen (London, 1977). The lines in question appear on fol. 121va.

[23] Dieter Mehl notes that 'the narrator repeatedly interrupts the narrative with his own comments', and that throughout these intrusions 'he clearly stands on the side of his two protagonists' (e.g. lines 414, 527, 597, 691–93, 705 and 757). See *The Middle English Romances of the Thirteenth and Fourteenth Centuries* (London, 1968), pp. 85–93, at p. 92.

the sustaining of another, with the implication being that controlling the audience's interpretation of the early whiff of erotic 'syn' is central to the text's moral agenda.

Sir Corneus, which follows *Lybeaus Desconus* in Ashmole 61, arrives at a surprisingly similar moral considering just how different it is in narrative form. Its Arthurian setting and tail-rhyme metrics give it immediate romance associations,[24] but it is essentially a comic negative exemplum – 'A gode ensample I wyll you sey', it begins (line 10; fol. 59v) – that uses the magic drinking horn motif to expose the cuckoldry of Arthur's court.[25] All of Arthur's knights have been proved cuckolds by the magic horn, and when Arthur himself tries his luck he spills as well. Guinevere blushes for shame (her only appearance in the story, lines 187–88; fol. 61v), and with a laugh Arthur joins the 'freyry' (line 215; fol. 61v) of cuckolds in a mirthful dance. On the surface it is a story that makes light of sexual infidelity, its irreverent tone and mild vulgarity being very different from *The Erle of Tolous*, but there nevertheless remains a serious moral undertow. As Blanchfield puts it, the exemplum illustrates how cuckoldry levels rank, much like death.[26] When Arthur is caught out the knights think the king is 'there awne brother' (line 182; fol. 61r, a phrase used twice more in the tale, lines 216 and 236; fol. 61v), and in a collective utterance they assert both their unity and their shared feebleness:

> 'Go we, lordingys, all same,
> And dance to make us gle and game,
> For cokwoldys have no galle'. (*Sir Corneus*, lines 202–204; fol. 61v)

The final line here is both comic and biting, reminding the reader just how far the greatest British king has fallen, and why. The comedy is part of its secularism, but in the context of Ashmole 61 the serious moral reverberates with corresponding religious exempla. Immediately following *Sir Corneus* are two cautionary tales, *The Jealous Wife* (item 22) and *The Incestuous Daughter* (item 23), both of which are quite

---

[24] The title, also suggestive of romance, is editorial. Sir Corneus, one of Arthur's knights, is identified as the author of the tale (lines 244–49).

[25] Ashmole 61 contains the only surviving witness of this text and there is no known source, though many analogues. The closest may be the thirteenth-century Anglo-Norman *Lai du Cor*, in which Arthur, after failing to take a clean drink, nearly stabs Guinevere before he is restrained. Malory's analogous episode, taken from the prose *Tristan*, sees the horn originally sent by Morgan le Fay to Arthur's court, but is then redirected by Lamerok to Mark's in order to catch Isode in her adultery. Here it is the ladies who drink, and when only four of one hundred pass the test Mark has to be talked out of sending them all to the stake. The other magical device used to detect unfaithful women is the magic mantle. Ulrich von Zatzikhoven's *Lanzelet* (which he claims to have translated from an Anglo-Norman original) includes a magic mantle that only fits truly blameless women. In this instance, however, it is used to show the perfection of Iblis, the heroine (*Lanzelet*, lines 5679–6228). A similar mantle also appears in the widely popular tale of Craddock's wife. The story survives only in the Percy Folio's *The Boy and Mantle*, in which all the women of Arthur's court, save Craddock's wife, fail the test. The boy also produces a magic drinking horn, though with very similar results. Caxton says in his preface to the *Morte Darthur* that Craddock's mantle can be seen at Dover Castle, along with Gawain's skull. See *The Anglo-Norman Text of Le Lai du Cor*, ed. C.T. Erickson, ANTS 24 (Oxford, 1973); *Le Roman de Tristan en Prose*, ed. R.L. Curtis, 3 vols (Leiden, 1963–85), 2:129–31; Malory, *Morte Darthur*, ed. Shepherd, pp. 268–69 (VIII:34); Ulrich von Zatzikhoven, *Lanzelet*, trans. Thomas Kerth (New York, 2005), pp. 92–98; *Bishop Percy's Folio Manuscript: Ballads and Romances*, ed. John W. Hales and Frederick J. Furnivall, 3 vols (London, 1867–68), 2:301–11.

[26] Blanchfield, 'Rate Revisited', p. 213.

serious in showing the dangers of a number of sexual sins. Added to these, *The Sinner's Lament* and *The Adulterous Falmouth Squire* (items 35a and 35b) are both invested in showing in explicit detail the eternal consequences of extra-marital affairs. Considering these five exempla together, some fifteenth-century readers might have found the jokes of *Sir Corneus* decidedly un-funny; at least, it is safe to assume that they would likely have been more attuned to the seriousness of its underlying moral than if it were read in isolation.

It is in this context, and the moral calibration it recommends, that I would like to consider the behaviour of Gyngeleyne in *Lybeaus Desconus*. Blanchfield notes the 'marked unsuitability' of the romance in its manuscript context, especially because of its proximity to the exemplary moral flavour of *The Erle of Tolous*. In fact, every other non-didactic narrative in Ashmole 61, she argues, has some obvious moral point, and in this regard *Lybeaus* stands alone as 'long-winded and shallow'.[27] Part of this perceived shallowness, perhaps, comes from those characteristics often found in Middle English translations of French romances, such as abridgement (often at the loss of logical coherence), psychological simplification and a greater emphasis on action and general knockabout adventure. But part, too, must come from the resulting lack of moral subtlety, or even the refusal to acknowledge potential moral complexities at all. The romance might not be noteworthy for its piety or its exemplification of Christian virtues, as George Shuffelton argues, but this is simply part and parcel of its wholesale levelling of the action's moral implications.[28]

Perhaps nowhere is this better witnessed than in the hero's dealings with women. As in the thirteenth-century *Le Bel Inconnu*, the Fair Unknown sets out with a damsel to rescue the Lady of Synadone.[29] Elyn, the damsel, mocks the young and untried Gyngeleyne en route, but following a victorious early outing against Sir William Dolebraunce the two make up:

> He and meyden bright
> Made together that nyght
> Game and grete solace.   (*Lybeaus Desconus*, lines 472–74; fol. 43r)

---

[27] Blanchfield, 'Rate Revisited', pp. 212–13; also, 'An Idiosyncratic Scribe', pp. 66–67. The moral lessons of Ashmole 61's entertaining narratives, as summarized by Blanchfield, are: '*Sir Isumbras* (penance redeems pride); *Carpenter's Tools* (drink ruins industry); *Sir Corneus* (cuckoldry levels rank); *The Erle of Tolous* (fidelity rewarded); *Sir Cleges* (justice served); *Sir Orfeo* (power of love triumphs); *King Edward*, the extant text (the treachery of drink)' ('Rate Revisited', p. 213). It also might be noted that *Lybeaus Desconus*'s critical reputation has been less than sterling. It got off to a bad start when Chaucer included 'sir Lybeux' (VII. 900) in the roll-call of famous knights in 'Sir Thopas', and even its modern editor characterizes the composition as 'consistently inept and careless'. See *Lybeaus Desconus*, ed. M. Mills, EETS OS 261 (London, 1969), p. 89.

[28] See Shuffelton, *Codex Ashmole 61*, p. 473.

[29] The romance now attributed to Renaut de Bâgé accords with the Middle English version in many details, though it seems likely that the latter either draws on additional sources or is based on a now-lost French text that bears an unknown relationship with the surviving *Le Bel Inconnu*. See Renaut de Bâgé, *Le Bel Inconnu (Li Biaus Descouneüs; The Fair Unknown)*, ed. Karen Fresco, trans. Colleen P. Donagher, music ed. Margaret P. Hasselman (New York, 1992), pp. xxi–xxii. The Fair Unknown story was very popular in Middle English: *Lybeaus* finds analogues in *Sir Perceval of Galles*, *Sir Degaré*, Malory's 'Tale of Sir Gareth' and Book I of Spenser's *Faerie Queene*.

Maldwyn Mills notes that this 'can hardly be anything other than a night of love-making'.[30] Of course 'game' carries a range of connotations in Middle English, but when used in the context of night-time activities between a man and woman the general implication seems pretty clear – what the *MED* reservedly calls 'amorous play' ('game', n. 2d.). The suggestion is further supported when Gyngeleyne later refers to Elyn as his 'lemman' (line 849; fol. 46v), though this fact the hero himself soon forgets. When the two come to the Yl d'Ore Gyngeleyne is bluntly propositioned by a beautiful lady:

> Sche proferd hym at a word
> Ever more to be hyr lord
> Of cyté and of castell. (*Lybeaus Desconus*, lines 1507–509; fol. 52v)

The lady is called Denamowre in Ashmole 61, though in the other manuscripts she is 'la Dame d'Amore' – Rate's form, perhaps intentionally, losing the name's erotic connotations.[31] If this is a mild form of scribal bowdlerisation for household tastes it is soon followed by a more drastic revision. Compare:

> Lybeus grantyd hyr in haste
> And love to hyr he caste.
> For ever at the last
> Sche dyd hym traye and tene...
> (*Lybeaus Desconus*, Ashmole 61, lines 1510–13; fol. 52v)

> Lybeous graunted hir in haste
> And loue to hir ganne caste,
> For she was bright and shene.
> Alas she hadde be chaaste!
> For euer at the laste
> She dyde hym traye and tene.
> (*Lybeaus Desconus*, Lambeth Palace 306, lines 1473–78; fol. 95v)[32]

The two lines missing from Ashmole 61 may have also been missing from Rate's exemplar, though it is at least as likely that Rate cut them himself, finding them rather too heavy-handed in the suggestion of a sexual relationship. Blanchfield finds Rate's editing patterns throughout the manuscript to be purposeful and slanted towards a religious or family preaching bias, and if pre-marital sexual activity was not bad enough, now the hero is not even true to his first 'lemman'.[33]

It might be argued that Gyngeleyne seem less culpable considering Denamowre 'bleryd hys eye' with illusions to make him believe he is in paradise (lines 1526–30; fol. 53r), but when the logic of this enchantment breaks down in the following two stanzas one is quickly reminded that he assented to her love in the first place. After

---

[30] Mills, *Lybeaus Desconus*, p. 58.
[31] Mills's edition reproduces the texts of London, BL MS Cotton Caligula A.2 and London, Lambeth Palace Library MS 306. The Percy Folio version (London, BL MS Additional 27879) can be found in *Bishop Percy's Folio: Manuscript, Ballads and Romances*, ed. John W. Hales and F.J. Furnivall, 3 vols (London, 1866–68), 2:404–99. The romance also survives in London, Lincoln's Inn MS Hale 150 and Naples, Biblioteca Nazionale MS XIII.B.29.
[32] From Mills, *Lybeaus Desconus*, p. 163.
[33] Blanchfield, 'The Romances of Ashmole 61', pp. 74–79.

more than three weeks of this revelry he happens across Elyn, during which encounter she berates him for leaving the Lady of Synadone to languish in prison, and for dishonouring himself 'For the love of a woman/ That mych of sorcery can' (lines 1538–39; fol. 53r). After hearing these words he 'thought hys herte wold breke/ For that gentyll dame' (lines 1545–46; fol. 53r), though it is not entirely clear if the 'gentyll dame' is the Elyn he has betrayed or the Lady of Synadone he has forgotten about.[34] In any case the suggestion that he is under some sort of enchantment has all but evaporated. And while in the Cotton and Lambeth manuscripts there is at least a hint of a covert escape from the Dame d'Amoure (Lambeth Palace 306, lines 1512–13; fol. 96v), in Ashmole 61 Gyngeleyne simply rides off:

> He toke with hym hys stede,
> Hys armour and hys other wede,
> And rode forth in same.
>
> (*Lybeaus Desconus*, lines 1547–49; fol. 53r)

Thus the next adventure begins, and his amorous relationship with Denamowre is not mentioned again. Indeed, when they reach the city of Synadone Gyngeleyne sends Elyn into town while he fights the giant Lamberte (lines 1586–91; fol. 53v), and she also is never heard from again. That the hero, too, has managed to forget about her for the second time becomes clear when he learns that the Lady of Synadone is an heiress: 'That lady wyll I wynne!' (line 1790; fol. 55r) – a vow he is at least brave enough to keep.

At the end, though, the romance's handling of Gyngeleyne's response to the erotic changes tack. When Mabon and Irain are defeated and Gyngeleyne has broken their enchantments by kissing the 'worme', the Lady of Synadone appears:

> Bot sche was all nakyd
> As the clerkys hyr makyd;
> Therfor Lybeus was wo. (*Lybeaus Desconus*, lines 2078–80; fol. 58r)

The tail line here is suggestive of the sort of gallantry one ought to expect from romance heroes, and it marks a shift in the romance's roughshod approach to the appropriate chivalric treatment of women, even if Rate took some pains to tone down the explicitly erotic. The story ends with a proper marriage back at Arthur's court, but there is still a final twist. Gyngeleyne's mother appears at the wedding to tell Gawain that he is Gyngeleyne's father, to which he gives the terse reply 'That lykes me' (line 2203; fol. 59r).[35] The happy reunion is complete when Gawain shares the news with the bride and groom: 'He that hath thee wedyd with pride', Gawain says to the Lady of Synadone, 'I gate hym under a forest syde/ Of a gentyll lady' (lines 2207–209; fol. 59r). This belated emphasis on family must have recommended the romance to Rate, as otherwise there would seem to be few explanations for what

---

[34] Cotton Caligula A.2 and Lambeth Palace 306 avoid the confusion since his heart breaks 'For sorowe and for shame' (Lambeth Palace, line 1511; fol. 96r). The 'gentyll dame' in these texts (line 1514) is the Dame d'Amoure he escapes from.

[35] This ending is only witnessed in Ashmole 61, the Percy Folio and Naples, Biblioteca Nazionale MS XIII.B.29.

would have done.³⁶ The happy ending, however, is not as rosy as the romance would have us assume, for what the reunion exposes is the abandonment of Gyngeleyne's mother in the first place.³⁷

But like father like son, we might say, this being just the final instance of the romance's depiction of ungallant knightly behaviour, and of the text's refusal to deal with the moral implications of that. The only time the hero acts with a broadly chivalric sense of sexual propriety is with the Lady of Synadone, the romance laying the groundwork for the proper and sanctioned union that culminates the hero's quest, as if to suggest that sexual encounters only require care when the politics of marriage and succession come into play. This is perhaps a rather cynical reading of the romance, but it is one prompted by its position in Ashmole 61. Read in isolation, the hero's promiscuity might have been considered an acceptable element (perhaps even a fantasy element) of the knight-alone romance, and the marked absence of moral concern part of the secularism and escapism of its form. However, following in the footsteps of one of the more morally conscious and sophisticated Middle English romances, *The Erle of Tolous*, Gyngeleyne's laddish ungallantry comes across as shallow indeed. A fifteenth-century audience conditioned to read for the exemplary may well have found something anti-heroic in the carelessness with which he treats his amorous partners, much like Arthur and his knights in *Sir Corneus*. The difference, though, is that in reading for the moral an audience could have come away from the laughs of Arthur's cuckoldry with an edifying message – and one that accords with the other exempla and entertaining tales scattered throughout the manuscript. Of course there are many texts in the manuscript that could have been read in conjunction with *Lybeaus*, as readers dipped in and out of the book, but it is worth noting that next to the other romances in the manuscript not discussed here – the piety of Isumbras and Cleges, and the utter faithfulness of Orfeo – Gyngeleyne's behaviour still does not have much to recommend it. It would certainly be a stretch to class Gyngeleyne as an anti-hero, but compared with the other romance heroes in Ashmole 61 he is certainly far from exemplary.

Cambridge, University Library MS Ff.5.48

This small paper manuscript of about 1475 is the work of four or possibly five scribes. Like Ashmole 61 it was likely put together for use in a lay household, and in fact it shares a number of texts with Ashmole 61 (as with many other fifteenth-century household books), suggesting a network of shared exemplars circulating

---

³⁶ Blanchfield makes this point, 'The Romances of Ashmole 61', p. 67. In terms of its moral stance, certainly, *Lybeaus* is an odd fit in the manuscript, but, like *The Erle of Tolous* and *Sir Corneus*, it is at least entertaining. As Shuffelton says, too, it is one of the romances that 'flatter the ambitions of renegade youth', a model fantasy of social ascendency. See 'Is There a Minstrel in the House?', p. 59. For a reading of the romance's ideological investments, see Stephen Knight, 'The Social Function of the Middle English Romances', in *Medieval Literature: Criticism, Ideology and History*, ed. David Aers (Brighton, 1986), pp. 99–122, at pp. 104–108.

³⁷ Gawain's impregnation of the lady in a forest setting has rather sinister generic reverberations. The 'fairi knyghte' who rapes the Fair Unknown's mother in *Sir Degaré* does so while she is lost in a forest (lines 79–108), and the rapist knight in 'The Wife of Bath's Tale' encounters his victim while 'ridynge fro ryver' (III. 884), for instance. See *The Middle English Breton lays*, pp. 89–144, at pp. 103–104; also, Corinne Saunders, *The Forest of Medieval Romance: Avernus, Brocéliande, Arden* (Cambridge, 1993); *Rape and Ravishment in the Literature of Medieval England* (Cambridge, 2001).

individually or in small groupings.³⁸ Indeed the five distinct sections that now make up the manuscript may have themselves circulated independently for some time, though they would have been bound together at a relatively early date, probably somewhere in the north.³⁹ As with Ashmole 61, too, the collected 31 items would have catered to a medley of household needs and interests, from the carnivalesque *Tournament of Tottenham* (item 12) to *The ABC of Aristotle* (item 2), from the fabliau *The Tale of the Basin* (item 11) to *A Lament of the Blessed Virgin* (item 15). It is at the end of this collection that *Thomas of Erceldoune* appears (item 30), the manuscript's only romance.⁴⁰ Of course any attempt at defining romance would locate *Thomas* on the generic fringe, though the fairy mistress and the adventurous journey help keep it close to a certain horizon of romance expectations. It should be noted, however, that its rhyming quatrains and use of repetition suggest affinities with the ballad, like the quatrains of *Robin Hood and the Monk* that follow (item 31).⁴¹ The narrative of Thomas and the fairy, moreover, take up only the first fit, the remaining two being

---

³⁸ In the first major study of the manuscript Janay Young Downing argued that it was the commonplace book of the Lancashire cleric Gilbert Pilkington, with a short booklet from another scribe (fols. 79r–94v) bound with it. However, the number of hands now recognised (Downing only identified two) makes its origin as a commonplace book unlikely, and the only evidence of Pilkington's involvement is the colophon to the *Northern Passion*: 'Explicit Passio Domini Nostri Ihesu Christi Quod Dominus Gilbertus Pylkyngton' (fol. 43r). Certainly, this could indicate that Pilkington was one of the four or five scribes, but it could just as well be the case that an unknown scribe copied the colophon from his exemplar, taking Pilkington to be the author of the *Northern Passion*. See Downing, 'A Critical Edition of Cambridge University MS FF.5.48', unpublished doctoral dissertation (University of Washington, Seattle, 1969), pp. xxviii–xxxiii. For a good description of the manuscript see Furrow, *Ten Fifteenth-Century Comic Poems*, pp. 45–52.

³⁹ For more on Ff.5.48 as a household book, and on the circulation of exemplars, see Carol M. Meale, 'Romance and its Anti-Type? *The Turnament of Totenham*, the Carnivalesque, and Popular Culture', in *Middle English Poetry: Texts and Traditions: Essays in Honour of Derek Pearsall*, ed. by A.J. Minnis (York, 2001), pp. 103–27, esp. pp. 110–17.

⁴⁰ *Thomas* survives in four other manuscripts: Lincoln Cathedral MS 91 (the Lincoln Thornton); London, BL MS Cotton Vitellius E.10; London, BL MS Lansdowne 762, and London, BL MS Sloane 2578. A version is also copied in one early print by Matthew Walbancke: *Sundry strange prophecies of Merline, Bede, Becket and others* (London, 1652). Unfortunately the *Thomas* section of Ff.5.48 has been much damaged by water, and by a chemical substance used by Robert Jamieson in a failed attempt to enhance the lettering when he edited the texts for his *Popular Ballads and Songs* (1806). Apparently the paper has deteriorated even further since James Murray edited it in 1875, as many lines are now entirely illegible. Here I will cite from Murray's edition; for other texts in Ff.5.48 I will for convenience adopt Downing's line numbering. See *The Romance and Prophecies of Thomas of Erceldoune*, ed. James A.H. Murray, EETS OS 61 (London, 1875), pp. lvi–lxi. For a modern edition of the early print see William P. Albrecht, *The Loathly Lady in 'Thomas of Erceldoune', with a Text of the Poem Printed in 1652* (Albuquerque, 1954).

⁴¹ Thomas may have originally descended from, and existed alongside, a ballad version of the same story; presumably it would have borne some relation to *Thomas the Rhymer*, recorded as ballad 37 in Child's collection. See *The English and Scottish Popular Ballads*, ed. Francis James Child, 5 vols (Boston, MA, 1882–98; repr. New York, 1965), 1.317–29. See also E.B. Lyle, 'The Relationship between *Thomas the Rhymer* and *Thomas of Erceldoune*', *Leeds Studies in English*, NS 4 (1970), 23–30; also, Richard Firth Green, 'The Ballad in the Middle Ages', in *The Long Fifteenth Century: Essays for Douglas Gray*, ed. Helen Cooper and Sally Mapstone (Oxford, 1997), pp. 163–84, esp. pp. 168–69.

the prophecies, much like the prognostications found in items 3, 18 and 26.[42] Of all the texts in Ff.5.48, though, *Thomas*'s most obvious affinities are with the exemplum of *The Adulterous Falmouth Squire* (item 14). In what follows I want to consider how this exemplum would have inflected a fifteenth-century audience's reading of Thomas's ungallant behaviour, and also how other relevant texts – like *The ABC of Aristotle* and *The Tale of the Basin* – might have shaded a reader's reception of the romance's hero in this context.

In days gone by of romance scholarship, when Celtic source-hunting was still fashionable, critics working on *Thomas* wrestled with the perceived problem of the text's mixture of Christian and Celtic elements. One solution, generally shared, was that *Thomas* was originally a story of the fairy-mistress type, and that the *Falmouth Squire* narrative was somehow grafted onto it to give us that curious mingling in which the fairy realm exists in some proximity to heaven, purgatory and hell.[43] My purpose is not to demonstrate any sort of textual indebtedness of one text to the other, nor am I interested in *Thomas*'s 'Christian' (as opposed to pagan) elements; rather I would like to suggest that the concentration of motifs and devices common to these texts might have encouraged a reading of the two texts as a pair.

The strongest similarity between these texts is that the visions in both are diegetically 'real'; that is, the protagonists are actually taken to the otherworld rather than having it shown to them in a vision or dream.[44] In *Falmouth Squire*, a youth wishing to know the fate of his father in the afterlife is visited by 'on in a qwyte surplisse' (line 91; fol. 68v) who acts as his guide:

> He led hym tille a cumly hille.
> Þe erth opeynd, in þei ȝede.
> Smoke and fyre þer can out welle,
> And mony gostes gloyng on glede.
>
> (*Falmouth Squire*, lines 97–100; fol. 68v)

A parallel quatrain in *Thomas*:

> She led hym to þe eldryn hill,
> Vndurneth þe grenewode lee,
> Wher hit was derk as any hell,
> And euer water tille þe knee.
>
> (*Thomas of Erceldoune*, lines 169–72; fol. 121r)

---

[42] Item 3, *Prognostications from the Amount of Thunder in the Months of the Year*; item 18, *Prognostics for the Year, According to the Day on which the New Year Falls*; item 26, *Prognostications about the Seasons of the Year*.

[43] Studies discussing this connection include Josephine Burnham, 'A Study of Thomas of Erceldoune', *PMLA* 23 (1908), 375–420, at pp. 408–11; Albrecht, pp. 26–27, 70; David C. Fowler, *A Literary History of the Popular Ballad* (Durham, NC, 1968), pp. 184–87; Ingeborg Nixon, 'Thomas and the Lady: Some Aspects of the Narrative Element in *Thomas of Erceldoune*', in *A Literary Miscellany Presented to Eric Jacobsen*, ed. Graham D. Caie and Holger Nørgaard (Copenhagen, 1988), pp. 52–66; E.B. Lyle, 'The Visions in *St. Patrick's Purgatory*, *Thomas of Erceldoune*, *Thomas the Rhymer* and *The Dæmon Lover*', *Neuphilologische Mitteilungen* 72 (1971), 716–22.

[44] In this group belongs *St. Patrick's Purgatory* as well. See Lyle, 'The Visions in *St. Patrick's Purgatory*', pp. 717–18.

This stanza from *Thomas* is not entirely the work of the original scribe. A different hand, presumably an early reader, has written 'hill' in the margin to the right of a crossed-out final 'tre' in line 169, and similarly in the next line 'tre' has been crossed out and 'lee' written in. More substantially, line 171 reads 'It was derk as mydnyght myrke', but this has been partially erased and in the same revising hand 'Wher hit was derk as any hell' has been written unevenly in the right margin. It may be that this reader was only interested in making his or her version accord with another available copy (both the Lincoln Thornton and Lansdowne 762 give 'Eldone hill' in line 169), but this hypothesis does not hold with what the reader did to line 171. The readings in Lincoln Thornton and Cotton Vitellius E.10 accord with the original in Ff.5.48, and Lansdowne 762 gives 'In weys derke þat was full ylle'. Certainly, it cannot be ruled out that this reader used hill/hell to fix the defective rhyming of the original, but this seems unlikely; someone as fastidious as that would have been very busy throughout the *Thomas* of Ff.5.48, and indeed throughout many other works in the manuscript, but this has not happened. Rather, with the otherworld entrance at a hill, and the use of an infernal rather than a midnight simile, it seems possible that at least one early reader had read *Thomas* with *Falmouth Squire* in mind, and the changes he or she made would have meant that readers to follow would have been more likely to do the same.[45]

However, *Falmouth Squire* is an 'insampulle' (line 53; fol. 67v) illustrating the dangers of lust – the 'lest of alle' the deadly sins but 'for to drede' nonetheless (line 4; fol. 67r) – and it is this same sin that gets Thomas into trouble. Things start out well enough; when Thomas first sees the lady he kneels to ask for the intercession of the 'qwene of heuen' (line 88; fol. 119v), but she appropriately answers: 'Quen of heuon am I noght,/ I toke neuer so hye degre' (lines 91–92; fol. 120r). Thus one of the first things we learn about Thomas is that he is a good Catholic with proper devotion to the Virgin, and that this fairy mistress, of 'anoþer cuntre' (line 93; fol. 120r), knows her right place in the metaphysical scheme of things. But then comes an about-turn; Thomas immediately follows up with a proposition: 'gif me leve to lye þe by' (line 100; fol. 120r). However, the lady says this is 'foly', and that 'þat wolde for-do my bewte' (lines 101, 104; fol. 120r). Thomas persists, and again she says 'þou wilt me marre,/ But ȝet þou shalt haue thy wille' (lines 117–18; fol. 120r), but again Thomas does not listen:

> Down þen light þat lady bright,
> Vndurneth a grenewode spray;
> And, as þe story tellus ful right,

---

[45] There are other points of contact between these texts. After visiting hell the boy in *Falmouth Squire* proceeds to paradise, where he enters a 'fayre erbere' where the 'popynjay' and 'nyȝttyngale' sing (lines 145–56; fols. 69r–v). When Thomas enters the earthly paradise he too hears the 'popyniay' and 'nyghtyngale' in a 'faire herbere' (lines 177–84; fol. 121r). More significant (in part because not conventional in medieval dream vision gardens) is the fruit Thomas tries to pick from one of the arbour's trees. The lady says: 'If þou pulle, þe soothe to sey,/ Þi soule goeth to þe fyre of hell' (lines 189–90; fol. 121v). In *Falmouth Squire* the boy also encounters a supernatural tree, and while *Thomas* only alludes to the forbidden fruit of the Garden of Eden, in this text the boy sees the tree itself, bleeding red from the place where the fateful apple was plucked (lines 157–76; fol. 69v). It is perhaps no coincidence that immediately following the fruit-picking test in *Thomas*, the hero is given his visions of the Christian otherworld realms.

vij tymes be hir he lay.
She seid, thomas, þou likis þi play:
What byrde in boure may dwel with þe?
Þou marris me here þis lefe long day,
I pray the, Thomas, let me be!

(*Thomas of Erceldoune*, lines 121–28; fols. 120r–v)

Helen Cooper aptly calls this 'sexual bullying', since it is not strictly rape, but nor is it a freely willed choice on the part of the lady.[46] The comically gratuitous 'vij tymes' and the potentially light 'þou likis þi play' hardly conceals the damage done. He has marred her ('Þou marris me here'; repeated from line 117), and to make things worse his seven efforts have taken the 'lefe long day' – i.e. the livelong day, a phrase that in Middle English has a sense of tediousness or drudgery about it.[47] In the Lincoln Thornton and Lansdowne 762 the sex is a 'synne' (line 104), but the allegation still seems clear enough even in Cotton Vitellius and Ff.5.48, where it is not explicitly linked to 'sin'. Cooper identifies it as the sin of lechery, but also notes that it is the lady who suffers through a hideous transformation, not Thomas: 'hir een semyd out [...] Þe too shanke was blak, þe toþer gray/ And alle hir body like þe leede' (lines 132, 135–36; fol. 120v).[48] As Cooper says elsewhere, Thomas's encounter with the lady is entirely opportunistic, and throughout the exchange there is not even the pretence of any emotion for her.[49] Certainly, part of the fantasy of the romance is that he is ultimately rewarded for this affront, as she returns to her former beauty while he enjoys the delights of the fairy realm, and he ends up with the gift of prophecy to boot. But how would a fifteenth-century audience, conditioned to read

---

[46] Helen Cooper, *The English Romance in Time: Transforming Motifs from Geoffrey of Monmouth to the Death of Shakespeare* (Oxford, 2004), p. 214. The quasi-rape of supernatural (or magical) women is actually not that uncommon in romance. Famous examples include the Breton lay *Graelent* and the twelfth-century *Partonopeu de Blois*, along with its fifteenth-century English translation. A 'real world' analogue comes from Wace's *Roman de Rou*, in which he records the account of a mysterious woman who, with a single kick, hurls a knight into the branches of a tree *after* he had raped her. She vanishes quite quickly after (III, 561–610). This strange phenomenon could be related to what Corinne Saunders calls 'the eroticism of force'. See *French Arthurian Literature IV: Eleven Old French Narrative Lays*, ed./trans. Glyn S. Burgess and Leslie C. Brook (Cambridge, 2007), pp. 351–412; *Partonopeu de Blois*, ed. Joseph Gildea, 2 vols (Villanova, 1967–68); *Partonope of Blois*, ed. A. Trampe Bödtker, EETS ES 109 (London, 1912); Wace, *The Roman de Rou*, ed. Anthony J. Holden, trans. Glyn S. Burgess (Jersey, 2002), pp. 118–21; Corinne Saunders, 'Erotic Magic: The Enchantress in Middle English Romance', in *The Erotic in the Literature of Medieval Britain*, ed. Amanda Hopkins and Cory James Rushton (Cambridge, 2007), pp. 38–52, at pp. 42–44.

[47] *OED*, s.v. 'livelong'.

[48] Cooper, *English Romance in Time*, p. 214. For lines 135–36 I am quoting from the original scribe. These have been half-erased and replaced with 'Þe too þe blak, þe toþer gray/ Þe body bloo as beten leed'. The transformation through no fault of her own obviously recalls Melusine, but perhaps a more acute parallel comes from that half-exemplum, half-romance *The Awntyrs off Arthure*, in which Guinevere's mother, suffering the pains of purgatory, appears to her daughter and Gawain: 'Bare was the body and blak to the bone' (line 105). Her chief sin was also sexual misconduct: 'That is luf paramour, listes, and delites,/ That has me light and laft logh in a lake' (lines 213–14). See *The Awntyrs off Arthure at the Terne Wathelyne*, in *Middle English Romances*, ed. Stephen H.A. Shepherd (New York, 1995), pp. 219–43.

[49] See Helen Cooper, 'Thomas of Erceldoune: Romance as Prophecy', in *Cultural Encounters in the Romance of Medieval England*, ed. Corinne Saunders (Cambridge, 2005), pp. 171–87, at p. 179.

for the moral and potentially with *Falmouth Squire* in mind, begin to think about this troubling sexual encounter?

Item 2 in Ff.5.48 is *The ABC of Aristotle*, a 'rewle' of good behaviour ('gode maner') intended for – crucially – 'clerkes and knyghtes a thowsande' (line 4; fol. 8v). The overarching sentiment here is that 'to myche of euerythyng was neuer gode' (line 7; fol. 8v), and in the first two letters one finds the kind of excesses reminiscent of Thomas's bad behaviour:

> A. to amerows, to aunterows
> B. to bolde, ne to besy, ne bourde not to large.
>
> (*ABC*, lines 14–15; fol. 8v)

The alphabet goes on, urging moderation in all things ('a measurable meyne', line 35; fol. 9r), its morals throughout being as rigid as its form.[50] Yet the articulation of moral propriety in *Falmouth Squire* is certainly no less severe. When the boy enters hell he sees souls in 'gret paynyng', including his father:

> He saw his fadur how he brent
> And be þe memburs how he hyng.
> Fendis bolde with hokis kene
> Rent his body lith from lith. (*Falmouth Squire*, lines 103–106; fol. 68v)

The burning and his being torn limb from limb are merely side attractions here; what really catches the imagination is the Dantesque way in which the punishment matches the crime. Of course the sin here is lust, in particular 'spouse-breke', and what makes matters worse is that he will hang by his genitals (upside-down, presumably?) for all eternity. If every blade of grass on the earth was a priest, the father explains, all of their prayers combined still could not release him from his torments. In fact, in an inversion of purgatorial doctrine, the more the boy prays for his soul, the father's 'peynes shalle be more and more' (lines 125–36; fol. 69r).

Such a hard line on illicit sexual practices can be found elsewhere in Ff.5.48, such as in *The Incestuous Daughter* (item 8), an exemplum on the importance of confession after committing a variety of sexual sins. Yet in a more secular vein, and closer to the *Thomas* narrative, is *The Betrayed Maiden's Lament* (item 27). This lyric tells of one Sir John (the stereotypical name for a clerical lecher) who rapes a woman he 'caght' at a well: 'He leyde my hed again the burne;/ He gafe my maydenhed a spurne' (lines 8–9; fol. 114v).[51] Apparent in the first-person narration is a remarkably vivid sense of the woman's anger, both at Sir John and the resulting pregnancy: 'I go with childe, wel I wot./ I schrew the fadur þat hit gate' (lines 19–20; fol. 114v). The eternal consequences of sexual sin may be terrifying indeed, but such sin also has consequences in the here and now. Real consequences, however, are precisely what the *Thomas* narrative lacks. Thomas does make a connection between his behaviour and his apparent abduction by the now-hideous lady – 'I trow my dedis wil wyrk me

---

[50] Nicola McDonald makes a similar point in her discussion of this text. See 'A York Primer and Its Alphabet', pp. 194–97.

[51] Neil Cartlidge gives a critical edition of this text in '"Alas, I Go with Chylde": Representations of Extra-Marital Pregnancy in the Middle English Lyric', *English Studies* 79 (1998), 395–414, at p. 404.

woo' (line 166; fol. 121r) – but as mentioned above everything turns out happily for Thomas in the end.

The major medieval form that revels in sexual impropriety, and that consistently makes light of erotic bad behaviour, is the fabliau. Ff.5.48 has one such narrative, *The Tale of the Basin* (item 11), in which a husband seeks the help of his brother, a parson, when he suspects his spendthrift wife of adultery with the priest, also named Sir John. Through a 'priue experiment' the parson makes the husband's chamber pot extremely sticky, and as expected the priest eventually ends up with both hands stuck to the pot, naked. The wife jumps out of bed to help, also naked, and she too has her hands caught. In trying to help, the house wench (naked as well) ends up attached, and eventually so too the clerk (clothed) and the carter (also clothed), who hits the wench on the 'towte' with his shovel, which becomes attached both to his hands and to her rump. Finally the parson and the husband arrive to witness the comic dance. Much like the father in *Falmouth Squire*, Sir John is threatened with a punishment appropriate to his crime: 'Þou shalle lese þine harnesse or a hundur pounde' (line 208; fol. 61r). As it turns out, though, all ends well. The priest leaves the country for shame, and the husband and wife make up: 'Thus þe godeman and his wife/ Levyd togedur withowt stryfe' (lines 219–20; fol. 61v).

What sort of moral might a lay household audience arrive at after a narrative such as this? The story is both anti-clerical and anti-feminist, but despite the husband's threats no punishments are actually doled out. Much like *Thomas*, though contrary to many texts in Ff.5.48 discussed above, *The Tale of the Basin* is not interested in giving an example of the consequences of sexual sin; in fact it works hard to avoid them, as even the £100 payment is never said to have been paid. However, at the last the story does manage to uphold fidelity in marriage as central to the happy ending. Here the sexual licentiousness is only part of the wife's excesses that were leading the family to ruin, and that required the husband (who had been given the family inheritance) to borrow money from his younger and un-endowed brother. In many ways *The Tale of the Basin* exemplifies the moral message of *The ABC of Aristotle* – that the key to good behaviour is the curbing of one's desires. Put another way, if *Sir Corneus* from Ashmole 61 is a comic exemplum on the social dangers of sexual sin, then *The Tale of the Basin* is an exemplary comic tale on the same topic.

Thus, even in this single manuscript there are many ways early readers could have contextualized Thomas's ungallant behaviour, though (much like in Ashmole 61) the surrounding texts, contra *Thomas*, all appear to hold an underlying moral consistency. As with Ashmole 61, too, audiences attempting to calibrate their understanding of this behaviour would have had available to them a great number of combinations and orders of texts in Ff.5.48, and indeed other texts not found in the manuscript. However, even this awareness of a broader generic context need not take us too far from Ff.5.48. Readers who would have laughed at *The Tournament of Tottenham* (item 12) and *The Feast of Tottenham* (item 28) would have had a keen understanding of chivalric expectations and the conventions of romance, and what they would have thought of Thomas's bad behaviour would have been at least partially influenced by how much they thought the expectations of chivalry could be brought to bear in Thomas's case. Granted this, the argument of this chapter has been that non-romance texts in the immediate manuscript contexts of both romances under discussion may have also played significant roles in influencing the reception of

Gyngeleyne's and Thomas's ungallant escapades. What this reveals is how a habit of reading for the moral can be fostered in a context of miscellaneous exempla and other morally focused texts. But while the moral exemplarity of romances may not always be as clear-cut as those of the texts surrounding them, it certainly was not a foreign notion in the later fifteenth century that romances should be read as exemplary. As Caxton puts it in his lament at the conclusion of *The Order of Chivalry*:

> O ye knyghtes of Englond, where is the custome and usage of noble chyvalry that was used in tho dayes? What do ye now but go to the baynes and playe atte dyse? And some not wel advysed use not honest and good rule ageyn alle ordre of knyghthode. Leve this. Leve it and rede the noble volumes of Saynt Graal, of Lancelot, of Galaad, of Trystram, of Perse Forest, of Percyval, of Gawayn and many mo. Ther shalle ye see manhode, curtosye and gentylnesse.[52]

A look at texts like *Lybeaus Desconus* and *Thomas of Erceldoune*, however, suggests that Caxton may have had an overly idealistic conception of heroic behaviour in romance (or at least in the sales-minded rhetoric of his epilogue that was the conception he wanted to promote). Some heroes, like the Earl in *The Erle of Tolous*, toe a relatively straight moral line when it comes to appropriate behaviour toward women, but if this is the generic rule then there are many exceptions to it. Indeed, what *Lybeaus* and *Thomas* show is that readers may not always see 'curtosye and gentylnesse' in romance, particularly when proximal to a wide range of texts of moral exemplarity. But the fundamental incongruity of an ungallant romance hero might also have been what morally minded readers would have found most interesting about these texts, their moral messiness exposing the tensions between the chivalric ideal and the complexities of lived experience, the kind of tensions that make romances worth reading.

---

[52] *The Order of Chivalry*, p. 99; *Caxton's Own Prose*, p. 126.

14
Sons of Devils

Neil Cartlidge

The ultimate anti-type in medieval culture is, perhaps by definition, the figure of Antichrist, who owes his place in the Christian imagining of the events leading up to the end of the world precisely to the way in which he both impersonates and inverts Christ's role as the principal hero of the Gospels; and I shall argue in this essay that he is also therefore implicitly the ultimate prototype for all the various figures in medieval romance whose being or ancestry is specifically represented as demonic. In the version of events imagined in the treatise *De ortu et tempore Antichristi* attributed to Adso of Montier-en-Der (ca. 920–992), which was to become 'one of the most influential compilations of Antichrist lore' in the Middle Ages,[1] Antichrist claims 'I am the Christ promised to you, who am come for your salvation';[2] and he pointedly opposes Christ's miracles with a series of 'great and unheard-of miracles' of his own, including apparent raisings of the dead.[3] At the same time, Antichrist's features are mapped onto Christ's only in such a way as to emphasize how completely he contradicts them. He is a reflection of Christ, not just in the sense that his image corresponds to Christ's, but also in the sense that the image is utterly reversed.[4] Antichrist is named as he is:

> quia Christo in cunctis contrarius erit et Christo *contraria faciet* [Judges 2, 17]. Christus uenit humilis, ille uenturus est superbus. Christus uenit humiles erigere, peccatores iustificare, ille e contra humiles eiciet, peccatores

---

[1] R.K. Emmerson, *Antichrist in the Middle Ages: A Study of Medieval Apocalypticism, Art, and Literature* (Manchester, 1981), p. 77. Cf. Bernard McGinn, who says that Adso's work 'set the standard Western view for centuries to come': *Antichrist: Two Thousand Years of the Human Fascination with Evil* (New York, 1994), p. 6.

[2] *Adso Dervensis: De ortu et tempore Antichristi*, ed. D. Verhelst, CCCM 45 (Turnhout, 1976), pp. 1–30, at p. 27, lines 143–44; trans. John Wright, in *The Play of Antichrist* (Toronto, 1967), pp. 101–110, at p. 107.

[3] Adso, *De ortu et tempore*, pp. 24–25, lines 72–73; trans. Wright, p. 104. There is an implicit reference here to Matt. 24, 24.

[4] Cf. Emmerson, p. 20: 'The medieval tradition basically portrayed Antichrist as a diabolical parody of Christ'; and McGinn shows that from relatively early on in the Christian tradition, Antichrist was seen as 'Christ's Alter Ego' (*Antichrist*, pp. 33–56). Stuart Clark describes Antichrist as 'that supreme inversionary symbol', in *Thinking with Demons: The Idea of Witchcraft in Early Modern Europe* (Oxford, 1997; repr. 2005), pp. 349–50.

magnificabit, impios exaltabit semperque uicia, que sunt contraria uirtutibus…

> because he will be contrary to Christ in all things, that is, his actions will be contrary to Christ. Christ came as a humble man; he will come as a proud man. Christ came to raise up the lowly, to pass judgment on sinners; he, on the contrary, will cast down the lowly, glorify sinners, exalt the impious and always teach vices which are opposite to virtues.[5]

Thus, unlike most of the figures discussed in this book, Antichrist's motives are in no sense mysterious or morally ambivalent. What makes him so troubling a figure is that, even though he is generally understood to be absolutely evil (literally the incarnation of evil), he nevertheless assumes characteristics that in other contexts would tend to be markers of exceptional or heroic status – in such a way as to make those characteristics themselves seem potentially suspect.

For example, one of the aspects in which Antichrist both imitates and opposes Christ is in his apparently supernatural conception:

> sicut in matrem Domini nostri Iesu Christi *Spiritus sanctus uenit* et eam *sua uirtute obumbrauit* et diuinitate repleuit, ut de Spiritu sancto conciperet *et quod nasceretur* diuinum esset ac *sanctum* [Luke 1, 35], ita quoque diabolus in matrem Antichristi descendet et totam eam replebit, totam circumdabit, totam tenebit, totam interius et exterius possidebit, ut, diabolo cooperante, per hominem concipiet et quod natum fuerit totum sit iniquum, totum malum, totum perditum.

> just as the Holy Ghost came into the womb of the Mother of our Lord Jesus Christ and covered her with His strength and filled her with divinity, so that she conceived from the Holy Ghost and what was born was divine and holy: so also the devil will go down into the womb of Antichrist's mother and fill her completely, possess her completely inside and out, so that she will conceive by man with the devil's assistance, and what is born will be completely foul, completely evil, completely ruined.[6]

The effect of this story is to make the motif of supernatural conception itself seem rather ambivalent; and indeed it could be argued that the legend of Antichrist's birth is so particularly disconcerting (if not downright disturbing) because of the way it seems to constitute a ghastly parody of the story of Christ's Incarnation.[7] Antichrist

---

[5] Adso, *De ortu et tempore*, p. 22, lines 2–7; trans. Wright, p. 102.
[6] Adso, *De ortu et tempore*, p. 23, lines 31–38; trans. Wright, p. 103.
[7] The parallel is made very explicit in a number of medieval texts: e.g. *Cursor Mundi*, ed. Richard Morris, EETS OS 57, 59, 62, 66, 68, 99, 101 (London, 1874–93), lines 22067–74: 'And als it in vr leuedi light,–/ Þe hali-gast thoru godds might,–/ […] Right sua þe deuil sal descend,/ In anticrist moder lend'; Henri d'Arci's Life of Antichrist, ed. L.E. Kaster, 'Some Old French poems on the Antichrist: I. The Version of Henri d'Arci', *MLR* 1 (1906), 269–82, lines 39–43: 'E si cum ly seint espirit vint en Marie/ Kant ele conceüt […] Autresi li malfé en Antecrist descendera'; and the life of Antichrist found in Paris, BNF MS f. fr. 1526, ed. Kastner, 'Some Old French poems on the Antichrist', *MLR* 2 (1906), 26–33, at pp. 26–31, lines 17–20: 'Ausi com Dieu de grace empli/ La vierge de qui il nasqui,/ Celle dont Antecrist nestra/ Del deable plainne sera.'

is given an apparently unworldly origin to match Christ's own birth partly because it is a logical development of the principle that he is Christ's anti-type in all things and partly because it permits a connection to be made with a key passage in the Letters of St Paul. As St Paul puts it, 'the son of perdition' is 'that wicked one [...] whom the Lord Jesus shall kill with the spirit of his mouth; and shall destroy with the brightness of his coming, him, whose coming is according to the working of Satan'.[8] This figure was traditionally identified both with 'Antichrist', who is named in the Bible only in the Letters of John (1 John 2, 18–22, 4, 1–3; and 2 John 7), and also with the seven-headed beast envisioned in the Book of Revelation (Rev. 13, 1), who is able to 'make war with the saints, and to overcome them' and to whom power is given 'over every tribe, and people, and tongue, and nation' (Rev. 13, 7–8).[9] Equated in this way with the 'son of perdition', Antichrist always stood at least figuratively and spiritually for the 'son of the Devil', but medieval writers also seem to have been increasingly willing to contemplate the possibility that he was also literally and physically conceived by the Devil – in this way providing a direct contrast with Christ as literally and physically conceived by the Holy Spirit.[10] Elsewhere in his treatise Adso is even even prepared to describe the 'son of perdition' explicitly as 'the son of the Devil' (*filius perditionis*, id est, filius diaboli').[11]

However, Adso is also careful to qualify this identification with the assertion that Antichrist's symmetry with Christ is, in fact, much less precise than it might appear to be. Just as his raising of the dead turns out to be just an illusion – a macabre manipulation of bodies that are (and actually remain) dead, rather than a genuine reconferral of life – so too his supernatural paternity turns out to be more apparent than real. Adso insists that, whereas Christ is indeed directly conceived by a supernatural power (that is, the Holy Ghost), Antichrist is conceived only by an ordinary human being – albeit with the Devil's active involvement in the process. According to Adso, Antichrist's conception is only unusual in that it occurred in a context of such utter sinfulness that the Devil somehow managed to enter his mother's womb at this very moment of conception, and in this way to endow the child conceived with something of his own power. Yet the more that Adso qualifies and complicates his suggestion that Antichrist's birth might be regarded as a sinister parallel of Christ's, the more it becomes clear quite how deeply engaged he is, at least subliminally, with this very possibility. After all, even authorities as eminent as St Augustine, St Bonaventure and St Thomas Aquinas were prepared to discuss quite seriously the possible mechanisms by which demons might at least appear to be able

---

[8] 2 Thess. 2, 3: 'homo peccati filius perditionis'; and 2 Thess. 2, 8–9: 'et tunc revelabitur ille iniquus quem Dominus Iesus interficiet spiritu oris sui et destruet inlustratione adventus sui eum cuius est adventus secundum operationem Satanae'. This is glossed as a reference to the Antichrist by several of the early Christian writers, including Tertullian, in *De carnis resurrectione*, cap. 24, *PL* 2, col. 829, and St Jerome, *Ep.* 121 (*Ad Algasiam*), *PL* 22, 1036; see further Emmerson, pp. 17–22, 37–39, and the references given at p. 251, n. 7. As Adso explains, the extraordinary circumstances of the Antichrist's birth provide the reason 'why that man is called the son of destruction, because as far as he can he will destroy the human race' (Adso, *De ortu et tempore*, p. 23, lines 39–40, trans. Wright, p. 103).
[9] Emmerson, pp. 22–23.
[10] Emmerson, pp. 81–83.
[11] Adso, *De ortu et tempore*, p. 26, lines 127–28, trans. Wright, p. 107.

to procreate with human beings.¹² From this perspective, it would be no great leap to consider the possibility that similar powers might also be credited to the 'prince of demons'¹³ himself – the Devil. Adso insists that Antichrist's paternity is human after all, not because it would be at all illogical for Christ's 'contrary' to be literally the son of Satan in the same way as Christ is the son of God, but because he is clearly appalled by the consequences of such a deduction. What it would imply is that the Devil has the power to breach the rules of nature just as readily as God can, that his power in this respect is equal to God's, and that the very characteristics that mark Christ out as God's own son could just as well indicate some kind of indebtedness to the Devil. The solution to this problem that Adso offers – the curiously anatomical scenario according to which the Devil somehow enters the womb at the very moment of conception – is all the more frightening for being so precisely and physically invasive. Indeed, the way in which the Devil is supposed to have effectively hijacked this particular sexual act could even be regarded as a kind of metonymical rape – a violent appropriation, not just of human bodies, but of the very processes of nature. In the end, Adso only succeeds in reassuring us that Devil is not literally the father of Antichrist at the expense of suggesting that he is capable of invading individual bodies and interfering with natural processes in a fashion that is – if anything – even more sinister.

Antichrist's shadow inevitably falls, more or less darkly, on all the various sons in medieval romance who are born as a result of some sort of supernatural union. In several such stories, there seems to be an implicit recognition that there is a danger of appearing to imitate or anticipate the scenario of Antichrist's birth, and a corresponding willingness to incorporate what might be seen as a prophylactic emphasis on Christian ritual. For example, in the Middle English romance *Sir Degaré*, the eponymous protagonist's mother is a princess who is unlucky enough to be separated from her companions in a forest.¹⁴ Here she encounters a 'gentil, yong and jolif' knight, wearing a scarlet cloak, who tells her that he is 'a fairi knyghte' and that he has loved her 'mani a yer', but also that 'Thou best mi lemman ar thou go/ Wether the liketh wel or wo' (lines 91–108). Despite her tears, and her attempts to flee, he rapes her, and then confidently predicts that the offspring of their union will be a boy (i.e. the eponymous Sir Degaré himself), in such a way as to suggest that the birth is, like Antichrist's, ineluctably fated to occur:

> 'Lemman,' he seide, 'gent and fre,
> Mid schilde I wot that thou schalt be;
> Siker ich wot hit worht a knave…' (*Sir Degaré*, lines 115–17)¹⁵

---

¹² On this point, see Neil Cartlidge, '"Therof seyus clerkus": Slander, Rape and *Sir Gowther*', in *Cultural Encounters in the Romance of Medieval England*, ed. Corinne Saunders (Cambridge, 2005), pp. 135–47, at pp. 138–41. See also Nicolas Kiessling, *The Incubus in English Literature: Provenance and Progeny* (Pullman, WA, 1977), pp. 21–42; Andrea Hopkins, *The Sinful Knights: A Study of Middle English Penitential Romance* (Oxford, 1990), pp. 165–67; Dyan Elliott, *Fallen Bodies: Pollution, Sexuality, and Demonology in the Middle Ages* (Philadelphia, 1999), esp. pp. 52–60.

¹³ For this phrase, see Matt. 12, 24.

¹⁴ *Sir Degaré*, ed. Anne Laskaya and Eve Salisbury, in *The Middle English Breton Lays* (Kalamazoo, MI, 1995), pp. 89–144.

¹⁵ Cf. also the Old French *Tydorel* (which also describes a woman's seduction by a supernatural/fairy knight) ed. and trans. Glyn S. Burgess and Leslie C. Brook, in *French Arthurian Literature IV: Eleven Old French Narrative Lays* (Cambridge, 2007), pp. 326–47, at lines

It is perhaps precisely in order to dispel the uncomfortably Antichrist-like connotations of this scenario that, when the princess is recovered by her father's followers, she is immediately taken to an abbey where she hears Mass:

> Thai browt hire into the righte wai
> And comen faire to the abbay,
> And doth the servise in alle thingges,
> Mani masse and riche offringes… (*Sir Degaré*, lines 145–48)

The 'mani masse and riche offringes' seem designed to emphasize, not just the court's relief at the princess's return, but also to neutralize the rather diabolical implications of Sir Degaré's conception – that is, as the result of an act of extreme wickedness (a violent rape), committed by a being who is, by his own admission, not human.

No rape is involved in the Old French lai *Yonec*, but the emphasis on the prophylactic functions of Christian ritual is here even more pronounced.[16] In this text Yonec's mother is a young woman imprisoned in a tower by her jealous husband. She is one day visited at her window by a large bird resembling a hawk, which, coming into her room, then metamorphoses into a beautiful fairy-knight. This mysterious visitor declares his love for this lady in terms similar to those used by the fairy-knight in *Sir Degaré*: 'I never loved any woman but you, nor shall I ever love another' ('Unques femme fors vus n'amai/Ne jamés autre ne amerai', lines 129–30). He too is later able to predict that their child will be a son (lines 327–28). Yet he also seems to be rather perturbed by the possibility that his shapeshifting powers might be read as an indication that his nature is diabolical, rather than merely otherworldly. It is apparently this particular suspicion that he attempts to allay by asking the lady to summon her chaplain to administer the eucharist to him in her presence:

> Ne vodreie pur nule rien
> Que de mei i ait acheisun,
> Mescreauncë u suspesçun.
> Jeo crei mut bien al Creatur […]
> Si vus de ceo ne me creez,
> Vostre chapelain demandez;
> Dites ke mal vus ad susprise,
> Si volez aver le servise
> Que Deus ad el mund establi,
> Dunt li pecheür sunt gari;
> La semblance de vus prendrai,
> Le cors Damnedeu recevrai,
> Ma creance vus dirai tute;
> Ja de ceo ne seez en dute! (*Yonec*, lines 146–49, 155–64)

113–15: 'De moi avrez .I. fiz molt bel,/ Sel ferez nomer Tydorel;/ Molt ert vaillanz et molt ert prouz' ('You will have by me a very handsome son,/ And you will call him Tydorel;/ He will be very valiant and very brave'.)

[16] 'Yonec', ed. Alfred Ewert, in *Marie de France: Lais* (Oxford, 1952), pp. 82–96; trans. Glyn S. Burgess and Keith Busby, *The Lais of Marie de France* (Harmondsworth, 1986), pp. 86–93.

> I would not on any account want guilt, distrust or suspicion to attach to me. I do believe in the Creator [...] If you do not believe this of me, send for your chaplain. Tell him that an illness has come upon you and that you want to hear the service that God has established in this world for the redemption of sinners. I shall assume your appearance, receive the body of Christ, and recite all of my credo for you. Never doubt me on this count.

This assertion of Christian belief hardly seems compatible with the adulterous (and therefore implicitly sinful) relationship into which the mysterious knight wants her to embark; and indeed it creates some considerable strain in the narrative. In order to take the sacrament from the lady's chaplain without exciting suspicion, the knight has to engage in yet more magical shapeshifting, this time into the lady's own likeness. The sheer determination with which the whole episode seems to be levered into the narrative clearly reflects something more than mere unease about the essentially pagan origins and associations of fairies. Indeed, nowhere in *Yonec* does the narrator or any of the characters express any explicit disapproval of the fairy-knight's otherworldliness as such – even when the lady follows him into his own country, where she finds him alone in a strange city constructed entirely out of silver.[17] If anything, the knight's uncanniness is presented, not as a cause for concern in itself, but only as a reason for finding him all the more glamorously attractive. *Yonec* underlines the fairy-knight's Christianity, not because of any anxiety that fairies might be un-Christian, but specifically in order to emphasize that they are not diabolical. This emphasis is motivated, in turn, by a recognition that it is precisely when supernatural beings are said to engender extraordinary sons by seducing or assaulting earthly women that there is the greatest risk of inviting uncomfortable comparisons with the conception of Antichrist.

If medieval romances seem to become sensitized to possible parallels with stories about Antichrist's supernatural paternity, then, conversely, some of the Antichrist-texts themselves seem to recognize the validity of such parallels by adopting motifs from romance in their depiction of the seduction and rape of his mother. In the Old French *Jour du Jugement* play, for example, the devil appointed to beget the Antichrist (a certain Engignart) introduces himself to her by claiming to have come 'D'estrange terre [...] pour aventure querre' ('from a foreign land [...] in search of adventure', lines 303–304).[18] He goes on:

> Si vous pri, par grant courtoisie,
> Que vous m'amie estre veilliez
> Et pour vostre amy m'acueilliez.
> A amy me veilliés saisir,
> Pour faire de vous mon plaisir,
> C'est ce que d'amours doit venir.
>
> Thus I beg you, with utmost courtesy,

---

[17] Indeed, as Elliott points out, it is the lady's jealous husband who is explicitly associated with Hell (*Fallen Bodies*, p. 59; 'Yonec', lines 86–88).

[18] Ed. Jean-Pierre Perrot and Jean-Jacques Nonot, *Le Mystère du Jour du Jugement: Texte original du XIVe. siècle* (Chambéry, 2000); trans. R.K. Emmerson and David F. Hult, *Antichrist and Judgment Day: The Middle French 'Jour du Jugement'* (Asheville, NC, 1998).

> to agree to be my lady
> and to accept me as your beloved;
> grant that you will take possession of me as you would a lover
> so that with you I will fulfill my pleasure;
> this is what should come from love.   (lines 306–11)

Here the devil poses as an exotic but still distinctively chivalrous suitor – a mysterious knight-adventurer not at all unlike the supernatural fathers of Yonec and Degaré. Moreover, just like the two fairy-knights, Engignart is able to predict, with apparent confidence, that the child of the union will be a son: 'A vous un fil engendreray/Qui avra mont tres grant puissance' ('I shall beget with you a son/ who will have tremendous power', lines 318–319). From this perspective, it appears that romances dramatizing the appearance of glamorously unworldly suitors have to work so hard to play down comparison with the Antichrist-legend at least in part because they already contain so many elements in common with scenarios of Antichrist's conception; and it is for the same reason that Engignart's strategy of appropriating the discourses of romance seems so natural in the context.

However, there is one particular figure frequently recurrent in romance whose association with Antichrist is so powerful that, even from relatively early on in his development as a literary character, he seems to have become closely associated with Antichrist. This figure is Merlin. Robert de Boron's version of his life begins with an account of how the devils were so upset by Christ's Harrowing of Hell that they gathered together in a kind of parliament to discuss what to do next:

> Mout fu iriez li annemis quant Nostre Sire ot esté en enfer et il en ot gité Adan et Eve et des autres tant com li plot. Et quant li enemi virent ce, si en orent molt grant merveille et s'asemblerent et dirent: 'Qui est cist hom qui nos a esforciez?'

> The Enemy was filled with rage when Our Lord descended into Hell and freed Adam and Eve and as many more as he pleased. When the demons realised what had happened they were bewildered, and gathered together and said: 'Who is this man who has committed violence against us?'[19]

Merlin is conceived as a direct result of the devils' attempt at creating a man to play precisely the role that is, ultimately and superlatively, Antichrist's own – that of false prophet:

> 'Mais coment porriens nos avoir un home qui pallast et deist noz sens et noz pooirs et nostre afaire si com nos l'avom? Car nos avons pooir de savoir toutes choses faites, dites at alees, et se nos avoiens .I. home qui de ce eust pooir et qui seust ces choses, et il fust avec les autres homes en terre, cil les

---

[19] Ed. Alexandre Micha, *Robert de Boron: Merlin: Roman du XIIIe. siècle* (Geneva, 1979), 1/1–5. The translation given here is based on Nigel Bryant, in *Merlin and the Grail: Joseph of Arimathea: Merlin: Perceval: The Trilogy of Arthurian Romances attributed to Robert de Boron* (Cambridge, 2001; repr. 2003), pp. 45–114, at p. 45. However, I have modified Bryant's text in recognition of the variation created by the fact that Bryant's translation is based, not on Micha's edition, but on the one by Bernard Cerquiglini, *Robert le Boron: Le roman du Graal* (Paris, 1981), which is in turn based on a different manuscript from the one chosen by Micha.

nos porroit mout aidier a engingnier, ansi com li prophete nos engingnoient qui estoient avec nos [...]' Lors dient tuit ensamble: 'Molt avroit bien esploitié qui en porroit .I. tel faire, que cil seroit mout creuz.' Lors dit li uns: 'Je n'ai point de pooir de concevoir ne de faire semence en feme, mes se je avoie le pooir, jel porroie bien faire, car je ai un femme qui fait et dit quant que je voil.' Et li autre dient: 'Il i a tel de nos qui puet bien prendre semblence d'ome et habiter a feme; mais il covient que il la praigne au plus priveement qu'il porra.'

But how could we find a man who'd speak out and explain our point of view, our prerogatives, and the case that we have? For we have the power to know all the things said and done in the past, and if we had a man who possessed this power and knew these things, and if he was with the people on earth, he could help us greatly in our schemes, just as the prophets schemed against us when they were with us [...]' Then they all said together: 'It would be a great deed to create such a man, for they would all believe in him.'

Then one of them said: 'I can't make seed or conceive a child in a woman, but if I had the power, I could certainly bring this about, because I have a woman who does and says whatever I want.' And the others said: 'There's one among us who can easily take on the appearance of a man and be intimate with a woman; but he should make sure to take her in the utmost secrecy.'[20]

This plan is successful only to the extent that one of the devils does succeed in fathering Merlin by an act of rape, for the child nevertheless escapes Hell's control. This is implicitly the result of his mother's prompt confession and penitence, and of her insistence on having him rapidly baptized – although, as it turns out, these measures in no way prevent him inheriting powers that are clearly diabolical in origin. In effect, Merlin comes into the world as a kind of experimental prototype of Antichrist – a prototype that, from the devils' point of view, turns out to be rather faulty, in the sense that, even from his infancy, Merlin feels no compulsion whatsoever to show any allegiance to his father's infernal kin. Yet Robert's Merlin is, at least in one respect, even more emphatically diabolical in his nature than Antichrist himself. He is literally a devil's child:[21] and Robert does not try to soften the philosophical and theological implications of this. He certainly makes no attempt to introduce anything like the anatomical or metaphysical qualifications that Adso thought necessary when describing the paternity of Antichrist.

At one level, Robert's characterization of Merlin as a son of a devil provides a convenient explanation for the very existence of Merlin's magical powers. The suggestion is that he derives them from the same source as the Antichrist's own apparently miraculous powers; and that he is a magician because he shares somehow in Antichrist's association with 'magicians, criminals, soothsayers, and wizards'.[22] Merlin's kinship with Antichrist perhaps also explains why he has particular gifts in

---

[20] Ed. Micha, 1/66–86; cf. Bryant, p. 46.
[21] Ed. Micha, 6/37–39 ('Icist deables qui ot pooir de converser et de gesir a femme fu tost apareilliez et vient a li en dormant, si conçoit'); cf. Bryant, p. 51.
[22] Adso, *De ortu et tempore*, p. 24, lines 51–52; trans. Wright, p. 103.

prophecy. Not only is the role played by Antichrist at the end of time particularly that of a 'pseudoprophet',[23] but also his sphere of activity must always lie, by definition, in the future (because after him comes only the end of time). The one motif that Robert could not have directly derived from the Antichrist-tradition is the suggestion that the devils' attempt at creating a false prophet came about as the result of a conference in Hell – since this idea is not to be found in any of the Antichrist-texts earlier than his own poem. However, it is a prominent feature of the Old French *Jour du Jugement* play, which begins with no fewer than eight different devils discussing Satan's plan to bring Antichrist into the world. It is as a result of this conference that Engignart volunteers to go into the world in order to seduce the Antichrist's mother. In other words, not only is Robert de Boron's Merlin clearly modelled, to some extent, on Antichrist, but it also seems that he succeeded in linking the two figures together so successfully as to encourage the flow of influence in the other direction, so that the *Jour du Jugement*'s Antichrist is clearly modelled, to some extent, on Merlin. The picture is complicated still further by the way in which the motif of the devil's parliament seems to have invited comparison with yet another distinct tradition in medieval demonology – that of the so-called *Satansprozesse*, in which the devils together resolve, not to create a false prophet, but to take legal action in Heaven.[24] This idea is developed at some length in the *Boek van Merline* by the Dutch poet, Jacob van Maerlant,[25] which is traditionally assumed to have been particularly influenced by the very widely circulated text now known simply as the *Processus Sathanae*, or 'Satan's Law-Suit' (which is still extant in at least 44 medieval manuscripts and 26 early printed editions).[26] In fact, the direction of influence could just as well have been the other way around; so that, in this respect too, romance-traditions about Merlin's diabolical ancestry probably contributed at least as much to the development of medieval demonology as they borrowed from it.

The diabolical ancestry that Robert de Boron imagined for Merlin clearly provides him with his sinister charisma and uncanny foreknowledge, but not, apparently, with any reasons for shame or self-doubt. The paradoxes of Merlin's nature tend to be dramatized in medieval literature only outwardly, in enigmatic utterances and

---

[23] According to Bruno of Segni, Antichrist is 'called the false prophet because he pretends to be Christ' ('vocatur [...] pseudopropheta, quia se Christum esse mentitur' (*PL* 165, col. 695, cited by Emmerson, pp. 23, 247).

[24] The two most significant texts in this tradition are the *Processus Sathanae* and the *Processus Belialis*, neither of which has been printed since 1611. The *Processus Sathanae* has recently been surveyed by Carmen Cardelle de Hartmann, in *Lateinische Dialoge 1200–1400: Literaturhistorische Studie und Repertorium* (Leiden, 2007), pp. 305–20. No such survey exists for the *Processus Belialis* (but I have so far collected references to 95 medieval manuscript copies of it, with the expectation that many more will emerge); nor has any detailed critical study of this text ever been written. In the absence of one, the best introduction to the text is provided by Norbert Ott's study of the medieval German translations, *Rechtspraxis und Heilsgeschichte: Zu Überlieferung, Ikonographie und Gebrauchssituation des deutschen 'Belial'* (Munich, 1983). Both Cardelle de Hartmann and Ott essentially follow the line of interpretation established by Roderich Stintzing in *Geschichte der populären Literatur des Kanonischen-römischen Rechts in Deutschland* (Leipzig, 1867; repr. 1959), esp. pp. 259–79.

[25] Ed. Timothy Sodmann, in *Jacob van Maerlant: 'Historie van den Grale' und 'Boek van Merline'* (Cologne, 1980): see esp. pp. 161–89 (lines 1608–2581).

[26] Cardelle de Hartmann's list of early printed editions runs to 25 items; but it does not include the edition printed at Memmingen by Albert Kunne in ca. 1500. The reference to Berlin, SBB-PK, lat. fol. 628 is an error: the manuscript in question is Berlin, SBB-PK, lat. fol. 650.

capricious interventions in the Arthurian world, not in the depiction of any tensions within his character.[27] His divided nature (part-human, part-demon) seems to produce no division of personality, no conflict of motives or allegiances, no shame or fear, indeed no stress of any kind. His conscience seems entirely untroubled by the fact that the source of his prophetic and magical powers lies in Hell; and, whatever the ultimate morality of his various manipulative interventions in the Arthurian world, they apparently cost him no effort of will to achieve. It could perhaps be argued that in this respect, Merlin is simply illustrating a healthy confidence in the exorcising functions of baptism, as if baptism in itself were capable of resolving all of the moral and philosophical difficulties created by his demonic paternity.[28] Or else, his extraordinary conception could be read as a signal that he is so utterly exceptional, so utterly unrepresentative of human nature in general, as to provide no basis for any kind of generalization about the relationship between humankind and the supernatural. Yet it could equally well be argued that it is precisely in Merlin's determined inscrutability that his real provocativeness lies. He is such a powerful and fascinating figure in medieval literature, not despite the nonchalance with which he wields his infernal powers, but largely because of it.

There are, however, two medieval romances that do interpret the motif of the demonically-conceived hero as the starting-point for the development, in each case, of an emotional and spiritual drama. These are the Old French *Robert le Diable* and the closely related Middle English *Sir Gowther*, both of which deliberately foreground the protagonist's shock at discovering the truth about his parentage and his subsequent feelings of guilt and shame.[29] They also attempt to provide some mechanisms for resolving the paradoxes of their protagonists' diabolical ancestry, even suggesting some answers along the way to the questions raised by the very possibility that devils can have sons among the human race. For example, how much of our nature is really inherited, and to what extent do we necessarily inherit sin? What exactly does it mean to be 'human' anyway, and is human nature in itself a good thing? How far is our behaviour constrained by our inborn characteristics and are there limits on the amount that people can change? How much can be achieved by penitence and in what ways should penitence be expressed? What part in the moral economy of the world is played by miracles and to what extent do miracles confirm – or contradict – human beings' capacity to exercise free will? And, if it is possible for evil to confer on certain individuals superhuman powers, is it also the case that good can do the same – i.e. that God's cause (and not just the Devil's) has its superheroes?[30] In effect, both Robert le Diable and Sir Gowther are presented as anti-types, and in a fashion that is particularly pointed, since the figure whose characteristics they both mimic and, in significant ways, contradict, is Antichrist himself.

---

[27] On this point, see Gareth Griffith's chapter on Merlin above, cap. 6.
[28] On the place of exorcism in the sacrament of baptism, see Hugh of St Victor, *De sacramentis*, part 6, cap. 10, *PL* 176, 456–57.
[29] *Robert le Diable: Roman d'aventures*, ed. E. Löseth (Paris, 1903); *Sir Gowther: Eine englische Romanze aus dem XV Jahrhundert*, ed. Karl Breul (Jena, 1886) and also ed. Maldwyn Mills, in *Six Middle English Romances* (London, 1973), pp. 148–68 (which is the edition from which I cite).
[30] Both Robert and Sir Gowther ultimately develop such penitential velocity, as it were, that they even finish their lives as saints: see *Robert le Diable*, lines 5065–78, and *Sir Gowther*, lines 721–26.

Sons of Devils

In *Robert le Diable*, Robert's conception is a consequence of his mother's frustration at being unable to conceive a child: in her desperation she prays to the Devil for his help in giving her a baby. There is no suggestion that he, or any of his servants, literally supplants the lady's husband in Robert's conception, but it is emphasized that 'Diables, qui le sot bien faire,/ Fu conselleires de l'afaire' ('the Devil, who knows very well how to do this, was an advisor in this matter', lines 67–68). In other words, the Devil here is somehow able to manipulate the process in a fashion that distinctly recalls Adso's description of his interference in Antichrist's conception. Indeed it seems likely that the *Robert*-poet's formulation was specifically intended to suggest this parallel – i.e. that the Devil is depicted here as 'conselleires de l'afaire', not in order to play down his involvement in Robert's conception, but in order to play up the possibility of a parallel with Antichrist. The English text, by contrast, states straightforwardly that its hero, Sir Gowther, is the son of a fiend. His conception comes about as a result of his mother's encounter, in an orchard, with 'a mon… That hur of luffe besoghth', who is also 'as lyke hur lorde as he myght be' (lines 65–67). After this impostor 'had is wylle all don' (i.e. after he rapes her), he reveals himself to be 'a felturd fende' ['a shaggy fiend']; and, just like most of the supernatural fathers discussed in this chapter, he seems capable of predicting that their union will result in a child (and indeed to know that the child will be a boy): 'Y have geyton a chylde on the/ That in is yothe full wylde schall bee/ And weppons wyghtly weld' (lines 73–75). Sir Gowther's close relationship with Merlin is explicitly emphasized, not just in the sense that they are both sons of devils, but also (according to this poet) sons of the same devil, and therefore half-brothers: 'This chyld within hur was non odur,/ Bot evyon Marlyon halfe brodur,/ For won fynd gatte hom bothe (lines 94–96). As Andrea Hopkins suggests, 'When the narrator of the poem tells us that the devil who begot Gowther is the same one who begot Merlin, he may well mean us to understand that the Devil is making another attempt to create Antichrist – this time a little more successfully.'[31]

Yet, unlike Merlin or Antichrist, neither Robert nor Sir Gowther seem to have any innate knowledge of their ancestry. As children, they express their demonic natures by being, not just precociously vigorous,[32] but also remarkably fierce and unruly. They are so vicious, even as babies, that Robert bites off his wetnurse's nipple and has to be fed through a funnel; while Sir Gowther (not to be outdone) kills no fewer than nine of his wetnurses before his first birthday – and then, when his mother tries to feed him herself, he bites off her nipple too ('He snaffulld to hit soo,/ He rofe tho hed fro tho brest').[33] As adults, Robert and Sir Gowther pursue careers of shockingly extreme violence, including, in both texts, the mass-rape and incineration of a whole convent of nuns. In *Robert le Diable*, this brutality is presented as something of a paradox:

> Si estoit biaus a desmesure
> De cors, de vis et de stature:

---

[31] Hopkins, *Sinful Knights*, p. 168.
[32] *Robert le Diable*, lines 119–20; *Sir Gowther*, lines 142–43.
[33] *Robert le Diable*, lines 105–112, and see also the more detailed text in MS B (i.e. Paris, BNF MS, f. fr. 24405), which Löseth prints in his apparatus; *Sir Gowther*, lines 115–29, quoting lines 126–27.

> S'est mervelle que mal faissoit
> Car a toute gent mout plaissoit.
> Hermites, encluses ne moigne
> Ne remanoit, tant i fust boine,
> Nes ochesist tout esraument... (*Robert le Diable*, lines 185–91)[34]

He was so extremely beautiful in physique, face and stature that it's amazing that his deeds were wicked, for many people found him very pleasing. There was no hermit, recluse or monk, no matter how virtuous, that he wouldn't immediately kill them...

The deduction that this remark seems to invite is that just as Robert's beauty is extreme, so too is his wickedness, which, in turn, seems to suggest that what supernatural paternity brings, above all, is a difference of scale. Being a supernatural figure, everything that Robert is and does is, as it were, supersized. Sir Gowther shares with Robert not just the compulsion to do evil, but also the tendency to extravagance:

> All that ever on Cryst con lefe,
> Yong and old, he con hom greve,
> In all that he myght doo. (*Sir Gowther*, lines 190–92)

Yet, when Robert and Sir Gowther experience their road-to-Damascus moments, and turn at last towards God, it is not, apparently, directly because of any sense of revulsion at the utter wickedness of their deeds. What prompts them to undertake their heroic deeds of penitence, in each case, is not a sudden onset of empathy for their victims, but rather the dramatic revelation of their own true identity – the discovery that they are, in fact, sons of devils. In other words, the catalyst is not so much a changed perspective on what they have done, as a changed perspective on who they are.

If Merlin's uncanniness resides largely in the insouciance with which he accepts his own identity – his apparent indifference to the fact that he is so closely related to Antichrist, both figuratively and familiarly – then *Robert le Diable* and *Sir Gowther* seem to offer a deliberately contrasting treatment of the motif of demonic parentage. In these texts even the very revelation of their implicit kinship with Antichrist is apparently so deeply traumatic that it leads to a fundamental reversal of their attitude to the world. When they discover their real identity – in each case, by threatening their own mother with a drawn sword – their reactions are, in fact, strikingly emotional. In *Sir Gowther*, 'Then weppyd thei bothe [i.e. Sir Gowther and his mother] full sare' (line 231); while in *Robert le Diable*, Robert's reaction to what his mother tells him is that:

> A grant deul mout et a grant honte.
> Il en pleure mout tenrement;
> L'ewe li file espessement
> Des ieus tout contreval la fache ... (*Robert le Diable*, lines 447–50)

---

[34] Sir Gowther is also notably beautiful, but this is not made clear until much later in the course of events (*Sir Gowther*, lines 336–38).

> This caused him great sorrow and shame. It made him weep piteously. The tears from his eyes trickled thickly all down his face…

This emotion is one in which the texts' readers are perhaps implicitly invited to share. The demonic ancestry of Robert le Diable and Sir Gowther is not a means of emphasizing their essential alienness, their fundamental difference from ordinary human beings. Instead, it is presented as a predicament that is still essentially human, and in such a way as to make them, in effect, representative figures. The challenges that these two (anti)heroes face may differ in scale from those of other people, but not in kind – or this, at least, is what the two texts seem to suggest. The trauma of discovering that one's father is a devil is, of course, hardly an ordinary problem. Yet it is perhaps only an extreme version of the trauma that every medieval Christian was expected to deal with every day: the trauma of recognizing that the sinful nature for which every human individual will be held accountable on Judgment Day is also an inherited liability that cannot be lightly repaid – the debt of original sin.[35]

Both texts make it clear that the wickedness committed by their protagonists is a direct consequence of their sinister paternity. Robert's mother recognizes the evil of her child even while it is still in the womb ('Car el set bien Dieu n'i a rien/ Et que ja ne fera nul bien': 'for she knew very well that God had nothing to do with it and that the child would never do anything but evil', lines 71–72). It is also explicitly stated that his crimes come about as a result of diabolical influence. Robert's assaults on the clergy are 'par diablie' (line 330) and, in his attack on the convent, he is said to behave 'si com li fist faire diables' ('just as the Devil made him behave', line 350). Sir Gowther's behaviour is also put down to the influence of his fiendish father: 'Erly and late, lowde and styll,/ He wold wyrke is fadur wyll' (*Sir Gowther*, line 204); and the old knight who bravely rebukes him is only stating the literal truth when he tries to shock Sir Gowther with the suggestion that 'thou come never of Cryston stryn,/ Bot art sum fendys son' (lines 205–206). Yet this explanation of Robert's and Gowther's wickedness would seem to contradict the principle enunciated in the Bible that 'the son shall not bear the iniquity of the father, and the father shall not bear the iniquity of the son' (Ezechiel 18, 20). On the face of it, this passage would seem to constitute an authoritative denial of the possibility that a son might inherit his father's iniquity, even if the father happens to be a fiend. In fact, the point at issue here is the inheritance, not of evil as such, but of culpability for it. The general tenor of this passage in Ezechiel is not so much a denial of the heritability of sin, as a statement of the principle that, in God's estimation, there is no inherited sin that individual virtue cannot outweigh:

> Behold all souls are mine: as the soul of the father, so also the soul of the son is mine: the soul that sinneth, the same shall die. And if a man be just, and do judgment and justice, […] he shall surely live, saith the Lord God. […] But if he beget a son, who, seeing all his father's sins, which he hath done, is afraid, and shall not do the like to them […] this man shall not die for the iniquity of his father, but living he shall live. […] And you say: Why hath not the son

---

[35] Cf. Hopkins, p. 170: 'The Gowther we see to be the son of a devil and the most sinful man imaginable – perhaps even the Antichrist – is moved to escape the burden of his inherited sinful nature and attain grace; but he is also Everyman, who has inherited Original Sin, and seeks to escape from the burden of his naturally sinful flesh.'

borne the iniquity of his father? Verily, because the son hath wrought judgment and justice, hath kept all my commandments, and done them, living, he shall live' (Ezechiel 18, 4–19)

Moreover, this assertion that sons do not 'bear the iniquity' of their fathers is apparently at odds with another passage in the Bible (Exodus 34, 6–7), in which God is addressed as the one 'who takest away iniquity, and wickedness, and sin, and no man of himself is innocent before thee, Who renderest the iniquity of the fathers to the children, and to the grandchildren, unto the third and fourth generation.' Here, on the other hand, is what seems to be a clear statement that children do 'bear the inquity' of their ancestors, after all.

The discrepancy between the two passages is so conspicuous that some churchmen specifically acknowledged the difficulty that it creates. St Gregory the Great, for example, cites the two passages in his *Moralia in Job*, adding that, 'In utraque igitur hac sententia dum dissimilis sensus invenitur, auditoris animus ut discretionis viam subtiliter requirat instruitur' ('the sense that emerges from these two statements is contradictory, so that anyone hearing and thinking about them is required to use some subtlety in searching out a means of interpretation').[36] In what he goes on to say, he suggests a distinction between, on the one hand, 'original sin' (which is inherited by definition, since it is the reflection in every human being of Adam's fault), and, on the other hand, sin as a property of each individual (which might be inherited in the sense of being a genetic trait or proclivity, but for which each individual is nevertheless personally accountable); and it is by means of this distinction that he attempts to 'save the appearances'[37] of the two passages:

> Peccatum quippe originale a parentibus trahimus; et nisi per gratiam baptismatis solvamur, etiam parentum peccata portamus: quia unum adhuc videlicet cum illis sumus. Reddit ergo peccata parentum in filios, dum pro culpa parentis, ex originali peccato anima polluitur prolis. Et rursum non reddit parentum peccata in filios: quia cum ab originali culpa per baptismum liberamur, jam non parentum culpas, sed quas ipsi committimus, habemus. Quod tamen intelligi etiam aliter potest: quia quisquis pravi parentis iniquitatem imitatur, etiam ex ejus delicto constringitur. Quisquis autem parentis iniquitatem non imitatur, nequaquam delicto illius gravatur.

We derive original sin, of course, from our parents, and, unless we are freed from it by the grace of baptism, we bear with us the sins of our parents themselves – in the sense, that is, that we were previously one [substance] with them. 'He renders the sins of the fathers to the children', in the sense that, as a result of the parent's guilt, the soul of the child is polluted by original sin. At the same time God does not 'render the sins of the fathers to the children', in the sense that when we are freed from original guilt by baptism, we are no longer responsible for the sins of our fathers, but only for those sins that we ourselves have committed. However, this might be interpreted in another way as well, in that whoever imitates the iniquity of an

---

[36] St Gregory, *Moralia in Job*, Book 15, 51, *PL* 75, 1110.
[37] For this phrase, see C.S. Lewis, *The Discarded Image: An Introduction to Medieval and Renaissance Literature* (Cambridge, 1964; repr. 1994), pp. 14–15.

evil parent is implicated in his sins too; but whoever refuses to imitate their parent's iniquity, is by no means burdened by his crime.³⁸

This distinction was later drawn rather more sharply by St Anselm, who explicitly differentiates between original sin and what he calls 'personal' sin.³⁹ Yet since he also insists that it is impossible 'to assert that original sin exists in an infant before he has a rational soul', it would seem to follow that the only sin an infant could inherit is the original sin that it derives from Adam (as opposed to the sins of any more immediate ancestor). St Anselm even goes so far as to consider the possibility that 'original sin is not sin absolutely speaking, but sin with the qualification "original", in the sense that a man in a painting is not really a man but a painted man; then surely it would follow that an infant that has no sin but original sin is free from sin'.⁴⁰ This line of argument would seem to rule out the idea that anyone could inherit evil so directly from their parents as to make them, even as babies, conspicuously wicked – which is clearly the conceit that is dramatized in the ferocious *enfances* of Robert le Diable and Sir Gowther. St Anselm's formulation here would also seem to contradict Adso's explanation of Antichrist's birth, since, not even when a child is conceived in utter depravity is it necessarily predisposed to depravity (except in so far as it shares in the original sin that it derives from Adam). In fact, St Anselm is ultimately much more willing to consider the possibility of inherited evil than these particular arguments would suggest – partly because he too wants to find a way of reconciling the two passages from Ezechiel and Exodus, and partly because he is keen to emphasize the extent to which Christ's own nativity was uniquely free of sin. The theory that he eventually suggests is complex, and apparently somewhat speculative, but it does seem to leave the door open to the possibility that evil can be transmitted from parents to children:

> Si autem peccata parentum aliquando nocent animabus filiorum: hoc modo potius fieri existimo, non quod ea illis deus imputet, aut quod eos in aliqua delicta propter parentes inducat, sed quoniam, sicut saepe meritis parentum

---

³⁸ St Gregory explicitly considers the involvement of demons in this context – not, however, as producers of wicked children, but as thieves of innocent ones: 'Quid enim est quod parvuli filii plerumque a daemonibus arripiuntur, nisi quod caro filii ex patris poena multatur? In semetipso enim percutitur pater iniquus, et percussionis vim sentire contemnit. Plerumque percutitur in filiis, ut acrius uratur; et dolor patris carni filiorum redditur, quatenus per filiorum poenas mens patris iniqua puniatur.' ('For how can it be that small children are often seized by demons, unless the father's punishment is being inflicted on the body of the child? It is because when the wicked father is punished directly, he deigns not to feel the force of the blow. Often he is punished by means of his children, so that the pain is keener, and the father's sorrow is rendered to the bodies of his children, so that by means of his children's sufferings a wicked father's mind might be chastised'.)

³⁹ Anselm, *Liber de conceptu virginali*, ed. F.S. Schmitt, *S. Anselmi Cantuariensis Archiepiscopi Opera Omnia*, 6 vols (Edinburgh, 1946–61), 2:135–73, cap. 23, p. 165: 'Est peccatum a natura […] et est peccatum a persona. Itaque quod est a persona, potest dici "personale"'; 'there is the sin committed by the nature, and there is sin committed by the person. Therefore what is committed by the person can be called "personal"' (trans. Brian Davies and G.R. Evans, *Anselm of Canterbury: The Major Works* (Oxford, 1998), p. 382).

⁴⁰ Anselm, *Liber de conceptu virginali*, cap. 3, 2:142: 'Si vero dicitur originale peccatum non esse absolute dicendum peccatum, sed cum additamento "originale" peccatum, sicut pictus homo non est vere homo sed pictus homo: profecto sequitur quia infans qui nullum habet peccatum nisi originale, mundus est a peccato'; trans. Davies and Evans, p. 361.

filios iustorum a peccatis eruit, ita filios iniustorum eorum meritis in suis aliquando derelinquit. [...] Namque satis videtur susceptibilius quod deus animam peccatricem, cui nihil praeter poenam debet, propter parentum peccata in suis dimittat peccatis ut pro ipsis puniatur, quam quod eam alienis oneret, ut pro illis torqueatur. Ita igitur sine repugnantia et originale peccatum est idem in omnibus, et 'filius non portabit iniquitatem patris' [...] et redit deus peccata parentum filiis 'in tertiam et quartam generationem'...

However, if the sins of parents do sometimes harm the souls of their children, I think it rather comes about in this way: not because God imputes the sins to them, or because he leads them into any transgression because of their parents, but because, as he often rescues the sons of the just because of the merits of their parents, so he sometimes leaves the children of the unjust in their sins because of their parents' deserts. [...] For it seems more reasonable that God should leave in its sin a sinful soul on account of its parents' sin – after all he owes it nothing but punishment – so that it is punished for its sins, than that he should burden it with others, so that it should suffer for those. Thus, therefore, it can be said without contradiction that original sin is the same in everyone, and that 'the son will not bear the iniquity of the father' [...] *and* that God visits the sin of parents on their children 'unto the third and fourth generation'....[41]

St Anselm's treatment of the question of whether or not evil is heritable thus ultimately creates – or at least leaves – a number of conspicuously grey areas; and it could be argued that it is precisely these grey areas that *Robert le Diable* and *Sir Gowther* choose to exploit. Just as St Anselm is prepared to admit to some uncertainty about God's attitude to the transmission of sin across generations, so too the two romances rely for their drama on the fact that the implications of their heroes' demonic paternity are by no means clear-cut. In the circumstances of their birth and their outward characteristics, they certainly share much with Antichrist, and yet, unlike him, the use to which they put their abilities is significantly not predetermined. In the end, virtue does triumph over heredity, but only as a result of decisions that the two protagonists make as individual human beings – in defiance of any pressure that heredity might be supposed to exert. In this respect too, *Robert le Diable* and *Sir Gowther* could be said to mirror the overall balance of St Anselm's thought – in which redemption is achieved only by the exercise of free will, whereas sin of itself ultimately has no substantial existence: it is essentially 'nothing'.[42] For all the self-conscious sensationalism with which the two romances present their use of the motif of demonic paternity, they do in the end offer what amounts to a finely balanced recapitulation of the position that most medieval theologians took – i.e. that heredity can be a powerful influence, even if its mechanisms remain troublingly difficult to define, but that its influence is in any case always balanced by every human individual's capacity for virtue, so that sin itself is therefore not essentially heritable. It is perhaps precisely because Robert and Sir Gowther are initially so alien and so Antichrist-like, that their ultimate rehabilitation is so reassuring, for if even the sons

---

[41] Anselm, *Liber de conceptu virginali*, cap. 25, 2:168–69; trans. Davies and Evans, p. 385.
[42] Anselm, *Liber de conceptu virginali*, cap. 5, 2:146–47; trans. Davies and Evans, pp. 364–65.

of devils can choose virtue and find grace, then there must be hope for each and everyone of us. Indeed, as the pope reassures Sir Gowther once he has been rehabilitated, 'Now art thou Goddus chyld/ The thar not dowt tho warlocke wyld' (*Sir Gowther,* lines 667–68). In other words, his repentance and penance mean that he is now no longer the devil's child at all, but God's; and this in turn means that there is no need even for him – and therefore, by extension, for any of us – to fear the Devil's power.

Index

The ABC of Aristotle 212, 213, 216, 217
Acre, Fall of (1291) 173, 174, 182, 191
Adso of Montier-en-Der
  on the Antichrist 221–2, 233
  De ortu et tempore Antichristi 219, 221
The Adulterous Falmouth Squire 208, 213, 214, 216, 217
Ælfric, *Catholic Homilies* 55
Aelius Donatus 10
Aeneas, *Livre du Cuer* 166
Aeneid
  allegorical reading of 10–11
  redemption 10
Ætheling, Edgar 71
Agravain, killed by Lancelot 84
Ailred of Rievaulx, *Vita* 67
Albina
  and Albion 53
  anti-hero 52
Alexander A manuscript 31
Alexander B manuscript *see Alexander and Dindimus*
Alexander and Dindimus 31, 38
Alexander the Great 4, 27–41
  anti-hero
    Alexandreis 27–8, 40
    Confessio amantis 35
    Fall of Princes 35
    Historiarum 31, 32
    Old English Orosius 31–2
    Polychronicon 31
  Aristotle's advice to 37
  Dicts and Sayings of the Philosophers 38
  explorer
    Alexandreis 39–40
    'The Monks Tale' 40–1
  hero
    Alexander and Dindimus 38–9

    Alexandreis 28, 36, 39–40
    Book of the Duchess 29, 30
    Confessio Amantis 35
    Fall of Princes 35
    House of Fame 29, 30
    Kyng Alisaunder 34–5
    Old English Orosius 31–2, 32
    Polychronicon 31
    Prose Life of Alexander, Darius incident 36
    'The Monks Tale' 29–30, 30, 32, 35
    The Wars of Alexander 36–7
    'Widsið' 33
  knighthood 35
  Kyng Alisaunder 29
  luck of 29
  'Manciple's Tale' 29, 30
  ruler of the world, *Alexandreis* 30, 40
Alexander Romance 9, 31, 35, 36, 39
Alexandria, crusade against 180–1
Ambroise, *Estoire de la Guerre Sainte* 188–9
Anglo-Saxon, and republicanism 46
Anglo-Saxon Chronicle 72
  manuscripts 60
Angrés of Windson, Count 97
Anselm, St, on inherited sin 233–4
Antenor 53
anti-heroes 52–3
  and Englishness 56–7
  see also under individuals, e.g. Alexander the Great
anti-heroism
  dramatic possibilities 1–2
  Livre du Cuer 159, 167
  medieval British romance 51–3
Antichrist, the 219

Adso of Montier-en-Der on 221–2, 233
Merlin, kinship with 225–7, 230
motives 219–20
son of the Devil 221, 222, 224, 229
supernatural conception 220–1
see also Devil
Anturs of Arther see Awntyrs off Arthure
Aquinas, Thomas, St
on prophecy 107
Summa Theologiae 107
Arfderydd, Battle of (575) 101
aristocracy, and romances 4
Aristotle, in *The Dicts and Sayings of the Philosophers* 37
Arthour and Merlin romance 94, 100
Arthur, King 55, 110
anti-hero 91, 124, 125–6, 127
conception 109
Cornwall, associations 93–4
as Herod-figure 92
murdered by Mordred 88–9
Arthur of Little Britain 203
Arviragus, King
Historia regum 49–50
Roman de Brut 49, 50
Astley, John, Sir 201
Athelston 131
Aucassin et Nicolette 160
Awntyrs off Arthure 92, 119, 127
Gawain 125

Bakhtin, Mikhail 143
Bale, John 46
Beaumont, Francis, *The Knight of the Burning Pestle* 134
Bede, St, *Historia ecclesiastica* 55
Le Bel Inconnu 208
Benoît de Sainte-Maure, *Chronique des ducs de Normandie* 17
Bernard of Clairvaux 177–8
The Betrayed Maiden's Lament 216
Beues of Hamtoun 97
Bevis of Hampton 131, 174
Boeve de Haumtone 76, 174
Brut, prose romance 46
Brut narratives 46

Burgh, Benedict 37

Caesar, Julius, in *Roman de Brut* 49, 50
Camille, in *Roman d'Eneas* 16
Camlann, Battle of (537) 81, 94
cannibalism, Richard the Lionheart 175–6, 197–9
Cassibellaunus 48, 49
Castleford's *Chronicle* 46
Catharism 109
Caulier, Achilles, *L'Hospital d'Amours* 165
Caxton, William 30, 37, 173, 183, 203
translator, *Order of Chivalry* 202, 218
Chanson d'Antioche 173
Chanson de Jerusalem 173
Chanson de Roland 173, 192
chansons de geste 186
character types, textual dimensions 2
charivari 136–7
Chartier, Alain, *Belle Dame Sans Merci* 165–6
Chaucer, Geoffrey
Alexander the Great
Book of the Duchess 29, 30
House of Fame 29, 30
'The Manciple's Tale' 29, 30
'The Monk's Tale' 29–30, 32, 35, 40–1
Canterbury Tales 133
Gawain, *Squire's Tale* 121
Le Chevalier à l'épée 119, 128
Gawain 122–3
chivalry
failure to practise 201–2
Guy of Warwick 176
and lawlessness 142
and Pentecostal Oath 202
Ralph the Collier 154, 158
and romances 201
The Tale of Gamelyn 141–2
Chrétien de Troyes
Chevalier au lion 111
Erec et Enide 203
Gawain 121
Perceval 126
Yvain 121, 122

Christine de Pizan 192
Clarel, King 192
　captives, treatment of 193
　capture 192, 193
　nobility 192, 194
　Otuel, battle with 192, 193, 194
Cleanness, Belshazzar's Feast 151
clergy, in *The Tale of Gamelyn* 138–9, 144
Cligés 97
Comnenus, Manuel, Emperor 179
Constantinople, sack of (1204) 179
Cornwall
　associations
　　Arthur 93–4
　　Mordred 94, 96
　　post-Conquest disaffection 94–5, 97, 98
Cortés, Hernán 53, 54
courtesy books 152, 153, 158
crusade romances 173, 174
　'recovery literature' 178
　Saracens in 192
Crusaders 4, 173–83
　heroes 173
　see also Saracens
crusades
　critique of, in *Guy of Warwick* 180–1
　failure, reasons for 182–3
　and personal redemption 174
　and violence 177, 178, 180

Damascus, Sultan of 190–1
Dame Ragnelle 124, 127
Danishness, Harold Godwineson 75
Devil, the 229
　　Antichrist, father of 221, 222, 224, 229
　　and heroes 4
　　and Merlin's origins 103, 107, 108, 109, 225–6
　　Turnus as 11
　　see also Robert le Diable
The Dicts and Sayings of the Philosophers
　Alexander the Great 38
　on Aristotle 37
Dido 23, 24

Domesday Book 65
Douglas, Gavin 146
Drances 21
　Turnus, opposition 18
Drayton, Samuel, Hengist, *Poly-Olbion* 45, 56
Dudo of Saint-Quentin 53
　De moribus 51
Dunbar, William 146

Edward the Confessor, King 60, 61, 67
　death 62
　Osbert of Clare's *Vita* 66
　reputation 65–6, 72
Edward I, King 59
Eleanor of Aquitaine, Henry II, marriage 23
Emma of Normandy 61
Englishness
　and anti-heroes 56–7
　pre-/post-Conquest 72
　variable identity 54, 55, 57
Epistola Alexandri ad Aristotelem 39
The Erle of Tolous 204, 208, 211, 218
　sexual fidelity 205–7
Estoire de Merlin 86
Estoire del Saint Graal 86
Eustace of Blois 3
Eustace the Monk 5
Exeter Book 33

fabliau 2, 212, 217
Facetus cum nihil utilius 153
The Feast of Tottenham 217
Ferumbras 186, 189–90
fiction, historiography, meeting place 22
Firumbras 186, 189
Fortescue, John, Sir, *De Laudibus Legum Angliae* 46
Foxe, John, *Acts and Monuments* 45
Freeman, Edward A. 59
Fulgentius
　Aeneid, allegorical reading of 10
　Expositio continentiae Virgilianae 10
Fulk Fitzwarin 5

Index

Gaimar, Geffrei, *Estoire des Engleis* 53, 97
gallant, meaning 202
Gamelyn 4, 129–44
　banquet 137–8, 140
　greenwood 144
　justice, enforcement of 142–3
　outlaw 140–1, 144
　pestle, use as weapon 133
　violence 129–30, 131, 132–3, 136–7, 140, 142–3
　wrestling 135–6
Ganhumara 82
Gawain of Orkney, Sir 2, 3, 5, 115–28
　amatory adventures 120, 121, 122
　　Lancelot of the Laik 127
　ambivalence, *Morte Darthur* 116–18
　courage
　　Awntyrs off Arthur 125
　　Golagros 126–7, 128
　　Lancelot of the Laik 126, 128
　courtesy, *Squire's Tale* 121
　Erec et Enide 121
　Gesta Regum Anglorum 120
　Golagros, conflict 127
　hero, *Golagros* 128
　Historia 120
　hybridity 118
　killed by Mordred 85
　knighthood, perfect 126
　Layamon's Brut 120–1
　literary treatment 119–20
　loyalty 121
　Modena Cathedral, door sculpture 120
　and the Pentecostal Oath 117
　pre-Malory history 119–21
　reputation 118–19, 121–5
　　Le chevalier à l'épée 122–3
　　Sir Gawain and the Green Knight 123–4
　Roman de Brut 120
　Scottish affiliation 119, 125–8
　Yvain 121
Geoffrey de Villehardouin, *Chronicle* 180

Geoffrey of Monmouth 3, 54
　Historia regum Britanniae 19, 46, 52, 56, 99
　　Arviragus 49–50
　　Gawain 120
　　Hengist 47
　　Hengist and Horsa 50
　　　manuscripts 51
　　Merlin 102–3, 105
　　Mordred 81–2
　　Prophetiae Merlini 100, 110
　　Romans 48
Geoffroi de Charny 187–8, 195
Gerald of Wales, on Harold Godwineson 73
A Gest of Robyn Hode 139, 141
Gesta Regum Britannie 94
Godfrey de Bouillon 173
Godfrey de Bouillon, hero 173
Godric of Cornwall, Earl 97
Godwine, Earl 60–1
Godwineson, Harold *see* Harold Godwineson
Golagros
　Gawain, conflict 127
　loyalty 127
Golagros and Gawane 119, 126, 127, 128
Gower, John, *Confessio Amantis*, on Alexander the Great 35, 37
Gray, Thomas, *Scalacronica* 94
greenwood, the
　fellowship of 140–1
　Gamelyn's 144
　loyalty in 141
Gregory I, Pope 7
　and Judas, legend 88
　Moralia in Job 232
Gui de Warewic 76, 174, 176
　Mordred 96
Guinevere 90, 92, 98, 115, 207
　ambivalence 93
　Lancelot, affair with 126
　lechery 92–3
　Mordred, incest with 87
　reputation 84
Guy of Warwick
　criticism of 195–6

motivation, transformation of 180, 181
Triamour, battle 194
Guy of Warwick 131, 174, 200
  chivalry 176–7
  critique of crusades 180–1
  Mordred 96
  'recovery literature' 176–7, 179
  violence 178–9
Gyngeleyne, Sir 4, 203, 208, 209–11

Hall, John Lesslie, 'The Calling of Hengist and Horsa' 43–4
Hamilton, William, Vortigern and Rowena, painting 44–5
Harald Hardrada, King of Norway 61–2, 66
Harold Godwineson 3
  anti-hero 63, 67–8, 68–9, 77
  claim to English throne 61
  Danishness 75
  Gerald of Wales on 73
  hermit 78–9
  hero 63–4, 76
    Polychronicon 73–4
    South English Legendary 71
    Vita Haroldi 77–8
    Waltham Chronicle 70
  hybridity 62, 63, 66–7, 69–70
  John of Worcester on 63–4
  'last English king' 59–60
  marginality 72, 73, 79–80
  pilgrim phase 76
  post-Conquest survival legend 74–80
  Turnus, identification with 22
  Vita Haroldi 75–6, 77
  William of Malmesbury on 63
Havelok 97, 131
Heart (*Livre du Cuer*) 167
  and heroism 168
  hybridity 159
  journey 162–3
  linguistic discoveries 163
  romance model 163
Hengist 43–57
  anti-hero 3, 52, 54, 55

  Historia Brittonum 43
  Roman de Brut 51
  hero
    'Hengist and Mey' 44
    Historia regum 47
    Poly-Olbion 45
    Roman de Brut 51
  hybridity 46, 51, 55–6
  literary transformation 46
  loyalty 51
  wanderings 52
Hengist and Horsa
  heroes
    Historia regum 50
    Roman de Brut 50
  Jefferson on 44, 45–6
Henry of Huntingdon
  Epistola ad Warinum 91, 94
  on the Norman Conquest 69
Henry II, King 95
  and Aeneas's victory 22–3
  Eleanor of Aquitaine, marriage 23
  as usurper 23
Henry III, King 67, 95
Hereward the Wake 5, 53
  loyalty 72
Hermann of Laon 93
heroes
  allegorical 168
  Crusaders 173
  and the Devil 4
  ill-behaved 203
  Saracen
    converts 186–92
    non-converts 192–9
  werewolf 5
  see also individuals, e.g. Alexander the Great
heroism
  and Heart 168
  instability of 169
  Livre du Cuer 166–7
  as paradigm 1
  and romances 228
Higden, Ranulf, *Polychronicon* 30, 46, 54
  Alexander the Great 31
  Harold Godwineson 73–4

Historia de Preliis 31, 35, 36, 38, 39
historiography, fiction, meeting place 22
Holinshed, Raphael, *Chronicles* 46
Horsa 43
    see also Hengist and Horsa
hospitality
    Sir Gawain and the Green Knight 150, 152
    Tale of Ralph the Collier 149–54, 158

identity formation, and *Richard Coer de Lyon* 175
Igerne 109, 110, 113
The Incestuous Daughter 207, 216
Ironside, Edmund, hero 53

The Jealous Wife 207
Jean de Joinville, *Life of Saint Louis* 178
Jefferson, Thomas 56
    on Hengist and Horsa 44, 45–6
Joan of Laval 169
John of Boundes 131, 132, 142, 143
John of Bourbon 161, 162
John of Cornwall 110
John of Fordun 89
    Chronica gentis Scotorum 125
John, King 95
    treachery 199
John the Reeve 146, 149, 151, 154
John, Seneschal of Hainault 165
John of Salisbury 23
John of Worcester, on Harold Godwineson 63–4
Jonas, Earl of Durras 180
Jour du Jugement 224–5, 227
Judas, and Pope Gregory, legend 88
Just War concept 177–8
Justinus, *Epitoma historiarum Philippicarum* 30, 31

King Edward and the Hermit 146, 149, 151
King Edward and the Shepherd 146, 151
King Horn 131
King Richard 96
The King and the Shepherd 149

The King of Tars 190–1
king-in-disguise story 146, 147, 155
kitchen implements, as weapons 133–4
knighthood 3, 5, 176
    Alexander's 35
    Gawain's 126
    Kaeuper on 133
    principles of 202
    Ralph's worthiness of 147
Knights of the Round Table, multinational 55
Knut, King, anti-hero 52
Kyng Alisaunder 29, 34–5, 39

Le Lai du Cor 93
A Lament of the Blessed Virgin 212
Lamorak de Galys, killing of 115
Lancelot of the Laik 119
    Gawain 126, 128
Lancelot, Sir 33, 202
    Guinevere, affair with 126
    kills Agravain 84
    Livre du Cuer 163, 164, 165, 166
Lancelot (Vulgate Cycle) 85
    Merlin 104
    Mordred 85–6
Langtoft, Peter
    Chronicle 46
    Harold Godwineson, Chronicle 68–9
lawlessness, and chivalry 142
Laȝamon's Brut 46, 85, 89, 99
    Gawain 120–1
Lestoire de Merlin (Vulgate Cycle) 104, 112, 113
Llull, Ramón, *Order of Chivalry* 202, 218
London 75, 97, 98
love visions genre 159–60
    Livre du Cuer 159
    symbolism 160
Lovelich, Henry, *Merlin* 100
loyalty 1, 147
    Gawain's 121
    Golagros's 127
    in the greenwood 141
    Hengist's 51

Hereward's 72
Ralph the Collier's 154–8
Sir Gawain and the Green Knight 154, 155
women's 123
Lybeaus Desconus 203, 204, 205, 210, 211
  bowdlerising 209
  shallowness 208
Lydgate, John 37
  Alexander the Great, *The Fall of Princes* 35

Maerlant, Jacob van, *Boek van Merline* 227
La Malinche 53, 54
Malory, Thomas, Sir 33
  Morte Darthur 84, 100, 113, 202, 203
  Gawain 116–18
Mannyng, Robert 68, 93
  Chronicle 46
manuscripts
  Anglo-Saxon Chronicle 60
  Bodleian Library MS Ashmole 61: 203–11
  Cambridge University Library MS Ff.5.48: 211–18
  Historia Regum 51
  Processus Sathanae 227
  see also Nowell Codex
'Matter of England', romances 131
Maximilian I, Emperor 168
Mélion 5
Melusine, and house of Lusignan 53
Merlin (Myrddin) 4, 5, 99–114
  ambivalence 114
  ancestry 102
  Antichrist, kinship 225–7, 230
  demonic origins 103, 107, 108, 109, 225-6
  divided nature 228
  as diviner 100
  exit-strategies 112–13
  Historia Brittonum 102
  Historia regum 102–3, 105
  humour 108–9
  hybridity 102–3, 108, 114

Lancelot 104
  magic, practice of 104–6
  Merlin 105, 108
  monarchy, relationship to 110–11
  narratives of 111–12
  prophecy 100, 101, 106, 108, 110
  shapeshifting 105
  sources 99–100
  and Stonehenge 105–6
  as warrior-prince 102
Merlin romance 100
Mexico, foundation narrative 53, 54
Mickle, William Julius, 'Hengist and Mey: A Ballad' 44, 56
Middleton, Thomas, *Hengist, King of Kent* 45
Milan, Edict of (313) 177
Milton, John 46
mirror for princes, *Roman d'Eneas* as 20, 24
Modred *see* Mordred
Mordred (Modred) 3, 5, 81–98
  adultery 93
  ambivalence 89–92, 98
  ancestry 85–7
  anti-hero 84–5, 98
    Gui de Warewic 96
    Guy of Warwick 96
    Historia regum 81–2
    Roman de Brut 83–4
  as archetype 96–8
  Arthur, murderer of 88–9
  Cornwall, association with 94, 96
  Ganhumara, love for 82–3
  Guinevere, incest with 87
  hero 81, 89–90
  incestuous birth 86–7
  kills Gawain 85
  Lancelot (Vulgate Cycle) 85–6
  Morte (alliterative) 87, 90
  Morte (stanzaic) 87
  redemption 3
  seizure of throne 87
Morgawse 115–16
Mort Artu (Vulgate Cycle) 86, 87, 88, 89
Morte Arthur (alliterative) 91

Mordred 87, 90
Morte Arthur (stanzaic) 84, 91, 94
  Mordred 87
Morte Arthure (alliterative) 84, 85, 94
Morte Darthur (Malory) 84, 100, 113, 202, 203
Myrddin see Merlin

Nennius
  Hengist, *Historia Brittonum* 43
  Historia Brittonum 92
    Merlin 102
Norman Conquest, Henry of Huntingdon on 69
Normans
  as mixed people 54
  Saxons, connections 52
  Trojan ancestry myth 51–2
Nowell Codex 39

Order of the Bath, oath 201
Orosius, Paulus, Alexander the Great
  Historiarum adversus Paganos 31, 32
  Old English Orosius 31–2, 32
Osbert of Clare, *Vita* of Edward the Confessor 66
Ote, Sir 140, 141–2, 144
Otuel 186–7
  Clarel, battle with 192, 193, 194
Otuel a Kniȝt 186, 188, 192
Otuel and Roland 186, 188
outlaw, Gamelyn as 140–1
outlaws
  fellowships 139
  as heroes 5
  tales 141, 142, 144

Palomides 164
Paris, Matthew 68
  La Estoire de Seint Aedward le rei 67
Pellinore de Galys 116
Pentecostal Oath
  and chivalry 202
  and Gawain 117
  and treatment of women 201
  and violence 177
Perceval 112

pestle
  as phallic symbol 134–5
  as weapon 133, 134
Petit traitise de nurture 152, 154
Processus Sathanae, manuscripts 227
prophecy
  Aquinas on 107
  Merlin 100, 101, 106, 108, 110
Prose Lancelot 90
Prose Life of Alexander, Darius incident 35–6
Prose Tristan 87

Queste del Saint Graal 118

Ralph the Collier 4, 145–58
  chivalry 154, 158
  fight with Saracen Magog 155, 157
  hospitality 149–54, 158
  hybridity 158
  knighthood 158
    worthiness of 147
  loyalty 154–8
  proverbial speech 153
  story 145
'recovery literature'
  crusade romances 178
  Guy of Warwick 176–7, 179
  meaning 174
  Travels of Sir John Mandeville 182
redemption
  Aeneid 10
  Mordred 3
  personal, and crusades 174
  Robert le Diable 234
  of sinners 224
  Sir Gowther 181–2, 234
Refusal (*Livre du Cuer*) 159, 167
René d'Anjou
  burial place 169
  Livre du Cuer 3, 159–69
    anti-heroism 159, 167
    Arthurian heroes 164–5
    heroes/anti-heroes blurring 164–5
    heroic romance model 160, 161, 162, 163
    heroism 166–7

introspection, invitation to 168, 169
love vision 159–60
narrative voice 161
prose letter 161, 162
republicanism, and Anglo-Saxon 46
Richard Coer de Lyon 174, 174–5, 200
and identity formation 175
see also Richard the Lionheart
Richard of Cornwall 95, 96
Richard II, Duke 61
Richard the Lionheart 2, 173
cannibalism 175–6, 197–9
see also Richard Coer de Lyon
Robert de Boron
Joseph of Arimathea 109
Merlin 86, 91, 99, 100, 103, 105, 108, 109
Robert Fitz Walter 95
Robert of Gloucester 93, 94
Metrical Chronicle 46, 92
Robert le Diable 228, 229–30, 234
Robert le Diable 4, 233, 235
demonic conception 229
redemption 234
violence 229–30, 231
Robert of Mortain 95
Robin Hood, tales 129, 131
Robin Hood and the Monk 212
Roman d'Eneas 3
composition date, and regime change in England 23
as mirror for princes 20, 24
Romance of Duke Rowlande and Sir Ottuell 186, 187, 188, 193
romances
and anti-heroism 1–2
and aristocracy 4
and chivalry 201
collections 203–18
and heroism 228
'Matter of England' tales 131
meaning 160fn1
as naïve texts 1
violence in 177
see also crusade romances
Romans

Historia regum Britanniae 48
Roman de Brut 49
Round Table, Knights of the 55, 116, 119, 127
see also Pentecostal Oath
Russell, Frederick, *The Just War in the Middle Ages* 177

Saladin 198
Saracens 4, 185–200
in crusade romances 192
see also Crusaders; heroes, Saracen
Satansprozesse 227
Saxons, Normans, connections 52
Secretum Secretorum 37
shapeshifting
Merlin 105
Yonec 223–4
Short English Metrical Chronicle 46, 55
genealogical amalgamation 56
Siege of Milan 174
sin
inherited
Anselm on 233–4
overcoming 231–2
original, and personal, distinction 232–3
The Sinner's Lament 208
Sir Cleges 204
Sir Corneus 204, 205
analogues 207fn25
sexual fidelity 207, 217
Sir Degaré, demonic encounter 222–3
Sir Ferumbras 186
Sir Gawain and the Green Knight 118, 119, 123–4, 128, 203
hospitality 150, 152
loyalty 154, 155
Sir Gowther 4, 233, 235
demonic conception 229
redemption 181–2, 234
violence 229, 231
Sir Gowther 174, 228, 230, 234
violence 181, 182
Sir Isumbras 174, 204
Sir Orfeo 204
Solomon and Marcolf 158

South English Legendary, Harold Godwineson 71
The Sowdone of Babylone 186, 190
Spenser, Edmund, *Faerie Queene* 45, 168
Stamford Bridge, battle 61, 72, 76
Stonehenge, and Merlin 105–6
Stowe, John, *Chronicles* 46
Suite du Merlin 85, 86, 92, 112
The Sultan of Babylon 174

The Tale of the Basin 212, 213, 217
The Tale of Gamelyn
  bloodshed, absence of 133
  chivalry 141
  clergy, view of 138–9
  manuscript survival 130–1
  violence 129–30, 131, 132–3, 136–7
The Tale of Ralph the Collier
  Christmas setting 147–9
  king-in-disguise story 147, 155
  sources 146, 149
  summary 145
Theseus, *Livre du Cuer* 166
Thomas of Erceldoune 4, 214–16, 216–17
Thomas of Erceldoune 203, 212
  Adulterous Falmouth Squire, affinities 213–14
The Tournament of Tottenham 134, 212, 217
The Travels of Sir John Mandeville, 'recovery literature' 182
Trevisa, John 30, 73
Triamour
  Guy of Warwick, battle 194
  nobility 195
Tristan 118
Tristan, in *Livre du Cuer* 161, 163, 165
Turnus 3, 9–25, 164fn13
  anti-hero in *Roman d'Eneas* 9–24
  as the Devil 11
  Drances, opposition 18
  hero in *Aeneid* 9, 11, 12–14
  literary transformation 21, 24–5
  Rage, in Fulgentius 10

Uther 56, 105, 109, 110, 113

violence
  and crusades 177, 178, 180
  Guy of Warwick 178–9
  justification for 178, 180
  and Pentecostal Oath 177
  Robert le Diable 229–30, 231
  in romances 177
  Sir Gowther 181, 182
  Sir Gowther 229, 231
  Tale of Gamelyn 129–30, 131, 132–3, 136–7
Virgil, *Aeneid* 3
  Turnus 9, 11, 12–13, 14
Vita Haroldi, Harold Godwineson 75–6, 77–80
Vortigern 43, 50, 51, 102, 108, 110
  and Rowena, Hamilton's painting 44–5

Wace
  Roman de Brut 19, 22, 46, 56, 99
    Arviragus 49, 50
    Battle of Hastings 64–5
    Gawain 120
    Hengist and Horsa 50, 51
    Julius Caesar 49, 50
    Mordred 83–4
    Romans 49
Waldef 96, 97
Walter of Châtillon, *Alexandreis* 27, 30, 36, 39, 40
  knowledge of, in England 29
Waltham Chronicle 75
  Harold Godwineson 70
The Wars of Alexander, Darius incident 36–7
The Wedding of Sir Gawain and Dame Ragnelle 119
William the Conqueror 22
  anti-hero 52
William of Malmesbury
  Gesta Regum Anglorum, Gawain 120
  on Harold Godwineson 63
William of Palerne 5
William of Poitiers 65

William Rufus, King 95
William of Tyre, *Historia rerum* 173
'wizard', meaning 100
women
  loyalty of 123
  treatment of, Pentecostal Oath 201
wrestling
  A Gest of Robyn Hode 136

Gamelyn 135–6
Wulfstan, St, *Life* 71–2
Wyntoun, Andrew 125

Yonec, shapeshifting 223–4
Yvain 111, 121–2
Yvain, Gawain 121

Volumes Already Published

I: *The Orient in Chaucer and Medieval Romance*, Carol F. Heffernan, 2003
II: *Cultural Encounters in the Romance of Medieval England*, edited by Corinne Saunders, 2005
III: *The Idea of Anglo-Saxon England in Middle English Romance*, Robert Allen Rouse, 2005
IV: *Guy of Warwick: Icon and Ancestor*, edited by Alison Wiggins and Rosalind Field, 2007
V: *The Sea and Medieval English Literature*, Sebastian I. Sobecki, 2008
VI: *Boundaries in Medieval Romance*, edited by Neil Cartlidge, 2008
VII: *Naming and Namelessness in Medieval Romance*, Jane Bliss, 2008
VIII: Sir Bevis of Hampton *in Literary Tradition*, edited by Jennifer Fellows and Ivana Djordjević, 2008
IX: *Anglicising Romance: Tail-Rhyme and Genre in Medieval English Literature*, Rhiannon Purdie, 2008
X: *A Companion to Medieval Popular Romance*, edited by Raluca L. Radulescu and Cory James Rushton, 2009
XI: *Expectations of Romance: The Reception of a Genre in Medieval England*, Melissa Furrow, 2009
XII: *The Exploitations of Medieval Romance*, edited by Laura Ashe, Ivana Djordjević, and Judith Weiss, 2010
XIII: *Magic and the Supernatural in Medieval English Romance*, Corinne Saunders, 2010
XIV: *Medieval Romance, Medieval Contexts*, edited by Rhiannon Purdie and Michael Cichon, 2011
XV: *Women's Power in Late Medieval Romance*, Amy N. Vines, 2011
XVI: *Heroes and Anti-Heroes in Medieval Romance*, edited by Neil Cartlidge, 2012
XVII: *Performance and the Middle English Romance*, Linda Marie Zaerr, 2012
XVIII: *Medieval Romance and Material Culture*, edited by Nicholas Perkins, 2015
XIX: *Middle English Romance and the Craft of Memory*, Jamie McKinstry, 2015

www.ingramcontent.com/pod-product-compliance
Lightning Source LLC
Chambersburg PA
CBHW051609230426
43668CB00013B/2043